Cilla Snowball

ADVERTISING WORKS 9

ADVERTISING WORKS 9

Papers from the IPA Advertising Effectiveness Awards

Institute of Practitioners in Advertising, 1996

Edited and introduced by

Gary Duckworth

NTC PUBLICATIONS LIMITED

First published 1997 by **NTC Publications Limited**
Farm Road, Henley-on-Thames, Oxfordshire RG9 1EJ, United Kingdom
Telephone: 01491 411000

A CIP catalogue record for this book is available from the British Library

ISBN 1 899314 60 1

Typeset by NTC Publications Ltd
Printed and bound in Great Britain
by Biddles Ltd, Guildford and King's Lynn

Contents

IPA
Advertising Effectiveness Awards
1996

FOUNDATION OF THE AWARDS

Prior to 1980, there was virtually no case history material demonstrating advertising effectiveness, anywhere in the world, which was both published and sufficiently rigorous in its analysis and presentation of data to be convincing. This was a major barrier to justifying the industry's services to its customers, and to the promotion of best practice and a more accountable culture within the advertising industry itself.

These Awards were designed to help fill this vacuum and have done so very successfully since 1980, producing a fresh tranche of effectiveness cases every two years. The demands for proof are considerably more rigorous than those made by effectiveness awards in the USA and Europe. Elsewhere, the Advertising Federation of Australia (from 1990), the Canadian Congress of Advertising (from 1992), the Institute of Canadian Advertising (from 1995), the Advertising Agencies Association of New Zealand (from 1995) and the Institute of Advertising Practitioners in Ireland (from 1995) have based their awards on the UK IPA format.

The evidence from a study among the British marketing community, undertaken by the IPA early in 1996, indicates that this award scheme is now viewed as pre-eminent in the field of UK awards.

THIS BOOK

This book represents several things.

First of all, it is the formal record of the prize-winning entries of the ninth biennial IPA Advertising Effectiveness Awards. It contains 20 detailed case histories which add to the bank of over 160 published in the previous eight *Advertising Works* volumes.[1]

---

1. The definitive information resource is the IPA's Advertising Effectiveness Data Bank which contains not only all the prize winners from the competition's inception, but all entries of merit – a total of well over 600 papers. Anyone may access any paper for a small fee, and an index on disc is available from the IPA. For further information contact: Institute of Practitioners in Advertising, 44 Belgrave Square, London SW1X 8QS Tel: 0171 235 7020 Fax: 0171 245 9904.

Second, this book is a record of an evolving advertising industry dealing with new challenges. A week is a long time in politics, and the 16 years since the competition was inaugurated is certainly a long time in advertising. One of the main shifts that has taken place is that new types of brand owner are making significant and highly profitable use of advertising investment. These prize-winning cases show some very fine examples of telecoms, retailers and services using advertising successfully, in addition to fmcg brands which have historically formed the backbone of this competition.

In many respects the marketing world has become more complex over the last 16 years. In particular the effect of the punishing recession of the early part of the '90s has been to impel companies both to cut their cost base and to seek ways of constantly building and evolving their competitive edge. In addition, drivers of change such as deregulation, innovation in distribution systems (particularly direct ones), and new technologies coming on stream – including new media – have created many fresh opportunities.

In this new climate there is pressure to innovate to stay ahead, but advertising has retained a central role because, while business structures may change and market opportunities shift, there is every sign that brands retain their ability to influence consumer choice to brand owners' advantage. And, while advertising is increasingly deployed to work harmoniously with other forms of marketing instrument, it remains the single most potent tool available for the creation, shaping and direction of powerful brands.

Close scrutiny of all forms of investment and a growing trend to zero-based budgeting, means there has also been increased pressure for all forms of marketing expenditure to demonstrate accountability. So the original aims of these awards set out in 1980 – with their emphasis both on learning and accountability – have lost none of their relevance in the transformed marketing climate of the late 1990s.

1. To generate a collection of case histories which demonstrates that, properly used, advertising can make a measurable contribution to business success.

2. To encourage advertising agencies (and their clients) to develop ever-improving standards of advertising evaluation and, in the process, a better understanding of the way advertising works.

In fact, given the developing sophistication of thinking and complexity of practice in modern marketing, this book provides immense benefit in setting out current exemplars of best practice in detail. So, thirdly, this book is a handbook to show not just *what* happened, but also *how* – the background of analytic thinking and the 'process' that enables agency and client working together to produce successful business results from advertising that is well planned, powerfully executed and rigorously evaluated.

THE PRIZE STRUCTURE

In 1994 the number of categories in the Awards scheme was rationalised – the number of primary categories was reduced to three. This did not change overall eligibility to enter or the total number of Awards available, but removed anomalies and provided a more coherent basis for judging. The six categories from 1992 (New brands; Established; 'Longer and Broader'; Smaller Budgets; European; Special including Financial) became three, structured in terms of the three main roles of advertising: to launch a new brand, to change the position of an established brand, or to build or sustain a brand over the longer term.

The three category definitions were retained for the 1996 competition and their attendant entry figures were as follows.

1. **New brands/advertisers,** including established brands with no significant previous advertising (23 entries).

2. **New campaigns** for previously advertised brands, resulting in significant short-term changes in their business performance (32 entries).

3. **Advertising over the longer term,** showing a benefit to a brand or business over several years (15 entries).

Each category typically has one gold, two silvers and three bronzes, and the Grand Prix – the paper which in the opinion of the judges exemplifies the best overall – is chosen from among the golds.

A second change in 1994 was the introduction of Special Prizes, to be given over and above category awards, designed to recognise particular types or aspects of entries the IPA wished to encourage, recognising the way that the use of advertising was evolving. Six Special Prizes were available:

- Integration with other marketing tools
- Direct response
- Limited budgets
- Best use of media planning
- European (multi-country) campaigns
- Innovative contribution to client's strategy.

Entries to the Awards must be in the form of written papers, up to 4,000 words in length (6,000 for multi-country entries), not counting appendices and charts. Each entry form must be countersigned by the agency's chief executive and by a competent representative of the client, by which act copyright is passed to the IPA. The criteria on which entries are judged are perhaps best explained by quoting from the actual instructions given to judges. These are substantially the same as those formalised in 1990 by Paul Feldwick of BMP DDB, who has played a major role in shaping the competition.

Notes for Judges

1. The main criterion for judging is simple: how convincing is the case put for the specific contribution of advertising to business success? The onus is on the author to anticipate questions and counter-arguments. Papers fail because they do not consider all the relevant facts, or present data in a obfuscatory way (on purpose or through carelessness). If you – as a sceptical but not necessarily 'expert' reader – feel reasonably convinced that it was indeed the advertising that produced the results claimed for it, then the paper is a contender.

2. However, when you read the papers you will find it not quite so simple. In some cases it is almost absurdly easy to demonstrate the advertising effect (eg for a 'partwork' magazine or direct response-based cases). In other cases, isolating the effect can be fiendishly difficult: car campaigns are a good example. Clearly it would be absurd and contrary to the spirit of the awards only to reward simple and obvious entries. We therefore find, in practice, we have to judge the arguments relative to the difficulties they have faced, both in terms of the advertising task and the evaluation of its effects.

3. Effectiveness in these awards is defined as contribution to the business. This does not mean that measures such as awareness or brand image are irrelevant – far from it, they are often vital – but there needs to be some sort of argument which links those to business objectives, ultimately in terms of sales or profitability. We also need to be careful that we do not reward only short-term paybacks – the long-term competitiveness, resilience and leverage of the brand can be at least as important. (This is especially true, of course, in the 'long term' category.)

4. Papers will obviously be less likely to convince if they are poorly written or presented. Good clear English, clarity of argument and good presentation of data all help. You should expect to see a clear exposition of the background to the campaign, the development of the strategy, and a clear statement of what was actually done and when (creative work and media plans), as well as the review of the performance.

5. You are not expected to be an expert in statistical modelling. Papers which use such techniques still have a duty to be intelligible to the general reader. Authors who make vague claims about models without presenting sufficient detail and technical evidence do not help their case.

6. You should not be influenced by whether you personally liked or hated the advertising, or whether it was 'creative' or not; you should judge the argument objectively. An author may, as part of these cases, show that 'creativity' contributed to the effectiveness: that is a different matter.

7. 'Bonus points' should certainly be added for papers which add something new to our knowledge, or make an original point. They must of course conform to the basic criteria as well.

These criteria show the difference between these awards and other advertising industry awards (which generally focus on the recognition of original thinking and craft skills); ie their single-minded focus on the demonstration of effectiveness. This difference is reinforced in the fact that, as in previous years, the majority of the judging panel was drawn from outside the advertising industry.

THE 1996 ENTRIES

The 1996 entries were again excellent both in terms of quantity and quality – 70 case histories were finally submitted to the judges. The total number of entries going forward to the judging stage was similar to 1994:

Year	'90	'92	'94	'96
Entries	87	80	73	70

It would appear that the overall number of entries has plateaued, down from the heady year of 1990 when the economy and the advertising industry went into recession. It may also be that the introduction of 'How to Win' seminars sponsored by the IPA from 1994 onwards has tended to reduce the number of entries because they have placed great emphasis on the need for cases to be substantiated by robust evidence. As with any other activity that requires time and talent, it costs money to evaluate advertising effectiveness properly, and it remains the case that very many successful advertising campaigns are inadequately monitored due to lack of resources or difficulty in collecting data. However, one of the continuing delights of the competition is the regular appearance of papers from small-scale advertisers who demonstrate that innovative thinking about evaluation techniques can nonetheless overcome scarce resources.

While the number of entries may have plateaued, participation in the competition has broadened: papers were entered by 34 advertising agencies in total, and the list of entries, as in previous years, comprises some of Britain's biggest advertisers drawn from very diverse arenas – National Savings, British Telecom, Nestlé, Renault, Procter & Gamble, Safeway and Whitbread – as well as many smaller companies. Virtually all of these made a good case that the advertiser's money had been well spent. The 20 cases, from 12 agencies, which emerged as Award or Special Prize winners represent real excellence in terms of the judging criteria laid down and the judges distributed awards broadly in line with the number of entries to each category. In the judges' view, although a number of papers demonstrated considerable merit in media planning, none was felt to be particularly outstanding, so sadly the Special Prize for media planning has not been awarded this time.

I earlier alluded to the way many of these prizewinners demonstrate the effective use of advertising by what would be considered non-traditional advertisers. In this respect it is interesting to note that the three category gold winners comprise two telecoms companies – BT and Orange – and one financial service company – Barclaycard. The list also includes a Scottish legal firm, Ross Harper, and even the BBC.

The table on page xii (compiled from the winners) shows that, while fmcg brands are still by far the leading category, they by no means dominate the picture. The overall spectrum is one of increasing diversity.

Category	No. of awards	Award winners
Fmcg	7	Felix, Walkers, Murphy's, Gold Blend, Stella, Philadelphia, ICBINB!
Telecoms	3	BT Consumer, BT Business, Orange
Automotive	3	Daewoo, Renault Clio, AA
Financial	2	Frizzell, Barclaycard
Fashion	2	Reebok, De Beers
Retail	1	Safeway
Other	2	BBC Education, Ross Harper

What this represents is a shift in the advertising marketplace. Fmcg brands still account for a significant share of advertising expenditure, but in the long term their share is diminishing as the newer kinds of brand owner use advertising as an important weapon in the competitive armoury, realising that brand investment and brand strength can make a significant difference in markets that are becoming more hard-fought, more fast-moving and more turbulent.[2]

New roles for advertising, new forms of evaluation

These new advertisers bring their own agenda. They are more complex businesses; a bank will operate in a variety of markets – mortgages, loans, current accounts etc – and will normally target businesses as well as consumers, homeowners and students. So advertising is frequently given a broader set of roles to play. Or advertising may even be used in an entirely different and innovative way.

The result is that the art of advertising evaluation has been continuously evolving because of the complexity of the decision chain, and the fact that the consumer 'interaction' with the brand prior to purchase is usually much more lengthy and involved.

For fmcg brands, the evaluation task is never easy, but it is usually facilitated by data relating to specific aspects of the consumer buying process – rates of sale, distribution, purchasing behaviour etc – which help to isolate the advertising contribution within the mix. And there is no unpredictable intervening variable like a telephone sales person, or a dealer, whose contribution to a sale is very difficult to quantify.

A hazard to evaluation which can emerge in complex businesses is the sheer volume of different kinds of data. Having too much data can be as much a barrier to successful evaluation as having too little, because it makes it difficult to see the wood for the trees.

The BT Consumer paper which is this year's Grand Prix winner deals very impressively with this more complex agenda. In one respect the paper is a classic example of strategic orthodoxy – the attempt of a very dominant market leader to build revenue by attempting to expand the size of the overall market. What marks

---

2. Over the period 1982 to 1995 food and drink's share of total advertising expenditure fell from 15.5% to 11.9%. Automotive rose from 7.1% to 11.3% and financial from 13.7% to 17.9%. (Source: Advertising Association.)

it out though is the boldness of the strategy. It is a commonplace that advertising is frequently used to change attitudes and thereby modify behaviour. But instead of trying to change our attitudes about the phone, strategic insight recognised that how we use it is determined by far more fundamental, deeply rooted cultural attitudes about the value of talking, especially among men, who frequently do not feel at ease with discursive telephone conversations, and this 'dampening' attitude affects the behaviour of women within the household.

The advertising very boldly tackled this issue head on and produced a shift in attitude and behaviour which grew the 'talking' market – hence building BT's revenue.

The case is also a great example of evaluation. Usage of telephone time in general is influenced by many factors as well as our attitudes, eg the growth of fax machines, answerphones and second lines. These are exactly the kind of complicating factors prevalent with 'new' brands discussed above, and make the task of isolating the advertising contribution very difficult. Econometric analysis is frequently used in IPA papers because it provides a means of understanding the relative contribution of a large number of variables in the marketing mix. Econometrics was used among other evidence here, but what singled out the paper was the lucidity and clarity of the exposition which made it highly readable for the non-technical reader.

It is no mean feat to take in this case an immense body of data, to simplify it and make its meaning comprehensible. And it will become increasingly necessary the more we need to understand how complex businesses operate.

Whatever means of advertising evaluation we develop, it is of central importance that our thinking and methodologies, no matter how 'clever', remain accessible to a wider audience, otherwise we will be in danger of losing conviction and trust. The paper is a very fine model in this respect.

A number of other papers offer valuable insights into evaluation: the Ross Harper/Legal Aid study is a model of a campaign on a very limited budget. The BBC Education campaign won one of the two Special Prizes awarded for Direct Response as an excellent example not only of response analysis but also the calculation of payback in an area fraught with difficulty. And finally, the BT Business paper provides some highly imaginative insights into assessing the value of leads generated by advertising in a complex sales process.

Thinking yourself ahead

Marketing life is more interesting because of the way new brands constantly break through in established marketplaces where many have ceased to believe there are fresh opportunities. And, while much attention is paid to product innovation as a means to succeed, far too little weight is given to the power of innovative thinking as a means of stealing competitive advantage. Too often, when faced with a particularly tough problem or target, companies have the knee-jerk reaction – 'we must do some research' – yet what many of these cases show is that we will often get far more powerful strategies if our first reaction is to say, 'we must do some thinking'.

Felix offers a classic case study in a very established fmcg market, where an existing brand moved from middling status to brand leadership by identifying an opportunity in consumers' heads – a brand personality with a high degree of empathy with cat owners – embodying the mischievous, characterful persona which many cat owners believe their pet possesses.

Similarly, Daewoo, as the fourth Korean entrant to the crowded UK car market, was hardly a brand endowed with prospects to an outside onlooker. Yet, by identifying an unmet need among private car buyers for a pleasurable buying and owning experience, and developing an offer to meet those needs, it created a very new kind of brand – more of a service brand than a traditional car brand – and hence set a new consumer agenda.

The Safeway paper is a very welcome prizewinner. Despite the fact that retail has for many years been a major advertising category, it is the first time that an effectiveness award has been won by a retailer of such stature. Clever targeting thinking, in conjunction with service innovations at store level, actively positioned the brand as meeting the needs of families with young children, hence creating a distinctive and motivating platform within one of the toughest and most competitive markets in the country.

The value of innovative thinking is frequently not confined to the 'external' world of the consumer. The AA paper won the Special Award for Innovative Contribution to the Client's Strategy. 'The fourth emergency service' enabled the entire *organisation* to see itself in a new light, and this had an impact right down the marketing chain to how the telephones were answered and the van livery. In a world where advertising is increasingly used by service companies we need to be aware that the brand is an experiential totality: the galvanising power of the brand proposition can be as relevant internally as it is externally.

None of the above are simple achievements resulting entirely from an interesting new idea. They are all examples where client and agency worked together to *apply* the thinking. In a sense anyone can have a good new idea: what is also required is commitment, confidence and partnership to see it through to fruition.

So often innovation is misrepresented as the result of wild lateral thinking which disregards orthodoxy – the cerebral equivalent of throwing away your old flannel trousers and donning purple latex flares. But all of these examples seem to owe their success to the identification of a consumer need or opportunity. The signs are that successful innovation comes to those who know their marketing first principles.

'Only advertising can do this'

Integration has become one of the leading strands of marketing thinking in the '90s. Its rise can be traced to two driving factors: the increasing variety and sophistication of below-the-line marketing techniques; and the greater appreciation of the value of leveraging the brand proposition through all levels of the marketing mix. But, while it is true that marketers have a greater choice of instruments and techniques to achieve their goals, the unique properties of advertising are very well demonstrated in this collection.

As Chris Baker wrote in the introduction to the 1994 volume:

'Advertising can of course be justified simply in "cost per thousand" terms (ie the cost of delivering the desired message to a given audience), but its real uniqueness stems from two related factors: (i) its power to grab people's attention, excite their interest and capture their imagination; (ii) its ability to create an atmosphere in which the other elements of the mix become more effective, and it simply becomes easier to do business.'

The current movement towards integration also makes evaluation tougher in that, if integration is working properly, the effect of the advertising input will inevitably be more difficult to disentangle.

Orange came late into the mobile phone market: many commentators believed there was no further opportunity, and actively dismissed the new company's prospects. Nonetheless there was a major opportunity because none of the existing companies had created a brand which stirred the imagination of the consumer sector. Through innovative thinking and a strongly branded campaign, Orange was enabled to 'own' the future and create a highly successful entry despite the strong positions of the established players. The paper also deals well with evaluating the advertising variable within an integrated marketing mix.

Human beings are complex animals to describe, but one thing that unites us is what psychologists call 'affect' – a disposition to become emotionally involved with the world around us, reflected in our relationships, the soaps we watch, or the team we support. A number of the cases demonstrate what might be called the pure power of a strong creative idea: the ability to encapsulate a brand message and *at the same time,* to create an emotional involvement with the brand well beyond that which any simple rational benefit or product can provide, hence providing a competitive advantage deriving from perceptual differentiation.

Barclaycard is a classic example of advertising used highly effectively in a defensive role. Barclaycard could easily have fallen by the wayside in a market that was characterised by a very large number of rival credit card entrants, as the eventual demise of Access shows. Yet the brand survived and prospered with a high-profile campaign which maintained the brand's saliency and gave it a distinctive and popular identity. This kept it perceptually apart from the morass of cheaper competitors. And, while the advertising communicated specific product benefits available to Barclaycard users, none were in themselves unique or potent enough to sustain the brand's success.

Other campaigns exemplify the same point: the Renault Clio – a perfectly serviceable but anonymous small car – has been supported from launch to well into the second stage of its product life cycle by a long-running campaign, which has given it a very distinctive identity in the small car sector.[3] Philadelphia has been able to build its penetration and usage in an fmcg category that could easily long ago have been ceded to own-label. And Gold Blend is an excellent example of a campaign idea that borrows from a very well-established vehicle for our emotions – the TV soap – and weaves a brand positioning skilfully into this framework.

One of the signs of a truly powerful creative idea is its ability to travel: as

3. See also: 'Renault Clio: Adding value during a recession', *Advertising Works 7.*

international campaigns increase in number, our reliance on the creative imagination for ideas which communicate across frontiers will grow. Diamonds are the supreme example of perceived added value: viewed from a 'product' perspective they are an allotrope of carbon, differing only marginally from a lump of charcoal. From a human perceptual perspective they have been viewed as one of the most precious and mesmerising commodities throughout history. But, like any commodity low on functional value, they are vulnerable in a recession. The De Beers campaign is a fascinating example of one that touched people's emotions – not only in Europe – but across the world in fundamentally different cultures, including South Africa, Japan and the Gulf states.

Looking beyond: lessons for the future

Marketing life has undoubtedly become tougher since the late '80s. More competitive conditions mean we have to reach higher standards to create success. The most important lesson emerging from these papers is the need to extract the maximum value from every aspect of the marketing mix – real product innovation, imaginative consumer insight and innovative thinking combine with creativity to create powerful brand campaigns. Power derives not just from the creative idea itself, but from its magnification and multiplication through the media delivery and the exploitation of leverage at all points of the consumer encounter. The ability of advertising to act as the public synthesis of what the brand stands for, and at the same time to be the fulcrum maximising leverage of all the other elements, remains supreme.

A final thank you

None of these studies would have been possible without great effort and time put into them by the agency and client concerned. It goes without saying that praise and thanks are due to all the authors. But no serious case study can be written without evidence, and we owe a great debt to the client companies and their research agencies for exposing their strategies and making their information available. It takes bravery and generosity to do this. Without it, the learning and inspiration which this book provides would simply not exist.

A Short Guide To The Case Histories

New brands or advertisers

Orange – How two years of advertising created twelve years of value (pp3–28)

Period: April 1994–March 1996

Media: Television, Press, Outdoor

The Judges' View: This paper was a clear winner in its category. It was particularly admired for some insightful strategic thinking which identified a sizeable opportunity for the Orange brand, even though it was a late entrant to the mobile market and was initially written off by many commentators. None of the existing players had yet created a brand identity which captured the consumer imagination, and this paper offers an excellent example of how insightful consumer thinking led to a brand identity that provided a strong competitive advantage, allowing Orange to catch up and overtake the existing players in a very short space of time. The strongly branded campaign which ensued enabled specific elements of the brand's offering – both brand and tactical – to be communicated at all levels of the marketing mix. The paper is an excellent example of how to deal effectively with the issues surrounding advertising evaluation within an integrated marketing framework.

Advertising that builds strong customer relationships? That'll be the Daewoo (pp29–52)

Period: 1994–96

Media: Television, Press, Radio, Outdoor

The Judges' View: This paper was admired for its imaginative strategic thinking which developed the positioning of 'The customer focused car company', in response to a very challenging target set by the client. The campaign became the most successful car launch ever. The innovative positioning influenced the way the whole company ran its operation, creating results well beyond conventional expectations. Advertising was employed in a multiplicity of roles – for example, putting the corporation on the map and building a database via a direct dialogue with consumers, as well as communicating the brand's overall proposition, all within a very highly integrated communication framework. Hence the judges also decided to give this paper the Special Award for Integration.

Felix Advertising 1989–95: How the cat that crept got the cream   (pp53–82)

Period: 1989–96

Media: Press, Television, Outdoor

The Judges' View: The Felix study was appreciated as an excellent example of how it is still possible for an outsider brand in a mature market to topple a brand leader previously thought impregnable. The weapon used was brand identity – by tapping into the emotions of cat owners and their feelings about their cats' 'personalities', Felix became a brand with a powerful emotional pull, built round the character of the 'Felix' cat. Starting with only a very small budget and some very imaginative media thinking in national press, the brand property was invested in with cumulatively greater effect, year on year, demonstrating the value of consistency as well as insight in creating success.

BBC Education – Ignore it. It'll go away   (pp83–106)

Period: February 1995

Medium: Television

The Judges' View: This was an exciting and different kind of case history – well written and a pleasure to read. Strategically, it exemplifies how the use of emotion can create breakthrough response levels. It tells a very interesting human story of how advertising relying on the use of emotion, and the concern parents have for their children, was used to generate thousands of requests among the 'difficult' target of adults with literacy problems. The analysis of response and the calculations of payback are very fine examples of the application of high-quality analytic thinking to direct response issues.

Frizzell Insurance – When the customer is not always right   (pp107–136)

Period: September 1994–December 1995

Media: Television, Radio, Press

The Judges' View: This paper offers an excellent analysis of how advertising was used to defend and grow Frizell's business in a market that rapidly became more competitive as the number of 'direct' entrants grew. Analysis of the client's current customer base demonstrated that Frizzell had built success and a distinctive business based on more 'conservative' customers. What was particularly impressive was the way advertising was used to filter out undesirable (high-risk) applicants, hence maximising conversion rates and getting the maximum value from the campaign investment. The paper offered a highly readable analysis of the value of the advertising's contribution.

Reebok – From relegation zone to championship contention   (pp137–160)

Period: 1994–95

Medium: Television

The Judges' View: This case was felt to be a very good example of how advertising can be used to take an established brand into a new market sector. The paper was appreciated for its clear and detailed dissection of the way that trade stocking policy creates an artificial barrier to entry in the competitive football boot market. Advertising was used to create a step shift in trade attitudes so that the brand was enabled to leap over the barrier. This, combined with offtake uplifts, strongly drove its brand share. A fine example of a situation in which the advertising played a vital role in the distribution chain long before the campaign was ever seen by its target group.

New campaigns for previously advertised brands

BT – It's good to talk   (pp163–186)

Period: 1995

Media: Television, Press

The Judges' View: This paper was felt to be exemplary in virtually every respect. It offers an excellent exposition of a bold and innovative strategy. The analysis shows how the deeply rooted and culturally defined 'dampening' attitudes of men to discursive telephone conversations have an impact on their own telephone usage, which tends to be restricted to 'functional calls'. These attitudes also repress the calling behaviour of other members of the household. The advertising tackled these attitudes head on, and had a highly beneficial impact on both attitudes and usage, thus generating strong incremental revenue growth for BT. At the same time a complementary campaign was used to address perceptions of the cost of using the phone which were significantly out of line with reality.

Generating a shift of this magnitude is an impressive achievement in itself but, with great rigour and clarity, the paper deals extraordinarily well with the complexities of demonstrating advertising contribution in a market where so many other variables impact on phone usage, such as the growth of second lines, fax machines and answerphones. Econometrics is frequently used in IPA papers to isolate the relative contribution of a significant number of variables, but this paper shows how econometrics can be used to provide convincing evidence in a way which is readable and comprehensible to the non-technical reader, and which cleverly interleaves statistical analysis with qualitative interpretation.

Safeway – 'Effective...moi?' (pp189–202)

Period: 1994–95

Medium: Television

The Judges' View: Retail advertising has been a vibrant growth category for years, but it is the first time that a paper of this stature has been entered for the awards. The thinking of the paper was appreciated for the way it gave Safeway a differentiated positioning as 'mother-and-child friendly'. This, in conjunction with initiatives at store level, enabled the brand to take a clear positioning in the competitive UK marketplace for the first time. The advertising also built brand affinity because the 'Harry' campaign captured the public imagination. The paper has a crystal-clear demonstration of the way the campaign shifted Safeway's image, and how it influenced the store's position on shoppers' repertoires.

Walkers Crisps – Garymania! How an already successful brand benefited from famous advertising (pp203–230)

Period: 1994–95

Medium: Television

The Judges' View: One of the issues created by success is how to build growth even further. It is so easy to assume that a brand leader has reached some kind of ceiling, and that all marketing can do is to maintain its leadership. This paper is an object lesson in how a brand that already dominated its marketplace through product and distribution strengths, was propelled forward to even greater success by a powerful advertising idea that captured the public imagination and appealed to all the types of buyer in the market. The paper impressed the judges not only for the way that the advertising effect was demonstrated, but also for the way it displayed how the popularity of the Lineker campaign worked at many levels and built distribution as well as rate of sale.

AA – 'No more Mr Nice Guy' (pp231–250)

Period: 1993–96

Media: Television, Press

The Judges' View: This paper offers a fine example of the role advertising can play in a service organisation. The 'fourth emergency service' positioning had a strong consumer effect, stabilising a decline in consumer share and, importantly, enabling the AA to maintain margins by boosting its image as a professional and responsive organisation, in a market where it was coming under increasing competition from the RAC and lower-price operators. What particularly singles out the paper is the demonstration of how the advertising had a galvanising internal effect as well, boosting morale and enabling the organisation to present itself in a more dynamic way at all levels of the consumer experience. Hence it was given the Special Award for innovative contribution to the client's strategy.

How BT made advertising work smarter, not just harder (pp251–272)

Period: 1994–95

Media: Television, Outdoor, Press

The Judges' View: This thorough paper demonstrates the value of advertising in defending the share of the dominant brand – BT – against the growth of competition in the business telecommunications sector. The strategy provides an interesting example of how the positioning of the BT brand was tuned to demonstrate the relevance of BT's offer to the business community, not just in terms of telecommunications, but in the developing area of PC-based communications. With some imaginative analysis, the paper demonstrates very well how, in a business context, the leads generated can be followed through to assess ultimate sales impact.

Murphy's – 'One brand's weakness, another brand's strength'   (pp273–306)

Period:	1993–95
Media:	Television, Press
The Judges' View:	One of the most difficult marketing problems is to enter a category where the brand leader is all-powerful. This is the case with the stout market and Guinness. The paper provides a fascinating analysis of how the Murphy's brand identity was constructed, relating both to the needs and identity of the male target group, and built on a product truth. It is an excellent example of the power advertising has to carve out a competitive positioning – both differentiating and motivating – where many might have thought that the long-established dominance of the brand leader precluded any serious brand competition.

De Beers – 'Hard Times: Selling diamonds in a recession'   (pp307–346)

Period:	1992–96
Media:	Television, Cinema
The Judges' View:	This paper was the clear winner of the European prize. It tackles a blend of industry, corporate and product branding issues which are discussed in an international setting and draws materials/analyses from sources beyond the diamond market. It describes how De Beers was able to buck the general downward trend in the purchase of luxury goods during the recession by 'turbo charging' the emotional response to the advertising of diamonds and combining this with a new media strategy of television and cinema where couples would be viewing together in an audio-visual environment. The campaign was tracked across the major international markets for both consumer and trade effectiveness.

Ross Harper – Creating a legal precedent   (pp347–362)

Period:	1994
Medium:	Television
The Judges' View:	This paper was the outstanding candidate for the limited budget special prize. It has a clear, direct style and details how Ross Harper was the first law firm to advertise Legal Aid on television in Scotland. The creative work addressed a range of misperceptions about Legal Aid and the use of solicitors in general. The commercial contained an 0800 number that was also listed in *Yellow Pages*. Although the total television budget was only £82,500, the campaign generated an estimated £600,000+ in legal fees for Ross Harper – a payback of 7.2.

Advertising over the longer term

Barclaycard – Put it away Bough!   (pp365–386)

Period: 1990–95

Medium: Television

The Judges' View: The judges felt that this Barclaycard paper was a prime example of one of the key themes of the 'long and broad' category, and indeed one of the key questions in business today – how to manage change.

The paper describes a typical scenario facing most brands and products, which is repeatedly described in many of the other papers: increased competition (30 cards in 1990, 500 by 1996), increasing commoditisation as cards rely on price and promotion for short-term advantage, increasing co-positioning (eg General Motors card). In other words, Barclaycard faced constant threats and constant change.

How should a brand react? Adapt to every change? Reduce advertising expenditure and move it into other activities? Fight on price?

The answer provided in the Barclaycard case very much revolves around creating a continuous and distinctive human presence which consumers can relate to. Empathy, even in the finance market, can go a long way.

The paper clearly demonstrates that the Rowan Atkinson Barclaycard campaign is the most famous and best-liked advertising in the market and, as such, provided a long-term platform which could be used to dramatise Barclaycard's unique product properties and get them noticed and appreciated.

An example of what might have been is given in the paper's use of Access which was forced to adopt a far less consistent approach to brand management.

Also of interest is the fact that the paper accepts that 'there is no point in trying to eliminate the effect of other marketing activities' in the traditional 'effectiveness awards style'.

As such, the paper begins to give us some lessons in best practice, in how to demonstrate advertising's effectiveness in the context of a fully integrated marketing programme.

All in all, in the judges' view, this paper tackled an extremely complex case in an extremely complex market and gave us convincing proof that advertising works in helping companies to manage change.

Love Over Gold – The untold story of TV's greatest romance   (pp387–404)

Period: 1987–95

Medium: Television

The Judges' View: The IPA judges saw in this Gold Blend case a fine lesson in how to move with the times.

One of the most interesting and surprising facts in this paper is that Gold Blend was originally launched in 1969. This makes it nearly as old as *Coronation Street*.

It is testimony to the advertising's ability to evolve therefore, that the brand still seems as fresh and contemporary as *Brookside*.

Again, the same characteristics of success show through – an emotional bond created beyond the core rational quality promise, a brand fame that lives beyond the advertising and in the public arena of headlines, sitcoms and even daily gossip – ('would she, wouldn't she?'), a use of that property to support and focus tactical and promotional activity, and therefore a delicate balance between consistency and flexibility.

The advertising and the brand has consistently evolved and in so doing helped build the brand's volume by some 60% at a time when the market was static or declining.

The campaign and its structure – advertising as soap opera – has got to be one of the definitive pieces of advertising of the last decade and the figures show it achieved both popular acclaim and brand success.

Kraft Philadelphia – The Philadelphia story   (pp405–428)

Period: 1987–95

Medium: Television

The Judges' View: For the IPA judges, 'The Philadelphia Story' was a simple but telling tale of advertising's ability to build a strong and lasting bond with its public.

The 'Philly Girls' campaign is one of those pieces of advertising, like others in this category, that manages to exist outside the commercials that created it. Indeed, it would be true to say that the two secretaries have become, in their own endearing way, popular icons. They live in our lives and change with us like long-term friends, popping in and out of our home via the TV screen, and always with something fresh and relevant to tell us.

This paper describes how this brand property was first developed and then used to manage the brand's development over 12 years, and through many different stages; first developing the brand positioning, then launching a new variant, then resisting new manufacturer and retailer brand entrants into a growing market, and finally developing new usage occasions.

As such it gives lessons on how to achieve consistency while adapting to change. As Ronnie Bell, MD of Kraft Jacobs Suchard UK, says in the introduction:

'Over the last decade the Philly girls have become one of the great advertising properties in the UK food business. They have created a strong brand with the British public while proving a flexible communication vehicle for developing and growing the Philadelphia brand.'

The value of that clever balancing act is revealed in Philadelphia's 50%+ market share and 20%+ price premium to own-label.

If you want to consider the scale of this achievement take a look at Figure 17 in the paper which shows own-label with only a 21% share of the soft cheese market (Philadelphia's sector) and 64% of the hard cheese sector!

Stella Artois – Seven Years in Provence   (pp429–458)

Period: 1990–95

Medium: Television

The Judges' View: One of the most difficult questions advertisers often face in managing change is, 'when shall I change my successful advertising?'.

This case gives interesting insights into how to go about answering that deceptively simple question.

During the mid-'80s Stella's 'Reassuringly Expensive' press campaign had perfectly captured the spirit of the times, and received much industry acclaim, in terms of marketing, creative and effectiveness awards. More importantly, the campaign had achieved great brand success, making Stella number one in the UK premium lager market.

However, taking a step back and looking at the long-term trends allowed the brand guardians to see that key fundamental drivers in the market had changed: penetration levels, the profile of drinkers, the number and nature of competitors, marketing spend, etc.

From this clear and incisive analysis, the agency and client were able to make the decision that the advertising also needed to change to reflect this.

As a result Stella was able to maintain its relevance to a new generation and new range of premium lager drinkers.

Interestingly, it did this not by changing everything and starting all over again but rather by retaining a clear sense of its core values and identity: quality, a 'gold standard', continental, classic, etc while shedding some of its previous outward expressions of those values: 'for flash gits', 'only for people with money', 'drunk to show off rather than because it's worth it'.

Stella therefore has retained its dominance as market leader in a vastly larger and more competitive market by keeping a balanced long-term perspective on the change around it, rather than hiding from it, or reacting to every fad and short-term diversion.

A blind taste test shows how much advertising and the brand have achieved.

The product comes last in blind tests. Add the name and it becomes first choice and leader in quality dimensions! A clear example of brand potency overcoming the limitations of product reality!

I Can't Believe It's Not Butter!
From extraordinary launch to long-term success (pp459–472)

Period: 1991–96

Media: Television, Press

The Judges' View: I Can't Believe It's Not Butter! had to deal with change even before its launch. The judges saw this case therefore as another valuable lesson in how to deal with a constantly shifting marketplace – use it to your advantage! Rather than being defeated by change, the agency and client embraced it as an opportunity.

The original breakthrough for the ICBINB! positioning came out of adversity. A dispute over the use of the word butter led to a TV ban only days before the launch. Existing US TV launch work had to be replaced by press. The press courted the controversy rather than trying to ignore it and, in so doing, caused headlines, and created an irreverent stance versus butter which, later, came through in the 'Cow World' TV campaign and the whole brand personality.

The judges also noted that it was probably no coincidence that ICBINB!'s advertising shared an ability, along with other winners in this category, to make itself bigger and more famous than, in a sense, the product alone warrants. This paper therefore illustrates that it is worth remembering that brands survive on the air of publicity and publicness not just in the intimacy of the one-to-one private relationships with their actual consumer.

However, ICBINB! did more than just create its own 15 minutes of fame. It took it and created a unique personality, founded in quirkiness and irreverence, and created an enduring brand personality that rose above the usual function-bound, chemical confusions of this market. And so again this paper illustrates the value of creating a consistent *emotional* appeal which can then be used flexibly to launch product variants, develop promotions and resist new competitors in a way that builds that personality rather than fragments it.

As an interesting aside, wouldn't it be fascinating to re-run this case with the shelved US TV advertising in place as originally planned. Imagine a world without 'Cow World'. Ponder what would have happened to the brand without this barmy army to support it.

'Vive la Clio' – How image leadership created a long-term success story (pp473–494)

Period:	1992–95
Media:	Television, Press, Outdoor
The Judges' View:	As the Volkswagen Golf case clearly demonstrated in the 1992 Advertising Effectiveness Awards (see *Advertising Works 7*), managing change in the car market means fighting against inevitable decline. This year's model is quickly superseded by a competitor's launch. Innovation is the norm and, once advertising has launched the model, very quickly its job becomes simply to slow down the law of atrophy.

This case demonstrates that advertising can do more than this. By building a clear position as 'image leader' the Renault Clio managed not just to slow decline but actually to build market share in every year after its launch.

The advertising, therefore, can be seen to have worked in defiance of the normal market cycle and, interestingly, in defiance of the pattern of every other European country in which the Clio was launched.

The difference was 'Papa and Nicole' – another British advertising institution. 'Papa and Nicole' perfectly reflected the Clio's positioning as 'the small car with big-car refinement', aimed at both a younger and older market.

It then reflected its 'big idea' status by being flexible enough to manage that image over time – adding sportiness, launching new upgrades, etc.

The client and agency now face another problem – should Nicole live on to the next model launch? On the evidence of this paper the answer is yes – she is too valuable a property to not allow her to grow up.

IPA ADVERTISING EFFECTIVENESS EXECUTIVE COMMITTEE

Chairman: Hamish Pringle – Chairman & Chief Executive, K Advertising

Gary Duckworth – Chairman, Duckworth Finn Grubb Waters

Graham Bednash – Managing Partner, Michaelides & Bednash

Stephen Woodford – Managing Director, WCRS

Mark Robinson – Business Development Director, Publicis

Nigel Maile – Group Finance Director, Bartle Bogle Hegarty

Paul Feldwick – Executive Planning Director, BMP DDB

James Best – Chairman, BMP DDB

Steve Gatfield – Chief Executive, Leo Burnett

Peter Field – Executive Director of Planning, Grey

Nick Kendall – Group Planning Director, Bartle Bogle Hegarty

Simon Marquis – Editorial Director, Haymarket Marketing Publications

1996 IPA ADVERTISING EFFECTIVENESS AWARDS JUDGING PANEL

Chairman: Lord Allen Sheppard

Convenor of Judges: Gary Duckworth – Chairman, Duckworth Finn Grubb Waters

Howard Barrett – Partner in Business Consulting, Arthur Andersen

Emily Bell – Media Business Editor, the *Observer*

Stewart Butterfield – Director of Sales and Marketing, Channel 4

Janet Hull – Consultant Director of Advertising Effectiveness, IPA

Nick Kendall – Group Planning Director, Bartle Bogle Hegarty

Seamus McBride – Marketing Director, Bass Brewers Limited

David McNair – Chairman of the ISBA Executive

Charlotte Pinder – Independent Consultant

Terry Prue – Senior Partner, HPI Research Group

Professor Mark Uncles – Heinz Professor of Marketing, Bradford University

Rosi Ware – Managing Director, Millward Brown International

ACKNOWLEDGEMENTS

The success of the 1996 IPA Advertising Effectiveness Awards owes a great deal to *Marketing* magazine for being the principal sponsor of the Awards presentation, for producing and distributing the awards supplement in its own and its sister publication, *Campaign*, and for supplying free advertising space.

The IPA would also like to thank the following companies whose support helped make the presentation possible:

Bartle Bogle Hegarty

BMP DDB

Leo Burnett

Channel 4

ITV

KPMG

Maiden Outdoor

Millward Brown

Mirror Group Newspapers

The Marketing Forum

Taylor Nelson/AGB

J Walter Thompson Co Limited

Many people worked hard to make the awards a success, especially Graham Bednash, Chairman of the Advertising Effectiveness Awards Committee, Gary Duckworth, Convenor of Judges, and Stephen Woodford, whose agency WCRS devised the advertising campaign. From the IPA, particular thanks are due to Tessa Gooding, Janet Hull, Lynne Robinson, Jean Aligorgi, Rachel Edwards and Linda Calderwood-Lea.

Prizes

CERTIFICATES OF COMMENDATION

The launch of Hep30: 'How naked ground workers worked'
Hamish Pringle and Scott Paton
  K Advertising for Hepworth

*'Where there's muck there's brass' – How advertising helped build Huggies'
business*
Janet Grimes and Simeon Duckworth
  Ogilvy & Mather for Kimberly-Clark

Number two or die
Clare Nunneley and Sigrid Jakob
  Bartle Bogle Hegarty for Lukcy Lotteries

It could be you: Launching the world's leading lottery
Mike Solloway
  Saatchi & Saatchi for Camelot

Match of the day – How quorn burgers and Ryan Giggs changed the way we eat
Mark Ellis and Peter Knowland
  Abbott Mead Vickers.BBDO for Marlow Foods

Listen to the animals
Sarah King and Magnus Willis
  Abbott Mead Vickers.BBDO for RSPCA

**New campaigns from previously advertised brands which resulted in significant
short-term effects on sales or behaviour**

GOLD

BT – It's Good to Talk
Max Burt
  Abbott Mead Vickers.BBDO for BT

SILVER

'Effective…moi?'
John Ward
  Bates Dorland for Safeway Stores plc

Garymania!
Gavin MacDonald and Jeff Lush
  BMP DDB for Walker's Snack Foods

BRONZE

'No more Mr Nice Guy'
Jon Leach and Roger McKerr
  HHCL and Partners for the Automobile Association

How BT made advertising work smarter, not just harder
Paul Jeffrey
  BDDH for BT

Murphy's: One brand's weakness, another brand's strength
Giselle Okin
  Bartle Bogle Hegarty for the Whitbread Beer Company

CERTIFICATES OF COMMENDATION

Appreciating your local water company
David Lavelle
  TBWA for Anglian Water

British Airways World Offers: 'Where is everybody?'
Sarah Ryder
  M&C Saatchi for British Airways

'Soft spreads and hard battles'
Anthony Tasgal
  Euro RSCG Wnek Gosper for the Butter Council

Fighting cancer with more than medicine
Fiona Bioletti
  J Walter Thompson for Cancer Relief Macmillan Fund

The co-operation of brand and product advertising
David Simoes-Brown
  BDDH for the Co-operative Bank

Hard times – Selling diamonds in a recession
Merry Baskin
  J Walter Thompson for De Beers

'Hello Hello': The story of a unique poster event (Kaliber)
Andrew Crosthwaite
  Euro RSCG Wnek Gosper for Guinness Brewing GB

Lil-lets: 'How the brand that whispered, prospered'
Deborah Mills and David Hall
  Rainey Kelly Campbell Roalfe for Smith & Nephew

'No use crying': How advertising prevented milk from getting spilt
Rachel Hatton
  BMP DDB for the National Dairy Council

National Savings – Off the backburner and into the heat of recession
Ev Jenkins
  McCann-Erickson for the Department for National Savings

How the hut hit back
Jeremy Thorpe-Woods
  Abbott Mead Vickers.BBDO for Pizza Hut UK

Creating a legal precedent
Diane Lurie
  The Morgan Partnership for Ross Harper

The dying days of a brand – How a new approach to advertising made a contribution to the Vauxhall Cavalier
Cressida Winch
  Lowe Howard-Spink for Vauxhall Motors

Advertising campaigns which benefited a business by maintaining or strengthening a brand over a longer period

GOLD (THE CHARLES CHANNON AWARD)

Barclaycard – Put it away Bough!
Paul Feldwick, Sarah Carter and Louise Cook
  BMP DDB for Barclaycard

SILVER

Love over gold: The story of Gold Blend
Colin Flint
  McCann-Erickson for Nestlé

Kraft Philadelphia: The Philadelphia Story
Bridget Angear and Nick Johnson
  J Walter Thompson for Kraft Jacobs Suchard

Stella Artois: Seven years in Provence
Jon Howard, Andy Palmer and George Bryant
  Lowe Howard-Spink for the Whitbread Beer Company

BRONZE

I Can't Believe It's Not Butter!: From extraordinary launch to long-term success
Jacqueline Feasey
  McCann-Erickson for Van Den Bergh Foods

'Vive la Clio' – How image leadership created a long-term success story
Michael Ellyatt
  Publicis for Renault UK

CERTIFICATES OF COMMENDATION

Potatoes: Britain's buried treasure
David Simoes-Brown
   BDDH for the Potato Marketing Board

Switch – How advertising helped to change the nation's spending behaviour
John Atmore
   Collett Dickenson Pearce for Switch Card Services

Special prizes

INTEGRATION WITH OTHER MARKETING COMMUNICATION TOOLS

Advertising that builds strong customer relationships? That'll be the Daewoo
Rachel Walker and Chris Forrest
   Duckworth Finn Grubb Waters for Daewoo Cars Ltd

DIRECT RESPONSE

Ignore it. It'll go away
Christopher Zelley-Beattie
   Bartle Bogle Hegarty for BBC Education

Frizzell Insurance: When the customer is not always right
Diana Redhouse and Les Binet
   BMP DDB for Frizzell Financial Services

EUROPEAN

Hard times – Selling diamonds in a recession
Merry Baskin
   J Walter Thompson for De Beers

LIMITED ADVERTISING/RESEARCH FUNDS

Creating a legal precedent
Diane Lurie
   The Morgan Partnership for Ross Harper

BEST USE OF MEDIA PLANNING

Not awarded

THE MARKETING AWARD FOR INNOVATION

'No more Mr Nice Guy'
Jon Leach and Roger McKerr
   HHCL and Partners for the Automobile Association

Section One

New brands or advertisers

1

Orange

How two years of advertising created twelve years of value

INTRODUCTION

This paper necessarily deals with advertising's contribution to Orange's success over its first two years (April 1994–March 1996). Using a range of data, it will demonstrate how advertising achieved a performance far in excess of payback.

This paper also seeks to view Orange's advertising in a broader context, demonstrating how the campaign helped create long-term brand value and secure the destiny of a brand which, at launch, few people thought would survive.

Uniquely among IPA case studies, we are in a position to put an authenticated value on the future worth of advertising. We can do this because, whilst Orange's actual future is yet to happen, its financial future was determined in May 1996. This was when the company was successfully floated on the Stock Exchange using Discounted Cash Flow methodology, a type of valuation which bases the worth of a company on projected sales and revenues (to the year 2005 in the case of Orange). It is on these projections that we will base our calculation of advertising's long-term contribution.

This paper will, therefore, conclude with two separate valuations: one relating to the first two years of advertising (April 1994–March 1996), and one relating to the next ten. It is worth noting that this second valuation is no less realistic for being derived from a projection. Orange achieved an actual rather than theoretical value of £2.45 billion on the strength of its future sales – a future in which advertising played a material role (see Figure 1).

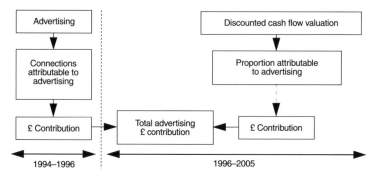

Figure 1: *Advertising's 12-year contribution*

3

MARKET CONTEXT AT LAUNCH

In the light of Orange's success, it is now difficult to appreciate fully the immense problems which the brand faced when it was launched in April 1994.

Conditions could hardly have been more hostile. Cellnet and Vodafone had ten years of market dominance behind them, with full national coverage and millions of captive subscribers on their analogue networks. Both had also successfully developed low-user tariffs as part of a pre-emptive strategy to block entry into the consumer market and had assiduously strengthened their dominance of the business market through the development of their digital (GSM) networks.

TABLE 1: NETWORK COVERAGE AT TIME OF
ORANGE LAUNCH (APRIL 1994)

Orange	c 50%
Cellnet Analogue	98%
Cellnet GSM	c 95%
Vodafone Analogue	98%
Vodafone GSM	c 95%
One-2-One	c 30%

Source: Network Coverage Maps

The old duopoly, therefore, represented a hugely formidable opponent, more than capable of squashing a fledgeling network at birth. Which is why, six months before Orange's launch, Mercury One-2-One decided to adopt an entirely different approach. With an infant network of approximately 30% coverage, it recognised the impossibility of competing with Cellnet and Vodafone directly and, instead, developed the famous free-call strategy alongside a regionalised approach to coverage build. The strategy was to prove immensely successful in gaining connections.[1]

Orange, which launched with approximately 50% coverage was, therefore, faced with a daunting challenge. From the old and the new it had seen most of its competitive opportunities closed off, it was late, had an eccentric name and came from Hutchison, the warren which had bred the unlucky Rabbit. Commentators queued up to write it off:

'Hutchison Whampoa's billionaire owner Li Ka-Shing is reported to be under pressure to quit the UK telecommunications business...'

The Times, 5 April 1994

'It would be a brave man who would bet on the Hong Kong company seeing to the end of the decade.'

Investor's Chronicle, June 1994

---

1. Between September 1993 and March 1994, One-2-One gained 64,000 subscribers. This is more than twice the number achieved by Orange in its first six months.

'Andrew Harrington, telecommunications analyst at Salomon Brothers is adamant that Orange will not be a success in Britain.'

South China Morning Post, 16 October 1994

GETTING THE STRATEGY RIGHT

One consideration dominated the launch and strategic development process. How could Orange overcome, or minimise, the huge disadvantage of being last? BSB's experience of being last in satellite was hardly a reassuring precedent.

But all was not doom and gloom. Orange did have a number of important competitive features. Most notably, it offered per-second billing and inclusive minutes which, for most users, would save 20 to 40% per month versus Cellnet and Vodafone. Given this cost advantage, a value for money/'we're cheaper' strategy was the obvious route. For a variety of reasons it would also have been a disastrous one.

Firstly, Orange was not cheapest (One-2-One was). Even if it had been, a lower cost of usage argument would have pitched Orange directly against one of Cellnet and Vodafone's greatest strengths, namely exceptionally low entry costs. Whereas most of Vodafone or Cellnet's analogue handsets fell into the £49.99–£99.99 price range, Orange's cheapest handset at launch was £249.99.

Above all, however, a cost-led strategy would have been disastrous because it would have squandered the one advantage of being last: the opportunity to avoid the mistake the others had made.

THE CATEGORY MISTAKE AND ORANGE'S OPPORTUNITY

This 'mistake' was to allow what should have been a highly popular and exciting category to become both commoditised and compromised. With the partial exception of One-2-One, the mobile phone category was more or less devoid of branding and brand values. Cellnet and Vodafone's duopoly mentality had resulted in a mobile phone 'ghetto', characterised by confusion, distrust and a tangle of complicated tariffs, deals and price claims.

The last thing Orange should do was emphasise its similarities by focusing on cost. Instead, its opportunity was to escape the ghetto by being the first to develop a fully rounded brand identity. This brand identity, moreover, could be built on the market high ground which had been left so conspicuously unoccupied by the competition. Once the high ground was secure, Orange would then be able to deliver its price-based message from a position of brand strength rather than commodity weakness.

HIGH GROUND POSITIONING RESEARCH

In order to identify precisely what Orange's high ground positioning should entail, an extensive programme of qualitative research was undertaken. This research consistently identified that the benefits of mobile telephony had immense appeal, it was the day-to-day reality that turned people off.

The task, therefore, was to find an expression of these benefits that would allow Orange to position itself well above the limitations of the existing market. Through an iterative process of concept development, the following expression was arrived at and was to become the Orange brand vision:

> 'There will come a time when all people will have their own personal number that goes with them wherever they are so that there are no barriers to communication. A wirefree future in which you call people, not places, and where everyone will benefit from the advances of technology.'

BEING FIRST RATHER THAN LAST

The two key words in Orange's brand vision are 'wirefree' and 'future', since they enabled Orange to distance itself entirely from the vocabulary and associations of the existing market. Indeed, psychologically, they allowed Orange to create a new category away from the two existing types of telephony.

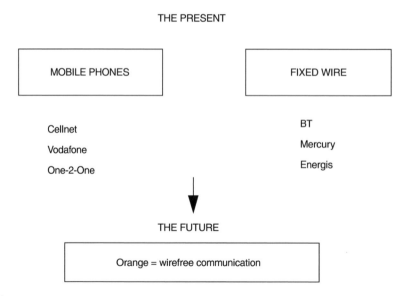

Figure 2

By defining its own category, Orange could be first rather than last: the first mobile phone company to benefit from the advantage of a fully rounded brand identity. The task for advertising was to bring the new category and the new brand to life. The advertising proposition read, simply, as follows:

'The future is wirefree and it's Orange.'

Orange's desired personality was to be forward-thinking, refreshing and dynamic. As we shall see from the tracking results, this was precisely the personality that advertising helped it to achieve.

There was only one executional guideline: Orange's advertising must never feature anything remotely resembling a mobile phone.

MEDIA STRATEGY

Given the doubts which surrounded Orange at launch, the most important task for media was to imbue the brand with as much confidence as possible.

This core strategic requirement was translated into a highly assumptive multimedia schedule. Rather than dominate one medium, Orange would dominate them all with posters heralding each new campaign theme, TV communicating core brand benefits and press providing detailed messages in the information-led environment of newspapers. This integrated approach has been rolled out across five phases of activity:

TABLE 2: MAJOR PHASES OF ACTIVITY

Phase 1	Launch	April–July 1994
Phase 2	Numbers	October 1994–February 1995
Phase 3	Capacity	May–October 1995
Phase 4	Savings	October–December 1995
Phase 5	Coverage	January–March 1996

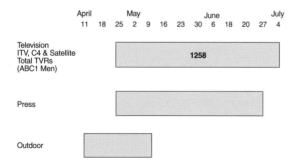

Figure 3: *Phase 1 media plan*

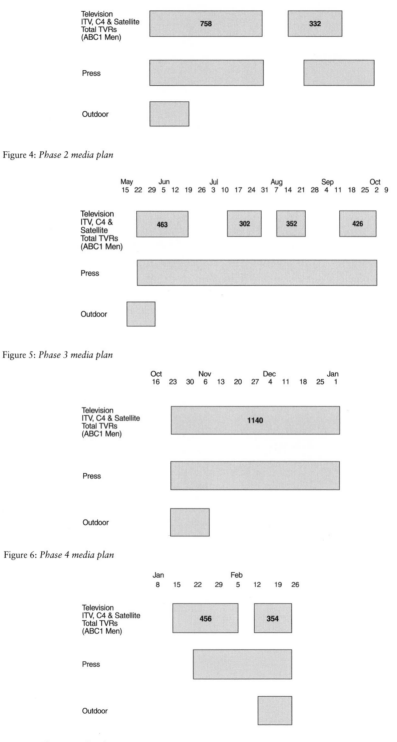

Figure 4: *Phase 2 media plan*

Figure 5: *Phase 3 media plan*

Figure 6: *Phase 4 media plan*

Figure 7: *Phase 5 media plan*

PHASE 1 ADS

PHASE 2 ADS

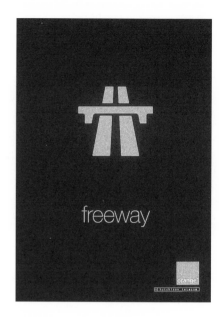

PHASE 3 ADS

PHASE 4 ADS

The efficiency of the chosen media solution is emphatically demonstrated by Millward Brown's tracking survey which shows how advertising helped Orange achieve a position of enviable pre-eminence in the public consciousness, so much so, that, after only two years, Orange enjoyed greater awareness than either Cellnet or Vodafone.

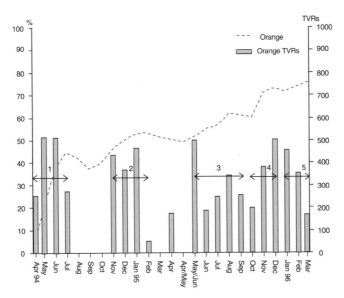

Figure 8: *Spontaneous awareness of mobile phone companies*
Source: Millward Brown

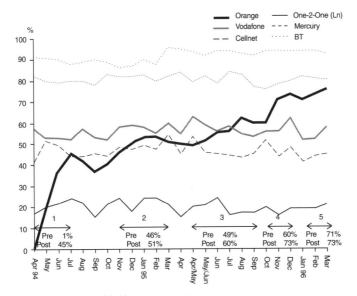

Figure 9: *Spontaneous awareness of mobile phone companies**
Source: Millward Brown
* Awareness is tracked in Orange coverage areas, except for One-2-One which is London only.

More remarkably still, the combined impact of Orange's multimedia strategy resulted in higher overall advertising awareness than BT, whose vast £90 million advertising budget dwarfed that of Orange (see Figures 10 and 11).

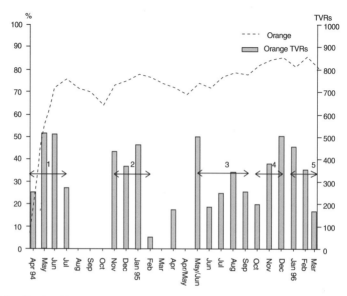

Figure 10: *Total media advertising awareness*
Source: Millward Brown

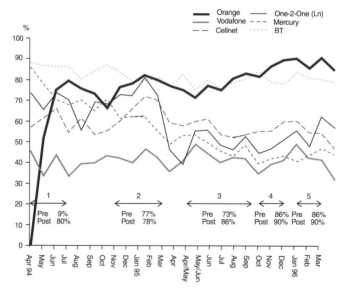

Figure 11: *Total media advertising awareness*
Source: Millward Brown

These remarkable levels of awareness enabled the campaign to achieve the rare distinction of becoming a public property. From the *Sun* to the Telegraph it became a part of journalistic currency, further enhancing the value of the advertising investment.

It is a popular misconception that Orange achieved this remarkable prominence by vastly outspending its competitors. In fact, Orange's budget was not dramatically greater than either Cellnet or One-2-One's, once their pre-emptive activity in the six months prior to Orange's launch is taken into account, and One-2-One's massive spend in London is compared on a like-to-like basis with Orange's.

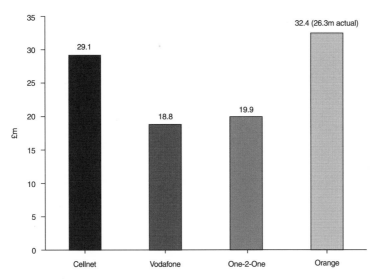

Figure 12: *Total advertising expenditure – September 1993 to March 1996 (£m)*
Source: Register/MEAL (Orange's actual spend was £26.3 million.)

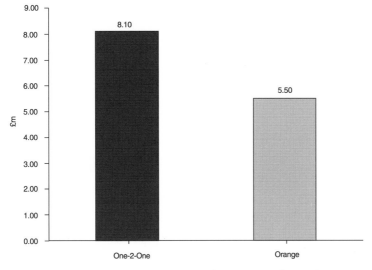

Figure 13: *Orange and One-2-One TV spend in London – September 1993 to March 1996 (£m)*
Source: Register/MEAL

The extraordinary impact of Orange's advertising, therefore, was not achieved by sheer weight of activity but by the quality of the media and creative solution. This is borne out by Millward Brown's Awareness Index, where Orange consistently outperforms all competitors:

TABLE 3: AWARENESS INDEX

| | April–March 1996 | |
	Min	Max
Orange	7.0	16.0
Cellnet	3.0	8.0
Vodafone	1.0	2.0
One-2-One	3.0	6.0

Source: Millward Brown

So, Orange's advertising was more impactful and more productive than any other advertiser in the category. But did it get its messages across?

The next section shows how saliency was combined with highly successful communication.

TRACKING RESULTS: THE COMMUNICATION AGENDA

Orange's communication agenda can be divided into three broad categories:

1. key image dimensions;

2. network benefits and credentials;

3. value for money credentials.

Whilst all activity reflected a consistent set of values, the messages varied depending on time of year, competitive context and stage of brand development. The most important distinction was between fourth-quarter activity and rest of year, the latter focusing on thematic network benefits, the former focusing more firmly on value-for-money messages during the key Christmas sales period. This approach can be presented schematically as follows:

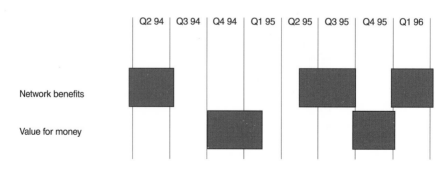

Figure 14: *Orange communication schematic*

Earlier, we highlighted how essential it was for Orange to be more than a cost-based brand. Through its commitment to sustained brand-building activity before and after its value campaigns, Orange successfully elevated itself above the market and, as we will demonstrate, substantially enhanced the effectiveness of its Christmas messages.

We will now examine advertising's effect on the three broad categories outlined above.

KEY IMAGE DIMENSIONS

Three key image dimensions have been tracked since launch:

1. sets the standard for the future;

2. leads the way in new technology;

3. is dynamic.

All three proved highly responsive to advertising. This is illustrated by Figure 15 which shows how their average score improved during each phase of activity.

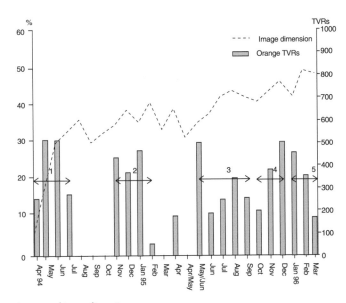

Figure 15: *Orange's averaged image dimensions*
Source: Millward Brown

The net result of this very positive performance was that Orange entirely transcended the competition (Figure 16).

Advertising clearly helped secure a very potent brand image, giving Orange an immense competitive advantage.

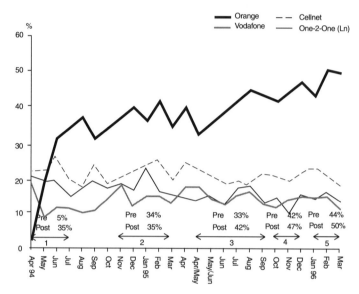

Figure 16: *Averaged image dimensions*
Source: Millward Brown

VALUE-FOR-MONEY CREDENTIALS

The three key value dimensions tracked by Millward Brown are as follows:

1. good value for money;

2. offer fair and reasonable prices;

3. lower running costs.

Figure 17 demonstrates that, on these measures as well, advertising proved to be exceptionally effective.

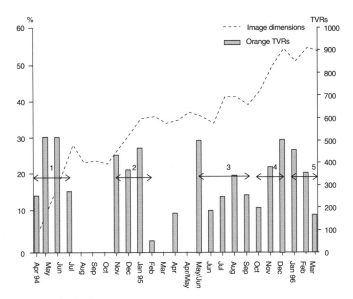

Figure 17: *Orange's averaged value dimensions*
Source: Millward Brown

It is important to note how, having plateaued at 25%, it is the two Christmas bursts (2 and 4) which had the greatest impact on value perceptions. This was precisely the strategic intention as set out in the Orange communication schematic (Figure 14). We shall see later how the success of the fourth-quarter phasing was also reflected in sales results. It is further endorsed by the following quote:

> 'Orange has been particularly successful in developing strong associations with value for money. This has been achieved not only because of the success of the fourth-quarter campaigns in communicating this message, but also because the core values established from previous advertising have provided a solid framework around which the price message has been able to crystallise.'

Richard Davies
Director, Millward Brown

The impact of advertising is accentuated even further when we look at the competitive picture, with Orange achieving an emphatic lead over Cellnet and Vodafone. Most impressively of all, Orange eventually succeeded in outstripping One-2-One, despite its free calls and a sample limited to its London heartland (Figure 18).

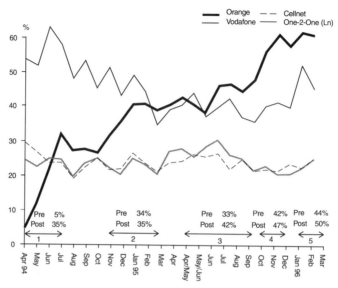

Figure 18: *Averaged value dimensions*
Source: Millward Brown

NETWORK BENEFITS AND CREDENTIALS

Alongside key image and value dimensions, it was important to communicate key technological and service benefits. This was done with great effectiveness, as illustrated in Table 4.

For the sake of simplicity we have taken awareness levels pre and post the main burst of activity for each message.

TABLE 4: AWARENESS LEVELS

	Pre activity %	Post activity %	Change %
Per-second billing	34 (Oct 1994)	63 (Feb 1995)	+85
Caller ID	18 (Jun 1995)	31 (Aug 1995)	+72
Inclusive minutes	17 (Oct 1994)	35 (Feb 1995)	+106
24hr replacement	23 (Jul 1995)	34 (Sep 1995)	+48
Capacity	14 (Apr 1995)	24 (Jul 1995)	+71
Wide coverage	29 (Jan 1996)	45 (Mar 1996)	+55

Source: Millward Brown

ADVERTISING AND SALES: THE PRIMA FACIE CASE

The tracking data provides compelling evidence that advertising played an instrumental role in shaping perceptions of Orange. Given that these perceptions were so favourable and so competitive, common sense would suggest that advertising had a significant effect on sales.

This impression is further strengthened by Orange's purchase intention scores, which ended significantly higher after each burst of advertising, giving Orange a clear lead over its competitors (see Figures 19 and 20).

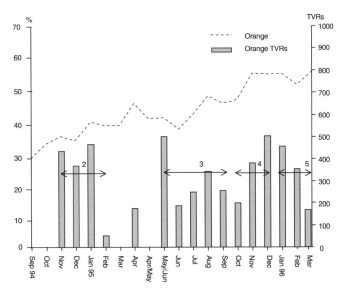

Figure 19: *Would seriously consider if buying a mobile phone**
Source: Millward Brown
* Purchase intention has only been tracked since September 1995.

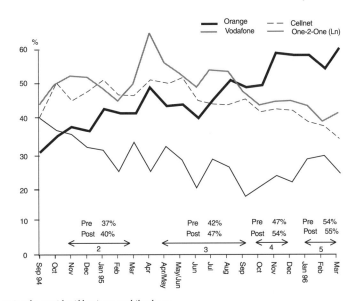

Figure 20: *Would seriously consider if buying a mobile phone*
Source: Millward Brown

These scores are reinforced by the fact that they reflect the market reality, with Orange outselling all its digital competitors.

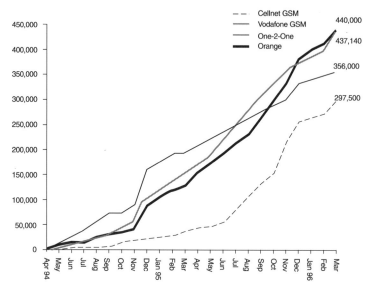

Figure 21: *Digital network connections since Orange launch*
Source: Fintech data

Taken as a whole, therefore, the tracking data makes a very strong prima facie case for a direct link between advertising and sales, showing how the campaign helped make Orange pre-eminent in terms of image, awareness, network benefits and value-for-money credentials, all of which has resulted in greater propensity to purchase.

We would now like to consider three final strands of evidence which make the case even more irrefutable:

1. expert opinion;

2. qualitative research;

3. econometric modelling.

EXPERT OPINION

One of the pleasures of working on Orange was to watch the gradual conversion of the Doubting Thomases. Bit by bit, as Orange's success became more and more inescapable, scepticism gave way to admiration, even from direct competitors:

'Orange's advertising has made its mark. It has served Hutchison well by helping to establish a distinctive brand personality.'

> Sholto Douglas-Home, BT,
> *Marketing Week*, 6 October 1995

'One of the great strengths of the Orange campaign has been its consistency.'

> William Ostrom, Cellnet,
> *Marketing Week*, 1 March 1996

More importantly, Orange's advertising success was enthusiastically endorsed by the trade. This was to represent a very important secondary contribution of advertising:

'The image and advertising of Orange is very, very powerful and it is part of what helped build the brand. It's a really aspirational product and service.'

> Charles Dunstone, MD, Carphone Warehouse,
> *Money Programme*, 10 December 1995

The national media also joined the chorus of praise:

'Orange is a relative newcomer, but it's an advertising triumph as though it's the only digital network.'

> *BBC1 6 O'Clock News*, 12 March 1996

'Orange's ad campaign has paid off.'

> *Independent on Sunday*, 28 January 1996

'Orange, unlike Vodafone and Cellnet, has established a strong brand image with its "the future's bright" catchphrase.'

> *The Times*, 29 February 1996

'The rise of Orange has been the catalyst that has taken the mobile phone out of its yuppie ghetto.'

> *Independent*, 20 February 1996

This last quote shows how successfully Orange achieved its strategic goal of extricating itself from the mobile phone ghetto.

The net result was that, even before flotation, Orange was hailed as an unqualified success. The turnaround had been remarkable:

'It is one of the most dramatic transformations in modern British corporate history. One moment Orange appeared to be an eccentrically marketed also-ran. The next, it was revealed as a big-time winner racing towards a flotation value of about £2 billion.'

> *Sunday Times, 3 May 1995*

QUALITATIVE RESEARCH

Qualitative research played an instrumental role in the Orange success story. On this basis, it is perhaps unsurprising that the brand and its advertising consistently met with very favourable responses in research groups.

Space prevents us from setting out a huge list of eulogistic quotes. One will be sufficient to give a flavour of the campaign's overall success in communicating a highly distinctive positioning:

> 'They seem confident, with a clear vision of the future. It's as if they saw what was wrong with the market and then came up with the solution.'

Respondent, 40–55 Male
Southgate, December 1995

ECONOMETRICS: THE CONSTANTS

In conjunction with the Orange market planning department, Millward Brown has constructed an econometric sales model designed to isolate all key variables and thus attribute a statistical value to advertising.

Before considering the variables it is important to define the constants, specifically:

— tariffs;

— technology;

— promotions.

TARIFFS

There were no significant tariff changes from Cellnet, Vodafone or Orange during the period in question. One-2-One did modify its free call strategy in autumn 1995, but by this stage Orange was competing primarily with Cellnet and Vodafone as a national network.

TECHNOLOGY

Whilst all four digital networks shared the same basic technology, there were some significant differences in the applications and features offered, with Orange offering the most advanced overall specification. Again, however, this was a constant factor in the market.

PROMOTIONS

We have already alluded to the fact that the mobile phone market was very dependent on deals, promotions and special offers. It would be impossible to find a day, let alone a week, when promotions from Orange's competitors were not happening. Although we do not have access to the exact information, we know from previous employees of Cellnet and Vodafone, that each brand spent at least £1.5 million per month on promotions.

In order to offset this competitive activity, from 1995 onwards Orange also adopted a constant promotional strategy – with one important difference. Rather than attempt to close sales with money-off promotions, Orange used promotions as a way of persuading would-be customers to subscribe to higher talk plans.

Promotions therefore were a constant which, in the case of Orange, were designed to affect sales value rather than sales volume.

ECONOMETRICS: THE VARIABLES

Beyond advertising, the main key market variables can be defined as follows:

1. Direct marketing and a DRTV pilot.

2. Sponsorship.

3. Below-the-line communications.

4. Organic market growth.

5. Handset costs.

6. Coverage growth.

7. Distribution growth.

8. Seasonality.

Each can be successfully accounted for or legitimately disregarded as not having a significant impact on sales.

DIRECT MARKETING

Orange's direct marketing investment was relatively small. There was one DRTV test, which did not prove significant enough to justify a second run. Mailing activity was similarly light, with only 310,000 mailings over two years. This is unlikely to have had a significant effect on sales.

SPONSORSHIP

Orange's main sponsorship commitment has been to cricket. In the summers of 1994 and 1995 this provided it with a substantial perimeter advertising presence. Among cricket viewers this is likely to have had some impact on saliency, but not before advertising had generated very high levels of awareness at launch.

BELOW-THE-LINE COMMUNICATIONS[2]

It is customary to view below-the-line activity as a variable whose beneficial effect should be discounted against advertising. This view is valid if the below-the-line activity works independently from advertising. In the case of most integrated campaigns, however, we believe there are three reasons why below-the-line effects should not be deemed advertising-deductible.

— First, they are not variable, they are invariable. Orange would never engage in non-integrated communication.

— Second, in many cases, the demands of retailers mean that a brand's below-the-line budget represents a sunk cost which can be spent well or badly. Successful integration means that the money is well spent. It would seem Draconian, therefore, to penalise advertising for what is essentially best practice in helping to make a non-discretionary budget work as hard as possible.

— Third, integrated campaigns tend to take their lead from advertising. Orange is no exception, with advertising setting the agenda for all through-the-line activity. To penalise advertising for the synergy it made possible would, again, appear unduly Draconian.

We are, essentially, making a global point about a changing communications market. Integrated below-the-line activity is increasingly becoming a part of best practice. In the case of those advertisers whose below-the-line budgets are largely non-discretionary, there seems little reason to discount the benefits of integration against advertising.

If, however, the orthodox view persists, then the only viable solution is to include Orange's below-the-line budget of £6 million in the overall campaign budget, taking the total cost from £26.3 million to £32.3 million. As we shall see later, this increased sum is still a mere fraction of the overall return generated by advertising.

---

2.   Definition: POS and collateral material in retailers and dealers.

REMAINING VARIABLES

The Orange Business Planning Model has been designed to account for the remaining key market variables listed earlier, and has done so successfully to a level of 98% explanation. Coverage, market and distribution growth are isolated within an overall Orange trend, whilst certain price reductions, like certain phases of advertising, can be seen to have an immediate impact on sales. Seasonality also emerges as a significant variable.

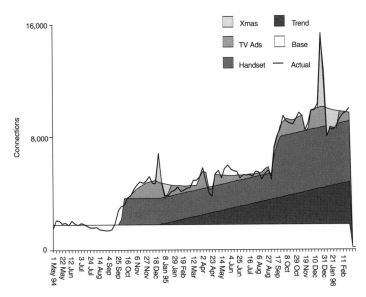

Figure 22: *Decomposition of sales variables*
Source: Millward Brown

RESULTS OF THE MODEL

Figure 23 overleaf highlights those phases of activity which the model identifies as being significant on a short-term basis. As can be seen, the two Christmas bursts had the most immediate impact. This underlines the strategic success of concentrating on value-for-money messages during the peak sales period.

The total number of connections attributable to the short-term effects of advertising is calculated by the Millward Brown model to be 61,000.

Allowing for cost of acquisition, and assuming network average revenue of £37 per month, the net value of these additional 61,000 connections amounts to £128 million. This is more than four times in excess of payback.

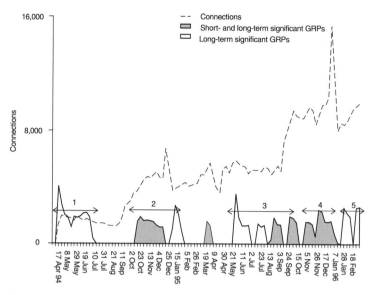

Figure 23: *Weekly connections versus Orange GRPs*
Source: Millward Brown

This figure, however, represents the minimum of advertising's contribution, since it relates simply to short-term effects. Millward Brown has constructed dozens of models for a wide range of clients and, as it explains here, generally finds that advertising's contribution is only realised over the long term:

> 'Our experience has shown, when measuring advertising effects, that it is often only when considering the long-term effects that advertising can be seen to pay for itself. To have an advertising effect in the short and long term is relatively unusual and obviously beneficial.'

Millward Brown
Presentation document, 4 April 1996

In assessing the overall contribution of advertising, therefore, it is clear that the short-term figure of £128 million needs to be supplemented with a corresponding value for advertising's long-term effects. Unfortunately, although Millward Brown is confident of advertising's long-term contribution, it cannot be precisely calculated because it is included in the broader underlying trend from which it cannot, as yet, be isolated:

> 'In the Orange model we can consider the trend to show the long-term impact of advertising, but also the contribution of other factors such as increased coverage.'

Millward Brown
Presentation document, 4 April 1996

We are unable, therefore, to give an absolute figure for advertising's total contribution between April 1994 and March 1996. We know, however, that the contribution will be substantially in excess of the £128 million identified by Millward Brown as advertising's purely short-term effect.

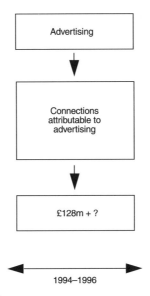

Figure 24: *Advertising's two-year contribution*

ADVERTISING'S LONGER AND BROADER CONTRIBUTION

As stated at the beginning of this paper, it is important to recognise advertising's broader contribution to a multi-billion-pound success story, and not just its narrower role in generating sales over a two-year span. The task of attributing a value to this broader contribution is considerably facilitated by the Discounted Cash Flow process which resulted in Orange's £2.45 billion flotation.

At least £1.45 billion of this sum was based on ten-year projections of revenue.[3] These projections were extrapolated from the performance of Orange over its first two years, a performance which was substantially enhanced by the 61,000 connections generated by advertising (or 14% of Orange's overall customer base).

The simplest and most logical way of deriving a formal value for advertising's broader contribution is to assume that advertising's share of the base should also represent its share of the projections. This would give it a 14% share of £1.45 billion, equating to a figure of £203 million.

Given that advertising's 14% share of the base is derived from a conservative estimate which excludes long-term effects, the figure of £203 million can be viewed as robust and, if anything, understated.

---

3. Orange was a loss-making company and had no more than £1 billion in fixed assets; its value beyond £1 billion, therefore, was derived entirely from projections of future revenues.

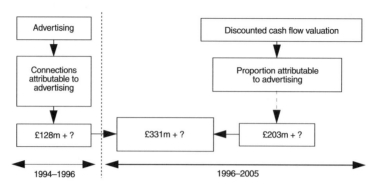

Figure 25: *Advertising's 12-year contribution*

CONCLUSION

The Future's Bright, The Future's Orange

In one sense this paper has been a conventional assessment of an advertising success story. Strategic and executional creativity have been combined with the rigorous use of data to produce a robust all-round case. But it is to be hoped that this paper has also moved one step beyond the conventional.

The circumstances of Orange's flotation have enabled us to quantify the long-term contribution of advertising in a quite unique way. We hope that this unprecedented aspect of the Orange paper will, to some small degree, prove a valuable piece of ammunition in the age-old debate regarding the long-term value of advertising.

By contracting twelve years into two, we have demonstrated not only that advertising is a sound investment, but that it can be one of the most productive investments a company can make. We have shown how a spend of £26.3 million generated a return well in excess of £300 million, building enduring brand values and brand assets.

At a time when the advertising industry is somewhat embattled, we hope that this case study is a celebration of one of advertising's greatest strengths: its ability to produce a disproportionate return on investment by building profoundly advantageous competitive differentials.

2

Advertising That Builds Strong Customer Relationships?

That'll be the Daewoo

INTRODUCTION

This is the story of how a car company with seemingly inauspicious prospects became the most successful marque launch since records began.

When Daewoo arrived in the UK, it had no predetermined marketing strategy, but it did have Korean management, which encouraged innovation and was willing to think beyond the boundaries of traditional car marketing.

Daewoo broke the widely accepted rules of car marketing to launch without dealerships and with atypical car advertising. It has been spectacularly successful because it obeys the most important marketing rule of all: the identification and satisfaction of unmet needs in its market. In this case those unmet needs were for hassle-free car buying and ownership.

Daewoo's extraordinary success has already attracted much praise, being voted the Marketing Society's 1995 Durables Brand of the Year, and being *Campaign*'s 1995 Advertiser of the Year.

In this paper we will show that the advertising agency made a defining contribution to the whole Daewoo offering, and developed a campaign whose effectiveness was crucial to Daewoo's rapid success.

IN THE BEGINNING

In July 1994, Daewoo Cars UK consisted of just a managing director, a deputy managing director and a marketing director, who had been in place for three weeks.

Every new car company has to overcome the problems of lack of awareness and risk aversion which are attached to such an expensive and important purchase.

But Daewoo's UK launch had its own additional problems. It was the fourth Korean entry into an already oversupplied market; its models were unexceptional, being based on 1980s Vauxhalls, and Daewoo had been set an extraordinarily ambitious sales target of 1% market share within three years.

Three previous Far Eastern entrants[1] provide benchmarks for this target:

— Hyundai had achieved 0.64% after 12 years;

— Proton had achieved 0.65% after 5 years;

— Kia had achieved 0.21% after 3 years;

— Daewoo's target was 1% after 3 years.

Source: SMMT, 12 months to December 1994

DAEWOO NEEDED A BRILLIANT MARKET ENTRY STRATEGY TO MEET ITS TARGET

Daewoo decided to involve advertising agencies, and its pitch brief recognised the value of a strong brand in becoming a mainstream volume player as soon as possible. It highlighted Daewoo's recent acquisition of European design facilities, which demonstrated the corporation's commitment to Europe and willingness to invest, and it suggested a positioning of 'The European Cars from Korea'.

DFGW'S PROPOSAL: THE UNMET NEED

Extremely challenging sales targets call for radical solutions. Our investigation indicated that there were unmet needs of a fundamental kind in the marketplace which represented a bigger brand opportunity.

It is car owners' collective experience that the process of buying and owning a private car is far from ideal. While drivers of company cars are relatively sheltered, almost all the buyers of private cars we spoke to in qualitative research had a horror story.

What people get:

— The car salesman who, true to stereotype, initiates a confrontational purchase experience.

— Hidden costs, eg delivery charges, number plates.

— A focus on one-off sales transactions, not customer care, hence poor after-sales service.

---

1.   The three Korean entrants preceding Daewoo were Hyundai (1982), Kia (1991) and Ssangyong (March 1995). Ssangyong in fact launched one month before Daewoo.

— Advertising that typically focuses on car performance and features fantasy portrayals of the driving experience.

A significant proportion of British car buyers are not car nuts. Millward Brown finds that 37% of car buyers regard their car primarily as a way of getting from A to B. They are more concerned with the day-to-day practicalities of car ownership than with car performance and engineering.

What people want:

— Hassle-free car purchase and ownership.

— No hidden costs.

— In short, a trusting relationship with car companies, not just a sale.

We therefore identified a huge opportunity for Daewoo to address these needs and become the most customer-focused and friendly car company in the UK, and hence set a new agenda.

We believed the Daewoo brand had the potential to fill this gap because:

— Being a new entrant meant no baggage of disgruntled customers.

— It is from the Far East, which is acknowledged to be leading most innovations in the car market.

— Although hitherto little known in the UK, it is one of the biggest corporations in the world, bigger than Coca-Cola and P&G, and this could provide reassurance.

ACTIONS SPEAK LOUDER THAN WORDS

Our qualitative research demonstrated the extent of cynicism that would greet any car manufacturer's assertion of customer focus. People feel they have been promised this before and the manufacturers and dealers have not delivered, so they have a 'won't get fooled again' attitude:

'They're all mouth and no trousers.'

Car buyer
DFGW Qualitative, July 1994

It was essential that Daewoo actually deliver its promises if it was to be, and be believed to be, customer focused. Daewoo would need to approach car marketing from a different point of view, engineering the company around a wider set of customer needs than all other car companies, which tend to concentrate on customers' product design needs. Essentially, Daewoo would need to sell car ownership as a *service* rather than cars as products.

DAEWOO'S RESPONSE TO OUR PROPOSAL: A BIG STEP

As it turned out, it was a meeting of minds. Daewoo's response to the agency's recommended brand positioning, was to consider *dispensing with dealers altogether*. The idea of selling cars direct was not new. But, in this instance, the agency had identified the huge opportunity available and the benefits to be gained from controlling all customer contact, so the client was all the more motivated to pursue this distribution route.

Direct distribution would create enormous short-term challenges, due to the slowness of distribution build. But Daewoo recognised it to be ideal for the long term, and had the confidence to break with the traditional ways of doing things. They were the right people with the right, supportive, innovative parent company to make it happen.

DAEWOO'S CLEAR BRAND VISION WAS A MOTIVATING FORCE

A torrent of innovations was developed in brainstorms for the total service that Daewoo would eventually provide.

Service Innovations Generated and Delivered

— Interactive in-store displays;

— Free collection and delivery for car servicing;

— Free café facilities;

— Free crèches;

— Free courtesy cars during servicing;

— Fixed, no-haggle prices;

— No delivery charges;

— Extended test drives;

— Location on retail parks;

— Three years full AA cover;

— Three years comprehensive warranty;

— Three years free servicing including labour and parts;

— Six-year anti-corrosion warranty;

— 30-day money back or exchange guarantee;

— All safety features as standard, eg airbags, ABS;

— Free customer helpline.

With the right positioning and the right offering, Daewoo was ready to meet the unmet needs.

So the advertising task was straightforward, right? Wrong. To meet the unmet needs in the market, the Daewoo brand needed to build long-term customer relationships.

However, we identified three potential barriers to customer relationships. Advertising was essential in overcoming every one of these barriers.

Barrier 1: Ignorance

'Daewho?'

Conventionally, it does not make sense to invest in advertising six months before a product goes on sale. It had never been done before in the car market.

But we had a daunting target of 1% in three years. We would also have far slower distribution build than usual for a marque launch, so people would need to be *more motivated* than usual to find a Daewoo outlet. Further to this, people are more receptive to brands they are familiar with. So, we decided to start building credibility early to help our sales momentum once the cars became available, and to help us to be taken seriously later on when we started saying new and different things.

Daewoo agreed with DFGW/CIA MediaNetwork that this brand building could begin before operational launch in order to accelerate early sales, which was testament to its commitment to the launch and willingness to listen to local advice.

Daewoo's corporate credentials were communicated in October 1994, six months before any cars arrived, through TV and press ads introducing the company's size and range of high-technology engineering products.

Barrier 2: Scepticism

'I bet they'll be just like all the others, they won't really understand what I want.'

Advertising had to convince a cynical audience that Daewoo really was going to be different. It wasn't just a gimmick.

CIA MediaNetwork proposed using advertising to act as consumer research to demonstrate Daewoo's willingness to listen. DFGW took this on to become the 'Daewoo Dialogue' campaign. The advertising invited people to tell Daewoo what they wanted from a car company. Those who responded were sent a questionnaire. This enabled us to:

— Seek ideas by asking people what they disliked about car buying and ownership and what they wanted from a new company.

— Be seen to ask – you cannot *tell* people you are customer focused – to be credible, you have to *show* them that you are.

— Build a database of highly predisposed responders to this campaign who would feel more 'ownership' of this new brand and hence facilitate more rapid sales growth when the cars went on sale.

Barrier 3: Apathy

'Why should I bother getting involved?'

We needed to overcome apathy at two distinct stages of the brand launch.

Encouraging People to Get Involved with 'Daewoo Dialogue'
We had developed an innovative role for advertising to act as consumer research, but developmental qualitative research on 'Dummy' (Dialogue campaign) told us that, although car owners liked to see manufacturers soliciting their views, most would not bother responding.

To boost response we needed to offer an incentive, but it had to be customer focused. Conventional incentives, eg 'win a car', would undermine the brand positioning by signalling that we were just like all the rest.

DFGW devised the customer-focused incentive of a chance to become one of 200 guinea pig Daewoo drivers who would be given a free car for a year's extended test drive. These 200 would also provide Daewoo with a valuable customer feedback panel.

Although the offer would sound like a huge commitment and be very motivating, Daewoo would get the cars back in a year, and hence only pay for a year's depreciation.

We alternated the incentivised ('Guinea Pigs') and unincentivised ('Dummy') executions in order to manage response.

The unanimity and scale of response (an astonishing 200,000 people), gave us our first indications of the potency of Daewoo's brand positioning.

Highlights from the 'Daewoo Dialogue' Campaign Response

The largest single survey of motorists' attitudes ever undertaken in Europe and (we believe) the world.

— 95% believe that car dealers should be more like other retailers and less like car salesmen.

— 84% say that the treatment they get from the dealer is *as important* as how they feel about the car.

— 78% notice that they are treated worse after buying a car than they were when they were making the original decision.

— 63% find showrooms intimidating and feel they always get subjected to hard-sell tactics.

Source: Arnold & Bolingbroke, February 1995

Encouraging Early Adopters

Qualitative research told us that many car buyers would be tempted to bide their time, and wait to see what became of Daewoo before making a purchase themselves.

A tactical promotion was therefore devised, to run in April 1995, promising the first 1,000 buyers a new, identical replacement N-reg Daewoo in August 1995 as a 'thank you' for taking the plunge.[2] This would accelerate early sales and create a significant volume of used Daewoos, enabling Daewoo to start building used-car brand values too.

After all this groundwork, the cars finally arrived in the country on 1 April 1995, and the first four showrooms opened. From the operational launch onwards we could set out the brand proposition.

OPERATIONAL LAUNCH

We Needed the Advertising Content to be Simple

Daewoo had developed a multitude of hooks. There was the potential trap of trying to put all Daewoo's hooks into one long commercial. But this would have been confusing.

In order to communicate a complex brand composed of many hooks,[3] in a simple way, we organised the hooks into four core brand values:

---

2. The 1,000 additional new car registrations in August generated by this promotion represent only a small proportion (5.6%) of Daewoo's total first-year registrations.

3. This use of a consistent brand perspective, manifested through many small hooks, has subsequently been labelled 'Velcro Marketing'. Ref: John Dalla Costa, IPA/Marketing Conference, June 1995 and *Admap*, January 1996.

TABLE 1: THE MOST CUSTOMER FOCUSED CAR COMPANY IN THE UK

Direct	Hassle free	Peace of Mind	Courtesy
Deal direct so can afford to be generous with no compromise to product	Interactive in-store terminals Free café facilities Free crèches Fixed, no-haggle prices Extended test drives Location on retail parks No delivery charges No commissioned salesmen	3 years comprehensive warranty 3 years full AA cover 3 years free servicing 6-year anti-corrosion warranty 30-day money back or exchange guarantee All safety features as standard: airbags, ABS etc	Free collection and delivery for service Free courtesy cars

Each of the four core brand values became the subject of a TV commercial. Two further commercials launched the customer hotline. Another communicated the tactical 'early adopters' promotion.

Press advertising used a consistent and distinctive layout that allows us to list Daewoo's many hooks without looking overcrowded.

In 1996, we continued to communicate core brand values in new executions. The agency also developed a second 'Dialogue' campaign, asking people to tell Daewoo about their maltreatment by the motor industry.

WE NEEDED A CREATIVE BREAKTHROUGH

People are not automatically attracted to a great offer in the car market, particularly when the value of the offer depends on your faith in the company's sincerity and longevity in the market. Even if the offer was for real, what is the point of three years free servicing if the company could go out of business within two years? Indeed, six of the marques launched since 1975 – Yugo, Sao, Lonsdale, ERA, Lincoln and Alpine – had been withdrawn.

Our early qualitative research identified the scepticism that would greet an unprecedented offer from an unheard of company:

'I smell a rat.'

Car buyer
DFGW Qualitative, February 1995

We needed a creative breakthrough – advertising which looked nothing like any other car campaign – to communicate that Daewoo really was different from all the rest, and to convey self-confidence, so that people would see the company as a long-term player.

Daewoo advertising avoids the typical car clichés and is deliberately down-to-earth and unpretentious. Our choice of subjects (eg highlighting the size of dealers' cut or hidden delivery charges), created a likeable, plucky, 'people's champion' brand which could evoke sympathy versus the big, bad motor industry establishment.

CONSUMER RESEARCH – 'DUMMY'

So, did you have any trouble from the salesman? Give you a proper test drive? What was the after-sales service like?
VO: Dummies can tell us a lot about safety... but they can't tell us much about service or test drives. Thank you. Thank you very little.

VO: We want to get our network right, so call and tell us how you want to be treated.

The biggest car company you've never heard of... would like to hear from you.

INCENTIVISED CONSUMER RESEARCH – 'GUINEA PIGS'

After 15 years of making cars all over the world, Daewoo are coming to Britain. And as part of the process, they're looking for guinea pigs to test drive 200 Daewoo cars for a year, free... Come on, you know that's not what I meant.

VO: If you'd like to be one of the 200 test drivers, call and tell us why we should pick you.
Daewoo. The biggest car company you've never heard of... would like to hear from you.

HASSLE FREE – 'DUSTCOVER'

Daewoo aren't just unveiling a new car, they're also unveiling a new way of buying a car... the whole family will be welcome

... there'll be interactive displays to help you choose... a café area to relax in..

and a kids' play area, where they play with their cars, not yours.
... But you won't find commissioned salesmen, just non-commissioned advisers. (Salesman) Hello, my name's... All this from a showroom? That'll be the Daewoo.

PEACE OF MIND – 'MECHANIC'

**EVERY NEW DAEWOO COMES
WITH A RATHER ATTRACTIVE EXTRA.**

Tempted? So you should be because all our models come with three years free servicing. No small print, no disclaimers, just free servicing including all labour and parts. (Apart from the tyres that is, they come with their own guarantee.) Unlike other car manufacturers this offer isn't for a limited period, nor is it an extra, hidden in the hiked up cost of the car. Our offer is the same right across the Daewoo range and is included in the fixed price you see on the cars in the showroom. Those prices range from £8,445 to £12,895 for the 3, 4 and 5 door Nexia and the Espero saloon. As if this isn't enough of an offer, we'll even telephone and arrange your car's service, then collect it from your doorstep leaving you with a courtesy car until yours is returned, if you wish. But what happens in between servicing? That's covered too. Every new Daewoo comes with a three year comprehensive warranty, three years Daewoo Total AA Cover and a six year anti-corrosion warranty. In fact, the only thing you do pay for is insurance and petrol. Take a look at the list and see for yourself. 1). 3 year/60,000 mile free servicing including parts and labour. 2). 3 year/60,000 mile comprehensive warranty. 3). 3 year Total AA Cover. 4). 6 year anti-corrosion warranty.

5). 30 day/ 1,000 mile money back or exchange guarantee. 6). Free courtesy car. 7). Pick up and return of your car for service if needed. Mainland UK only. 8). Fixed purchase price with no hidden extras. 9). Delivery included. 10). Number plates included. 11). 12 months road tax included. 12). Full tank of fuel. 13). Metallic paint included. 14). Electronic ABS. 15). Driver's airbag. 16). Side impact protection. 17). Power steering. 18). Engine immobiliser. 19). Security glass etching. 20). Mobile phone. 21). Free customer helpline. If you were glad to hear all this we'd be glad to tell you more, so please call us on 0800 666 222.

A car where the extras aren't extra? That'll be the Daewoo.

DAEWOO

TABLE 2: DAEWOO ADVERTISING ATTRIBUTES

Traditional car advertising	Daewoo advertising
Emphasis on car	Emphasis on company
Glossy	Down to earth
Uses epic music	Uses a voice-over
Fantasy driving sequences	Studio sets
Beautiful people	Robert ('bloke next door') Harley
Dominated by packshots of the car	Non-packshot visual with substantial copy

OPERATIONAL LAUNCH MEDIA STRATEGY

CIA MediaNetwork planned the media to help overcome the potential barriers we had identified.

— Ignorance. To continue to grow brand awareness rapidly, a large proportion of the spend went on TV.

— Scepticism. Consistency of presence would help to convince people that Daewoo is a long-term player in the market. TV was spread throughout the year and rolled out regionally as more showrooms opened. The press strategy was to own regular sites in key titles throughout the year.

— Apathy. We needed fast awareness build of four core values communicated by four different TV executions. The traditional route would have been to buy one space per break. But CIA MediaNetwork bought a pattern of five slots over two breaks, with two ads running in the first break, and three in the following break, for more rapid communication of our messages.

The effect of the break pattern was to have one promise building on the next, ending with an invitation to call.

Daewoo ad   Other ad

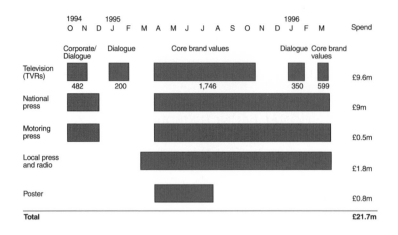

Figure 1: *Media plan*

To summarise, the three roles for advertising, against which it can be judged, were as follows:

Overcome Barrier 1, Ignorance: Build awareness and brand image
Overcome Barrier 2, Scepticism: Overcome distrust of Daewoo as a car company
Overcome Barrier 3, Apathy: Motivate to either visit or contact via advertising

The visit to a Daewoo showroom would then confirm the expectations set up by the advertising, giving the potential for a sale.

THE SALES, THE BRAND AND THE ADVERTISING ACHIEVEMENT

In this section we will demonstrate Daewoo's great brand strength and sales results beyond expectations.

We will show that *only advertising* could have accounted for the widespread and clear understanding of the brand. We will then show that *the strength of Daewoo's brand* was primarily responsible for the sales achievement. It follows that the advertising investment must be primarily responsible for the sales success.

The Sales Results were Unprecedented

Daewoo sold 18,005 cars in the first year, representing 0.92% market share, thus almost attaining the three-year target of 1% within just one year.

This performance places Daewoo up with, and indeed ahead of, many brands which have been established for far longer (Table 3).

TABLE 3: SHARE OF REGISTRATIONS APRIL 1995–MARCH 1996

	%
Honda	2.43
Volvo	1.87
Mercedes	1.71
Audi	1.44
Land Rover	1.30
Daewoo	0.92
Mazda	0.90
Suzuki	0.75
Hyundai	0.72
SEAT	0.67
Saab	0.63

(There are another 25 brands smaller than Saab in the market.)
Source: SMMT

This performance made Daewoo the most successful marque launch since 1975, which is the earliest year for which SMMT, the industry audit, holds data.

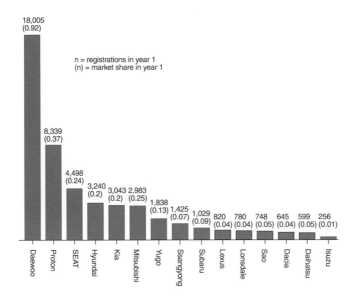

Figure 2: *The first 12-month performances by all new entrants since 1975*
NB: We have excluded the launches of ERA, Alpine, Suzuki and Lincoln, all of which sold fewer than 60 cars in their first year.
Source: SMMT

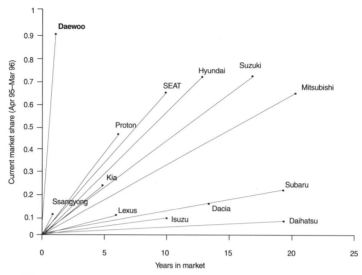

Figure 3: *Where all the new entrants since 1975 are now* NB: Yugo, Sao, ERA, Lincoln and Alpine have been withdrawn from the market.
Source: SMMT

None of the other new entrants have ever achieved Daewoo's first-year market share of 0.92%, despite their extra years in the market. What could have accounted for such rapid success? We believe that advertising was successful in overcoming all the potential barriers to a relationship that we had identified.

Barrier 1, Ignorance, has been Overcome

Brand awareness is near universal…

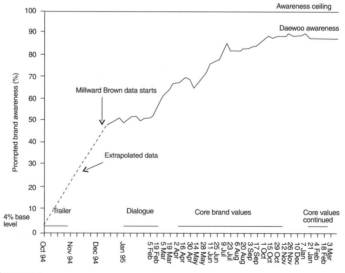

Figure 4: *Brand awareness*
Base: Adults 17+, drivers of new or used cars no older than four years, non-rejectors of Far Eastern marques, not expecting to pay over £13,000 for their next new or used car.
Source: Millward Brown, 8-weekly rolling data

People also feel that Daewoo makes cars that are becoming more popular. This is an important factor in people's likelihood to buy a car, since it makes the cars feel like a less risky purchase.

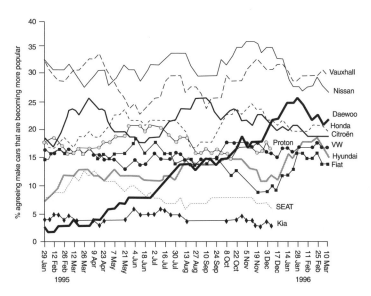

Figure 5: *Question: Which of these manufacturers do you think makes cars that are becoming more popular?*
Source: Millward Brown

Daewoo is seen as different from other car companies…

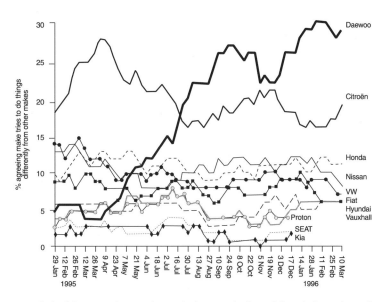

Figure 6: *Question: Which of these manufacturers do you think tries to do things differently from other makes?*
Source: Millward Brown

… it is seen as customer focused.

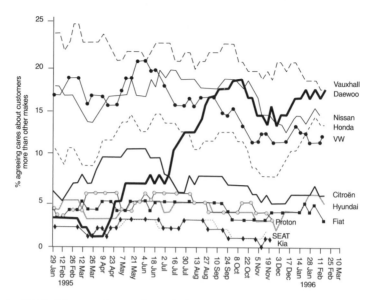

Figure 7: *Question: Which of these manufacturers do you think cares more about customers' needs than other makes?*
Source: Millward Brown
NB: The marques shown are all those selected for inclusion on the tracking study. They were chosen on the basis that they are relevant competition. Given limited space on the study only one of the top three marques, Vauxhall, was included. Proton, SEAT and Kia were dropped from the study in December 1995 because Daewoo had overtaken them on all important measures.

Barrier 2, Scepticism, has been Overcome

Remarkably for a car company, people feel that they can trust Daewoo:

'The impression I've had is that they're more honest than the others.'

'They're a good company...straight, with their cards on the table.'

'They won't rip you off.'

'They're not too glossy. I like that. They cut out all the bullshit.'

Non-Daewoo owners qualitative research
The Research Practice, March 1996

Barrier 3, Apathy, has been Overcome

Huge numbers of people have visited Daewoo showrooms. Daewoo estimates, on the basis of footfall counts, that 400,000 people visited its showrooms in the first 12 months.

We cannot assume that all visitors were in the market for a car, some may just have been coming in out of curiosity. However, to put the 400,000 visitors into perspective, they represent around 20% of the two million new car buyers every year.

Increasing numbers of people say they would consider Daewoo when they next come to buy a car.

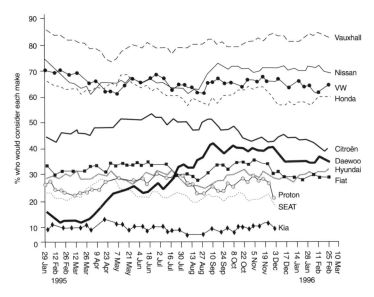

Figure 8: *All who would definitely, probably and might consider*
Source: Millward Brown

This places Daewoo's consideration ahead of several more established marques.

Advertising was Responsible for these Achievements

We believe that, from a zero base, such rapid and widespread understanding of the brand could only have been built by advertising. In this section we show several pieces of evidence to support this belief, and eliminate other potential causal factors.

1. The brand measures move in line with adspend (Figure 9).

2. The advertising cut-through (Figure 10).

3. The advertising is efficient in generating awareness: Millward Brown's Awareness Index measures the percentage increase in ad awareness that is achieved per 100 TVRs. Daewoo's Awareness Index of 12 is far higher than all other car brands on our study, so 100 TVRs against the Daewoo campaign works harder than 100 TVRs against any of the competitive campaigns we monitor.

TABLE 4: DAEWOO'S STRONG AWARENESS INDEX

	Awareness Index
Daewoo	12
Our car study mean	3

Source: Millward Brown

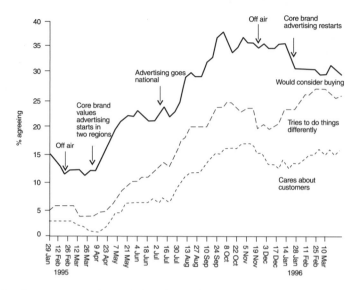

Figure 9: *The brand measures move in line with adspend*
Source: Millward Brown/Register MEAL

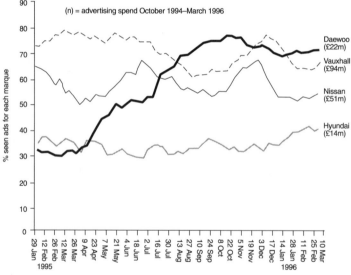

Figure 10: *The advertising cut-through*
NB: These are the only four marques for whom we have asked this question over the entire period
Source: Millward Brown, Register MEAL

4. The advertising was motivating: In a recent survey, 71% of Daewoo buyers questioned said that advertising had encouraged them to visit a Daewoo showroom in the first place.[4]

---

4.   Source: FDS, May 1996. Base: 120 Daewoo buyers, sampled randomly.

Also, 200,000 (1995) and 135,000 (1996) people responded to our 'Dialogue' campaign.

A further 289,000 have either phoned or written in response to other ads in the campaign,[5] giving a total of over 600,000 people responding.

People on this advertising-generated database are predisposed to the brand, as shown by the fact that 2,205, or 12%, of all Daewoo buyers featured on it prior to their purchase.

The evidence suggests that *advertising* was responsible for the brand effects shown. We can also show that *no other element* of the marketing mix could have been responsible.

PR

There has been much coverage of Daewoo in the national and motoring press. Inevitably, this will have had an impact on brand awareness and image. However, a large proportion of the PR has been about two subjects.

1. Praise for the advertising. For instance:

'The car may be ordinary but the campaign is extraordinary.'

Independent Weekend, 27 January 1996

'The Daewoo campaign was markedly different from traditional car ads.'

Guardian, 14 April 1996

2. Criticism of the cars. Daewoo's Espero and Nexia were based on 1980s Vauxhalls, and comment reflected this, for instance:

— *Autocar* (January 1996) rated both Daewoo's Nexia and Espero worst product in their sectors.

— *Top Gear* (March 1996) rated Daewoo Espero 12th out of the 12 family cars it reviewed.

Direct Marketing

Daewoo has sent mailings to a total of 600,000 people, approximately 300,000 of whom had made contact with Daewoo of their own accord first, by responding to advertising or visiting a showroom. The remaining 300,000 represent less than 1% of the adult population, and could alone not account for the strong tracking findings.

Neither PR nor direct marketing could have been responsible for Daewoo's brand image. Further, since the image is perfectly in line with our advertising

---

5. Source: Merit. Figure for 11-month period May 1995–March 1996, data unavailable for April 1995.

communication, we conclude that nothing other than advertising could have built such a strong brand in such a short period of time.

Could Factors other than Brand Strength have Accounted for
Daewoo's Rapid Sales Success ?

Were Daewoos irresistibly cheap?

Daewoo's prices are below average in the relevant market sectors by about 10%.[6] However, the cars were deliberately not priced at rock bottom. To do so would have firmly anchored the company as bargain basement, which limits share potential (eg Lada and Skoda) and is at odds with a value added proposition.

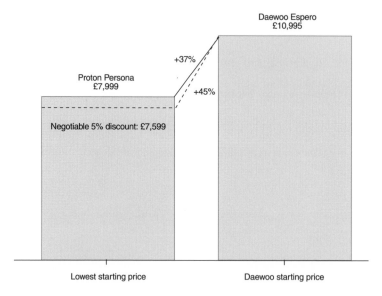

Figure 11: *Price difference between Daewoo Espero and cheapest model in upper medium sector*
Source: *Autocar*, March 1996

Daewoo's prices start at 37% above the lowest starting price in the upper-medium (Mondeo-sized) sector, and 92% above the lowest starting price in the lower-medium (Escort-sized) sector.

Daewoo's prices are fixed, whereas buyers of other marques can negotiate a discount of 5–10%. When this is taken into account, the difference between Daewoo's and competitors' starting prices is even greater.

---

6.   Daewoo estimate.

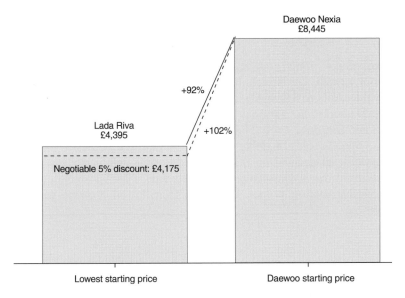

Figure 12: *Price difference between Daewoo Nexia and cheapest model in lower medium sector*
Source: *Autocar*, March 1996

*Daewoos are not the cheapest in the market, but was the
package with the cars irresistible?*

The Daewoo package is undoubtedly very generous, facilitated by having the
middleman (dealer) cut out.

Given this, would people have bought Daewoos in large numbers even without
any advertising? This is very unlikely for two reasons.

1. Advertising needed to tell people about the offer in the first place.

2. Advertising needed to convince people that Daewoo was a committed,
   differentiated long-term player for the offer *to be believed and have value.*

Daewoo's value for money stance has been communicated, but buyers give this
as only one of several brand-related reasons for visiting a Daewoo showroom.

TABLE 5: DAEWOO BUYERS' REASONS FOR VISITING A DAEWOO SHOWROOM
IN THE FIRST PLACE

	120 Daewoo buyers %
Because the cars are good value for money	88
The fact that they don't have salesmen pestering you	75
Because I thought I would like the cars	68
I thought they would be better at looking after their customers than other car companies	56

Source: FDS, May 1996

Did Daewoo have exceptional distribution?

Far from it.

Daewoo, unlike other new entrants, has had to build its own showroom network from scratch. On launch day, Daewoo had only four showrooms, and that number grew steadily to 18 by March 1996.

To give Daewoo the national presence it needed to service buyers' cars, it formed a joint initiative with Halfords. In contrast to fully equipped Daewoo showrooms, there is only a desk, two staff, and three courtesy cars to manage Daewoo servicing at each of the 136 Halfords stores involved. This began in July 1995, a quarter of the way into Daewoo's first year.

With 154 distribution points, Daewoo's distribution is some way below the industry average.

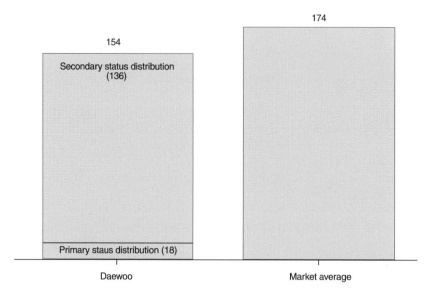

Figure 13: *Daewoo distribution*
NB: Given the nature of the Daewoo presence in Halfords, we are describing Daewoo's showroom distribution as primary-status distribution, and Halfords as secondary-status distribution.
Source: *Autocar*, March 1996

We have shown beyond reasonable doubt that only advertising could have accounted for the brand strength. We have also shown that only brand strength could have accounted for Daewoo's rapid success. We conclude, therefore, that advertising performed the dominant role in Daewoo's exceptional sales achievement.

QUANTIFYING ADVERTISING'S CONTRIBUTION

Car manufacturers entering a new market do not expect to generate profits in their first year, particularly if they are building their own distribution from scratch.

So, instead of the usual question for advertising effectiveness – what *extra* profit did the advertising produce – more relevant questions are:

— Did the advertising help the brand to exceed its targets?

— Did the advertising generate sufficient revenue to contribute to operational (before capital costs) profit?

The answer to both is a resounding yes.

Actual vs Planned Sales

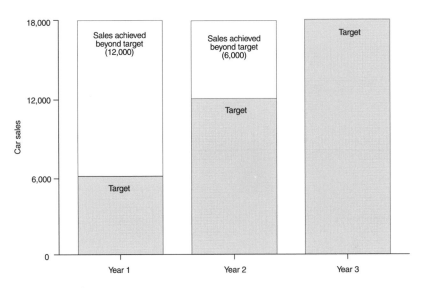

Figure 14: *Daewoo exceeds target in year 1*
Assumptions: Target was for steady growth across the three-year period. Conservatively assume Daewoo's current annual volume remains constant between years one and three, instead of growing from first year onwards.
Source: *Autocar*, March 1996

Daewoo exceeded its target, to reach almost 1% in one year instead of three. The additional volume, represented by the unshaded areas in Figure 14, is 18,000 sales.

The average cost of a Daewoo is £10,562. 18,000 additional cars at £10,562 each = £190 million.

Daewoo Buyers' Research

The advertising prompted 71% of Daewoo buyers[7] to visit a Daewoo showroom in the first place.

---

7.   Source: FDS owners study. Base: 120 Daewoo buyers, randomly sampled.

If we assume that those 71% of buyers would not have visited without advertising, then we can also assume that the advertising generated 71% x 18,005 sales = 12,784 sales.

The value of the 12,784 sales generated by advertising, at an average value of £10,562 each, is £135 million.

Comparison with Launch Performances by Other Marques

The three previous Far Eastern new entrants provide benchmarks for what Daewoo might have achieved without its positioning and advertising campaign.

TABLE 6: FIRST-YEAR RESULTS OF OTHER
FAR EASTERN ENTRANTS

Marque	First 12 months share
Proton	0.37%
Kia	0.20%
Hyundai	0.20%

Source: SMMT

We can use their share achievements to estimate the upper and lower values of the contribution made by Daewoo's positioning and campaign.

TABLE 7: UPPER AND LOWER VALUES OF DAEWOO'S CONTRIBUTION

	Share estimate	Volumes based on Apr95–Mar96 market size	Actual (18,005) minus estimated volume	Value at average cost of £10,562
Upper (Proton)	0.37%	7,200	10,800	£114 million
Lower (Kia/Hyundai)	0.20%	3,900	14,100	£149 million

Source: SMMT/DFGW

By this method, the lower value of the positioning and campaign contribution is £114 million, and the upper value is £149 million.

We cannot reveal Daewoo's profit margins per car, but we are able to say that each of the estimates for advertising contribution above are sufficient to have contributed to Daewoo's operational profit.

CONCLUSION

The Daewoo case shows that an unexceptional product can achieve exceptional sales results through insightful strategic thinking and advertising.

We have shown that the advertising agency was seminally involved in the development of the brand strategy.

Advertising established a differentiated and motivating brand.

The advertising campaign's effectiveness was crucial to Daewoo's success, and the advertising budget of £22 million generated up to £190 million revenue.

3

Felix Advertising 1989–95

How the cat that crept got the cream

INTRODUCTION

Can you think of a grocery brand in a mature and established market that, after spending years as a relatively insignificant minor player, suddenly started to grow rapidly, overtaking the market leader in less than five years? More specifically, can you think of a brand that has achieved all this without significantly revamping the product, with parity pricing and with, at best, parity levels of distribution to its rivals?

If you can't, here's one: Felix. This paper will show how advertising featuring a mischievous black and white cat was the catalyst to this remarkable success story.

THE WET CATFOOD MARKET

In 1989, when our story begins, the UK wet catfood[1] market was worth over £400 million a year. Although a mature market with almost 100% penetration among cat owners, it had grown steadily through the 1980s, driven by an increase in the cat population. This growth plateaued towards the end of the decade and during the period covered by this paper (up to August 1995[2]) the market was static.

The market was segmented as follows:

— Expensive super-premium brands, usually served as treats.

— Premium brands served daily.

— Sub-premium brands, which were less palatable[3] and cost significantly less than the premiums.

---

1. In volume terms, wet catfood accounts for roughly 88% of the catfood market, the remaining 12% coming in either dry biscuit or 'semi-moist' formats.
2. This cut-off point was chosen due to alterations in our principal data sources.
3. 'Palatability' is a reasonably objective index of product quality in the catfood market. Manufacturers tend to measure it in two ways: (i) using cat owners to assess in-home how much their cats appear to like unbranded samples, and (ii) in the laboratory (or 'cattery') by recording the speed and manner with which cats eat samples of products – known in the trade as 'cat attack'.

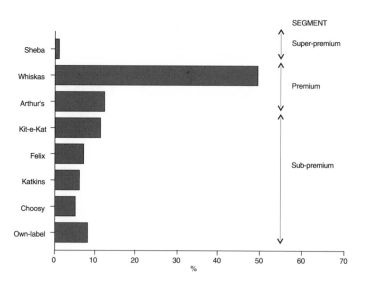

Figure 1: *Catfood brands volume share and market segment, year to January 1989*
Source: Nielsen

Whiskas Supermeat was the market leader with a share of nearly 50%. This premium brand had dominated the market since the 1970s and its position seemed as secure as Kellogg's Corn Flakes or Coca-Cola in their respective markets.

FELIX UNDER PRESSURE

Felix was bought by Quaker[4] in 1970 and positioned in the sub-premium market sector. The brand grew steadily through the early 1980s, helped by distribution gains but, by 1989, its share had levelled out at around 6.5%.

Although its share was steady, two trade developments raised the worrying possibility that Felix might start to lose listings:

— The major multiple retailers wanted to allocate more shelf space to the highly profitable super-premium sector (launched in the mid 1980s).

— They were also keen to sell more own-label catfoods.[5]

Felix was in a particularly weak position to face such a threat.

---

4. Quaker Petfoods was bought by Spillers in February 1995.
5. In 1989, the own-label catfood sector was relatively underdeveloped in comparison with other fmcg sectors.

— It came in only six flavours, making it a relatively uncompetitive range to stock.[6]

— Unlike all the other major brands, it had never received advertising support.

— From a consumer perspective, it lacked a distinctive identity.

Action had to be taken. As Quaker Petfoods' commercial director put it: 'The alternative of doing nothing would have meant we wouldn't have had a brand within two years.'[7]

THE FELIX RELAUNCH

Hence, the decision was taken to relaunch Felix in May 1989.

— The product was reformulated.

— Three new flavours were introduced.[8]

— The packaging was redesigned.

— For the first time in the brand's history, it received a £250,000 budget for advertising.

The relaunch marketing objective was to increase volume share to 10% over two years by getting non-users to try Felix and by building purchase levels among existing users. In reaching such a position the hope was that Felix would challenge Kit-e-Kat's placing as the third-largest brand in the market, thereby securing its listings and, ultimately, its long-term future.

DEVELOPING THE ADVERTISING

In January 1989, BMP was asked to develop the advertising for the relaunch. The primary advertising objective was to make Felix a credible brand, to endow it with an identity that would give non-users a reason to try it and users a reason to use it more regularly. This was a challenging brief!

All the major brands in the sector advertised heavily so there was no question that our combined media and creative solution had to be highly distinctive. If it was

---

6. By contrast, Kit-e-Kat came in nine flavours, Arthur's in ten and Whiskas Supermeat in twelve. (Source: *The Grocer Price List*, 1 April 1989).
7. *Marketing*, 3 December 1992.
8. Trout & Shrimp, Duck & Heart and Beef & Liver (replacing Liver). This took the number of flavours in the range up to eight.

not, our plaintive meowing risked being drowned out by the roar of our competitors, especially Whiskas which spent the equivalent of our entire budget every eight days.[9]

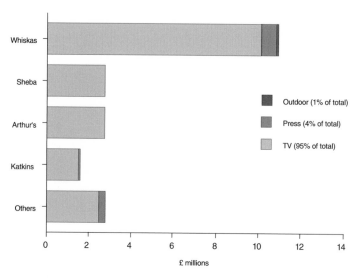

Figure 2: *Catfood brands adspend 1988*
Source: MEAL

To answer the trickier question of exactly what form this distinctiveness should take, we scrutinised our competitors' habits and got under the skin of cat owners.

The Creative Strategy

We found that most catfood advertising at the time sought to reassure owners that their cat would be eager to eat the brand being advertised.[10] It attempted to do this in a very rational manner using owner endorsements, lingering shots of catfood being forked from tin to bowl, and voice-over information about vitamins and minerals. These product stories were accompanied by idealised images of immaculately groomed cats and owners.

However, as soon as we started talking to owners, we realised that there was a gap between how these ads portrayed cats and how a great many owners actually felt about them.

---

9. Even Katkins, the smallest spender among our main competitors, spent around four times our budget annually.
10. This need to reassure was understandable; unlike dogs, who will eat almost anything, cats frequently turn up their noses at something that they were happy to eat the day before. However, owners are (excusably) reluctant to sample brands and flavours on behalf of their unpredictable pets.

At the warm-up stage of our first group discussion, we naïvely invited respondents to tell us what it was like having a cat – little knowing the difficulty we would have in getting them to stop! They reeled off dozens of amusing cat anecdotes.[11] This enthusiasm was shown by almost everyone we spoke to: they liked their cats *not* because they were affectionate bundles of pretty fluff (as represented in the competitive advertising), but because of their mischievous characters and frequently exasperating exploits.

Quotes from Cat Owners

'He's an absolute nutter, he terrorises the other cats.'

'My cat is a real cow first thing in the morning and it's bedlam.'

'They're mischievous, aren't they? Whatever you're doing they'll come and mither at you.'

'When they've done something wrong they give you a look that says "What are you going to do about it?"'

'They do what they want, when they want, and the odd thing is you forgive them for it. No idea why!'

Source: BMP Qualitative Research

We felt we had spotted a gap in the market: the most effective way to give the Felix brand a distinctive and motivating identity was to target these people and talk their language. We did not need to talk about vitamins, minerals and flavours to persuade them their cats would like to eat Felix, we could persuade them by showing we understood what cats were *really* like.

The Media Strategy

Before incorporating this learning into a creative brief we needed to have a clear idea about where the advertising ought to appear. Indeed, to maximise our limited budget, it was critical that our creative and media strategies reinforced each other as much as possible.

Initially, we could not afford to advertise on television – nor did we want to since that was where our competitors spent most of their money. Instead, we chose to start the campaign in national newspapers. No other catfood brands advertised in this medium so we would be able to dominate it as our own. Furthermore, by choosing to advertise in only a small number of titles, we could afford to maintain a continuous weekly presence all through the year. This allowed us to:

---

11. For example, about how little Rambo had swiped the Sunday roast off the sideboard, about Smudge's weakness for squirrels, or about Tibbles and her disastrous attempt to scale the Christmas tree.

— Echo the regular weekly timing of the catfood purchase cycle.

— Maximise the chances that advertising would catch owners when they were most vulnerable to brand switching.[12]

— Produce many *different* executions, to help flesh out the personality that lay at the heart of our creative strategy.

— Expose our target to a regular succession of executions, helping to boost Felix's brand stature in their eyes.

Despite these benefits, this 'targeted drip' approach was quite risky; the only way we could afford such a prolonged presence was to sacrifice coverage and appear in a limited number of newspaper titles. However, we believed the benefits of the strategy far outweighed any potential disadvantages: if 'Eight out of ten cat owners (who expressed a preference)' preferred Whiskas, we were happy just to talk to the two out of ten who did not.

We were now able to write the creative brief.

Creative Brief

Requirement
Black & white national press campaign.

Target
Cat owners, mainly women, who appreciate their cats for who they are.

Proposition
If your cat is like the Felix cat then he or she will like Felix catfood.

Support
Show the sorts of things mischievous everyday moggies get up to.
Show that those sorts of cats like to eat Felix.

Tone
Cheeky and down to earth.

---

12. Namely whenever their unpredictable cat started refusing to eat a brand it had previously liked.

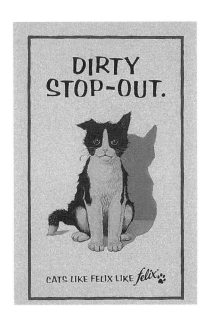

FELIX 'PERSONALITY' NEWSPAPER ADS

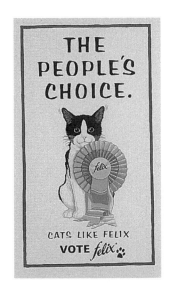

FELIX 'TOPICAL' NEWSPAPER ADS

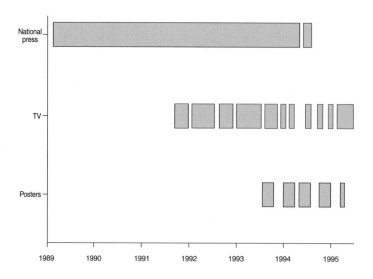

Figure 3: *Felix media plan: September 1989 to August 1995*
Source: MEAL

The Creative Work

We had found in research that many cat owners liked the black and white cat on the new Felix packaging. The creative team christened him Felix and decided to bring him to life.[13] The ads they came up with showed Felix either engaged in, or coming home from, various roguish tricks and, now, wanting to be fed. These featured the end-line *'Cats Like Felix Like Felix'*.

The team also created a series of cheekily topical ads, to be used on particular days during the course of the year.

CAMPAIGN DEVELOPMENT

Felix in the Newspapers

From mid-September 1989, Felix appeared in two daily titles.[14] As the brand grew, increased budgets allowed us to broaden our coverage, while maintaining frequency, by moving into additional titles.[15] The press buying brief was *be cheeky*: like hungry cats around meal times, the press ads popped up everywhere.[16]

---

13. After experimenting with photographs of black and white cats they decided an illustrated cat would – paradoxically – be more characterful. Certainly, it was much easier to 'direct' than a real cat.
14. The *Daily Express* and the *Daily Star*.
15. The *Daily Mirror*, the *Sun* and the *Daily Telegraph*.
16. In November 1992, we even bought every space in a single title, the *Daily Mirror*, a tactic subsequently adopted by Microsoft for the launch of Windows 95, Mercury for the launch of the Oliver and Claire campaign, and Pepsi for the launch of its blue can. We were, we believe, the first brand to do this.

Felix Goes On Telly

In October 1991, the budget became large enough for us to increase our coverage further by moving onto television. We still wanted to avoid the competition, create the impression among a discrete set of cat owners that Felix was a bigger brand than it actually was, and echo the catfood purchase cycle. So, instead of adopting a more conventional burst strategy, we continued with our tightly targeted drip approach.[17] Again, as budgets increased, we broadened our coverage by moving into additional programmes and dayparts.

Felix Goes Outside

From March 1993 the television and press work was supplemented by regional poster activity designed to boost brand awareness and further build Felix's brand stature.[18]

Spillers deserves praise for its audacity. It did not choose the obvious advertising solution. Instead, it consistently invested in work that broke many catfood advertising precedents:

— It did not show the product or talk about its contents.

— It focused on real rather than idealised cat behaviour.

— It illustrated these (ironically) with an 'unreal' cat.

— It appeared initially in a medium where catfood had never previously been advertised.

— It was bought in a manner where frequency and consistency of presence took priority over coverage.

RESULTS

Spillers' audacity has been extremely well rewarded.

---

17. Translated into the new medium, this initially involved buying one spot every week in *The Bill*, supplemented by further spots in the Breakfast TV daypart.
18. Again, as far as is possible with posters, we tried to use them in a suitably mischievous manner. For example, when one of our competitors sponsored the 1993 Cat Show at Olympia, the first thing spectators saw as they arrived and departed were two Felix ad vans parked outside the front entrance. This feat was topped at the same event two years later by our projecting Felix onto the exhibition hall itself.

'SMOOTH OPERATOR'

SOUND: Telephone rings

Hello...oh hi...yes...

Oh, I see...did you...?
SOUND: Dial tone.

Come on...

FVO: Cats like Felix like Felix.

Sales

There was an immediate uplift in Felix's sales after the advertising began in September 1989. Within only 16 months, eight months earlier than planned, the relaunch objective of achieving 10% share was met.

This growth continued: by August 1995, volume and value share had increased by a further 145% and 158% respectively (Figure 4).

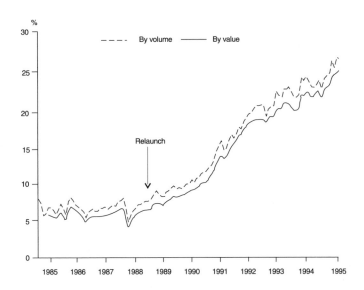

Figure 4: *Felix market share 1985–95*
Source: Nielsen

Felix did not simply catch up with the number-three brand, Kit-e-Kat, in December 1990 it overtook it. Then, 14 months later, it overtook the number two brand, Arthur's. And, in January 1994, it overtook the previously dominant market leader, Whiskas Supermeat.

It was not only by the standards of the catfood market that Felix's rate of growth was impressive: in 1991, Felix was the fourth fastest-growing brand in *any* grocery category; in 1992, the second fastest-growing brand; and, in 1993, the third fastest. This moved it from being the 80th biggest brand in the country before the relaunch to being the 27th biggest by 1995.[19]

---

19. This put Felix ahead of Gold Blend, Weetabix, Fairy Liquid, and Mars Bar. Source: *Checkout* magazine/Nielsen Biggest Brand Survey.

Consumer Behaviour

As planned, Felix's growth was driven both by large increases in penetration and loyalty levels. The brand's user base tripled in size (see Figure 5).[20]

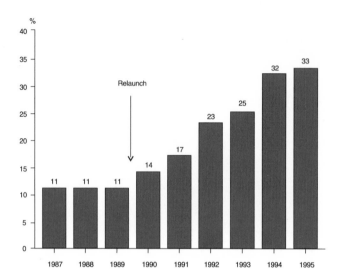

Figure 5: *Felix penetration 1985–95*
Base: Catfood buyers
Source: TGI

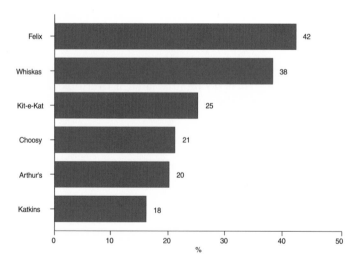

Figure 6: *Share of repertoire occupied by brand*
Base: All buyers of brand during survey period
Source: AGB Superpanel 20 w/e 27 August 1995

---

20. Since the TGI measuring year runs from April through to the following March, the 1989 figure can be regarded as a clean pre-relaunch measure.

And Felix's share of repertoire among catfood buyers doubled from 21% in 1988 to 42% in 1995, putting it ahead of all of its competitors (see Figure 6).[21]

Consumer Perceptions

In terms of how consumers view the Felix brand, spontaneous and prompted awareness increased significantly.

TABLE 1: FELIX BRAND AWARENESS

	November 1989 %	August 1995 %
Spontaneous	29	49
Prompted	87	94

Base: Housewives with cats
Source: Millward Brown

Perceptions of Felix's quality and stature, likewise, increased:

TABLE 2: THOSE AGREEING WITH FELIX BRAND IMAGE STATEMENTS

	November 1989 %	August 1995 %
'It is particularly good quality'	17	35
'It is becoming more popular nowadays'	9	18

Base: Housewives with cats
Source: Millward Brown

Furthermore, Felix was given a distinctive and highly characterful identity within the catfood market (see Figure 7).[22]

Overall, then, the marketing objectives following Felix's relaunch were not simply met, they were dramatically exceeded.

---

21. Source: AGB Superpanel, 28 w/e April 1988 versus 20 w/e August 1995.
22. We didn't have enough money to conduct awareness and image research before the relaunch and the advertising. The earliest measure we have comes from early November 1989, roughly six weeks after the advertising started. Accordingly, the baseline against which we are judging Felix's performance is likely to be higher than an absolutely clean pre-relaunch measure. This suggests that these figures underestimate the extent to which Felix's awareness and image measures have grown.

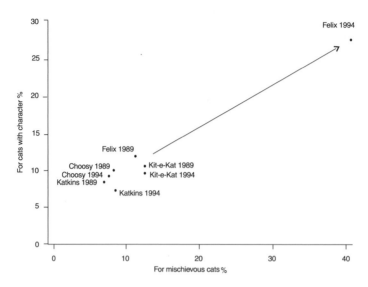

Figure 7: *Catfood brand identity Nov 1989 versus Nov 1994*
Base: % Housewives with cats who agree with image statement
Source: Millward Brown

THE CONTRIBUTION OF ADVERTISING

Felix's fortunes may have been transformed but what evidence is there to link this transformation of the brand to its advertising? We have four reasons to believe such a link exists.

— Consumers responded to the advertising exactly as we had planned.

— Cross-media and cross-regional analyses show correlations between the advertising and Felix's sales and penetration growth.

— We can rule out the contribution of non-advertising factors.

— Econometric modelling.

CONSUMER RESPONSE TO THE ADVERTISING

The newspaper and TV advertising was impactful, enjoyable, empathetic, and communicated clearly.

Within just two years of the start of the campaign, and only a month after it had first moved onto television, it had become the second most-noticeable catfood campaign (see Table 3).[23]

TABLE 3: ADVERTISING AWARENESS (IN ANY MEDIUM)

Whiskas	67%
Felix	30%
Kit-e-Kat	25%
Arthur's	21%

Base: Housewives with cats
Source: Millward Brown, November 1991

Crucially, for a campaign which was meant to tap into owners' positive feelings towards their cats, the advertising was enjoyed by cat owners (see Table 4). More specifically, over 50% of them spontaneously commented that they liked the Felix cat, and 30% said it reminded them of exactly how their cat behaves.[24]

TABLE 4: ENJOYMENT OF FELIX TV ADVERTISING

Enjoyed a lot	28%
Quite enjoyed	42%
Total	70%

Base: Housewives with cats who have seen Felix TV advertising recently[25]
Source: Millward Brown (campaign norm up to 7 May 1995)

In terms of communication, the Felix newspaper and TV ads established the type of cat which was most likely to want to eat Felix, as well as more 'generic' quality credentials (see Figures 8 and 9 overleaf).

Further evidence for the campaign's impact, enjoyability and clarity of message comes from qualitative research.

Consumer Comments on Felix Newspaper and TV Advertising

'The other adverts all look the same. I haven't seen a style like this before, it's quite a revolution.'

'You can relate to having a cat like that. I can see my cat in there, the way he jumps up.'

'It's part of the charm of the ad, he's got a character like a cheeky little child.'

'He's not one of those posh cats that lie around on the sofa. He's mischievous William Brown – I can see the catapult in his back pocket.'

'He's got that look on his face as if to say "Well, I've been out all night and now I want feeding!" '

---

23. Although, strictly speaking, this is more an indication of efficiency rather than effectiveness, it is worth noting that the Felix campaign has been a remarkably cost-effective generator of advertising awareness. For example, in May 1995 it was scoring 12 on Millward Brown's Awareness Index compared with Kit-e-Kat's 4 and Whiskas' 1.
24. Source: Millward Brown, May 1995. Base: Housewives with cats who have seen Felix advertising recently.
25. We do not have comparable quantitative data for the Felix press advertising.

'He always wants feeding and he always manages, whatever the situation, to be fed.'

'The food's so good he can't wait to get stuck into it.'

Source: BMP Qualitative Research 1990–95

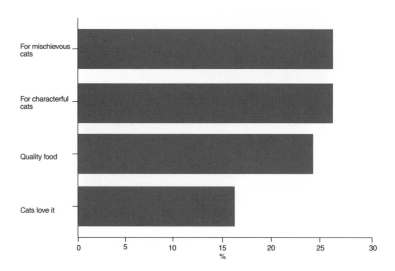

Figure 8: *Prompted impression: newspaper ads*
Base: Housewives with cats who have seen Felix advertising recently
Source: Millward Brown, June 1991

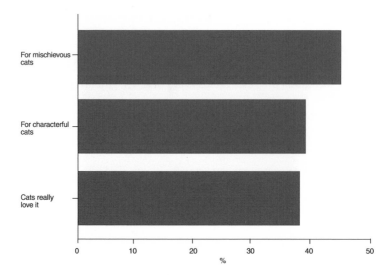

Figure 9: *Impressions from Felix TV ad*
Base: Housewives with cats who have seen Felix TV advertising recently
Source: Millward Brown, 13 March–7 May 1995

TABLE 5: FELIX BRAND IMAGE: ADVERTISING AWARE
VERSUS UNAWARE

Those who agree	Aware %	Unaware %
'It is for mischievous cats'	42	22
'It is for cats with character'	32	18

Base: Housewives with cats who do/do not recall having seen Felix TV
advertising recently, mean score September 91–July 95
Source: Millward Brown

Comparing perceptions of Felix's brand image among advertisement-aware versus unaware cat owners suggests strongly it was the advertising that built and reinforced the brand's distinct identity (Table 5).[26]

Taking all this information together, it is clear that the changes in consumer perceptions towards Felix are largely due to the advertising, which worked exactly as we had hoped.

CROSS-REGIONAL AND CROSS-MEDIA ANALYSES

During the period of our press advertising, before we began to advertise on television, the regional differences in Felix's share growth correlated with the regional differences in its newspaper advertising weights (Figure 10).

Again, prior to the move onto TV, Felix's penetration levels among readers of titles where we advertised grew faster than among readers of non-advertised titles (Table 6).

TABLE 6: FELIX PENETRATION AMONG READERS OF NEWSPAPERS
WHERE THE BRAND ADVERTISED

	Ever read %	Never read %
1989	11.6	11.2
1990	16.8	13.3
1991	21.4	15.6

Base: Housewives with cats who ever/never read the *Daily Mirror*, *Daily Express*, *Daily Star*.
Source: TGI

Following the brand's move onto TV, regional differences in the cost of airtime resulted in regional differences in Felix's share of voice. These correlate with regional differences in the brand's penetration growth (Figure 11).

---

26. The IPA's *Guide To Authors* stresses that 'differences in behaviour or attitudes between those who claim recall of advertising and those who do not will not be regarded as proof of advertising effectiveness, largely because of the contaminating influence of intervening variables like product usage and selective perception. Thus, while it is true that usage and perceptions of Felix's quality are higher among cat owners who are aware of its advertising, we *won't* cite this as evidence that the advertising was responsible. However, perceptions of *Felix's character* are highly unlikely to have been influenced by product usage, so we can legitimately claim that advertising is the only thing that can have driven these particular brand image dimensions.

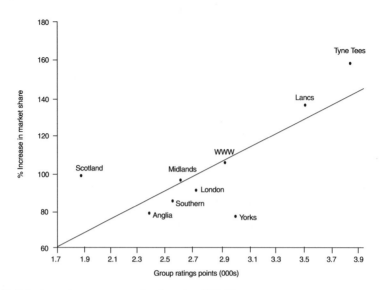

Figure 10: *Felix share gains versus press ratings by region, 1989–91*
Sources: Nielsen, BMP

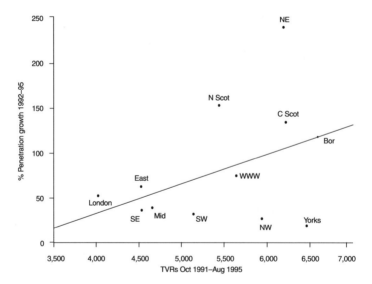

Figure 11: *Felix penetration growth versus TVRs by region*
Sources: MEAL, TGI

Overall, looking at the entire campaign period (up to August 1995), there was a 95% correlation between Felix's monthly share and the amount spent on advertising during the *previous* year (Figure 12).

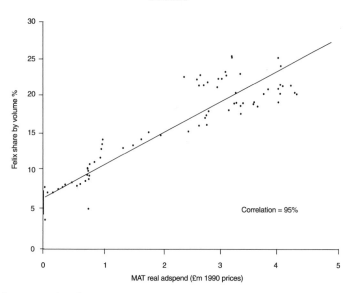

Figure 12: *Felix share versus adspend*
Sources: Nielsen, Register/MEAL

It appears, then, that there is very strong correlational evidence to link advertising to Felix's sales and penetration growth[27]. Can we make this evidence more compelling by ruling out other factors which might also have influenced that growth?

THE CONTRIBUTION OF NON-ADVERTISING FACTORS

Looking at all the non-advertising factors that might have exerted an influence, we found that, although some elements in the marketing mix could have contributed to brand performance, either individually or in combination, advertising is by far the strongest candidate when it comes to isolating the key driving factor behind Felix's success.

---

27. Further evidence – albeit inferential – for the effectiveness of Felix's advertising comes from the 1989 Choosy relaunch. A strong case has been made that the advertising accompanying that relaunch was effective (see 'The relaunch of Choosy catfood', *Advertising Works 6*, pp 302–322). Since Felix's growth considerably outstripped Choosy's in the 12 months post relaunch, when the brands are most comparable, it seems fair to infer that Felix's advertising was even *more* effective.

Non-advertising Factors that might have contributed to Felix's Growth

a)   The individual components of the relaunch: product reformulation, new
     flavours, new packaging.

b)   The *combined* effect of these components.

c)   Pricing.

d)   Trade presence: distribution and forward stocks.

e)   Range extensions.

f)   The UK black and white cat population.

g)   Competitive activity: promotions and advertising.

h)   The purchase of Quaker Petfoods by Spillers.

The Individual Components of the Relaunch

Product Reformulation
Perhaps Felix's success was due to straightforward product superiority, either in
terms of cat palatability or human appeal.

Although we do not have relative palatability data for all the major brands
covering the entire 1989–1995 period, we do have enough to draw some
conclusions. Felix's reformulation at relaunch improved its palatability, putting it
ahead of Kit-e-Kat. However, this advantage was only temporary. Within 11
months of the relaunch (and seven months after Felix began to advertise), Kit-e-Kat
too reformulated and caught up again. More importantly – contrary to some
reports – until summer 1992, Felix was consistently *less* palatable than Whiskas
Supermeat, the brand from which it appears to have taken most share up to that
date (see Figure 13).[28] So, this rules out product superiority as a factor.

As for human appeal, at the time of its relaunch, Felix's chunks-in-jelly format
was noticeably different from the meaty-loaf products of Kit-e-Kat, Whiskas
Supermeat and Arthur's. However, there are three reasons to believe that Felix's
cosmetic appeal was not the key driver of the brand's growth.

---

28.   Source: Quaker/Spillers cattery tests, March 1989, April 1990, February 1992, May 1992, June 1992,
      August 1992. Interestingly, in August 1992, Whiskas launched a new chunks variant, Select Cuts. This
      new product outperformed Felix cosmetically and in palatability terms, but its arrival on the market did
      not reduce Felix's rate of growth.

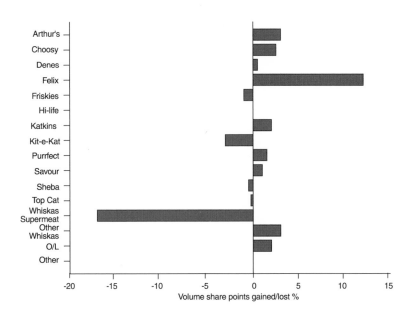

Figure 13: *Share gains April 1989–August 1992*
Source: Nielsen

— Felix had been in this format *unchanged* since September 1982.

— Katkins was also available in the chunks format, yet it did not enjoy similar growth.

— Whiskas, Kit-e-Kat, and Arthur's have all launched chunks-format brand variants since Felix's relaunch, yet none of these has grown to the same extent as Felix.

New Flavours
Cat owners want to give their cats a varied diet so it is possible that some of Felix's growth was driven by its availability in new flavours (Figure 14).[29] However, there are three reasons to believe that this was not a significant factor behind the brand's success. First, the sales for the flavours which had been available *before* the relaunch continued to grow after it.

Second, the *rate of sale* of Felix's original flavours also grew after the relaunch – indeed, by 1992, two of them had become the country's fastest sellers (see Table 7).

---

29. As well as the three flavours introduced at the relaunch, three more were launched in September 1991, and a further three in March 1993.

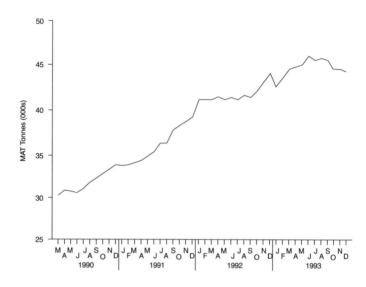

Figure 14: *Felix ex-factory sales, original flavours*
Source: Spillers

TABLE 7: ORIGINAL FELIX FLAVOUR'S RATE OF SALE RANKED VERSUS
OTHER CATFOOD BRANDS' FLAVOURS

	Pre-relaunch (Year to 6/88)	Post-relaunch 1 (Year to 6/91)	Post-relaunch 2 (Year to 6/92)
Chicken	33	15	1
Beef	28	16	2
Tuna	39	18	9
Rabbit	36	17	12

(ie in 1988 Felix Chicken was the 33rd fastest-selling flavour in the country, in
1992 it was the fastest seller).
Source: Nielsen
Base: 1988 and 1991 TOPS, 1992 Key Accounts

At no point between 1989 and 1995 did Felix have more flavours in its range
than any of its main competitors.

As for *type* of flavour, there is no reason to believe that Felix's flavours were
significantly more alluring to cat owners than those of its competitors.

Packaging
There is little evidence to suggest that Felix's packaging was a key driver of brand
growth:

— For much of the 1989–95 period, many of Felix's competitors enjoyed the practical advantage of having easy-to-open ring-pull tops.

— According to a quantitative study conducted by Quaker in spring 1989, the revised label did *not* increase owner's 'propensity to purchase' Felix.

— The post-relaunch label, while obviously different from the pre-relaunch design, still followed the conventions of the market.

Figure 15: *Felix pack design, pre-relaunch versus post-relaunch*

That said, Felix's packaging did differ from its competitors in one respect after the relaunch: a paw-print and the phrase 'Tasted and Approved' were printed on the can lid. It is possible that the introduction of this paw-print and phrase could have led to a one-off step change in Felix's performance. However, it is highly unlikely that such a minor difference could have driven Felix's growth for a full *six years*.

The Combined Effect of the Relaunch Components

It may be possible to discount the non-advertising relaunch components individually, but perhaps they worked together *synergistically*. Fortunately, there was a four-month gap between the relaunch and the start of the advertising which allows us to examine the relaunch effect in isolation.

The relaunched product had entirely replaced the pre-relaunch version on shelf by the end of May 1989. Figure 16 shows that, although Felix's share grew in June and July, it fell back in August and September, and did not start to rise again until the advertising began.

This suggests that there *was* a non-advertising relaunch effect but that it was relatively short-lived. Like the paw-print on the can lid, Felix's relaunch might explain a one-off step change in the brand's performance but not six years of sustained brand growth.

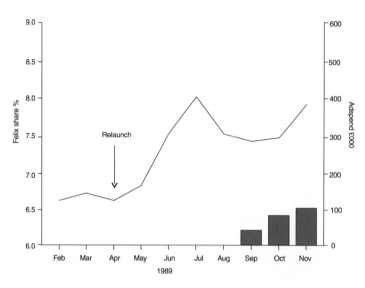

Figure 16: *Felix relaunch 1989*
Sources: Nielsen, Register/MEAL

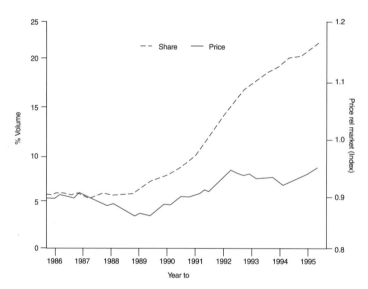

Figure 17: *Felix share versus relative price MATs*
Source: Nielsen

Pricing

Although the catfood market is highly price sensitive, price cutting did not drive Felix's growth: its price *increased* relative to its key competitors (Figure 17).[30]

Trade Presence

Distribution

Felix increased its sterling distribution between 1989 and 1995, but this increase does not appear to have driven the brand's growth. Indeed (as Figure 18 shows), distribution growth lagged *behind* share growth.[31]

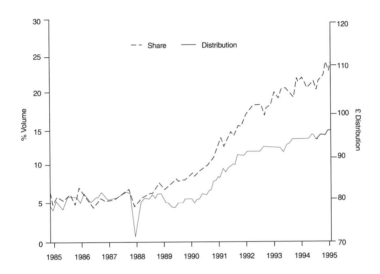

Figure 18: *Felix share versus distribution*
Source: Nielsen

Further evidence showing that distribution was not a factor comes from Felix's rate of sale, which has risen consistently since the advertising began (Figure 19).

---

30. This pattern of growth could be interpreted in another way: it might be argued that increasing the price improved consumers' perceptions of Felix's quality. This may or may not be true at a perceptual level, but econometrics shows that, all other things being equal, increasing price actually depresses sales. This is true of all catfood brands (and, indeed, nearly all goods and services). However, even if Felix was one of those rare products with a 'positive price elasticity', the price increase could still not explain its sales growth: prices started to rise about a year after the brand started growing.
31. This lag suggests that increases in Felix's sales may have driven the distribution gains.

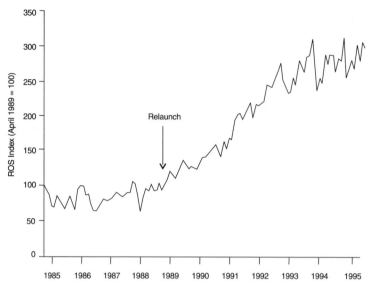

Figure 19: *Felix rate of sale*
Source: Nielsen

Forward Stocks[32]

Felix increased its share of forward stocks between 1989 and 1995 but there are two reasons to believe that this was not the primary driver of brand growth. First, growth of Felix's forward stocks *lagged behind* share growth (see Figure 20).[33]

Second, the brand was consistently 'underfaced' compared with its main competitors during its period of growth (see Figure 21).[34]

Range Extension

There have been two Felix range extensions since the 1989 relaunch:

— From May 1994, the brand was available in a chunks in *gravy* format in addition to its original chunks in *jelly* format.[35]

— From July 1995, the brand was available as a kittenfood variant.

These extensions may have contributed to some of Felix's growth between May 1994 and August 1995. However, since they only accounted for 14% of the

---

32. A brand's 'forward stocks' can be defined as the total number of cans on display in Britain's shops at any given time. 'Share of forward stocks' expresses that as a percentage of all the catfood brands on display.
33. Suggesting, as with distribution, that the brand's gains in shelf space have been driven by its growing rate of sale.
34. That is, it didn't receive shelf-space allocation commensurate with its volume share.
35. It was the fourth brand to enter this sub-sector of the wet catfood market after Whiskas, Kit-e-Kat and Arthur's.

brand's overall volume by this time, this contribution is unlikely to have been significant.

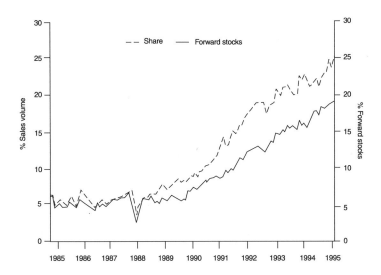

Figure 20: *Felix share versus forward stocks*
Source: Nielsen

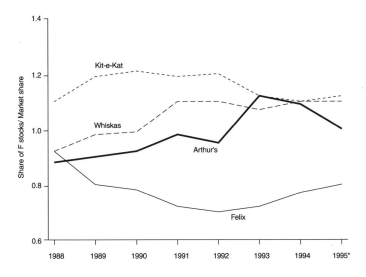

Figure 21: *Forward stocks to share ratio*
Source: Nielsen
* Year to August

The UK Black and White Cat Population

Felix's growth could have been driven by an increase in the proportion of black and white cats within the UK cat population. However, there is no reason to believe such a population increase occurred.[36]

Competitive Activity

Promotions

Between 1989 and 1995 there is no evidence that either the number of Felix promotions, or the rewards they offered, exceeded those of its competitors.

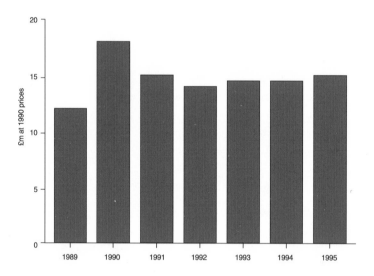

Figure 22: *Competitive adspend*
Source: Register/MEAL, AA

Advertising

Perhaps our competitors reduced their media budgets and we simply outspent them. This was not the case, apart from some fluctuation around 1989 and 1990, their combined spend remained broadly static (Figure 22).

The Purchase of Quaker Petfoods by Spillers

Following Felix's acquisition by Spillers in February 1995, it became part of the same catfood brand portfolio as Arthur's and Choosy, suggesting that some of its

---

36. Sources: the Cats Protection League, the General Council Of Cat Fancy, the Black and White Cat Club.

growth might have been due to the 'managed decline' of these brands. However, we can state that deliberate portfolio management was not a factor.[37]

Overall, then, we can discount all the factors which might have contributed to Felix's growth.

ECONOMETRICS

The direct and inferential evidence presented so far suggests strongly that advertising has played a key role in Felix's remarkable success. However, to dispel any remaining doubts, we constructed an econometric model of Felix's market share, taking account of all the factors which might have influenced sales over the last ten years. This model provides the final confirmation of advertising effectiveness, demonstrating that Felix's advertising did indeed have a strong and direct effect on the brand's sales.

RETURN ON INVESTMENT

Overall, the model estimates that the £17 million[38] spent on Felix's advertising between 1989 and 1995 increased sales by *£108 million*. Although we cannot reveal profitability figures, margins in the catfood market are sufficiently high for us to say that Felix's advertising more than paid for itself. Indeed, in investment terms, the return from advertising 1989–95 was almost *four times* greater than investing in the FT ordinary share index over the same period.

TABLE 8: COMPARATIVE RETURN ON INVESTMENT
PER ANNUM 1989–95

Felix advertising	49.6%
Shares	13.0%
Bonds	9.1%
Bank deposits	9.3%

Source: BMP Estimates

Furthermore, there are good reasons to believe that the true payback is even greater:

— The model shows that the advertising effect is quite long-lasting; even if the ads had stopped in 1995, they would still be generating extra sales for several years to come. Using a reasonable set of assumptions, modelling estimates that the

---

37. Given that we have already ruled out product quality, trade presence, advertising weight, and pricing as drivers of Felix's growth, it is hard to conceive what form such 'portfolio management' could have taken.
38. Source: MEAL/Media Register. This figure doesn't include production costs. However, these are more than counterbalanced by substantial discounts achieved in buying the Felix press advertising.

extra sales generated between 1995 and the year 2000 by previous advertising would probably be worth a further £90 million.[39]

— As well as direct advertising effects, the ads may have had an *indirect* effect on brand growth by helping to persuade retailers to stock more Felix.[40]

— Econometrics suggests that Felix's price elasticity has fallen since 1989, reducing the impact of price increases that have taken place since. Although we cannot quantify its contribution, it seems likely that advertising was partly responsible for this.

— All of the above calculations assume that, without advertising, Felix's sales would have been roughly static. However, there is good reason to believe that, had we not taken action in 1989, Felix might have eventually been delisted. In that case, advertising may have made the difference between having sales of £111 million a year and having no sales at all.[41]

CONCLUSION

IPA effectiveness papers often end with a pertinent marketing moral. In the case of Felix, it is hard to know which one to choose. We could stress the David and Goliath side of the story: that advertising can be an extremely powerful business tool in markets which appear to be 'sewn up', even when the budget is tiny in comparison with the competition. We could talk about the benefits of 'joined-up thinking', emphasising the integration of creative and media planning, where the latter is used as a tool to reinforce the content of the advertising rather than simply as a way of delivering it efficiently to the target audience. Or we could point out the virtues of a continuous but tightly targeted media presence, even when this means coverage figures end up looking a little thin.

However, if forced to highlight just one lesson from the Felix story, it would be that the advertiser who dares wins: breaking the advertising conventions of a market can be highly effective in business terms, provided your rule-breaking is based on rock-solid consumer insight.

---

39. 1990 prices.
40. The model shows that some of Felix's extra sales were due to increases in forward stocks. However, forward stocks in this market are principally determined by historic sales levels, suggesting that Felix's stock gains were largely a knock-on effect of the brand's early share gains. We know from the modelling that many of these share gains were, in turn, due to advertising, so some of the extra sales attributed by the model to stock gains were almost certainly due to advertising. Without modelling forward stocks, it is impossible to quantify this indirect effect, but it may well be as big as the direct effect.
41. Although the value of Felix's equity has not been formally audited it is also worth noting that in February 1995 Spillers paid £442 million for the Quaker Petfood business and its two principal brands, Felix catfood and Chunky dogfood.

4

BBC Education

Ignore it. It'll go away

BACKGROUND

The Scale of the Problem

In 1994, the Basic Skills Agency (BSA), whose mandate is to help increase overall levels of literacy in the British population, estimated that one in seven of the adult population of Britain, six million people, had difficulties with literacy skills, such as:

— being able to read an address in *Yellow Pages*;

— understanding a classified recruitment advertisement;

— reading First Aid instructions.

Moreover, research in 1993 (Bynner & BSA), demonstrated that there was an inter-generational effect upon literacy. Children in this research project were divided into quartiles according to reading ability – 72% of children in the lowest reading ability quartile had parents with reading problems.

There is a clear need to break this vicious circle of parents passing on illiteracy to their children. Therefore, we decided that the best way to address the overall adult literacy problem was to break that circle.

THE ROLE OF THE BBC IN PROMOTING ADULT LITERACY

This is an unusual paper in that it is about an advertising campaign featured on BBC Television.

BBC Education is a department of BBC Television. Its task is to commission educational programming, as dictated by the BBC's Government Charter. In addition, BBC Education develops campaigns for social issues singled out by the Government. An outside body is usually involved in such campaigns; for the BBC's 1995 adult literacy campaign, this was the Basic Skills Agency.

In the past these 'single issue' briefs have been addressed by producing a series of promotions, up to 90 seconds in length, which are then slotted into the BBC's programming schedule at convenient times. Such advertising campaigns are produced by the BBC to its own standards.

In the case of the 1995 adult literacy campaign, and as a departure from the norm, BBC Education decided to experiment by using an advertising agency. The BBC felt that the problem was sufficiently difficult to warrant outside help from experts. BBH was briefed in May 1994 to produce a campaign for February 1995, as part of a week of adult literacy programming on BBC radio and television. All the week's activities were designed to stimulate applications for a learning pack which parents with literacy problems could use to improve their own literacy skills at the same time as they helped their own children to read and write.

For internal reasons at BBC Education, none of the additional programming originally planned around the advertising happened, and efforts were concentrated around BBH's advertising campaign.

THE ADVERTISING CHALLENGE

The advertising challenge was to persuade as many parents with literacy needs as possible to apply for the learning pack.

At first sight, this might seem a simple task. Surely the target would jump at any chance offered to begin an illiteracy 'cure', especially in the form of a free learning pack?

The Barrier to Successful Communication

In reality, the advertising task was difficult. Admittedly people were aware of their literacy problem, because they dealt with it every day of their lives; reading street names and bus timetables or filling in forms and writing receipts. But there was one major barrier: persuading people to respond to advertising would be extremely difficult because of their strong tendency to ignore their own literacy problems.

> 'In general it's the ones that are not coming [to adult literacy programmes] that need more help, and that's a hard one to overcome.'

> Interview with Programme Co-ordinator, Family Literacy Works, BSA

The Reason the Target Ignores its Problem; the Stigma Attached to Illiteracy

Illiteracy is often seen as a sign of stupidity or mental deficiency. Any indication of difficulty in reading or writing carries great social stigma. The consequence is straightforward; people who have literacy problems are terrified of being 'found out'.

> 'People are unwilling to seek help...it is difficult to change a cycle of low expectation and failure.'

> Basic Skills, BSA

To seek help for poor literacy is potentially shaming, hence normally avoided.

'I was frightened of getting things wrong and making a fool of myself.'

Parent Interview, Family Literacy Works, BSA

BBH experienced confirmation of the effect of this stigma at first hand, when, for briefing purposes, we visited classroom programmes where parents were learning with their children. Although warned in advance of our visit, one father simply got up and left the room when we walked in, too embarrassed by his difficulties to discuss them with strangers.

The Strategies the Target uses to Conceal its Literacy Difficulties

Parents develop strategies to conceal their problem – even from partners; 'Can you read this for me? – I haven't got my glasses with me' or 'You do the road signs, I'll do the driving'.

In public situations, the strategies are more complicated and more vulnerable to failure: 'Excuse me, what *colour* tin does the masonry paint come in? – I can't find it anywhere'.

Shock Tactics Would Fail

Advertising had to overcome the effect of this stigma and conquer parents' tendency to ignore their literacy problems and remain passive. We doubted whether we could *shock* the target into action, as charity advertising might. The stigma attached to illiteracy had made this audience wary of revealing its difficulty. Shock tactics might drive them deeper into denial of the need to do anything about their problem.

'It is essential that these [the executions] offer encouragement and are not seen as parent-blaming.'

BBC Briefing Document

Traditional Direct Response Techniques were Unlikely to Help

We also doubted that simply providing information about a new learning pack, to drive response to an 0800 number in the normal way, would be enough to overcome our target's ingrained inertia. For this campaign, we needed to rethink received wisdom of TV direct response advertising.

'Traditionally, successful TV direct response campaigns are rational in approach and information-based. Facts and information are presented boldly and clearly. There is a reluctance on the part of creative directors in traditional advertising agencies to issue direct requests to consumers. They prefer more subtle persuasion, over a longer time scale. This is not the way to get people to reach for the phone. *Subtlety will not get a response* [BBH emphasis]. Issue a strong call to action...Sustain the response number on the screen for as long as possible. This means, at the very minimum, twice as long as it takes to read it out. Even more effective is to flash it up for this period three times during the ad...From the outset, make it clear that this is the sort of ad that a) incorporates a phone number and b) will offer the viewer some benefit...When promoting a product which may be unfamiliar to consumers, don't leave it to their imagination. Demonstrate the product and its benefits clearly.

A Guide to Direct Response Television Advertising, Merit Direct

It is not that these direct response guidelines are incorrect but, as with all rules, there are exceptions.

We were in no doubt that our target would reject any attempt simply to reason it into responding. Our target group had spent several decades deliberately ignoring information about how to tackle its literacy problems. Advertising had to do much more than announce new information about help offered and invite response in the normal way.

THE ADVERTISING STRATEGY

The advertising strategy was the culmination of long discussions with parents who themselves suffered from the consequences of poor literacy.

We knew that the stigma attached to illiteracy meant that our target was likely to ignore the campaign's offer of help.

Our creative solution to this issue was advertising that was highly empathetic and emotionally involving. Our target was so used to authority figures failing it, that it had grown to mistrust any outside body which offered help. Establishing an emotional connection was key to communicating that we understood their predicament. We wanted them to feel, 'yes, that's absolutely right, that's me'.

As a result, we believed, the target could be 'won over' and persuaded to ignore its problem no longer. It was by achieving emotional empathy with our target group, that we also believed we could prompt a response.

Empathy was achieved by the following three elements.

— Using parents' naturally protective attitudes towards their children. Parents told us repeatedly about their strong desire that their children should not endure the same misery that they had. That a parent's literacy could affect their children's welfare as well as their own provided considerable emotional resonance for our target.

— The dramatisation of real-life examples of problems described to us by parents with literacy problems, which rooted the campaign firmly in our target's own experience.

— A direct tone that dealt with the problem in a plain and unpitying manner. (During the briefing process, parents spoke of their natural fear of being 'talked down to' because they were 'stupid'.)

THE THREE EXECUTIONS

Avoidance of literacy problems took different forms so we realised that different executions were needed to achieve empathy with as many people as possible.

— In 'Wendy' a child talks aloud to her doll, finding reasons not to read to it. She is obviously mimicking her own mother.

— In 'Jack' a small boy lies in bed listening to repeated readings of a story his father has committed to memory and asks, 'Daddy, can't you read any other stories?'

— In 'Imagine' we depict problems in the daily life of a girl disenfranchised by her literacy difficulties.

— All three executions end with an 0800 number to order a free 'Read and Write Together' learning pack.

Our focus on parents' feelings and fears for their child was key. Hopes for their children were stronger than parents' own shame of their literacy problems.

RESTRICTIONS ON MEDIA PLANNING

The BBC's target audience was parents with literacy difficulties.

Of the total population, 22% have children under nine years (TGI), so of the six million people with literacy difficulties, around one million would be in our target audience. (This estimate assumes that the likelihood of having children is the same for those both with and without literacy difficulties.) In demographic terms, the target tended to fall into low-income groups and be aged 16–34.

Print campaigns were ruled out by the nature of the task; our target audience naturally does not read often. (Nine 25 x 4 b/w advertising insertions in the national press, however, targeted the education profession and those supporting 'grass roots' activities.)

But television is a particularly appropriate communication vehicle for addressing adults with poor literacy skills; a medium they feel comfortable with. Furthermore, television is ideally suited to emotion-based communication.

At first glance, airtime on the BBC might seem like a media 'gift' because there is no other advertising. But using the BBC presented difficulties of its own.

— It was impossible to plan a schedule as normal because there was no 'choice' of spots; timings depended on what the BBC had available.

— The sort of advance programming details from commercial networks were not available.

'WENDY'

VISION: A little girl inside her wendy house. She is playing 'mother' to her doll and doing the washing up.
SOUND: (Music): Eerie music-box chimes throughout.
(Little girl): Sorry darling, I can't read to you now, I'm busy.

SOUND: (Little girl): Hullo? – play with your toys love, we'll read later – now, where was I...

SOUND: (Little girl): If you're bored, watch the telly, you can see I've got a lot on (sighs).

SOUND: (MVO) If you can't find time to help them, your children may have problems learning to read.

VISION: She tucks her dolly in bed.
SOUND: (Little girl): Come on now love, bedtime. Perhaps we'll read tomorrow.
SOUND: (MVO) For your free 'Read and Write Together' pack call 0800 44 77 00.

'JACK'

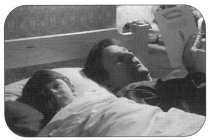

VISION: A small boy lies in bed as his father reads to him.
SOUND: (Father): 'Fee fi fo fum' said the giant as he climbed down the beanstalk…!

VISION: The boy is playing with a toy car as his father reads.
SOUND: (Father): 'Fee fi fo fum' said the giant as he climbed down the beanstalk…!

SOUND: (Father): 'Fee fi fo fum…'
(Son): Daddy, can't you read any other stories?

VISION: The father puts the book down on the bed and leaves the room.
SOUND: (MVO) People who find reading a struggle often read the same story again and again.

VISION: The father collects a 'Read and Write Together' pack from his letterbox.
SOUND: (MVO) Our 'Read and Write Together' pack can help.

VISION: His father is reading a new story to him.
SOUND: (Father): 'I'll huff and I'll puff…'
(Son): Dad, can we have fee fi fo fum?

VISION: Father pretends to shake the boy in mock frustration.
SOUND: (Father): Why you…

'IMAGINE'

VISION: A little girl is standing back from the small group of friends. They are reading a magazine in a newsagents.
SOUND: (Music) Classical strings throughout.

VISION: The girl is sitting in an exam. She is writing, erasing and writing again and again.

VISION: The girl is now a teenager at work. She hesitates before deciding where to place items on the shelf.

VISION: It is her wedding. Her husband points out where she should sign the register.

VISION: She is looking for the maternity ward in a hospital. A nurse points the way.

SOUND: (MVO) She may have your eyes and mouth, but she needn't have the problems you had getting someone to help you read.

VISION: Her daughter is left sitting in front of the television.
SOUND: (MVO) For your free 'Read and Write Together' pack call 0800 44 77 00.

So 31 potential spots were agreed with BBC Education to use as a 'hit-list'. BBC Education attempted to ensure that the advertising was broadcast around appropriate programmes. Half of the 25 spots on the final schedule matched this list.

TABLE 1: THE 'READ AND WRITE TOGETHER' CAMPAIGN

Stations	Dates	Number of spots	Time lengths	ITV equiv national spend*	TVRs
BBC1 & BBC2	11–18 February 1995	25	40	£662,000	220 against the target

* BBC/BBH estimates

THE RESPONSE

Based on response to previous BBC campaigns directed at encouraging adults to return to education and making allowance for the difficulty of motivating adults with poor literacy, the BBC set a target of 40,000 calls.

With only eight days of advertising and 25 spots, the television orderline took 321,049 calls.

The sheer scale of response, over eight times that expected, astonished everyone involved.

'It was a fantastically successful campaign, both in content and in numbers.'

Glenwyn Benson, Departmental Head, BBC Education

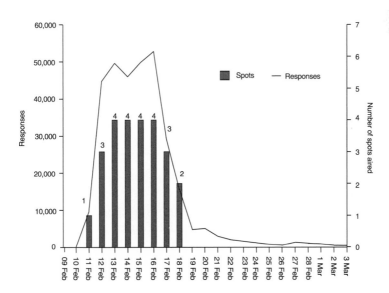

Figure 1: *Relationship between responses and spot timings*
Source: BBC/BBC Audiocall
NB: 280 calls were received on 9 and 10 February, a consequence of local activities

EVALUATING SUCCESS

Responses Track the Advertising

Figure 1 shows the relationship between TV advertising and orders for the learning pack.

Coinciding with the start of TV advertising, there was a jump to 9,735 telephone enquiries on 11 February, 44,830 enquiries on 12 February and so on until the eighth day when we received 15,598 calls. The day afterwards, call levels dropped off immediately.

Reply Card Information

Very few people cannot write at all, so each 'Read and Write Together' pack contained a response-paid card to help us understand more about the target audience – 3,750 reply cards were returned. The cards contained seven open-ended questions, one of which invited respondents to say how they had heard about the pack.

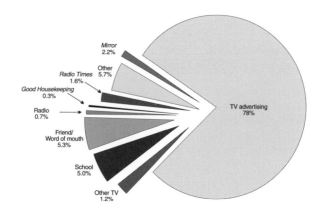

Figure 2: *How did respondents hear about the pack?*
Source: BSA Reply Card Analysis

Figure 2 indicates that 78% (over 250,000) of respondents said (unprompted), that they were motivated to apply for the pack by our advertising.

Figure 3 indicates that nearly 90% reported that they used the TV telephone number to order the pack.

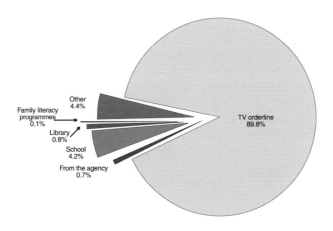

Figure 3: *How did you order the pack?*
Source: BSA Reply Card Analysis

THE SCALE OF THE ACHIEVEMENT

The timing of responses clearly indicated that the advertising was effective. What is particularly interesting about the campaign is the *scale* of the effectiveness.

A Better Performance than Commercial TV Direct Response Measures

In 1994 and 1995 Channel 4 and BT surveyed a series of direct response TV campaigns. They found the single highest response rate to be 0.36% of all adults watching a commercial, and the average response rate for the top ten campaigns surveyed to be 0.17% of all adults watching.

TABLE 2: COMPARISON OF 'READ AND WRITE TOGETHER' AND OTHER
DIRECT RESPONSE CAMPAIGNS

Campaign	% Response from all adults watching any one spot
Best ever response rate across all campaigns surveyed[1]	0.36
Average response rate across best 10 campaigns surveyed[1]	0.17
1995 'Read and Write Together' (17 February 1995)[2]	0.66

1: BT/Channel 4 joint 1995 DRTV Research.
2: This figure is a result of calculating total responses on one evening, as a percentage of total impacts on that same evening. This is a 'tougher' measurement than calculating responses as a percentage of coverage. For example, a respondent can receive three impacts from an ad, but can normally only respond once.

For a 'Read and Write Together' commercial, we recorded a response rate of 0.66%, almost four times that of the average commercial benchmarks.

The Advertising Outperformed Similar BBC Education Campaigns

'Read and Write' Versus Other Literacy Initiatives
The BBC's first project addressing adult literacy, 'On the Move', featured Bob Hoskins, in his first recognised role, as a removal man with literacy problems. Unfortunately, because it was broadcast in 1975, very little information about this campaign remains available. However, we do know that 'On the Move' generated only a third as many responses (120,000), even though 'On the Move' promotional material was broadcast over a longer period than our campaign.

'Read and Write' Versus Similar Adult Education Campaigns
A more recent comparison is available; 'Second Chance', which the BBC ran in 1992 and 1994, was aimed at encouraging adults, whose early experience of education had been unhappy, to return to learning. Both campaigns were broadcast on the BBC and featured a series of executions concentrated over a short period; Table 3 shows the similarities and Table 4 the differences.

TABLE 3: 'SECOND CHANCE' MEDIA DETAILS VERSUS 'READ AND WRITE TOGETHER'

BBC campaign	Media investment BBC/BBH estimates*	Time length	Number of spots
March 1992 'Second Chance'	£1,463,000	90 seconds	33
May 1994 'Second Chance'	£1,179,000	60 seconds	30
February 1995 'Read and Write Together'	£662,000	40 seconds	25

Source: BBC
* Estimates of costs from that year

TABLE 4: 'SECOND CHANCE' CAMPAIGN DETAILS VERSUS 'READ AND WRITE TOGETHER'

	'Read and Write Together'	1994 'Second Chance'
Audience size	1 million	7 million
PR coverage (recorded by BBC Press Department)	180 + articles	700 + articles
0800 number	Yes	Yes
Free pack	Yes	Yes
Supporting programmes	No	Yes

Source: BBC

As can be seen, 'Second Chance' had a number of advantages, which led the BBC to expect lower response to 'Read and Write Together'. Not only was our potential target audience smaller, but adults with literacy problems were less likely to 'come forward'. Admitting to a literacy problem is potentially much more shaming than volunteering for information about adult education.

Nonetheless, the response to 'Read and Write Together' was eight times greater than that for either 'Second Chance' campaign.

TABLE 5: RESPONSES COMPARED TO OTHER BBC CAMPAIGNS

BBC campaign	0800 responses
1992 'Second Chance'	56,933
1994 'Second Chance'	51,415
1995 'Read and Write Together'	321,049

Source: BBC

EXPLAINING THE SCALE OF THE RESPONSE

Three factors could have been responsible for the scale of the response:

— The nature of the product meant that the target could not resist the offer.

— The advertising was unfocused, drawing in responses from people of those parents without literacy problems.

— The advertising was particularly persuasive.

The Scale of the Response was not due to the Nature of the Product or Offer

We believe that the pack was well constructed and useful. Nevertheless, it is unlikely that response could have been driven by a demonstration of the pack alone. The pack only featured on screen briefly in one of the three executions, *Jack*, and in the others not at all. The voice-over and 'super' in all executions simply said: 'For your free "Read and Write Together" pack, call 0800 44 77 00'.

Throughout the campaign, the learning pack was never the focus of the advertising; establishing emotional engagement with the target audience was.

People without Literacy Problems were not Inflating Response Levels

The three executions were specifically designed to attract parents with literacy difficulties and to exclude others. A viewing of the executions will confirm the likelihood of this.

Television includes almost everyone in its reach. Had we simply attracted large numbers of responses from people outside our target? Two pieces of desk analysis indicated that this was not the case.

Regionality of Responses Corresponded with Areas of Lower Average Literacy

Postcodes were supplied by 225,678 of the respondents.

BSA research had shown a correlation between socio-economic class, general
level of education statistics and the possession of poor literacy skills. MORI
analysis of our respondents' postcodes showed an above-index response rate from
districts with a higher proportion of those most likely to experience poor literacy,
as Figures 4 and 5 show.

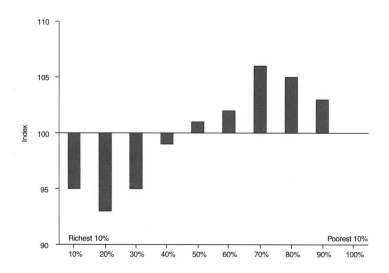

Figure 4: *Response indexed by average socio-economic level in postcode area*
Source: MORI

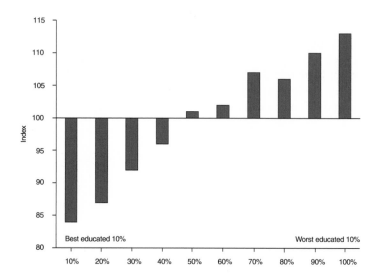

Figure 5: *Response indexed by average education level in postcode area*
Source: MORI

Using MOSAIC categories, which allocate various social 'identities' to each postcode, MORI's analysis also showed an above-index response rate from MOSAIC districts more likely to have lower literacy skills, and a below-index response rate for districts likely to be better off.

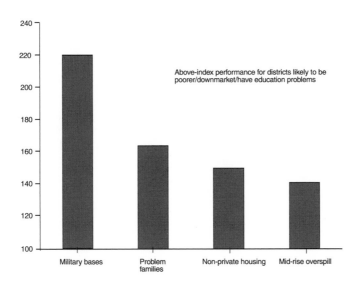

Figure 6: *Above average index of response by MOSAIC postcode area*
Source: MORI

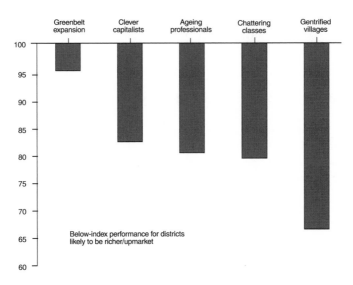

Figure 7: *Below average index of response by MOSAIC postcode area*
Source: MORI

Respondents were Parents

The reply card data confirmed that most respondents were parents and indicated the number of children in the household.

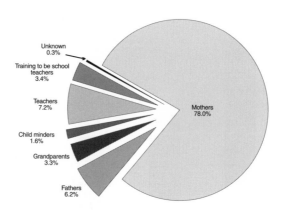

Figure 8: *Relationship between respondents and children*
Source: BSA Reply Card Analysis

Analysis of the postcodes demonstrated that we had overperformed in areas presumed to contain a larger number of our target audience. The reply card data indicated that we had reached parents.

Analysis of Respondent's Handwriting Proved Their Literacy Need

Analysis of respondents' handwriting as given on the reply cards represented a new and unusual method of exploring educational ability, and reassured us that we had attracted the correct type of respondents. The BSA analysed each one to identify whether the writer had literacy problems.

BSA Indicators of Poor Literacy Skills for Reply Card Handwriting Analysis

Grammatical errors:	'used it has a guide', 'Thank you for send it to me', 'am very greatfully for it'
Mixing upper and lower cases in individual words:	'tHanK You', use of 'i' for 'I'
Lower case for first letters of proper names:	'norwich', 'mrs. knight'

| Incorrect punctuation: | 'it gives you good idea's', 'because thats exactly what it does', 'its a good help to children and parents' |
| Incorrect spelling: | definate, relevent, mi, reconnising, differcult, intrested, brillant, untill, realy, usefull, parants, telivision |

NB: Each reply card contained between 30 and 50 words. There were 3,750 reply cards in total.
Source: BSA

The reply card analysis showed that 51% of the people who returned a reply card had significant literacy deficiencies.

But this was only 51% of those who returned a reply card, and almost certainly underestimated the scale of the literacy problem amongst our 321,049 responses, since:

— Return of the card was optional so the sample is very probably not representative. Many parents with the most severe literacy problems would not write a reply.

— The categories suggesting that the writer *did* have literacy needs erred on the side of caution. A single incorrect use of punctuation was not taken as an indication of problems. Moreover, errors that might conceivably be the consequence of regional variations or poor skills were not used as a certain indicator, eg *'it helps me to learn my child'*.

— It is likely that those who did reply made an extra effort not to make mistakes because responding on a semi-official form.

Nonetheless, the cards indicated that at least 51% of our 321,049 respondents had literacy difficulties.

By combining this 51% with the 78% of responses that the reply cards indicated were attributable to the advertising, at a bare minimum over 127,000 (321,049 x 78% x 51%) members of the target audience had taken steps to address their literacy problem, *directly* as a result of the campaign.

The Advertising was Particularly Persuasive

An RSGB Omnibus indicated that the advertising was particularly persuasive and that this was the primary reason for the scale of the response.

The Omnibus results demonstrated surprisingly high spontaneous awareness of the advertising, considering that the campaign achieved only 220 TVRs and was on air for only eight days (see Figure 9).

Prompted, the recall figure almost doubled. Recall among our target audience was even higher (see Figure 10).

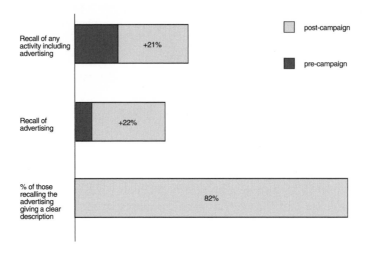

Figure 9: *Unprompted recall of advertising campaign*
Source: RSGB Omnibus, 1–5 February 1995/ 22–25 February 1995, sample 1,000, UK population weighted

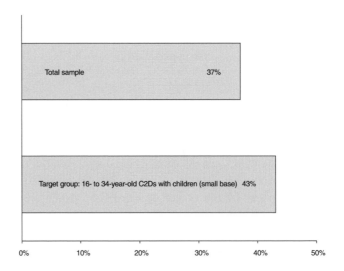

Figure 10: *Prompted recall of advertising campaign*
Source: RSGB Omnibus

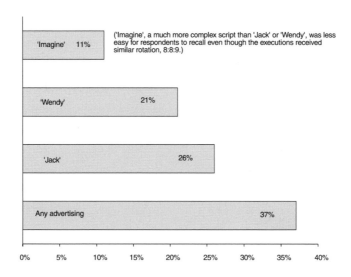

Figure 11: *Prompted recall of individual executions*
Source: RSGB Omnibus

Moreover, prompted recall data showed that all three executions could be recalled in some detail (see Figure 11).

(Incidentally, awareness levels outperformed earlier BBC campaigns that had used similar samples and methodologies and we would have gained a place in the Adwatch Top 20. Table 6 features campaigns with much higher media spends and, as a consequence, much higher TVRs.)

TABLE 6: AWARENESS LEVELS COMPARED TO
SIMILAR BBC CAMPAIGNS AND 'ADWATCH'

Campaign	% Awareness
1992 'Second Chance' (Television Opinion Panel survey, 3,170 viewers, awareness of the ads)	21*
1994 'Second Chance' (Television Opinion Panel, 3,170 viewers, awareness of any activity)	31*
Adwatch (Audience Selection, weekly list of Top 20 'best recalled' campaigns; first quarter 1996 average levels of all claimed, prompted awareness among sample of 1,000, weighted to reflect UK population, giving ads Top 20 entry)	37
1995 'Read and Write Together' (RSGB, all claimed, prompted, awareness, sample of 1,000, weighted to reflect UK population)	37

* Higher weights of advertising
Source: BBC / Adwatch

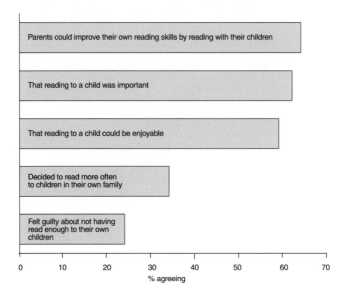

Figure 12: *Advertising's effect upon claimed intention and key communication dimensions*
Base: Those recalling the advertising
Source: RSGB Omnibus

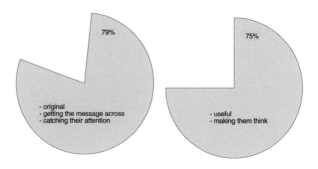

Figure 13: *Percentage agreeing that the advertising was...*
Base: Those recalling the advertising
Source: RSGB Omnibus

The RSGB results also indicated that parents had accepted the message and, even at this stage, reported an intention to change their behaviour (see Figure 12).

People's attitudes towards the executions were also extremely positive, indicating that they generated the empathy and warmth we had hoped (see Figure 13).

The levels of awareness and recall, and the positive attitude towards the advertising are indicators of the executions' ability to cut through and to persuade the target audience. The findings also suggested that we were generating empathy with the target group and that the audience understood the message of the campaign.

DISCOUNTING OTHER FACTORS

Local activities took place in schools and libraries organised as Family Literacy Week. It appears that these accounted for 30,000 additional 'bulk' orders direct to the BSA (additional to our 321,049 responses) but local activities seem unlikely to have driven our response levels significantly.

We knew that our target audience did not read often, so few responses would be generated by press PR (the reply cards reflect this). In any case, 'Read and Write Together' received less press PR than 'Second Chance' yet generated more responses.

Moreover, the campaign was supported only by editorial articles in *The Bookworm*, 4.25pm on Sunday 12 February 1995 and *Video Nation* 7.30pm on Tuesday 14 February 1995.

Given this limited support, it is hardly surprising that only 1% of reply cards cited 'other TV programme', and 0.7% 'radio', as the reason for calling. (Source: BSA reply card analysis).

('Second Chance' 1994 had three five-minute documentaries, two half-hour documentaries, and Channel 4 ran a series of films about unemployment and education – yet all of these taken together did not result in a higher response level.)

It was the BBC's firm belief that the advertising was the cause of the success of 'Read and Write Together':

'We were extremely pleased with such a high level of response, which vindicates the approach and the advertising responsible.'

Glenwyn Benson, Departmental Head, BBC Education

PAYBACK

TABLE 7: CAMPAIGN COSTS

BBH estimates of ITV equivalent media costs	£662,000
Television production costs	£140,000
Production, handling, postage for learning pack *	£875,000
Total campaign costs	£1,677,000

* We included the pack costs when calculating payback as the advertising alone could not 'cure' literacy needs, it only prompted the target to take first steps towards a 'cure' to obtain the learning pack

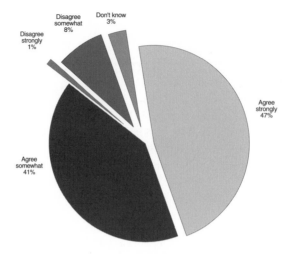

Figure 14: *Poor basic skills increase industry costs*
Base: Gallup survey of 400 UK companies
Source: BSA, The Cost to Industry

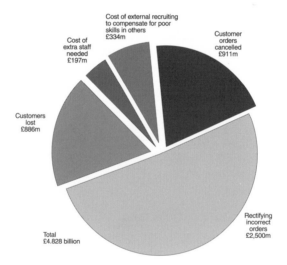

Figure 15: *Estimated costs to industry of poor basic skills*
Base: Gallup survey of 400 UK companies
Note: This £4.828 billion was felt to be an underestimate. For example, it did not include loss of future business or the costs of training staff who cannot cope with written materials.
Source: BSA, The Cost to Industry

THE COST TO INDUSTRY OF POOR BASIC SKILLS

It would be naïve to expect that a learning pack will change people's ability; all we can do is to move them up the literacy scale.

Nonetheless, by way of comparison with advertising investment, we have estimated costs to British industry of poor literacy in the UK workforce. The total cost is £4.828 billion.

If we divide this £4.828 billion total among individuals with poor literacy in the workforce, we can estimate what contribution each individual makes to the total.

In March 1994, the UK workforce was around 21.5 million people, but we estimate that only one in ten of the workforce has literacy problems, because our target group finds it more difficult to get a job.

Consequently, around two million workers have literacy difficulties. Each contributes around £2,450 a year to the total cost to industry of £4.828 billion.

If we could even begin to improve any of these workers' literacy skills, we could begin to reduce the cost to industry; for every worker whose skills improved, we could remove their contribution of £2,450 from the national total of £4.828 billion.

Or, put another way, if we could cut 0.035% from the cost of poor basic skills to industry, the money saved, in just one year, would be the payback for the advertising campaign.

This means that if only 690 of the 127,000 people with low literacy skills, who we know responded to our campaign, went on to 'cure' their poor literacy, we would see a return on the campaign investment in the costs saved to British industry.

Of course, taking this argument further, over a working life of 30 years, each worker would cost industry not £2,450, but 30 x £2,450, or £73,500. In that case we would need only 23 of our respondents at the start of their working life to improve their literacy in order to justify our investment...!

CONCLUSION

The BBC is the world's biggest, most experienced educational producer, broadcasting over 3,000 hours of education programming annually. Yet the advertising prompted the largest ever telephone response to a BBC television education campaign.

Advertising succeeded because it engaged the target audience's emotions, generating an empathy that drove it to respond.

By bringing to bear the skills of advertising to the campaign, the BBC's prediction of 40,000 calls turned out to be far too low. Advertising was so successful that, with only 75,000 packs printed, we had to call on further funds to supply the 321,049 packs eventually requested.

The campaign won *Marketing* magazine's 'Best Use of Telemarketing in Direct Response TV' award in 1995. In March 1996 BBC Education won a Royal Television Society Educational Award in the category 'Adult Education Television' for 'Read and Write Together', the first time this award had been given to an advertising campaign.

> 'The campaign not only exceeded our expectations, it was beyond anything we could have hoped for.'

> Fiona Pitcher, Executive Producer, BBC Education

But much more importantly, a large number of parents no longer felt able to ignore their literacy problem and did at least one thing about it, sending off for a learning pack.

5

Frizzell Insurance

When the customer is not always right

INTRODUCTION

This is the story of how advertising built a brand through selective targeting. By devising a campaign that was only motivating to a desirable target, we were able to attract profitable customers – and deliberately discourage others.

BACKGROUND

At the end of World War I, a young Scottish sergeant, Thomas Frizzell, left the Royal Flying Corps with the ambition of setting up his own insurance company.

He believed that, by offering not only excellent products but also the highest standards of service, he would set his insurance company apart from its many competitors. His conviction was justified. From its launch in 1923, at a time when the concept of customer care was relatively unknown, Thomas Frizzell's approach gave his company the impetus that saw it grow from modest beginnings with a staff of two, to becoming a leading provider of financial services.

Such growth was generated by clever marketing. Thomas Frizzell recognised that the future belonged to the car. He focused his business on motor insurance, and persuaded the Civil Service Motoring Association (CSMA) to become one of the company's first partners. This was a shrewd move: civil servants made profitable customers because they happened to be 'safe' risks. They were sensible, responsible drivers, who were prepared to pay for quality service and cover – and less likely to claim on their insurance. Over the years Frizzell gained additional 'safe' risks by concentrating recruitment not only on the Civil Service, but also on professionals such as teachers and other public servants. This was achieved by targeting 'affinity' group organisations (the CSMA, the NUT and NALGO), through organisational tie-ups, or through direct response ads in magazines such as *The Teacher* and *Public Servant*.

The business itself was handled directly from Frizzell's head office in Bournemouth, mainly over the telephone. This meant that Frizzell was actually in the vanguard of direct selling, 20 years before the likes of Direct Line.

FRIZZELL IN THE 1990s

By 1993, Frizzell had more than 600,000 customers, and an estimated company value of £108 million. True to the company's heritage, insurance (particularly motor insurance), remained Frizzell's main business, although banking and independent financial advice were also major profit contributors.

Frizzell's customers continued to be profitable. They remained low risk and, therefore, fairly claim free. But they were also profitable because they were extremely loyal to Frizzell, a characteristic which resulted in the company enjoying some of the highest renewal rates in the business. Nine out of ten customers renewed their policies annually. The average customer stayed for over 12 years. And some had been Frizzell customers for more than 55 years.

THE PROBLEM

The 1980s were good years for Frizzell, with the business growing strongly. But with the start of a new decade, the situation began to change dramatically. In January 1990, Direct Line launched its first TV advertising campaign.

Direct Line had entered the insurance market in 1985. The idea behind the business was simple and, ironically, it mirrored Frizzell's own approach. Rather than use traditional broking methods, it sold insurance direct to the public over the telephone from one centralised office. Unlike Frizzell, however, Direct Line underwrote its own insurance. The resultant cost savings were passed directly on to the consumer, enabling it to compete aggressively on price. By itself, this would probably have been a successful formula, but what made it so revolutionary was the decision to use high-profile TV advertising to generate business.

The successful formula of Direct Line was quickly imitated. Since 1990, 23 new 'direct' insurers have been launched, all offering cut-price insurance, and all advertising heavily. As the direct sector of the market has grown, prices have tumbled (Figure 1). Total expenditure on insurance advertising has increased by 216%, with a greater use of TV than previously (Figure 2).

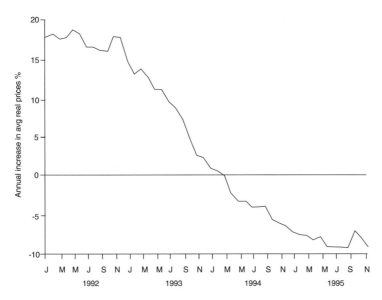

Figure 1: *Real premium inflation, motor insurance*
Source: SG Warburg, Advertising Association, CSO
Note: Data for household insurance not available

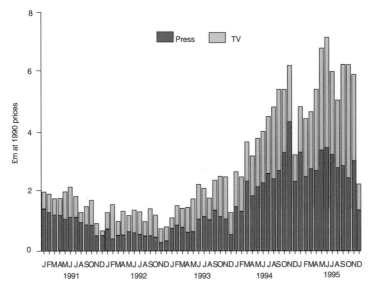

Figure 2: *Total real adspend, insurance market*
Source: Register/MEAL, Advertising Association

By 1994, Frizzell was facing a challenge. With more advertised firms to choose from, it was increasingly unlikely that new customers would turn to a relatively obscure company like Frizzell for a quote. This was reflected in a slow-down of enquiries (Figure 3).

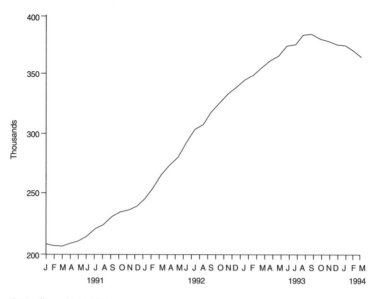

Figure 3: *Total Frizzell enquiries MAT*
Source: Frizzell

NEW MARKETING STRATEGY

Something had to be done. Even with a relatively loyal customer base, Frizzell's business would begin to shrink unless more customers were recruited. The only way to generate new business in sufficient volume was by shifting the focus away from affinity recruitment towards a broader target. Frizzell chose to commit itself for the first time in its 70-year history to mainstream consumer advertising.

THE SCALE OF THE TASK

The company was understandably nervous about committing itself to such an expensive new venture. Few people (apart from affinity group members) had heard of the company (Table 1):

TABLE 1: PROMPTED BRAND AWARENESS OF INSURANCE COMPANIES

	Motor %	Household %
AA	86	26
General Accident	83	66
Swinton	74	47
Direct Line	70	27
Commercial Union	65	69
Prudential	57	83
Sun Alliance	57	74
Churchill	47	22
Frizzell	16	11

Source: Audience Selection, 1993

Although not strictly speaking a new brand, Frizzell would probably be perceived as such by consumers. It was effectively a late entrant into an extremely competitive market. In addition, Frizzell was competing, on a budget of £1.7 million over the first year, with companies that traditionally invested heavily in consumer advertising (Table 2).

TABLE 2: TOTAL ADVERTISING EXPENDITURE 1990–94

Direct Line	£21.9m
Churchill	£16.6m
AA	£15.4m
The Insurance Service	£15.0m
Swinton	£13.3m

Source: MEAL

It was clear that, if Frizzell was going to be successful against the Goliaths of the insurance world, it needed an imaginative strategy.

BUSINESS STRATEGY

Product Focus

Advertising was to focus on Frizzell's core area of expertise – insurance – rather than the full range of Frizzell's services. Other product areas, such as banking, could be supported in time.

Enquiry Generation

The ultimate aim of the advertising was to generate significant numbers of enquiries. Moreover, for the brand to compete successfully in the future, not just short-term but long-term enquiry generation was vital.

Quality of Enquiries

There was concern that straightforward awareness generation could attract potential customers indiscriminately, including the wrong sort of people (higher risks, such as younger drivers and irresponsible householders). These people would be wrong for two reasons:

— it would be difficult for Frizzell to satisfy them on price;

— if they did take out a policy, they would be more likely to claim.

Since each unsuitable call still incurred handling time, all enquiries that did not lead to a sale remained a cost. Therefore, it was not enough to interest people in Frizzell. The ads had to interest the *right* people, and actively discourage everyone else.

The key measure of success here would be the 'closing rate' – the proportion of enquiries leading to sales. Frizzell's closing rates were traditionally high, because most enquiries were generated by word of mouth and affinity groups' recommendation. It was accepted that it would be difficult for advertising to match this. Nevertheless, it was important that the inevitable fall in closing rates should be minimised.

DIRECT RESPONSE OR BRAND BUILDING?

One way for Frizzell to generate awareness and increase enquiries was direct response advertising. Indeed, the majority of insurance companies were following the tried and tested direct response style: simple price messages, accompanied by a brand name, a telephone number, and an invitation to call. Apart from Direct Line, little attempt was made at brand building: all that was required was immediate response.

Frizzell rejected such an approach for the following three reasons.

i) Frizzell offered quality products, not cheap deals, being about 5% dearer than the competition.

ii) Frizzell wanted to position itself away from most other insurance advertising:

'We believe that an innovative positioning and strong creative approach, whilst initially riskier, may provide the greater long-term reward.' (Frizzell Advertising Brief, 1993)

iii) Most significantly, it was considered difficult for the normal type of direct response advertising to attract desirable customers, and discourage others. What was required was direct response advertising with a difference: a campaign that could build a distinctive brand and subtly signal the right response cues to the desired target at the same time. The advertising would, therefore, have to act as an attitudinal filter:

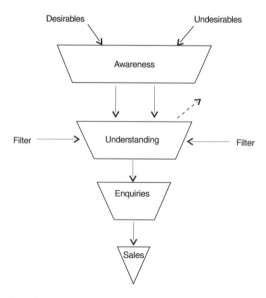

Figure 4: *Attitudinal filter effect of the advertising*

To achieve this, it was vital to understand the sort of person Frizzell wanted to target and, with them in mind, identify what positioning the brand should adopt.

DEFINING THE TARGET

We studied the characteristics of existing Frizzell customers. Research revealed them to be traditional, responsible people, the sort who might spend their time gardening, doing crosswords, reading and taking caravan holidays in the Dordogne. While many of them were older (over 35 years), and slightly upmarket, they tended to be defined more by attitude than socio-economics. They were conservative, loyal, risk-averse and cautious. And this affected their expectations of insurance. They wanted integrity and good service rather than cheap deals.

DEFINING THE POSITIONING

From our understanding of these 'Careful Planners', as we described them, we were able to discover the brand positioning that was most appealing to them – to potential like-minded customers – and least appealing to everyone else.

Among existing customers the company was seen as honest, expert, trustworthy and helpful. It was genuinely regarded as one of the best-kept secrets in financial services. Such respect was unusual in a market normally viewed with suspicion.

Attitudes towards Frizzell were encapsulated by the concept of *loyalty*. Our 'Careful Planners' respected the fact that Frizzell had some of the most loyal customers in the business. For them, loyalty to the brand signified excellent service and good-value products. It was also a quality with which they closely identified, valuing it in their own working and personal lives.

By contrast, loyalty was irrelevant to the 'high risk' consumer, more interested in financial deals. It was evident that such a positioning would provide us with the filter we needed.

TABLE 3: LOYALTY – THE DESIRED EFFECT

Existing customers	Reflects and enhances positive experience
Desirable potential customers	Proof of excellent service/product
	Proof of value for money
	A company we recognise as trustworthy
	Aimed at people like us
Undesirable customers	Not aimed at us

FRIZZELL INSURANCE '1957' 40 SECONDS

Music plays ('My Special Angel' by Malcolm Vaughan)

(MVO) In 39 years the world has seen many changes.

But Mr and Mrs Leverton are still with Frizzell Insurance.

FRIZZELL INSUARNCE '1965' 40 SECONDS

Music plays ('I'll Never Find Another You' by The Seekers)

The Beatles collect their MBEs.

First US space walk.

Mr Catherall slightly damages his Hillman Minx.

He calls Frizzell Insurance.

Who quickly despatch a claims form.

Mr Catherall. Still with Frizzell Insurance.

(MVO) In 31 years the world has seen a lot of changes. But Mr Catherall is still with Frizzell Insurance.

FRIZZELL
Direct Motor Insurance
0800 608 608
We'll make sure you never want to leave.

FRIZZELL INSURANCE '1970' 40 SECONDS

Music plays ('Everything Is Beautiful' by Ray
Stevens)

(MVO) In 26 years the world has seen many
changes.

But Mr and Mrs Saffin are still with Frizzell
Insurance.

CREATIVE BRIEF

As a result, the brief focused on loyalty:

TABLE 4: THE CREATIVE BRIEF

Key insight:	Customers who join Frizzell rarely leave
The target:	Desirables: Existing/future customers –
	sensible, cautious 'Careful Planners'
Not:	The undesirables: Those looking for cheap deals
Proposition:	When you join Frizzell, you will never want to leave
Support:	Highest customer loyalty rates in the business
	Friendly, caring, helpful staff with your interests at heart
	Quality products of excellent value

MEDIA CHOICE

Television was chosen as the best medium to dramatise the proposition and capture Frizzell's unique values. Radio and press were chosen as possible secondary media if the budget allowed.

ADVERTISING SOLUTION

The first creative work to be researched involved spoof romantic scenarios in which the intensity of relationship between the Frizzell customer and the company was dramatised.

This created a problem. Potential Frizzell customers found it too frivolous, both in tone and message, and this made them suspicious of a company of which they had never heard:

'I don't really trust them, these Frizzell people with their odd name, what do they know about insurance?'

'Careful Planner', BMP DDB Qualitative Research

By contrast, higher risk consumers, the very people Frizzell did not want to attract, found the proposed campaign extremely appealing. The brief was therefore revised to focus on longevity of relationship as a better expression of loyalty.

To help the creative team's understanding of the target's characteristics, film of family and friends who fitted both the desirable and undesirable profile was used to bring them to life.

The result was a campaign based on real case histories, involving customers like Mr Catherall, who had joined Frizzell at least 20 years earlier, and who had stayed ever since. The authenticity of the stories was supported by news footage and music from the appropriate period. The approach was warm and gentle. Both the message and tone proved extremely appealing to Frizzell's target: they appreciated the subtle humour and the use of nostalgia. They prided themselves on remembering key dates from their past. They believed the stories and identified with the characters portrayed. And, above all, they respected the emphasis on traditional values. By contrast, the undesirable found the idea not only unexciting – but also irrelevant.

TABLE 5: RESPONSE BY CONSUMER SEGMENTATION

Desirable 'Careful Planners':	It is charming – honest and involving.
	I would respond better to this sort of ad.
	I loathe most insurance ads ramming it down your throats.
	An honourable company with traditional values of service – in a world of sharks.
Undesirables:	It's simplistic rubbish. Frizzell, what have they got to offer?
	It's just boring – I can't be bothered.

Source: BMP DDB Qualitative Research, April 1994

Two television executions were developed, one focusing on motor insurance and one on household. Two radio ads, picking up on the theme of loyalty, were also recorded.

THE MERIDIAN TEST

The campaign initially ran in a test area so that the effect of Frizzell's first major advertising campaign could be carefully monitored. Meridian was chosen because the area includes Bournemouth, the home of Frizzell; it was hoped that the campaign would raise staff morale. It also happened to be Frizzell's strongest region (with highest awareness and a significant number of policy holders).

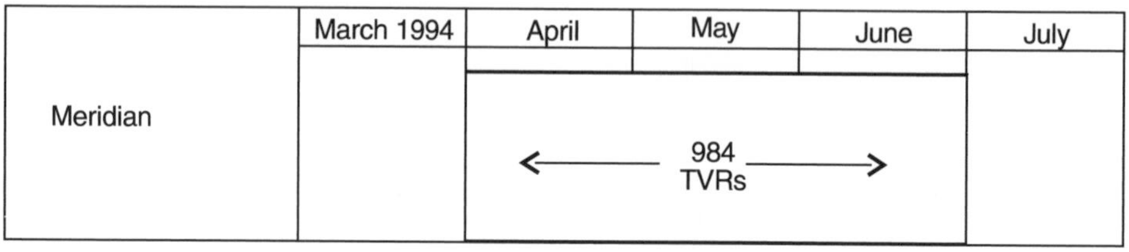

	March 1994	April	May	June	July
Meridian			← 984 TVRs →		

Figure 5: *Meridian test*
Source: BMP Media

The results of the Meridian test were encouraging. Prompted brand awareness (already higher in this region than others) increased dramatically. Equally important, the advertising had the right effect. Enquiries from the Meridian area increased while continuing to fall in the rest of the country (Table 6).

TABLE 6: MERIDIAN TEST RESULTS

	Pre (March 1994)	Post (August 1994)	% Change
Prompted brand awareness	47%	78%	+66
Enquiries in Meridian	6,114	6,356	+4
Enquiries in other regions	27,694	22,789	-18

Source: Frizzell/Millward Brown

Encouragingly, the advertising also appeared to be communicating the right message: brand image improved on four key dimensions (see Figure 6).

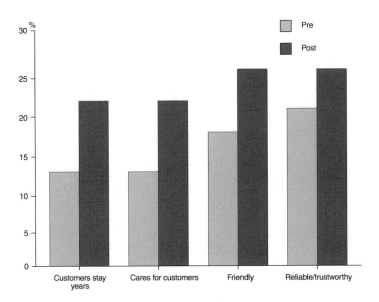

Figure 6: *Improvements in Frizzell's image in Meridian*
Source: Millward Brown

On the basis of these encouraging results, Frizzell extended the campaign nationally.

THE NATIONAL ROLL-OUT

The media strategy was planned around staggered regional bursts to avoid big peaks and troughs in total enquiry levels (hence utilising Frizzell's call-handling operation in the most efficient way).

The first regions targeted, in September 1994, were West Country, Anglia, HTV, Yorkshire and Tyne Tees. Meridian was also included for a second wave of advertising. Further activity extended the campaign to other areas, with national coverage (excluding Scotland) being achieved by summer 1995. The ads also ran briefly on satellite television during October and November 1994.

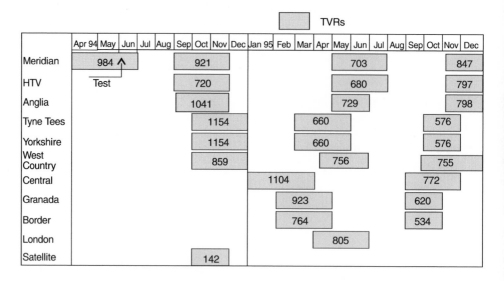

Figure 7: *Frizzell television roll-out*
Source: BMP Media

Initially, the motor and household ads ran at a ratio of 1:1. With the introduction of a second household ad in 1995, they ran at a ratio of 2:1, putting the greater emphasis on the household product.

OTHER MEDIA

The radio ads ran during November and December 1994 on Classic FM, in conjunction with Frizzell's sponsorship of the station's Travel Update. However, pressure on budgets led to the ads running for only four weeks.

Advertising ran in the national press from May to July 1995 to promote household insurance.

OTHER ACTIVITY

Frizzell continued direct response advertising in the affinity press. The company also continued its sponsorship of British Equestrian three-day eventing.

THE EFFECT OF THE ROLL-OUT

The Effect on Awareness

The roll-out produced even greater awareness shifts than the test:

TABLE 7: FIRST BURST RESULTS – PROMPTED BRAND AWARENESS BY REGION

	Pre 1st burst %	Post 1st burst %	% change
Meridian	47	78	+65
West Country	23	47	+104
Anglia	19	67	+253
HTV	25	55	+120
Tyne Tees	16	68	+325
Yorkshire	14	66	+371
London	22	54	+145
Central	16	58	+262
Granada	13	59	+154

Source: Millward Brown/Frizzell

Overall, awareness of the Frizzell brand at the national level increased by 200% during the first year of the campaign, going from 20% to 60%. The way that awareness built up over time, and the lack of any substantial drop in awareness when the advertising went off air in August 1995, suggested that awareness decayed slowly (less than 10% decay a month). The awareness gains appeared, therefore, to be quite long term (Figure 8).

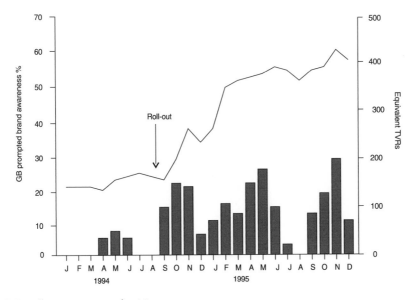

Figure 8: *Frizzell awareness versus advertising*
Source: Millward Brown, Frizzell

The Effect on Brand Understanding

The communication of the advertising was strong. Research revealed detailed recall of each scenario, indicating that people's involvement with the campaign was extremely high:

Sample Verbatims from Tracking Study

'It's set in the '50s or '60s, and it's all in multicolour. Coal falls on the hearth rug. They stuck with Frizzell. I had never heard of Frizzell before I saw the advert. They have been around a long time. They are reliable. People are happy with them and they will be around in the future.'

'It's the one where a man is driving a car and he hits a slippery bit and hits a wall. Then it shows 25 years later. He has lost his hair but he is still with them. I hadn't heard of them until I saw the ad. The music was nice. They have been going about 25 years. They are looking after their customers as they did years ago.'

'The one with the two old dears. They are talking in the garden. It seems to go back in time to show they have been around a long time. They came to be coloured as they aged, and they are still with them. They are friendly...they always give a reliable and quick service.'

' "Everything is beautiful" song and a fence being knocked down by some cows. They eat Mr Thing's runner beans. The couple change dramatically – a 25-year gap. The people have always been happy with the company and so stayed with them.'

Source: Millward Brown Tracking Study, 1995

Such involvement had a notable effect. After the first burst, Frizzell's image improved significantly (Figure 9).

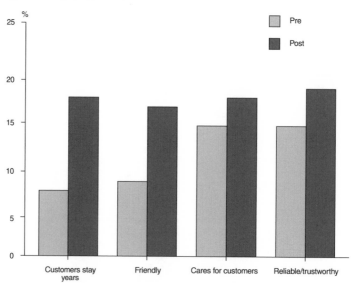

Figure 9: *Improvements in Frizzell's image in rest of country*
Source: Millward Brown
Note: During the advertised period, some regions only received four bursts of advertising and some only one or two bursts. To avoid complication we have therefore focused on image shifts for the first burst.

Further Indication of Impact

Internal company questionnaires revealed that the advertising had a positive effect on staff morale. The salesforce regularly reported comments of approval from customers. Frizzell also received many letters from customers complimenting them on the campaign. Additionally, at least two calls a week requested information about the music and films used in the commercials.

The advertising won two Bronzes at the 1995 British TV Awards for 'Best New Campaign'.

The Effect on Enquiry Volumes

There was also a marked turnaround in the level of telephone enquiries. The decline first appeared to slow and then to reverse (Figure 10).

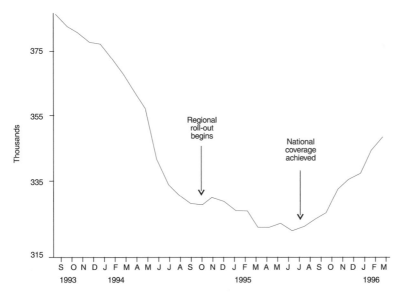

Figure 10: *Total Frizzell insurance enquiries, motor and household, MAT*
Source: Frizzell

Quality of Enquiries

The spectacular increase in awareness and enquiries that followed the advertising was extremely encouraging. But was it among the right people?

There was initial concern that Frizzell was receiving too many young (under 35-year-old) callers. Even though it had always been accepted that the target definition was one more of attitude than demographics, we needed to know whether the filtering of desirables and undesirables was really working. Frizzell therefore conducted a special survey involving psychographic analysis of those under 35-year-olds contacting Frizzell as a result of the advertising.

The findings revealed that over 83% of the callers in this group shared the 'Careful Planner' attitudes, and so fell within the target.

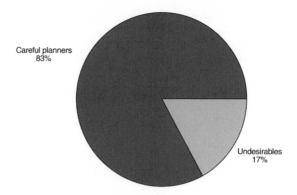

Figure 11: *Psychographic profiling of under 35-year-old enquirers*
Source: IRB International

Such evidence is supported by further analysis of the tracking data. This shows that while awareness grew generally, consideration of Frizzell for insurance only rose significantly among the desired target.

TABLE 8: AWARENESS AND CONSIDERATION OF FRIZZELL

	Pre %	Post %	Change %
Desirables: Careful Planners			
Prompted awareness	43	73	+70
Would consider Frizzell for motor insurance	22	45	+104
Would consider Frizzell for household insurance	17	38	+123
Undesirables			
Prompted awareness	47	80	+70
Would consider Frizzell for motor insurance	25	26	+4
Would consider Frizzell for household insurance	23	25	+8

Source: Millward Brown

However, the ultimate test of quality was the closing rate, the proportion of enquiries leading to sales. As we expected, the closing rate for advertising-generated enquiries was lower than for other enquiries – but only slightly. So the advertising was successful in generating 'quality' enquiries; further proof that the 'filter' worked as intended.

TABLE 9: PROPORTION OF ENQUIRIES LEADING TO SALES

	Advertising-generated enquiries	All other enquiries
Closing rate (Index)*	89	100

*Frizzell's closing rates and sales figures are confidential so cannot be disclosed.

POSITIVE EVIDENCE THAT ADVERTISING WAS RESPONSIBLE

We have four kinds of evidence (regional awareness, regional enquiries, phone call analysis and econometrics), to suggest that it was primarily advertising that affected brand response.

Regional Awareness

There is a strong correlation[1] between the size of the awareness shift in each region, and the amount of advertising to which the region was exposed (Figure 12).

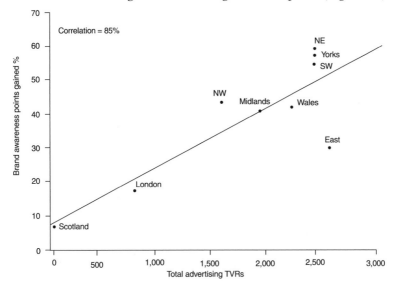

Figure 12: *Awareness shifts versus advertising, overall effect of a regional roll-out*
Source: Millward Brown, Frizzell, BARB
All data September 1994 to December 1995. Meridian is not shown because it had already been exposed to one burst of advertising and so cannot be compared to the other regions in a straightforward way.

In Scotland, where there was no advertising on ITV, awareness hardly changed. The slight shift that did occur was probably due to the small amount of satellite advertising that took place in autumn 1994.

Regional Enquiries

Regional analysis also shows that the advertising did increase enquiry levels. In 1994, roughly half the country was exposed to advertising, allowing us to compare advertised against non-advertised regions. Until the autumn roll-out, enquiry patterns in the two halves of the country were very similar (Figure 13). But as soon as the advertising began, the patterns diverged, with enquiries falling in the non-advertised regions, and rising in the advertised ones.

---

1.   Statistically significant at the 95% confidence level.

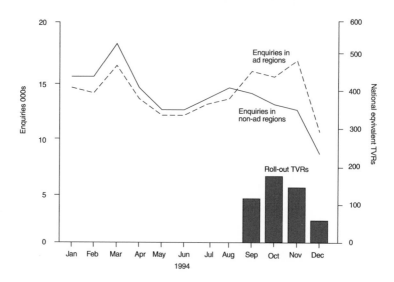

Figure 13: *Effect of roll-out on enquiries*
Source: Frizzell, BARB

Furthermore, there is a clear relationship between the amount of advertising each region was exposed to and the size of the enquiry uplift (Figure 14).

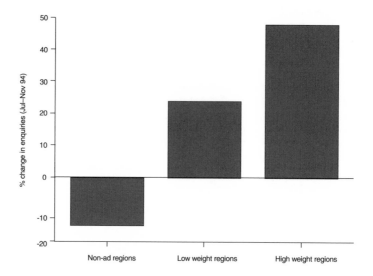

Figure 14: *Effect of roll-out on enquiries*
Source: Frizzell
Low-weight regions (HTV/South West): under 800 TVRs. High-weight regions (Meridian/Tyne Tees/Yorks/Anglia): 900–1000 TVRs

So, as with the Meridian test, the regional roll-out did appear to increase enquiry levels. Unfortunately, it is not possible to extend the regional analysis into 1995, because there were too few non-advertised regions that year to act as a control. But we can prove that the ads did continue to generate enquiries by looking at the log of phone calls made to the company.

Phone Call Analysis

Tracking revealed a significant increase in the number of people claiming to have heard of Frizzell from television advertising (Figure 15).

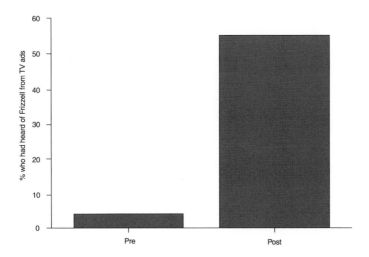

Figure 15: *Increase in awareness due to TV ads*
Q: 'How did you first hear of Frizzell?'
Source: Millward Brown

In addition, when people phone for insurance they are asked how they heard about Frizzell. Their answers are coded for analysis, providing a good indication of what prompted their call.

This revealed that:

i) there was a significant rise in the number of people saying that they were prompted by advertising;

ii) the flow of advertising-generated enquiries continued throughout 1995;

iii) there was an obvious relationship between the number of TVRs in any month and the number of enquiries generated;

iv) household enquiries rose dramatically following the greater support put behind the household executions in 1995.

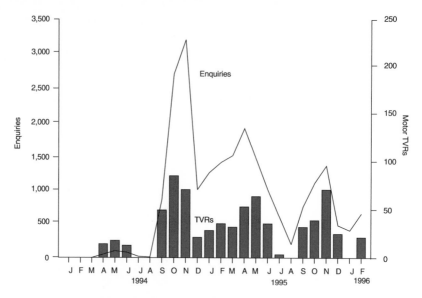

Figure 16: *Frizzell motor enquiries directly attributable to TV ads*
Source: Frizzell Phone Call Analysis

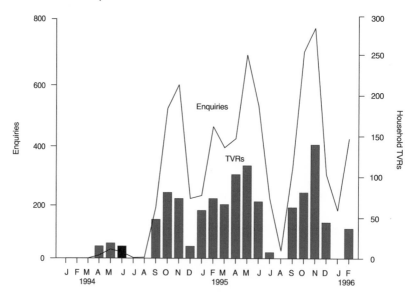

Figure 17: *Frizzell household enquiries directly attributable to TV ads*
Source: Frizzell Phone Call Analysis

Advertising-coded enquiries alone were enough to account for the turnaround in 1995. However, people are not always aware of, or willing to admit to, the influence of advertising, so the phone call analysis could underestimate the size of the advertising effect. Figure 18 confirms that this was the case. Comparing the results of the regional analysis with the call analysis reveals that the latter underestimated the effect by at least 47%. Also, looking at the unadvertised period of July to August 1994, it appears that the advertising effect decayed more slowly than the call analysis suggested.

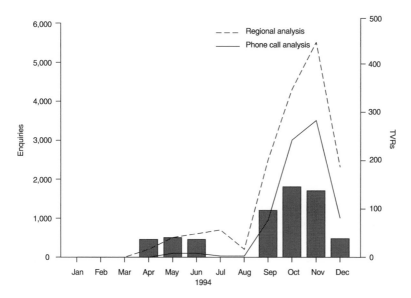

Figure 18: *Estimated enquiries generated by ads*
Source: Frizzell, BARB

So while the call analysis provided evidence that advertising did affect enquiries, it could only suggest a minimum effect. In order to estimate the true effect, we used econometrics.

Econometric Analysis

Econometrics had been successfully used in the planning process from the start of the campaign, enabling us to set targets, evaluate performance and forecast future trends. Analysis of the whole advertising period revealed that 100 TVRs increased enquiries by 2.2%, with the effect decaying away at 5% a month. This was entirely consistent with the slow decay rate observed for awareness.

The model also confirmed that the advertising was responsible for reversing the decline in enquiry levels. Without it, Frizzell's position would have continued to deteriorate (Figure 19). In all, advertising generated a total of 102,000 enquiries by December 1995, which accounted for 26% of all Frizzell enquiries that year.

Additionally, because the effect decayed away so slowly, enquiries would still be generated for the next two to three years, even if no advertising ran after 1995. We estimated that this effect would bring in an extra 205,000 enquiries, raising the total to 307,000.

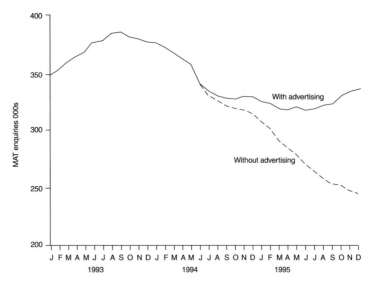

Figure 19: *The effect of advertising on Frizzell enquiry levels*
Source: Frizzell, Econometric Model

ELIMINATING OTHER INFLUENCES

Despite such positive evidence, we needed to be sure that there were no other factors assisting the enquiry increase. We analysed each of these in turn.

Car Sales

The car market was relatively static during the period when the advertising ran (Figure 20).

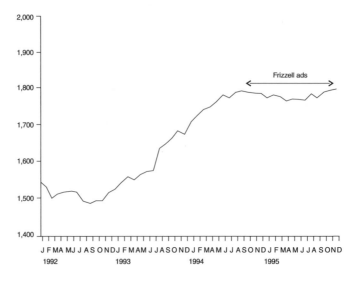

Figure 20: *New car registrations, MAT*
Source: CSO

Housing Market

The housing market continued to decline (Figure 21).

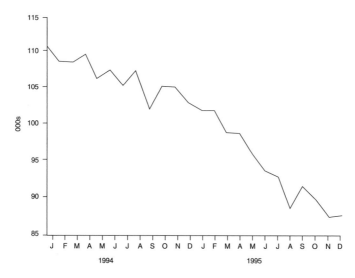

Figure 21: *The housing market, number of transactions*
Source: Inland Revenue (NB: Figures are for England and Wales – Scottish data unavailable)

Price

Experience shows that price does affect enquiries; as prices rise, people shop around more. But average prices fell throughout the advertised period, so this factor would have depressed enquiries, not boosted them.

Nor was it down to a reduction in Frizzell's relative price. Frizzell became less competitive (Figure 22).

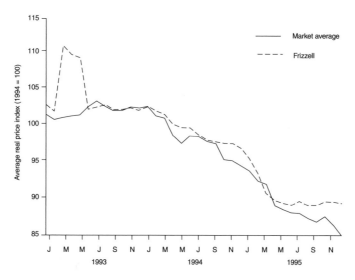

Figure 22: *Average real price of motor insurance*
Source: SG Warburg, Advertising Association, CSO, Frizzell

Easing of Competition

The market became more competitive, not less. After 1994, 15 new direct insurers entered the market, and competitive adspends tripled (Figure 23).

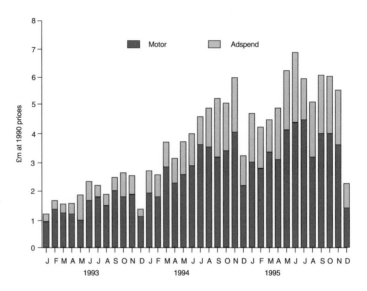

Figure 23: *Competitive adspend*
Source: Register/MEAL, Advertising Association

Improved Product or Distribution

There were no changes in Frizzell's policies, nor were there any changes in the method of selling or distribution. After all, Frizzell had been selling by phone since the 1960s.

Yellow Pages

One factor that could have increased enquiries was *Yellow Pages* advertising. Frizzell first went into *Yellow Pages* in 1993. Advertising now appears in all 73 GB volumes, and has recently started appearing in *Thomsons*.

Directories complement the role of brand-building advertising. Because people only purchase insurance once a year, there is often a gap between the time they are exposed to advertising and when they start calling for quotes. So, although the ads may leave them with a strong image of Frizzell, most of them will forget the telephone number by the time they need it. Directories fill that gap, helping awareness and image to translate into enquiries.

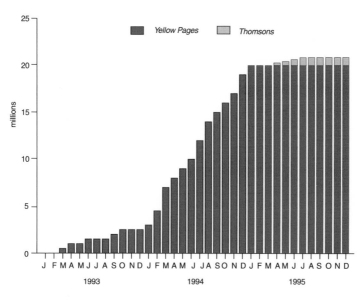

Figure 24: *Directories carrying Frizzell ads*
Source: *Yellow Pages, Thomsons*

But while directories might have enhanced the advertising effect, they could not have caused it for the following three reasons.

i) It was extremely unlikely that *Yellow Pages* could explain the increase in Frizzell's awareness and image – people only see the ads when they are about to call.

ii) Awareness and enquiry levels continued to rise strongly throughout 1995, yet directories coverage was static that year.

iii) The effect cannot explain the regional difference in awareness and enquiry levels discussed earlier. When the campaign first rolled out in 1994, advertised regions performed better than non-advertised regions yet, as Figure 25 shows, there was no difference in *Yellow Pages* coverage.

Other Activity

— Affinity budgets fell slightly in real terms during this period (Figure 26).

— The sponsorship of Classic FM's Travel Update appeared to have little effect.

— The British Equestrian Team was sponsored for two years before the advertising started, as well as throughout the campaign. This was unlikely to have affected the results.

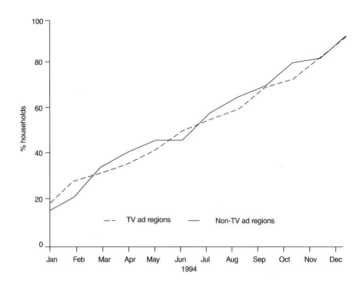

Figure 25: Yellow Pages *coverage, TV advertised regions versus others*
Source: *Yellow Pages*

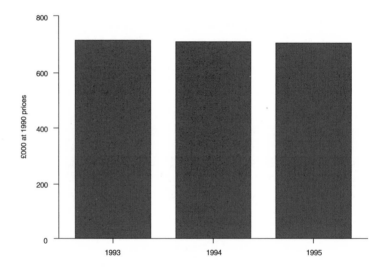

Figure 26: *Frizzell affinity advertising, real expenditure*
Source: Frizzell, Advertising Association

EFFICIENCY AND RETURN ON INVESTMENT

So the advertising fulfilled its objectives: raising awareness and understanding among the right people, and encouraging them to call. But just how cost efficient was it?

We believe that the advertising was very efficient. The tracking study gave the ads an Awareness Index of between 7 and 9 (depending on region), unusually high for financial sector advertising (Figure 27). Indeed, Millward Brown commented that it was 'one of the highest scores presented in the last five years'.[2]

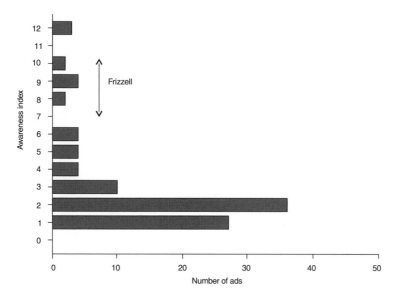

Figure 27: *Average levels of awareness index, insurance advertising*
Source: Millward Brown

Another way to gauge the efficiency of Frizzell's advertising is to compare it with another insurer. Following Direct Line's first burst of advertising, awareness in London grew from 24% to 42%, a 75% increase.[3] Frizzell's first burst, which ran at a similar weight, produced greater shifts in awareness, despite spreading its support over more TV regions (Table 10).

TABLE 10: AWARENESS OF FRIZZELL ADS

TV region	Frizzell awareness uplift (first burst) %
West Country	+104
Anglia	+253
HTV	+120
Yorkshire	+371
Tyne Tees	+325

So the creative approach was cost effective at raising awareness. But how did this translate into profit?

---

2. Dominic Twose, Millward Brown.
3. See Direct Line's 1992 IPA paper. Direct Line ran at a weight of 436 TVRs, with a spend of £500,000 in press. Frizzell's first burst had 433 TVRs with £46,000 on radio.

By the end of 1995, Frizzell had spent £6.6 million[4] on advertising. Econometrics revealed that this would generate around 307,000 enquiries. Our analysis of closing rates enables us to translate this into sales.[5] From this, given that 90% of customers renewed their policy every year, we can calculate the flow of income generated, and hence the total income that would be generated by the advertising over the next 15 years.

In addition, we can calculate the return on the original advertising investment. Without disclosing sensitive information, we can reveal that the stream of extra income generated is equivalent to a return on investment of 24.9% per annum. If Frizzell had invested the same £6.6 million in 15-year Government bonds, they would have only earned 8.3% per annum. Investing in advertising therefore made sound financial sense.

CONCLUSIONS

Two years after the start of its first television advertising campaign, the brand enjoys a position that would have delighted Thomas Frizzell. It is now recognised by over half the population and, most importantly, the brand offer is understood and appreciated by the 'Careful Planners' it seeks. Such success demonstrates the potential of 'direct response' advertising through the subtle use of brand values to generate desired enquiries and filter out the undesired. As the insurance market becomes increasingly competitive, with many companies struggling to retain their customers through unprofitable offers, Frizzell is in a good position. Perhaps as testimony to the strength of the brand, the friendly society Liverpool Victoria recently bought Frizzell Financial Services for £188 million, £80 million more than the company's previous owners, Marsh & McLennan, paid for Frizzell only four years previously.

---

4. Including production.
5. The exact sales figures are confidential.

6

Using Advertising To Improve Reebok's Performance In The Football Market

Or – from relegation zone to championship contention

BACKGROUND

The Reebok Brand

Reebok first came to prominence in the UK during the early 1980s, thriving on the back of four dynamics:

— The increase in health awareness and affluence which drove both sports participation and the whole sports shoe market;

— Its involvement at the birth of aerobics (initially Reebok was the only major brand to produce dedicated fitness shoes);

— Perceived American roots (despite being founded in Bolton!), which furnished Reebok with a sense of stylishness and fashionability, which was lacking in the established European brands;

— The brand's high price, which captured the 'badge'-wearing heartbeat of '80s Britain;

The upside of these factors was that Reebok soon established itself as number one in the market. The downside was that it left the brand with no real sports credentials (its association with the world of 'Jane Fonda workouts' did little to instil confidence in most men, as well as many women). As the market began to mature in the late '80s, and as consumer motivations changed, it became clear that Reebok's previous advantages were now its Achilles Heel.

At a time when consumers were looking increasingly for (sporting) credibility from their brands, Reebok was seen more as an 'expensive fashion accessory bought to satisfy personal vanity'.

At the turn of the decade Lowe Howard-Spink was appointed to help address this. Our brief was to develop advertising that built robust foundations for the Reebok brand, by providing those sports credentials it lacked. This we did with great success in two commercials – 'Shoes In Action' and 'Second Year Running'.

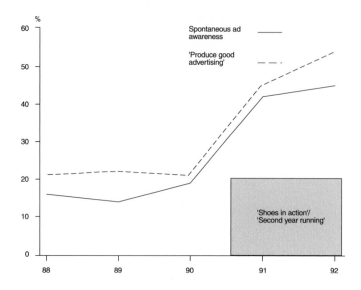

Figure 1: *Reebok advertising performance 1988–92*
Source: Marketing Focus

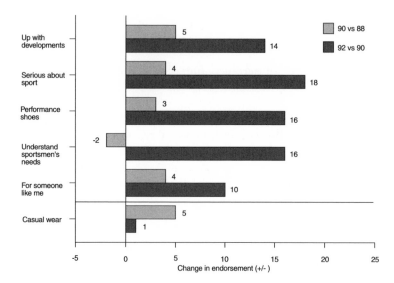

Figure 2: *Reebok brand image shifts 1988–92*
Source: Marketing Focus

Without going into details, it suffices to say that this advertising helped protect Reebok from erosion in overall brand appeal, allowing it to remain dominant to this day.

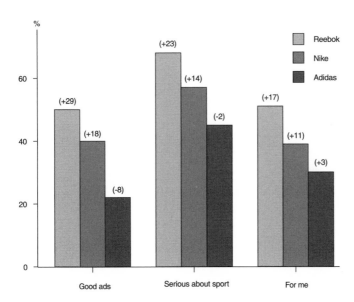

Figure 3: *Reebok brand image versus key competitors, 1995*
Source: Marketing Focus

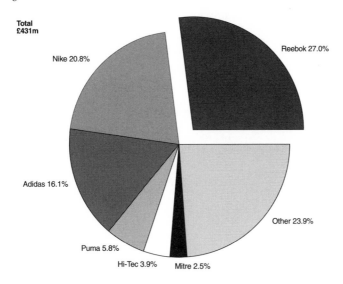

Figure 4: *UK sports shoe sales (MAT, Nov 1995)*
Source: Nielsen

The relevance of this may not be immediately apparent when considering Reebok's more recent footballing success. However, it has two important implications: it confirms the robustness of Reebok's general brand dominance and it shows that the right advertising can have an impact on performance. It is against this backdrop that Reebok's historic failure in football, and subsequent change in fortune, must be considered.

Reebok's Performance in Football

In 1992, football was the third biggest sports shoe sector and one of the fastest growing.

TABLE 1: SPORTS SHOE SALES BY SECTOR

| | £m MAT May 1993 | | |
	£m	%	year-on-year growth
Fitness	127.8	35	+2
Running	82.7	22	+18
Football	65.9	18	+27
Tennis	42.2	11	-10.2
Basketball	22.7	6	+11.7
Outdoor	19.7	5	+54.7
Squash/Badminton	9.3	3	-18.4
Total	370.3	100	+9.4

Source: Nielsen

At that time though, Reebok was but a minor player; neither the original fashion-led success the brand enjoyed nor the credibility boost it subsequently received from advertising had an impact on performance.

TABLE 2: FOOTBALL SALES BY BRAND

| | % share MAT May 1993 | |
	Volume %	Value %
Mitre	20	16
Puma	15	16
Adidas	14	16
Patrick	9	8
Nike	6	7
Hi-Tec	6	5
Reebok	5	7
Other	25	25

(Note: 70% boots, 30% trainers)
Source: Nielsen

When compared with overall market dominance, performance on the football pitch was obviously not good enough.[1] Something had to be done.

---

1. At this time Reebok accounted for one in two of all fitness shoes sold and one in three of all running shoes, but only one in twenty of football boots.

Understanding Reebok's Footballing Problems

The roots of Reebok's poor performance lay in the dynamics of the football market, which are very different to those of other sectors.

Most significantly, football boots are, by definition, sport-only products. The consequent pre-eminence of product performance (versus the fashionability of the broader trainer market), results in highly brand-loyal, risk-averse consumers, who stick with what they know and trust. This innate conservatism is compounded by a bias towards the independent and mail-order trade sectors, which tend to stock only the big, established players.

Finally, the situation is not made any easier for smaller brands by an idiosyncratic trade sell-in mechanic. Because of its complexity, and the fact that sell-in will form an important part of this case, we will spend time explaining this.

Every October, Reebok presents to retailers its football range for next season. This does not appear in-store until August but, essentially, orders placed at this time are fixed. Reebok over orders by about 10%, but retailers cannot increase stock levels significantly after this. Consequently, trade behaviour is totally dependent on past performance, with a 12-month lag. Good consumer sales in the preceding season mean improved trade sales for a product that will not appear until the next season. The reverse is true for poor sales. (Unsold stock is cleared at reduced prices in late spring or returned to make way for the new season's range.)

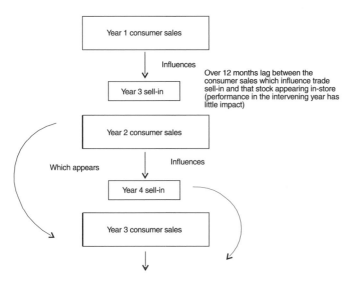

Figure 5: *Relationship between consumer and trade sales*

The problem is that, together with conservative consumer and trade attitudes, this maintains the status quo. Big brands remain successful; small brands like Reebok remain marginalised (unless they can engineer a step-change improvement).

This situation was worse for Reebok in 1993 than for most small brands. Beyond its size, it also lacked any association with football. It was a recent market entrant seen as lacking in heritage and credibility; its product was considered poor quality and, in the specialist context of football, it still carried unhelpful 'fashion' associations. This meant that, at best, Reebok was not considered and, at worst, it was actively rejected.

The Task Facing Reebok

Under its own steam, Reebok would clearly go nowhere fast in football. To succeed, the brand needed an outside catalyst to bring about the required step change.

The target to aim for was the 10% share barrier. Though something of a chicken-and-egg situation, breaking this double-figure ceiling seemed to be the key to reaching 'critical mass'.[2] But this would require Reebok to double its share and leap-frog three competitors.

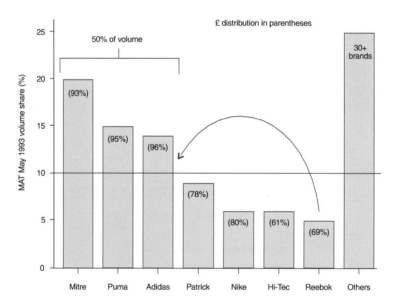

Figure 6: *Becoming a contender – the extent of Reebok's task*
Source: Nielsen

Star Endorsement: Off-the-Peg Credibility?

Reebok's solution to this conundrum was star endorsement, which research consistently showed was a primary motivator for teenagers (the core boot market). The objective was to gain appeal and credibility by association. This led Reebok to sign the up-and-coming young star of British football – Ryan Giggs – in early 1993.

However, despite Giggs' popularity and high awareness of the sponsorship among consumers, there was no evidence of the desired catalytic effect.

---

2.   This is proved by the three big brands: Mitre, Puma and Adidas. All have over 10% share and 90% £ distribution, and account for over 50% of volume.

TABLE 3: REEBOK'S FOOTBALL PERFORMANCE
PRE AND POST SIGNING UP GIGGS

	Pre-Giggs June 1992–May 1993	Post-Giggs June 1993–May 1994
Volume %	5	5
Rank	7	7
Value %	7	7
Rank	5	5

Source: Nielsen

This was not simply a function of constrained volume. Reebok did enjoy share gains over the period, but only when price-promoted in the end-of-season sale. The relationship between movements in Reebok's price premium (versus key competitor average) and movements in share shows this clearly (Figure 7).

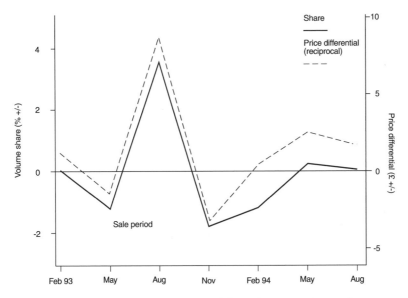

Figure 7: *The relationship between share movements and price differential movements (reciprocal)*
Source: Nielsen

But these price-led improvements were not sustained. In fact, in a market growing 10% year-on-year, Reebok only managed 2% growth, and that from a very low base. Giggs alone did not seem to be enough to force a step change re-evaluation of the brand.

The reason for this was easy to identify: most consumers still did not naturally think of Reebok when buying boots. Preconceptions were so firmly rooted that Reebok could not get on shopping lists, even with Ryan's help; and if not on the list there was little chance of catching the eye among the clutter of the average sports shop.

The implications of this surfaced during the October 1993 sell-in; volume sales to the trade actually declined by 21%. Clearly, star endorsement alone was not enough of a catalyst; the vicious circle remained unbroken. An alternative strategy was required, so Reebok turned once more to advertising and LH-S.

THE ADVERTISING

What Advertising had to Achieve

The task was clear: advertising had to provide the step-change catalyst that Giggs' endorsement alone could not.

Once in the market there was, of course, a desire for continued growth. However, the immediate objective was to force reassessment and get Reebok on the shopping list of the core 12- to 24-year-old consumer. If the boots then delivered, which Reebok were confident of, there was significant potential for repurchase the following season. The vicious circle would then become a virtuous one.

Strategic Development

It was felt that the simplest way to create belief in Reebok's footballing credentials would be to link the brand with the considerable, but still untapped, potency of Giggs – Reebok had been right to sign him; what was now required was proper exploitation

This seemed easy enough. However, from talking to consumers, it was clear that other factors were also important. First, we would have to demonstrate an understanding of football; to show that Reebok was a *fan* of the Beautiful Game. Second, football's 'gang' mentality meant advertising would also need to cross boundaries of team affiliation to maximise appeal.

While confident that any advertising produced would capture the 'spirit' of the game, the issue of tribalism gave rise to concerns about Giggs' appropriateness as an advertising 'star' in some quarters. However, both consumers and retailers allayed our fears: Ryan was one of those rare players whose appeal crossed all boundaries.

His ability was obvious, but unlike some 'stars' featured in football ads, he did not antagonise. This meant that his skill could be appreciated regardless of team affiliation. Add to this his teen-idol appeal, and without doubt he lived up to his media sobriquet, 'the new George Best'. That he played for Manchester United was the icing on the cake.

Creative Development

When writing the creative brief things were kept very simple, focusing on the core idea that...

'Ryan Giggs wears Reebok football boots'

...and the fact that, in terms of brand personality, Reebok needed to be portrayed as a true footie fan.

Given this, the creative solution was perfect. Taking the perennial playground (and pub) debate of who would be in your 'best ever' side as their starting point, the creatives picked Giggs for a Manchester United 'Dream Team' alongside the likes of Best, Charlton and Law (the sub-text being that his inclusion was helped considerably by the fact that he wore Reebok boots). That the idea also tapped into the rise of the 'Fantasy Football' phenomenon, both in the national press and on TV, was an added bonus.

In creative development research the concept was extremely well received, clearly positioning Reebok as a 'proper' footballing brand.

'Reactions were universally positive…it showed Reebok understood football. The finished commercial was expected to be intriguing, original and watchable; one to be discussed with your mates.'

Fusion Research, February 1994

There had been some concern that the players featured were too old for the teen target audience (the explosion in boot sponsorship deals during the '80s precluded the use of recent players). Happily though, this underestimated the extent to which teenagers are immersed in footballing folklore. All knew of and admired Best, Charlton and Law, and most had heard of at least some of the other players featured.

Another concern was whether Giggs could credibly appear in the 'best ever' Manchester United side. Again though, this was unfounded. Even those who did question his inclusion saw it as justifiable advertising hyperbole.

Finally, and most encouragingly, respondents felt that a commercial of this type might make them (re)consider Reebok.

So, we seemed to have the required catalyst. All we had to do now was make it work in the real world.

PUTTING 'DREAM TEAM' ON AIR

The core advertising target was 12- to 24-year-old males: sports shoes' heartland. 'Dream Team' would be competing not only with other football activity, but also the background noise of the total sports shoe market, plus the whole gamut of 'youth' advertising. It was not an easy task.

The commercial broke in May 1994, on the weekend of the FA Cup Final, with activity through to the end of the year. This was followed by a small-scale satellite campaign in the autumn of 1995.

Over this period, Reebok was the heaviest-spending football brand (£1.6 million – mostly 'Dream Team' – plus a little specialist press). However, this must be offset against the heritage of Adidas and Puma (both reasonable investors in the category) and Nike's on-going heavyweight spend (£2.5 million between 1993 and 1995, plus unquantifiable poster activity).

TABLE 4: TOTAL MEDIA SPEND IN THE FOOTBALL MARKET

	1990	1991	1992	Spend (£000) 1993	1994	1995	Total
Nike	186	308	157	1,264	809	350	3,074
Reebok	0	0	0	0	1,343	246	1,589
Puma	0	2	18	581	191	542	1,334
Adidas	73	12	10	268	764	153	1,280

Source: Media Register

With production costs of £400,000, the total investment behind 'Dream Team' was £2 million. However, it should be pointed out that immediate payback was not a success criterion (this was never seen as a short-term investment). The real payback was expected in the longer term, from benefits that would accrue once Reebok was properly established as a serious player in the football market.

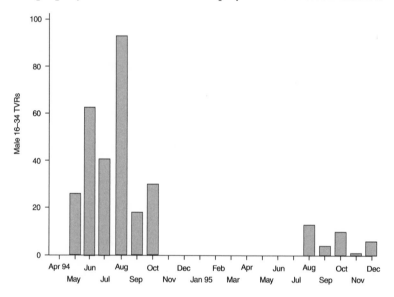

Figure 8: *Reebok football media plan*
Source: Media Register

ADVERTISING'S SUCCESS – ANECDOTAL AND INTERIM MEASURES

The Media

First indications of the impact 'Dream Team' would have came when the commercial was presented to the national media pre-launch. It created a huge stir, precipitating articles in all major newspapers (notably five pages in the *Sun*), a slot on *News At Ten* and unprecedented exposure on *Grandstand*, prior to the FA Cup Final in which Manchester United were appearing. Subsequently, the commercial has also appeared *twice* on BBC1's *How Do They Do That?*

The value of this coverage is estimated at £3 million, twice the actual media budget; in itself this is significant evidence of advertising potency.

The Advertising and Marketing Community

Positive endorsement was also received from the advertising and marketing community.

The commercial was crowned 'campaign of the week' in *Marketing*:

'A 60-second masterpiece…all sports fans will sit up and watch.'

Marketing, May 1994

'Pick of the week' in *Campaign*:

'Stunning…back of the net.'

Campaign, May 1994

As well as garnering editorial praise from the same source:

'A great, strong idea…you can debate the team selection, but it creates interest in an ad based on its own merits. All too rare.'

Campaign, May 1994

The Trade

Retailers were also smitten when presented with the commercial. But, ironically, the demand they thought the commercial would create presented something of a problem; because of pre-ordering they could not increase stock levels. To compensate, some of the major multiple chains actually increased the number of outlets stocking Reebok. This spread things more thinly than normal, but they believed it was better to have some stock everywhere than some places with none (Figure 9).

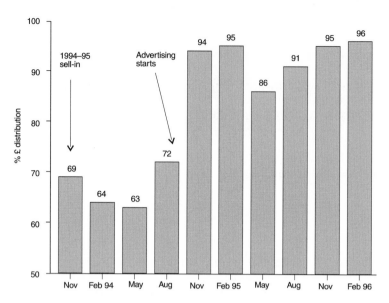

Figure 9: *Distribution of Reebok football products*
Source: Nielsen

The Consumer

Consumers were equally enamoured with 'Dream Team' when it finally appeared.

It proved highly impactful: over 75% of the core target recognised the commercial from stills, and nearly 50% could brand it correctly (Figure 10).

As a point of comparison, this was superior to two major competitive launches (most significantly Adidas' top-of-the-range Predator football boots), which were on air at the same time as Reebok.

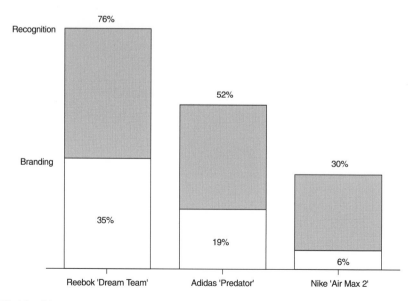

Figure 10: *Advertising awareness*
Source: Marketing Focus (15–24 males)

This superior awareness was mirrored by positive attitudes.

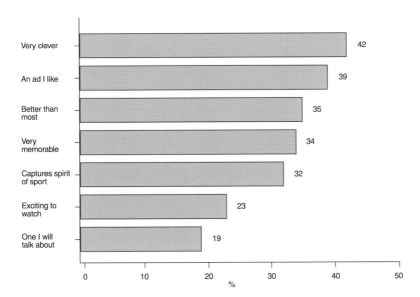

Figure 11: *Consumer attitudes to 'Dream Team'*
Source: Marketing Focus (15–24 males)

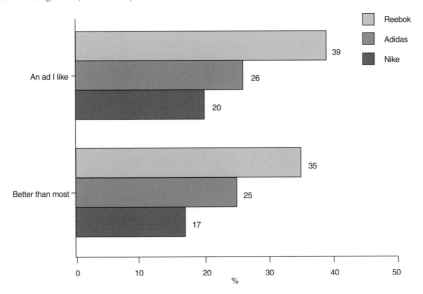

Figure 12: *Consumer attitudes (versus Adidas and Nike)*
Source: Marketing Focus (15–24 males)

Our message was getting through, but was it having any effect?

Effect on Brand Perceptions

The first sign of effectiveness was an improvement in Reebok's image on many key dimensions.

TABLE 5: IMPACT OF 'DREAM TEAM' ON REEBOK'S BRAND IMAGE

| | Brand image | | |
	Pre %	Post %	Change
Produces good advertising	37	52	+15
Wide range	59	69	+10
Choice of top sports people	53	63	+10
High-performance shoes	60	67	+7
Good value for money	21	28	+7
Well designed	58	64	+6
Understands sportsmen's needs	55	60	+5
Mostly for casual wear	45	36	-9
Expensive	72	62	-10

Source: Marketing Focus (15–24 males)

Purchase intention among football buyers also improved, from no consideration to top of the hit parade.

TABLE 6: PURCHASING BEHAVIOUR AMONG FOOTBALL PLAYERS

| | Would buy Reebok in the future | | |
	Pre	Post	Change
%	0	24	+24
Rank	=7	1	

Source: Marketing Focus (15–24 males)

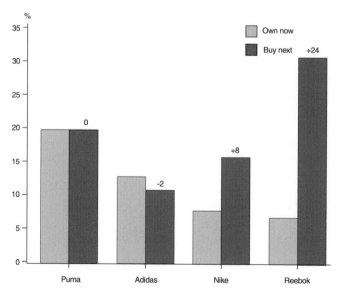

Figure 13: *Football boot purchase intention versus current behaviour*
Source: Match/Harpers (males 10–18)

Research conducted by the sports trade magazine Harpers showed a similar improvement (Figure 13).

So, intent was there, but were people buying in reality?

ADVERTISING'S SUCCESS – SALES PERFORMANCE

Consumer Sales

Advertising's impact on consumer sales was almost immediate. On top of increased distribution, rate of sale nearly doubled post-advertising year-on-year.

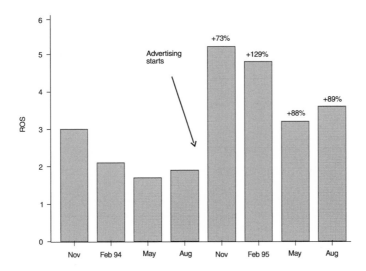

Figure 14: *ROS of Reebok football products*
Source: Nielsen

The result? Sales surged and, for the first time ever, Reebok sold out (including the 'slush' stock that had been held back). Retailers even managed to clear shoes from the previous year's range without cutting price. There were to be no stock returns this year! From 22,000 pairs in August 1994, volume rose by 282% the next period (Figure 15); key competitors' grew by only 73%.

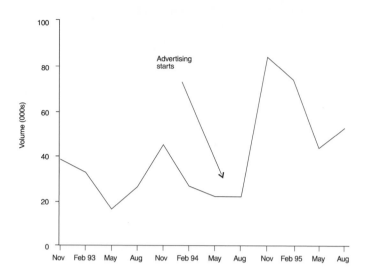

Figure 15: *Reebok's volume uplift post-advertising*
Source: Nielsen

As a consequence, share also improved, from 5% to 10%, as did rank position, from seventh to fourth; and this during the third quarter when the new ranges appear, and the bulk of volume is sold.

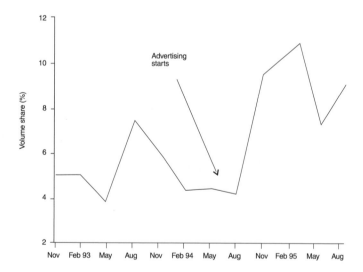

Figure 16: *Reebok's share uplift post-advertising*
Source: Nielsen

Within six months, therefore, Reebok had reached its objective: to generate a step-change improvement, breaking the 10% share barrier and gaining fourth place in the market.

In value terms, things were even more impressive; Reebok's share reached 14%, putting it in third place, only 2% points behind Puma (the gap had been 12 previously).

In fact, so great was Reebok's success during the first six months of the season, that 'out-of-stocks' reached 30% by spring 1995, causing the sales downturn that occurred during that period. However, sales have since rebounded to new heights, showing the robustness of Reebok's new-found appeal.

Discounting Other Factors

But could this sales improvement be attributed purely to advertising? The two factors which might also have played a role were product and price (bearing in mind that increases in distribution were themselves a function of advertising).

The product is easily discounted; it remained more or less the same year-on-year.

Could price, perhaps, have played a role, especially given the historically close relationship with share? The answer to this is an unequivocal no. Reebok's price premium (versus key competitor average) remained more or less consistent over the advertised period. If anything, price actually moved against Reebok during the quarter to November, the time of the biggest share uplift.

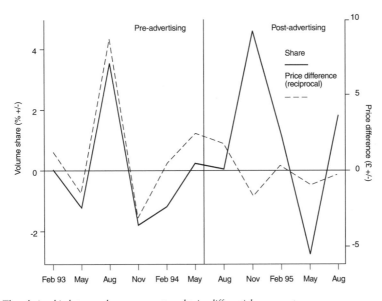

Figure 17: *The relationship between share movements and price differential movements*
Source: Nielsen

This left advertising as the only real impetus behind improved sales. And by inspection, advertising investment[3] clearly coincided with the initial step change share movement.

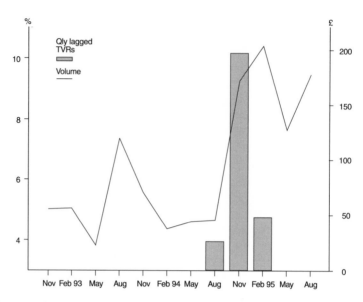

Figure 18: *The impact of advertising (Reebok's volume share versus quarterly lagged TVRs)*
Source: Nielsen

Quantifying the Uplift in Consumer Sales

So, advertising did seem to be responsible for the step change in performance, but can we quantify the extent of this? Assuming Reebok's share would have remained at best unchanged year-on-year *without* advertising, this equates to at least a 90% volume uplift.

Clear evidence, then, of a consumer effect. But what about the trade? Reebok's investment would only be repaid if retailers bought more of the product. It is here then that the real proof of success would be found.

---

3. Note: quarterly lagged TVRs have been used, both because impact on sales is never immediate in this market, and to offset the fact that sales data is only available on a quarterly basis.

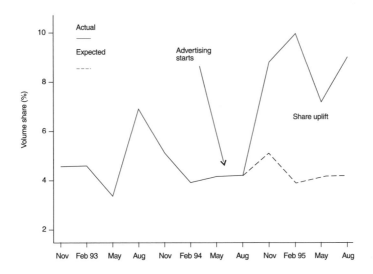

Figure 19: *Reebok's share (actual versus expected)*
Source: Nielsen

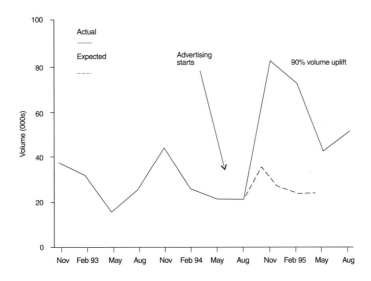

Figure 20: *Reebok's volume (actual versus expected)*
Source: Nielsen

Trade Sales

The first indications of advertising's effect on the trade came during the October 1994 sell-in (the '95/'96 range).

Though only two months into the advertising, and one month into the new season, Reebok's sales force found buyers far more receptive. The immediate consumer demand generated by the advertising had short-circuited the usual 12-

month lag between consumer and trade sales; almost overnight the brand had gone from difficult to sell to 'must stock'.

David Smith, one of Reebok's sales directors, said, 'I've never known a commercial have such an impact on retailer confidence and commitment.'

Whereas previously, a retailer might have stocked one or two Reebok products, they were now buying the whole range. The brand enjoyed its biggest commitment ever from multiples and prospered among independents and mail-order companies, football's conservative heartland. For example, in mail-order Reebok went from a couple of 'entries' to two or three pages of product.

The result? From a decline of 21% in 1993, sales more than doubled in 1994. Moreover, continued consumer demand throughout 1995 meant that volume again increased during the most recent sell-in period; ie a step change followed by continued improvement, the ideal result.

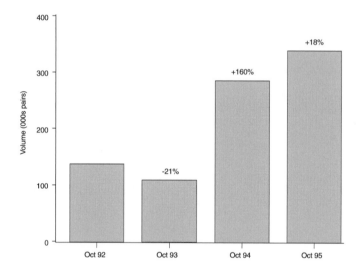

Figure 21: *Reebok's football sales into retailers*
Source: Reebok

Quantifying the Trade Sales Effect

When estimating what Reebok's sales to the trade might have been without advertising we will assume that movements would have mirrored consumer sales. In 1994, for example, Reebok's pre-advertising growth rate was 2%; we will assume similar trade growth. To predict 1995 sales we will assume that the ratio of Reebok's growth rate with the rest of the market would have remained constant.[4] Given competitive growth in 1995 of 23%, this equates to growth for Reebok of 4%.

---

4.   ie 2% in 1994 versus competitive growth of 10% = 0.02.

Based on these assumptions, sales without advertising over the two years would have been in the region of 229,000. Given actual sales of 627,000, we believe advertising generated a sales uplift of 174% (or incremental volume of 398,000).

PAYING BACK THE INVESTMENT

So, advertising had an identifiable effect on sales, both to consumers and the trade; but did this pay back the £2 million investment?

To answer this we need to reconsider the 1994 and 1995 sell-in periods. At these times, sales value increased first by 143% and then by a further 13%.

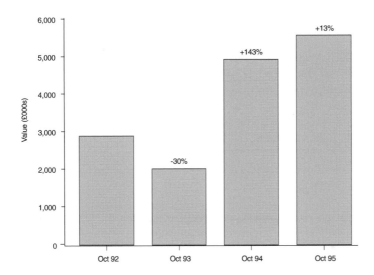

Figure 22: *Reebok's football sales into retailers*
Source: Reebok

To calculate the revenue uplift, we will make the same assumption used to calculate volume uplift.[5] This suggests an uplift in sales value due to advertising of 148%, or a revenue increase of £6.3 million.

But what does this mean for Reebok's bottom line?

Exact margins cannot be revealed, but taking a range within which the actual figure sits (35–45%) delivers incremental gross profit of between £2.2 million and £2.8 million.

Given investment of £2 million, this equates to a return of between £0.2 million and £0.8 million within two years.

So, advertising not only generated the required step change, it also had a big impact on Reebok's bottom line within a very short time period. The impact of

---

5.   ie 2% and 4.5% growth in 1994 and 1995 respectively.

advertising does not stop here though, we still have the longer-term effect to take into account.

THE POTENTIAL LONG-TERM EFFECT

Reebok's objective for advertising was never simply to make money in the short term, so rapid payback was as welcome as it was unexpected. The long-term effect was always a paramount objective; to emphatically break into the market and enjoy the benefits that accrue to 'proper' footballing brands.

The company's commitment to the long term, its desire not just to be in the Premiership but champions as well, can be seen in its continued investment.

As of March 1996, a second Reebok football commercial, 'Theatre of Dreams', went on air. This film continues the football fantasy theme and use of Ryan Giggs started by 'Dream Team'. The eternal fantasy captured this time is the daydream all football fans have to play like their favourite star. Giggs is that star while, to add spice and interest, the (quite genuine) fans are 'personalities' in their own right; people who might appear to have everything, but still want to be in Ryan Giggs' boots.

So, how can we calculate the long-term effect this commitment to advertising might have? By making a number of assumptions:

— that the football market will grow by 10% year-on-year to the end of the decade (possibly a conservative estimate);

— that without the initial investment in 'Dream Team', Reebok's growth would have remained, at best, at pre-advertising levels (ie 20% of market growth or 2% year-on-year);

— that, with advertising, Reebok sales will at least grow with the market;

— that Reebok will continue to invest in football at around the equivalent of £2 million (production and media) every two years.

Based on these assumptions, and again taking the range of margins used to calculate the return on 'Dream Team', a net return on investment up to 2000 of between £4.3 million and £7.5 million could be suggested.

And this is without taking into account the fact that Reebok's performance might actually improve further (ie continued upward momentum after the initial step change), something which already seems to be happening.

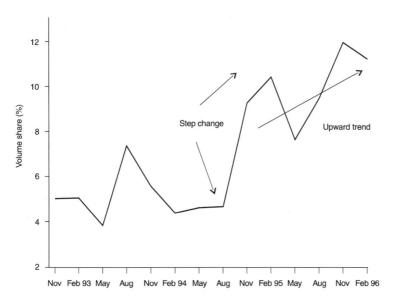

Figure 23: *Reebok's volume share: step change and continued upward trend*
Source: Nielsen

We will not attempt to quantify this additional uplift. It suffices to say that it could drive Reebok's return on investment beyond the £8 million mark.

CONCLUSIONS

Despite overall dominance in the sports shoe market, and successful brand advertising, Reebok was a minor player in the football category pre-'Dream Team'.

The appearance of the commercial radically changed this. As well as effectively doubling Reebok's available media budget through the PR it generated, it positioned the brand as a credible member of the football elite, causing significant consumer and trade reassessment.

In so doing, 'Dream Team' generated a step-change improvement in sales performance, more than paying back the investment it received. Looking forward to the end of the decade, it is possible that the net returns due to advertising could be in excess of £7 million.

By anyone's reckoning, this is clear and demonstrable evidence of advertising effectiveness.

Section Two

New campaigns for previously advertised brands

7

BT

'It's Good to Talk'

'Perhaps the word campaign does it an injustice…it is actually a piece of social engineering.'
(*Marketing Week*)

INTRODUCTION

This paper is unique. Having looked through the *Advertising Works* books, we have not found an example of a strong brand leader using advertising to grow an already buoyant market. We believe, therefore, that this paper will be the first to do so.

We will show that BT's past three campaigns designed to stimulate calls have done so, but that 'It's Good To Talk' has been by far the most effective, and has achieved a return on investment of 6 to 1.

It achieved this through a strategic and creative change of direction which involved for the first time addressing underlying attitudes which were restricting telephone usage.

To tell the story, we must go back to the biggest event in BT's recent past, its privatisation in 1984.

THE NEED TO GROW THE MARKET

Following privatisation, one of OFTEL's rulings was that BT should reduce its 'basket' of individual call charges. The level of required reduction has varied over time, but since 1993 has stood at RPI minus 7.5%.

Other measures encouraging competition were also introduced to force BT to reduce market share. For BT's residential division, the only way out of this enforced revenue decline was to grow the market. Its response was threefold:

1. to encourage adoption of products likely to stimulate calls (eg second phone points in homes, and answerphones)

2. to step up R&D to create new call stimulatory services (eg Call Return – 1471)

3. to use the power of advertising to stimulate calls.

THE EVOLUTION OF BT'S CALL STIMULATION ADVERTISING

There have been three campaigns over the period and, as we will show later, all have been successful. But all three operated to different strategies.

How the Strategies Evolved

'Beattie': targeting heavy users, prompting more calls from women
'Beattie' attempted to highlight the different types of calls in people's 'portfolio' (eg enquiries to shops, consolation calls, etc) in order to prompt people into making similar ones.

The target audience was heavier callers; mid-market 25- to 45-year-old housewives. For this reason, the campaign chose a loquacious housewife as a role model for heavier phone usage.

The campaign ended in 1992. BT felt that 'Beattie' and her family had become such famous individuals themselves, that the messenger seemed to be overwhelming the message.

Moreover, research showed that she was having an effect opposite to that intended. Her character had become a parody of the person that many people want to avoid calling. Rather than being a role model, for some she was the opposite because she compounded a negative stereotype of the 'wasteful' woman chatting 'aimlessly' on the phone.

'Get Through to Someone': strategic shift, positive role models…particularly men
So BT created a new campaign that provided people with more accurate positive role models of good phone behaviour, which would be capable of generating empathy with the viewer. Lighter-calling men, who BT felt offered call growth potential, were also targeted.

The campaign differed from 'Beattie' by providing the viewer with a more sensitive portrayal of positive phone behaviour. But it was similar in the sense that it was also designed to work by prompting people into action by reminding them of a certain type of call.

However, there was a growing belief at BT that, while 'Beattie' and 'Get Through to Someone' may have had some success in *prompting* calls, little had been done to change *underlying negative attitudes* that restrict many people's calling levels, and little emphasis given to promoting the positive value of phone communication. BT's expression of this latter point was:

'You get more out of your life, and your relationships, by communicating [through BT].'

In short, BT wanted to engineer a positive change in the way that our culture values phone communication.

So, BT put the account up to pitch in 1994, subsequently appointing Abbott Mead Vickers•BBDO.

'It's Good To Talk' (IGTT): major strategic shift, addressing underlying barriers to calling

The thinking behind 'It's Good To Talk' (IGTT) stemmed from research done in 1993. Women tend to spend more time just 'chatting' on the phone because they view the pleasure this can give as an end in itself. Men, however, view the phone more as a means to an end, a functional instrument for delivering rational messages. Therefore men's usage tends to be less frequent and their conversation tends to be more short and sharp.

Some men therefore find it difficult to understand women's behaviour, and in a large proportion of households try to restrict their partners' usage. In other words, they act as 'gatekeepers' to the phone.

They use cost as justification for this and cite much of women's usage as a waste:

> 'She spends her time just whittering away about absolutely nothing. I just can't understand it, and I tell her to get off the phone 'cos it's just money down the drain you know. She'll see her friend anyway when she picks our daughter up from school.'

> Source: AMV Qualitative

By standing over their families, tutting while they are on the phone, they reinforce the phone's image as a *'whirring meter'*, constantly clocking up more charges the more time they spend on it. Many women therefore feel guilty about their style of use and the cost, and restrict their own calling levels and their children's.

Diagramatically, we have 'gatekeepers' (usually men), who not only limit their own usage, but also impose control upon, and create inhibition in, the women and children in the household. These would-be key callers have weak arguments and defences against this control.

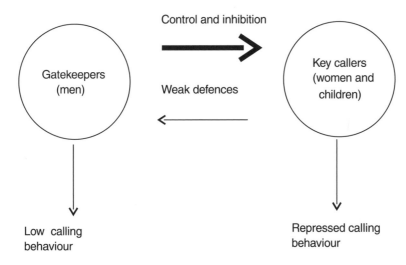

Figure 1

With this learning, we identified two opportunities.

Opportunity 1 – Promoting the value of female-style phone communication

We concluded that there was great potential for call growth if we could raise the value of female-style communication in men's eyes, by directly comparing its benefits to male-style functional usage.

— It would legitimise women's behaviour. This would free up restricted female users by softening the attitudes of the 'gatekeeper', and provide women themselves with ammunition for defending their usage.

— It would encourage men to reappraise their own behaviour.

Opportunity 2 – Reducing price perceptions

Given the prominence of cost as the 'gatekeeper's' rational justification to restrict usage, we needed to affect price perceptions, because they are less likely to criticise if they think calling is less expensive.

The reader might think that this should be happening anyway, because call prices were dropping regularly each year.

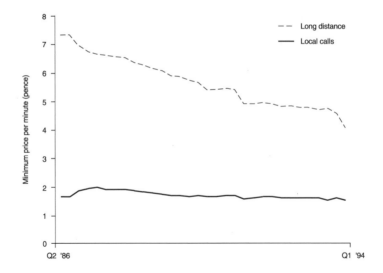

Figure 2: *Minimum price of BT calls (RPI adjusted)*
Source: BT

However, oddly, the number of people believing that prices were high had, for much of the last nine years, been rising!

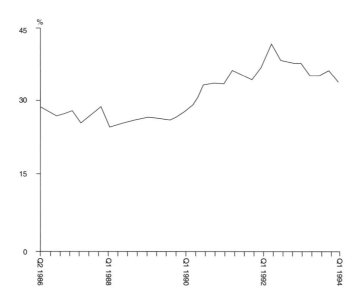

Figure 3: *Percentage of people agreeing that BT call charges are high*
Source: BMRB

Our explanation for this was as follows: Research showed that consumers do not know the cost of calls, and derive their perceptions of telephony costs from the *quarterly bill*, not individual call charges. The average bill had risen by 71% since 1986, and even when RPI adjusted by 12%.

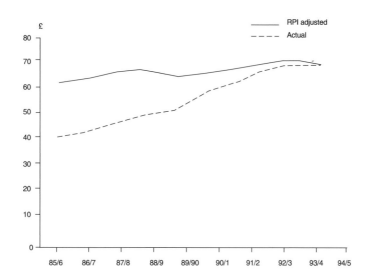

Figure 4: *Average BT quarterly phone bill (inc VAT)*
Source: BT

This was due to several factors. First, line rental – not part of OFTEL's formula – was rising faster than inflation. Second, call volumes were increasing, especially the more expensive international and premium rate calls. On top of this, in 1991, VAT increased from 15 to 17.5%.

In addition, competitors were fuelling BT's high price perceptions by marketing themselves as cheaper alternatives.

To counter this whole problem, BT had started advertising special offers and major tariff changes. This had apparently had some success because, as Figure 3 above also shows, price perceptions had *started* to fall.

Despite this fall, research revealed that people still overestimated the cost of a call by about 400%! It was clear that this needed urgent attention.

We concluded that, in order to bring price perceptions down more steeply, we needed to address these vast overestimates by relating the cost of individual calls to other purchases people make. Doing this would relate the somewhat abstract price per unit to real life.

The effect of this proposed new approach to communicating call charges sang through in our qualitative research:

> 'If you think of half an hour on the phone only costing you as much as the *Sun*, which I get every day, it makes you realise it is actually value for money.'

> Source: AMV Qualitative

Summary of the Advertising Brief for 'IGTT'

We aimed to persuade people to make more and longer calls, by primarily targeting households in which male 'gatekeepers' put pressure on 'key callers', their partners and children, to phone less.

We would achieve this by demonstrating the value of female-style calling, and illustrating that individual calls are as low in cost as other everyday purchases.

Our eventual aim was to ease the tension between 'gatekeeper' and 'key caller', thus releasing pent-up demand. We also thought that, if men believed the benefits, they would increase their calling levels too.

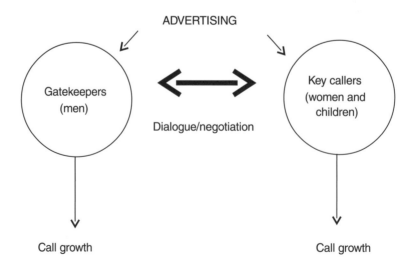

Figure 5

Creative Solution

Television: An Objective Guide to Better Communication
Our messages needed to be skilfully delivered, not only because we were challenging deeply ingrained attitudes, but also because some people hold a grudge against BT.

For this reason, we needed a campaign spokesman whose objectivity could increase the credibility of our messages; someone who people saw as 'one of us', rather than as a BT stooge.

Bob Hoskins was chosen because he met this criterion and, crucially, because he is well-loved by both sexes. Women find him endearing, and he can tell men to soften up because he, himself, is perceived as a hard man.

Bob is made more believable by playing the role of a Jiminy Cricket-type conscience figure, sitting unnoticed on people's shoulders and pointing out to us the benefits of good phone communication.

Non-Broadcast Media
The strategy behind the TV executions (highlighting the differences between the sexes) was also echoed in a national press campaign.

To reduce price perceptions, a poster campaign, comparing call costs to everyday low-cost items, was created (these comparisons were referenced by Bob in many of the TV executions).

Figure 6: *Media plan*

Media Laydown

BT invested £44 million in 'IGTT' between May 1994 and June 1995. The campaign maintained a consistent presence, apart from the three-month period February to April 1995, when it made way for national code change advertising. The campaign plan is shown above in Figure 6.

'BERYL'S BIRTHDAY'

Bob: Beryl doesn't look too happy does she? And you know why that is…

It's her birthday and the doormat's a bit light on birthday cards.

Actually, what really happened was this – there were plenty of cards and you know why?

Joan: It's me… mum. Don't forget Gran's birthday.

Joan: Helen, before you go on holiday, send Gran a card, all right?

Joan: I know you're broke Tom, so I've got a card – you can sign it when you come over, all right?
… I'd like to order some flowers, please.

Bob: Don't ask me why women ring around more than men – maybe they care more – I know one thing though – when they get on the blower, things happen.

Beryl: The flowers were beautiful and I had a lovely lot of cards…
Bob: It's good to talk.

'NOT TALKING FOR LONG'

Alex: Hi mum, it's Alex.

Bob: It's all right, he can't see me.
Alex: I'm just calling before we pop out to the cinema, see how you are…
Bob: Have you ever done that? I know I have. Before you say anything else you say, 'I can't talk for long, we've got to go out'.

You want to see how it feels on the other end.
SOUND: Phone rings.
Mum: Alex…Oh.

Bob: It's not on is it? Have you ever listened to a woman on the phone?

Wife: That dress you were looking for… did you find one with the neck you wanted… square wasn't it, not too low…
Alex's mother (laughing): Don't be daft, it's for whist not whistles…

Bob: It's kinder isn't it? And you don't have to rack up the phone bill to do it. Call at the weekend. Low weekend rates mean a 20-minute chat costs less than a bottle of lager.

Three minutes for 10p – that's the national weekend rate – so next time you call your Mum sit down and enjoy it.
Alex: I hear you're buying low-cut dresses…

Mum: Too late for that lad, my chest moved south about the same time as you did.
SOUND: Alex laughing
Bob: It's good to talk.

'POSTER ADS'

EVALUATING THE THREE CAMPAIGNS

We will now quantify the contribution of the three campaigns discussed above, and demonstrate how 'IGTT' has been the most successful.

BT Call Growth History

As mentioned earlier, after privatisation, BT had adopted a number of market growth measures. As far as calls-per-line were concerned, this strategy seemed to work. Figure 7 shows how, before privatisation, they were flat but started to rise subsequently.

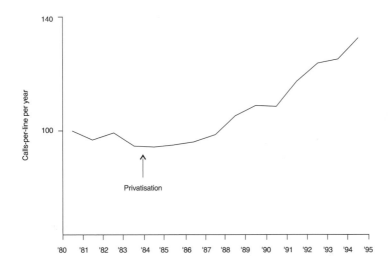

Figure 7: *BT calls per line 1980–95*
(Index 1980 = 100)
Source: BT

From April 1986, it was also possible to measure average conversation durations (see Figure 8 overleaf).

The duration pattern was different to calls-per-line, showing a downturn in the second quarter of 1991 and, subsequently, starting to rise from the second quarter of 1994. These movements needed explanation.

Nevertheless, despite durations falling, *total* volume (calls-per-line x durations) had risen 23% since 1986.

Figure 8: *BT average call durations*
Source: BT

What we did: The Approach

Proving advertising effectiveness here is a complex task because the telecommunications market has seen huge changes over ten years. Beyond the reduction in call charges discussed above, there has been a dramatic increase in the penetration of products and services.

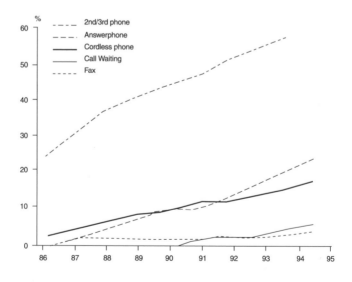

Figure 9: *Household penetration of products and services*
Source: BT/TGI

Also, BT now faces direct competition from new entrants like Mercury and cable companies, and indirect competition in the form of mobile telephony.

To complicate evaluation further, there has been an increase in products and services offered by businesses over the phone (eg pizza delivery) and a major recession.

In July 1995, BT and AMV•BBDO decided that the whole issue of effectiveness needed to be tackled in a comprehensive manner, and a joint project was undertaken with David Cowan Associates. Because of the task's complexity, econometric analysis was just not an option, it was a necessity.

First, in order to simplify the number of variables used in the analysis, we needed to strip out the effect of products and services, which are known to affect call volume.[1]

Second, given that the marketing objective was to grow the market (as measured on BT lines), we needed to decide if competition, which is mostly about switching customers from BT to cable or Mercury, was of relevance to our assessment.

If we could account for and then remove the effects of these, econometric analysis would then be left with the simpler task of disentangling the effects of price, advertising and the economy.

In other words, we were going to clear the ground for econometric analysis. Diagramatically, what we were trying to do is illustrated in Figure 10.

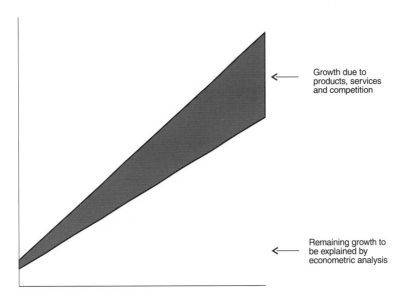

Growth due to products, services and competition

Remaining growth to be explained by econometric analysis

Figure 10: *BT volume growth*

---

1. Another reason for estimating and removing the effects of products/services before conducting multivariate analysis, was to avoid the phenomenon known to statisticians as multicolinearity. This occurs when variables move together. If this happens, as it does in this case, it is not possible to distinguish which variables are responsible for sales effect.

Clearing the Ground for Econometric Analysis

Stripping out the Effect of Products and Services

BT is in the unique position of having highly accurate 'purchase' data on every customer. We used this to measure the effect of product/service acquisition on phone bills.

As well as customers' bills, BT holds details of equipment hired and services subscribed to. With this information we set up 'before-and-after' panels comprising approximately 4,500 households for each product/service.

By comparing over three quarters the bills of 'acquiring' households with those of demographically matched control groups who were 'non-acquirers', we quantified the effect that products/services have on bills. Schematically, this is shown in Table 1.

TABLE 1: BEFORE-AND-AFTER PANELS

	Q 1	Q2	Q3
Sample A 'Acquirers' call bills	No device	Acquire device	With device
Sample B Matched 'Non-acquirers' call bills	No device	No device	No device

$$\frac{Q3\ (A)}{Q1\ (A)} \div \frac{Q3\ (B)}{Q1\ (B)} = \text{change due to acquisition}$$

Five panels were constructed in total, involving 22,500 households. The results are shown in Figure 11.

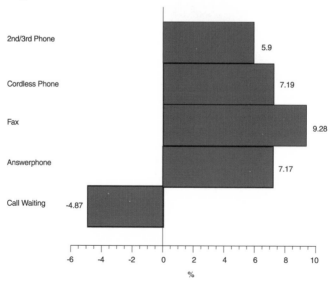

Figure 11: *Average change in bill size compared to control sample*
Source: BT/David Cowan Associates

With this highly accurate information, we quantified the contribution of products and services to call growth.

Could Competition have Grown Call Volumes on BT Lines?
We concluded that there were only two ways in which the above could come about:

— If households that switched to cable or Mercury were lighter users, this would have resulted in an apparent increase in the average call volumes of the BT households remaining. This was not the case. Analysis of the final bills of households who BT knew had defected to the competition shows that call volumes in these households are, on average, 5% *higher*. We therefore accounted for this in our analysis.

— Mobile phone penetration has increased dramatically over the period, and households now make additional calls to mobiles. But all of the data we are using to make our case *excludes* calls from fixed lines to mobiles.

However, we also asked ourselves whether calls involving mobiles generate extra fixed-line to fixed-line calls. A further BT panel analysis showed this not to be the case.

We therefore concluded that mobile competition could not have led to an increase in call volumes on BT lines.

To Recap this Section
We have shown how we calculated and removed the effects of products/services and fixed-line competition on calls-per-line and durations. We have also shown that mobile competition is not material to this enquiry. Having cleared the ground, we could now disentangle price, economic effects and advertising.

The Econometric Analysis

BT's business is complicated. There are over 40 different chargebands covering the many international destinations, premium-rate calls (eg chat lines), as well as the more common local and long-distance calls within the UK. We have concentrated on UK local and long-distance calls, which account for over 99% of volume.

Even with this restriction, the analysis was a complex one because we needed to construct *eight* different models, measuring both the impact on calls-per-line and durations for four combinations of rates and destinations, over the nine years of the three campaigns.

TABLE 2: THE EIGHT DIFFERENT MODELS

1. Calls-per-line
2. Durations   ⟶   Local calls, standard rate
3. Calls-per-line
4. Durations   ⟶   Local calls, cheap rate
5. Calls-per-line
6. Durations   ⟶   National calls, standard rate
7. Calls-per-line
8. Durations   ⟶   National calls, cheap rate

Descriptions of the Variables that went into the Models

Choosing the correct variables for a model is crucial, and naturally involved much discussion. There were core variables (price, advertising and the economy), whose precise forms needed to be decided, and other variables whose influence on calling needed to be investigated.

Price

We had to choose between using actual prices or price perceptions. As described earlier, while *actual* individual call prices had been falling, for much of the period *perceptions* of BT's call charges had not, because total bills were rising.

We decided to use price perceptions as the variable, on the grounds that, in this market, consumer demand is likely to be influenced by what people *think* prices are, rather than what they *actually* are.

The Effect of the Economy

There are several measures which could represent the effects of the economy on calling. We chose consumer expenditure, not only because the amount spent on telephone bills forms part of consumer expenditure, but also because phoning shops and businesses is a direct expression of economic well-being.

The Advertising Variable

An important decision was how to represent the well-known fact that advertising can have both immediate and lagged effects.

We felt that this would certainly be true of telephony advertising. We could envisage it stimulating a call to a friend, which would subsequently generate a cycle of return calls, which might peter out over time.

To model this effect, we assumed that only a proportion of a TVR has its effect in the period of spend. The rest of the effect is spread out over subsequent periods.

Other Variables

Other variables were examined, however we found only one which made a significant contribution, and this was that *durations* affect *calls-per-line*. (This is discussed further below.)

The Results of the Models

The models produced had a good fit with the data, accounting for a large percentage of the variation in call volumes. For example:

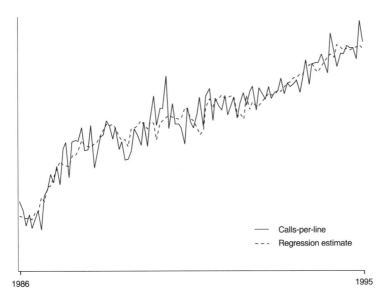

Figure 12: *Model 5: National standard rate calls-per-line versus regression estimate ($R^2 = 0.83$)*
Source: BT/ The Planning Business

Qualitative Interpretation

The models tell us much about how the markets work.

Our overall confidence in the analysis was enhanced because the models suggested that the markets work in ways which fit both with common sense and qualitative research.

— That durations affect the number of calls-per-line makes sense, because if you are an inhibited caller and make a long call, you will restrict the number of calls you subsequently make.

— We found that price perceptions and consumer expenditure affected local *durations*, but not local *calls-per-line*. We would expect this as, given the lower perceived cost of a *local* call, people are less inclined to think twice about picking up the phone, but as the conversation progresses, the 'whirring meter' worry increases.

— On *national* calls, price perceptions and consumer expenditure have an impact on calls-per-line *as well as* durations. This also makes sense. Given the higher perceived cost of *national* calls, people are likely to think more carefully each time they pick up the phone.

Quantitative Results

The net effect on total call volumes for each of the three campaigns is as follows:

TABLE 3: NET EFFECT ON TOTAL CALL VOLUMES

Campaign	Eventual % revenue return from 100 TVRs	Index (Campaign 1=100)
1. 'Get through to Someone'	0.44	100
2. 'Beattie'	1.05	236
3. 'It's Good To Talk'	1.75	398

Source: David Cowan Associates

The analysis demonstrated that all three campaigns had a positive effect, but that 'IGTT' achieved by far the highest return.

The models showed that if 100 ratings are spent in a month then, for 'IGTT', the eventual return over time is 1.75% of monthly sales.

PUTTING 'IT'S GOOD TO TALK' UNDER THE MICROSCOPE

So far, we have considered the effect of all three campaigns over the last nine years. From now on, we will concentrate on 'IGTT', the main subject of this paper.

Direct Evidence of IGTT's Impact

One of the problems of econometrics is that it inevitably involves an element of 'black box', where results arise out of 'correlations and best fits'. It is always reassuring to have direct evidence of effect. In this case, we have such evidence.

For the campaign's first three months, BT kept the Central TV region 'quiet' by withholding all ITV airtime (with C4, press and posters, Central received only 37% of the nationwide spend). Central's calling patterns are typical of the rest of the country. Even though this control region was not absolutely 'silent', a substantial increase in calls-per-line was seen nationally compared to Central.

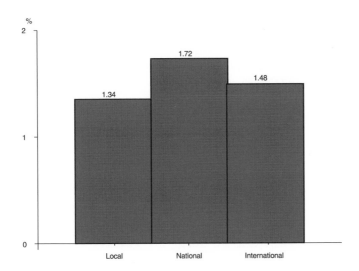

Figure 13: *'Quiet' region test: nationwide increases in calls-per-line versus Central 'quiet' region*
Source: BT

Unfortunately, BT did not have the technical capability to measure durations regionally. Nevertheless we still have direct evidence of 'IGTT's' effect on durations by looking at the national picture. As alluded to earlier in this paper, since the middle of 1994 there has been a prolonged rise in durations for the first time since records began. This coincided precisely with 'IGTT'.

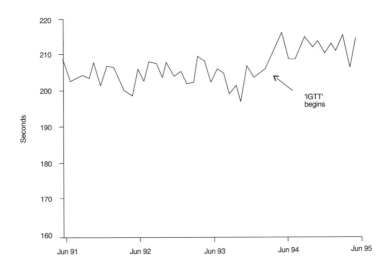

Figure 14: *BT average call durations*
Source: BT

Calculating the Payback of 'It's Good To Talk'

We have shown that 'IGTT' has generated a 1.75% sales uplift for every 100 TVRs spent. This amounts to an incremental value per TVR of £33,000. To arrive at an overall advertising-generated income over the period under discussion, we make the following calculation:

£33,000 (value per TVR)
times
10,566 (total number of 30-second equivalent TVRs)   = £297m
minus
£44m (media) and £8m (production)

NB: BT also advertises products and services, and international calls. We have not included this spend for two reasons. First, whilst advertising for products and services may encourage their adoption, their impact on calling has been factored out in the way described earlier in this paper. Second, international calls have been excluded from our models.

Given that no further variable costs are incurred, this £297 million is almost entirely incremental profit, and represents a return on investment of nearly 6 to 1.

In fact we believe this is an underestimate of 'IGTT's' contribution. Our analysis excludes any effect on BT's international calls, or its seven million business lines (research shows that many personal calls are made at work). We see no reason why 'IGTT' will not have affected these calls too.

Putting the Result in Perspective

In the context of other advertisers, 'IGTT' performs well:

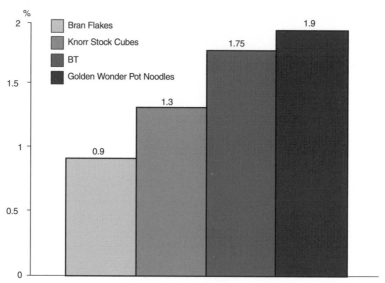

Figure 15: *Advertisers % sales returns on investment*
Source: *Advertising Works 3, 7, 8*

It is when this performance is combined with the huge size of BT's market, that the absolute return becomes so vast.

Beyond the strategic and creative relevance of the campaign, there are other reasons why BT's advertising is likely to be particularly effective. There is very low wastage of advertising monies because almost the whole audience uses the phone and, unlike most markets, there is a point of purchase in nearly every house.

Could Anything Else have caused the Uplift in Call Volumes During 'IGTT'?

Other BT Activity
Other significant marketing activity either declined or remained constant during 'IGTT'. Both BT's *corporate* and *business* divisions reduced the adspends behind their campaigns by approximately 50%, and there was no significant change in the strategies or level of investment behind below-the-line activity.

Competitive Advertising Activity
Because Mercury withdrew from the residential market during the period, other advertising in the telephony market was almost all to enrol mobile users. None of this is likely to have stimulated the BT network.

In any case, year-on-year, media-inflation-adjusted adspends from these advertisers actually *fell* by 6% during this time.

Weather
There is some evidence to suggest that bad weather encourages people to stay indoors and, hence, call more. However, over the period, temperatures and sunshine hours were *higher*, and rainfall *lower* (Source: Met. Office). If anything, this would depress calling.

Demonstrating IGTT's Effects through Consumer Data

The Campaign was Widely Noticed
In awareness terms, the campaign made a great impact. Soon after it broke, it reached number one in *Marketing*'s Adwatch Survey, and remained there for 22 of the next 30 weeks. This is a record.

People Claim to use the Telephone More
BT's tracking study has two behaviour statements relating to the advertising. Over the advertised period, agreement with these statements rose (see Figure 16 overleaf).

This is particularly impressive because, in most consumer studies, the public does not admit to being influenced by advertising.

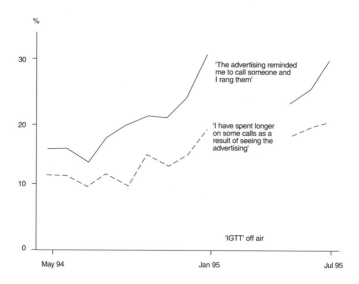

Figure 16: % claiming to use telephone more
Source: BMRB

The Advertising has Worked in the Way Intended

We could not track 'gatekeeper' *households*, because BT's advertising monitor interviews *individuals*, not family units. Instead, we looked for changes among demographic groups most likely to approximate to our target audience.

When the two behaviour statements discussed above are analysed by age and sex, we found that the biggest rises in claimed behaviour came from the group whose phone usage we would expect to be most repressed: women, especially those aged 35+.

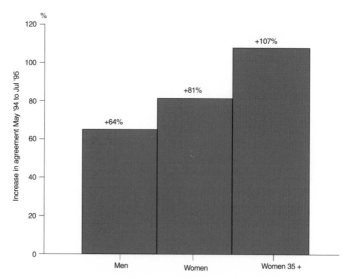

Figure 17: *'I have spent longer on some calls as a result of seeing the advertising'*
Source: BMRB

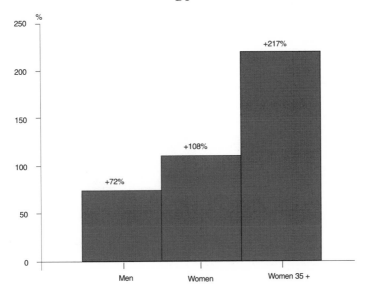

Figure 18: 'The advertising reminded me to call someone and I rang them'
Source: BMRB

BT also tracks the degree of relaxed attitudes towards using the phone with the statement 'It's fun to pass time chatting on the phone'. Agreement with this measure rose substantially (Figure 19).

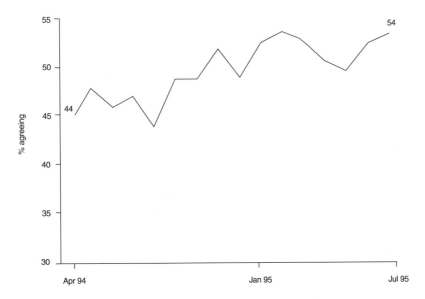

Figure 19: 'It's fun to pass time chatting on the phone'
Source: BMRB

As we would expect, movement was greatest among men, and especially older men, suggesting a particular softening in gatekeepers' attitudes towards chatting on the phone (Figure 20 overleaf).

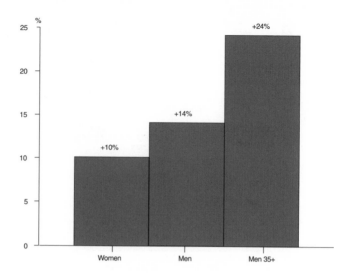

Figure 20: *'It's fun to pass time chatting on the phone'*
Source: BMRB

Correspondingly, if the gatekeeper has a more relaxed attitude, we would expect women to feel less guilty about using the phone. There has indeed been a small but significant reduction in the proportion of women feeling *'guilty about chatting on the phone'* (48% to 44%).

There has also been a Steep Fall in Price Perceptions

We earlier described how important price perceptions were, because they fuel 'gatekeeper' prejudices and create guilt amongst would-be callers. Figure 21 shows that, although the percentage of people saying call charges were high had been gradually falling since mid 1992, it began to fall steeply once our campaign began.

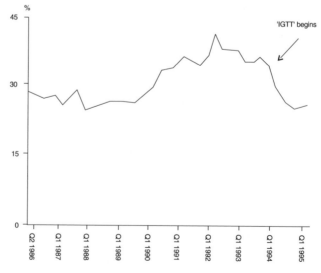

Figure 21: *Percentage of people agreeing that 'BT call charges are high'*
Source: BMRB

So is IGTT 'Social Engineering'?

Beyond the effects we have demonstrated on its intended target audiences, other evidence suggests that the campaign has worked in a wider way, and on a much 'higher' level, to raise the topic of good communication onto the agenda of 'things we should all be better at'.

The campaign has unarguably generated a *huge* amount of media coverage. But, more importantly, when 'It's Good To Talk' is referenced in the media, as often as not the point being underlined is a serious one: that we should be better communicators.

It does seem that Marketing magazine got it about right. The 'engineering' may have just begun, but 'IGTT' *is* more than an advertising campaign, it is indeed a piece of social engineering.

By raising the topic of good communication, BT is benefiting. As the following quotes illustrate, an increased understanding of the fact that it *is* good to talk, is leading more people to use the phone.

> 'Apart from a few people, we are all bad communicators, and what BT are saying is true...I was watching that ad just now and it made me feel guilty that I haven't spoken to my mother in the last three weeks. When I get home I'm going to.'

> 'Yes, it is good to talk, and I do admit that when I've seen Bob on the telly it makes me think how actually I'm a bit bad at it...and I ought to make more of an effort.'

> 'My son's schoolteacher tells her class every day that it's good to talk, and now when he wants to use the phone and my husband kicks up a fuss, he says "but Daddy, it's good to talk you know." What can you say, it's true?'

Sources: The Planning Partnership/AMV Qualitative

IN CONCLUSION

BT has historically invested heavily in advertising. This paper demonstrates how strategic and creative relevance made a large budget work harder to create a step-change in call volumes. Latest data shows the campaign's continued success beyond the period under discussion.

We have calculated a payback of 6 to 1. In fact, the campaign's return will be far greater than this in the long term. 'It's Good To Talk' is changing attitudes towards telephony, and the future benefit of this to BT will be huge.

BT's eventual goal is to change perceptions of telephony from a cost which should be minimised, to an investment in quality of life which should be valued. By helping to achieve this, the campaign is growing the market, and convincing the nation that it really *is good to talk*.

8

Safeway

Effective...Moi?

UNUSUAL SYNERGY

Grocery retail advertising has often been forced into stark and unacceptable choices: to either tactically drive sales (hand-to-hand combat), or to strategically alter or enhance the retailer's core image and values (the art of generalship).

The uniqueness of the Safeway campaign is its combination of tactics and strategy into one all-embracing campaign. A campaign which used Safeway's 'Boy-King', Harry, to warmly embrace messages ranging from loyalty cards to the launch of own-label, new in-store services and 'Offers of the Week'.

The resultant synergy has transformed a foggy and weak brand personality into a clearly positioned provider, pre-eminent in serving the needs of mothers with young children.

From 'overgrown delicatessen' to 'observant provider' in 18 months flat.

WELL BEHIND ON THE STRATEGIC GRID

Safeway's brand and advertising heritage before the 'Harry' campaign was something of a bare cupboard, stocked only with Hannah Gordon, a vaguely American heritage and a jingle. This was not surprising given an almost total advertising emphasis on 'line and price' special offers rather than 'filling the sponge' of the brand's equity.

It was also in sharp contrast to the market leaders.

Sainsbury's had invested for more than a decade in the best sound-bite written on value for money: 'Good food costs less at Sainsbury's'. Beautifully crafted press advertising had stressed the quality of its own-label, further enhanced by the 'Recipe' campaign on television. These recipes resolved the dilemma of quick and original mid-week meals, as well as stressing the *end benefit* of shopping in preference to the process itself.

Tesco, meanwhile, had invested in a Dudley Moore campaign which played to its less stuffy reputation and added a dimension of own-label quality and freshness to a long-standing 'pile-it-high, sell-it-cheap' heritage.

Figures on advertising spend during these years tell a story of a Safeway brand that had been consistently out-shouted by the competition (Table 1).

TABLE 1: SHARE OF VOICE 1989–93 (%)

	1989	1990	1991	1992	1993
J Sainsbury	23.7	17.7	22.5	23.9	28.6
Tesco	34.2	43.6	36.8	37.7	32.0
Asda	25.2	25.7	20.6	15.8	17.4
Safeway	16.7	12.9	20.1	22.7	21.9

To have several brand deficiencies is rare, but research carried out in late 1993 and early 1994 indicated that Safeway suffered exactly that fate. Its image was:

— poor value for money;

— a lot of smaller stores unlikely to have full range;

— poor own-label offering (not worthy to be called 'retailer brand');

— cold, distant ambience;

— for singles or couples, not families;

— no pre-eminence.

As a consequence, it failed to even audition for the repertoire of many shoppers.

THE KEY TARGET AND KEY INSIGHT

These qualitative findings led in turn to the hypothesis that Safeway's shopper profile might be abnormal in shape.

In particular, the hypothesis was understandably formed that it could have a weak penetration of the all-important family formers and rearers who represent the big-ticket shoppers in the sector.

Pinpointing the Penetration Weakness

To this end, in early 1994, a special analysis was commissioned from AGB of Safeway's brand share by age band (Figure 1). This showed clearly that, while Safeway's share peaked among 'DINKYs', at the point of family formation it dipped dramatically.

The problem was further compounded by the fact that demographically, over the years to 2001, the Safeway area of strength was set to decline by 21.5%, while the area of weakness would grow by 13.7%.

Qualitative work therefore now turned to concentrate specifically on the attitudes of these thirty-something family rearers.

It confirmed Safeway's vague and somewhat distant image; the brand came across as one that was *not popular with its peers* and associated with people who had higher disposable incomes, and therefore might border on being 'spendthrift'.

Safeway was seen as a place where its limited 'treat' range might 'be good for dinner party shopping' but not for a main family shop. The psychology of 'balancing the household books' was a very acute one for this life-stage and situation.

Many of the women interviewed had been working until recently, but had sacrificed their salary rather than their time with the children. This meant that they either had to restrict their shopping budgets or felt duty-bound to the sole, male bread-winner to curb any indulgence. In a more general, ideological sense there was a desire to either ditch the attitudes of 'the profligate '80s', or at least to appear to do so. Thus Safeway was in danger of being washed away as an expensive '80s relic in a tide of '90s value-consciousness.

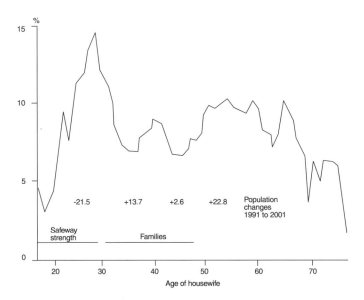

Figure 1: *Safeway share of age by housewife*
Source: AGB

Key Insight

Going shopping with young children not only felt like you had a different purse, it also felt like you'd joined 'the ranks of the discriminated-against minorities'. Research showed that supermarkets generically failed to react to the difficulties of shopping with young children.

Supermarkets were adult-centric.

This provided Safeway and the agency with an opportunity to present a supermarket that looked at the world through child-coloured spectacles. This meant not just warm feelings but well-observed realities:

— Mother-and-baby parking spaces and changing facilities;

— Crèches;

— Bag packers.

Importantly, this could *not* be done without also changing the bedrock requirements of:

— Range (definitive, not exotic);

— Value for money;

— Quality own-label (ie retailer brand);

— Special offers as 'magnets' to build store traffic (the evidence being that once in-store they would be cross-sold on to other items).

CHANGING THE MEDIA RULES

Line-and-price press advertising was the norm for grocery retail campaigns. It acted as a 'surrogate shop window'. Because all the competitors used it, there was a fear that to abandon it as a marketing weapon would reduce effectiveness.

Yet, past tracking of imagery over time showed that this approach had done nothing to address the weaknesses of the Safeway brand. It also appeared to have resulted in a relatively low spontaneous awareness, while, importantly, there was no evidence of consistent progress in like-for-like sales growth year-on-year.

We thus thought the previously unthinkable.

We decided to test the abandonment of tactical press advertising in favour of using television as the lead medium. We tested this idea in Scotland in mid-1994 and consequently achieved improvements in both overall brand awareness and specific points of communication.

The stage was set.

We would rewrite the rules and use television as the lead medium for the new national 'Harry' campaign.

This was a strategy which led to using television as a flexible medium for everything from brand ethos to weekly offers.

THE CREATIVE LEAP

The proposition of Safeway as 'the best ally a mother with young children can have' had many facets. One of these was that it had to overcome a weak or negative image. It therefore had to be both straightforwardly throat-grabbing and charming. It had to not just cajole but to change behaviour.

It had to persuade rather than just assert, to show a soft underbelly to the hard sell. It also had to be diverse without being fragmented.

Campaigns such as Red Rock Cider and Tango had dealt with the awkward business of delivering product information by being amusingly blatant and delivering the information twice over. We chose something less radical but equally charming. We chose, as Spielberg had done in his best films, to shoot everything from the perspective of a child.

Early script development showed that as a vehicle a two-year-old child could comment on a number of different communication tasks without getting in the way of the message – and could in fact raise the interest level of what was being talked about – a bag packer, for instance, not being the most intrinsically interesting thing to feature in a commercial.

Equally the Harry character provided a warmth and humanity that Safeway was lacking.

The charm of his insights into the adult world became the charm of Safeway's insights into the dilemma of the shopper.

Three initial films were made: a launch commercial concentrating on the new 'case' initiatives, another on own-label and a third on the refund-and-replace promise in relation to own-label quality. Within two weeks, however, five 10-second line-and-price commercials were also being aired, a total of £5.5 million being spent on this initial burst from 2 October to 3 December 1994.

Over the full 18 months, over 60 Harry films were made, covering a variety of product and price, and corporate initiative subjects. Every film was signed off with the line 'Lightening the Load' as a summation of the brand ethic.

THE MEDIUM IS THE MESSAGE

To unleash the full power and flexibility of Harry's insights and personality, we needed television, and lots of it.

Safeway increased its TV expenditure sufficiently to ensure an uplift in share of voice from 25% to 31% across the period of the campaign launch.

Ultimately, however, this campaign was about increasing Safeway's 'share of mind' rather than simply its share of voice.

The launch phase in toto had to embrace a wide range of objectives:

— Three 'brand' commercials embodying the new service ethos;

— The breadth of Safeway's Christmas price offers;

— The launch of Safeway own-brand cola.

The media task was therefore to balance the exposure requirements of 'brand' communication with the more tactical but pressing commercial imperatives of product promotion.

We started with a three-week high-density burst of activity for the three longer-time-length brand commercials, to establish the new store ethics and Harry's character.

We then utilised 10-second commercials, that were short celluloid stories in their own right, to gain frequency of exposure for more tactical messages.

This mixed use of time lengths, and the care taken to craft well constructed 10-second commercials as whole stories, rather than just apply the editor's scissors to cut-down longer films, paid off. Recall of individual 10-second executions proved to be very high, giving them the impact of 20- or 30-second commercials for a fraction of the cost.

SWITCHING ON THE HEART MONITOR

Courage and innovation need monitoring to ensure that they are correctly entrepreneurial rather than foolhardy.

Thus, Millward Brown produced a tracking study at regular intervals, while Taylor Nelson was commissioned to report on brand image dimension movements over time.

While both these companies have world-class reputations in their fields, we were also concerned to look closely at the precise way the campaign was being received, to monitor the heartbeat *and* do a brain scan. Alistair Burns was therefore also asked to look *qualitatively* at how the campaign was working.

An Immediate Response

Within three weeks of the inception of the campaign, Millward Brown showed a rise in spontaneous advertising awareness from 11% to 27%, and an increase in the Awareness Index from 3 to 5, a very high figure for a traditionally low-interest sector, and the highest in the category despite formidable rivals.

Over time (as Figure 2 demonstrates) the awareness level itself has outstripped all competitors to reach a peak of 66%, a *six-fold* increase on the original figure.

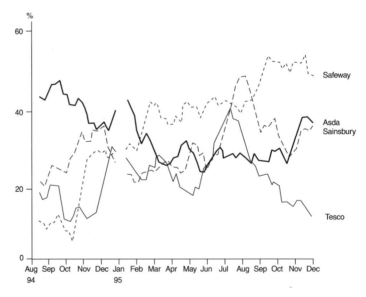

Figure 2: *Claimed advertising awareness – TV*
Source: Millward Brown

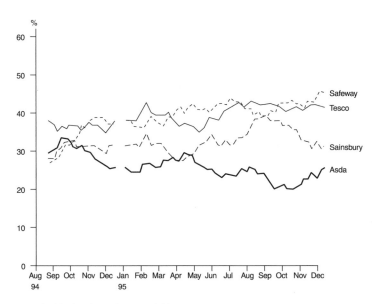

Figure 3: *Image – is ideal for families with young children*
Source: Millward Brown

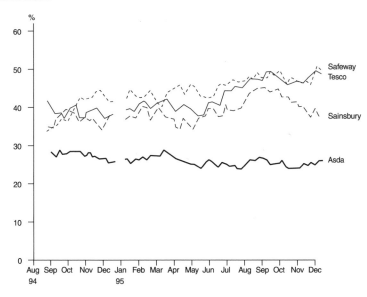

Figure 4: *Image – makes shopping easy*
Source: Millward Brown

Getting the Message Across

By the end of the first burst, Millward Brown's detailed recall and communication monitor also showed the creative vehicle communicating 'easy to shop with children' (55%), 'competitively priced own brand' (33%), 'child friendly' (44%) and 'family store' (25%).

Figure 5: *Supermarket image – is becoming more popular these days*
Source: Millward Brown

Over the full term of the campaign, image tracking by this company also showed marked improvements on 'ideal for families with young children' (Figure 3), 'makes shopping easy' (Figure 4), 'becoming more popular these days' (Figure 5) and 'good value own-brand' (Figure 6). On all except the last of these dimensions, the brand has now moved from last to first place in the market.

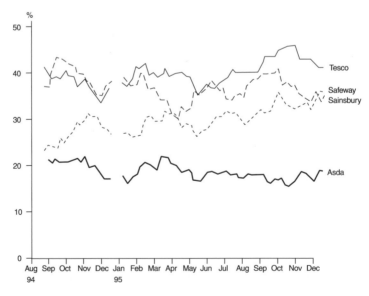

Figure 6: *Image – value own-brand*
Source: Millward Brown

Previous research having shown a somewhat cool and distant personality, two personality dimensions were also tracked by Millward Brown. Figures 7 and 8 also show how, on the dimensions of 'approachable' and 'caring', the brand has taken the lead in the sector.

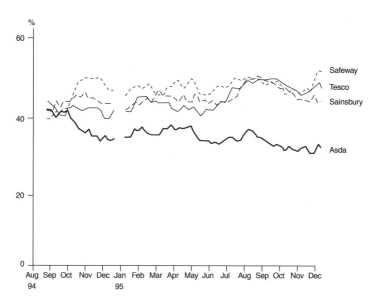

Figure 7: *Store personality – approachable*
Source: Millward Brown

Figure 8: *Store personality – caring*
Source: Millward Brown

Safeway had thus not only moved up in consumer minds, it had also moved closer.

Changing

Finally, having benchmarked the propensity to shop at Safeway on a five-point scale, Millward Brown was able to show how, over the period of the campaign, specific intentional attitudes to the brand had improved. Significant increases in 'it's my favourite supermarket' and 'I would certainly consider shopping there in the future' were reflected in a marked decrease in the score for 'it's a supermarket I would not consider' (Figure 9). Additionally, these intentions were clearly reflected in sales results.

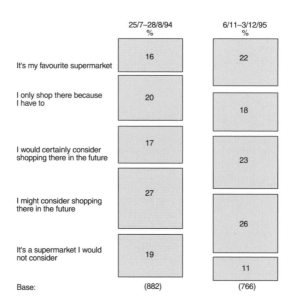

Figure 9: *Attitude to shopping at Safeway*
Source: Millward Brown

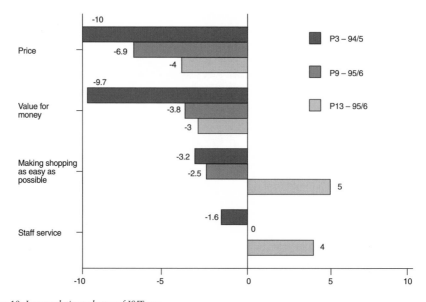

Figure 10: *Image relative to better of JS/Tesco*
Source: Taylor Nelson

Further Confirmation of Impact

These findings, in terms of image shift, are confirmed by the Taylor Nelson monitor that has been reporting throughout the campaign. Figure 10 shows how the competition's lead on price and value for money has been eroded by the campaign, while, in terms of specifically making shopping easier and staff service generally, Safeway has overtaken its rivals.

After nine months of the campaign's life, the Alistair Burns qualitative consultancy was commissioned to give us further insights on how the campaign was 'structurally engineered'. At a spontaneous level, Burns found accurate and enthusiastic recall coupled with strong branding:

'...as soon as you see him you know it's Safeway'.

The campaign was found to be enjoyable, memorable and popular without being patronising, and the main communication was perceived to be about being helpful and friendly, especially for those with small children:

'They put themselves out to help you.'

'They're more geared to children than the others.'

It seemed therefore, that on the basis of a range of both quantitative and qualitative data, the campaign was fulfilling the objectives set for it.

There remained one all-important question, however: could the campaign be shown to be having a positive effect on sales performance? Could it actually, therefore, change behaviour as well as mind-set?

COMMERCIAL RESULTS

Sales and market share results achieved since the start of the campaign provide strong circumstantial evidence that the advertising played the major contributory role in improved performance by Safeway.

In particular, it is worth noting that the only element of the marketing mix to undergo changes in weight, media emphasis and content was the advertising itself.

This is not enough alone to make an ultimately convincing case for clear correlation between a change in advertising policy and a sales uplift. For this, we felt we needed an econometric model.

Accordingly, The Decision Shop – an econometric consultancy – was commissioned to produce a model, in order to try and correlate various factors with sales performance. Seasonal (Christmas and Easter) factors were tested along with the full range of weather factors (there was an abnormally hot summer in 1995) and other key variables, such as price and share of advertising voice.

The model ran from the beginning of 1994 (well before the campaign broke in October of that year), until the spring of 1996, and would thus be able to measure the relative correlation between television advertising and sales for the period as a whole, *and* for the period of the new television advertising. We were determined to be rigorous.

An important potential way in which the data from this model might be 'skewed' concerned the actual retail estate of Safeway. Throughout any given year the company is active in launching new stores and refitting old ones in order to improve performance, and the result of this is invariably an increase in sales in the changed/new stores.

For this reason, therefore, all new and refitted stores were removed from the model sample. While it could be argued that this was 'unfair' to the advertising (in that only the 'weaker' store performance was being monitored), it remained our concern to screen out all extraneous effects that could perhaps artificially inflate the result.

The results eventually presented by The Decision Shop showed an R^2 percentage of 89.6, showing that the model was highly efficient in explaining all the variables at play. When set against actual sales performance, the model was also extremely accurate, with a fitted mean absolute percentage error of only 1.7%. The Durbin-Watson statistic was also well within the acceptable range at 1.7.

The clear finding of the modelling process was that the 'Harry' campaign had increased the advertising's positive elasticity in relation to sales. Taking the modelling period as a whole, the elasticity was 0.081. However, for the period of the 'Harry' advertising, it was 0.105.

The Decision Shop concluded that:

'...the "Harry" campaign on its own has twice the advertising effect on sales than pre and post combined...the campaign has significantly increased the Safeway advertising elasticity.'

TABLE 2: SAFEWAY UK VALUE 'CLEAN' STORES MODEL – POST-'HARRY'
1994 WEEK 40 TO 1995 WEEK 43 – OCT TO OCT

Variable	Elasticity	T-statistic
Average Safeway price	-0.456	2.2
Temperature	+0.026	1.8
Rainfall	-0.002	0.7
Safeway TV advertising 80% ret/m price+offer+loyalty	+0.105	2.7
Tesco TV advertising 90% ret/m loyalty	-0.004	1.5
Christmas	+0.816	18.8
Easter	+0.206	4.4
R^2 90.6%	FMAPE 1.9%	

These elasticity figures mean that, for instance, were the advertising budget to have been doubled during the 'Harry' period, Safeway would have seen a 10.5% increase in sales.

Taking the 1995/6 fiscal year figures as an example, this would have resulted in a £616 million sales boost for an additional television advertising outlay of around £22 million – representing a profit increase in excess of £42 million.

That Safeway's commercial performance did improve over the period in question there can be no doubt. Nielsen Homescan data shows that brand share increased from 8.0 to 8.8%. Given the size of this sector, as calculated by Nielsen, in absolute terms this represented additional sales of £820 million in 1995 – or, again, a profit boost in the region of £57 million.

At the same time, Safeway's own like-for-like sales showed a percentage year-on-year uplift range during 1995 of between 3.2 and 10.475% (the average was 7.68% by monthly period), compared to a range of from -2.6 to 2.85 during 1994.

It is also notable that, during the period of the campaign, Safeway's average basket size has increased by 12%, from £13.55 to £15.18, suggesting that the brand is increasingly attracting the more mainstream shopper over time.

These commercial results would not, we feel, have been possible without the changes in advertising role and media emphasis which took place in October 1994. Above all, we also firmly believe that what the advertising has done – as shown by the two independent quantitative monitors from Millward Brown and Taylor Nelson – is to give Safeway a vivid and warm *raison d'être*.

Picasso once said, 'It took me 60 years to see like a child'. It has taken this campaign 18 months to get the nation to see grocery shopping and Safeway through the warm, wry, honest eyes of a child. The result is a total change of mind-set and, more importantly, of behaviour.

9

Walkers Crisps

*Garymania! – how an already successful
brand benefited from famous advertising*

INTRODUCTION

This paper examines the effectiveness of BMP's advertising for Walkers Crisps since
its appointment in August 1994, a period which has seen Walkers transformed into,
arguably, the most famous and successful branded property in UK advertising.

THE HISTORY OF WALKERS CRISPS

Henry Walker's butchery business had flourished in Leicester in the 1930s.
However, with the advent of rationing, the Second World War brought severe
consequences to the whole food industry. Diversification was vital, and Henry's
range of choices was finally narrowed to one option – potato crisps.

By 1960, distribution was still confined to the Midlands, but sales nonetheless
trebled over the next decade.

The 1970s saw the start of a programme of regional expansion from Walkers'
Midlands base into Yorkshire, Anglia, Lancashire, Wales, London and the South.

In 1989, Walkers and Smiths Crisps moved under the umbrella of PepsiCo
Foods International. In 1993, the two brands were merged. With a turnover in the
region of £300 million, Walkers Crisps had become the biggest single food brand in
the UK.

THE SITUATION IN AUGUST 1994

By August 1994, Walkers had experienced two years of double-digit growth,[1] and
the brand's share had reached 22%, over three times that of its nearest branded
rival.

---

1. 11.2% year to August 1993, 17.5% year to August 1994. (All retail audit figures are derived from IRI
    Infoscan data, with all share figures based on the total market of crisps and other salty snacks, such as
    Hula Hoops, Quavers, etc.)

However, there were a number of clouds looming on the horizon.

Plateauing Distribution

A very significant proportion of the brand's growth over the last few years had been the result of distribution growth, particularly through regional roll-out. This was already coming to an end in the much larger Grocery channel, and was expected to do likewise in the Impulse channel soon after.[2]

March 1994 had seen the last (mainland) UK region succumb to the Walkers' bandwagon, with the launch into Scotland. This took national distribution to 95% in Grocery and over 60% in Impulse, in both cases nearing what appeared to be the 'natural' limit for the brand.

Growth through distribution gain as a result was unlikely to be as significant a contributor to the brand's success in the future.

Success of Promotions

However, beginning in March 1993, Walkers had embarked on a series of 'Instant Win' promotions which were dramatically successful, producing large and immediate uplifts in volume and ROS.

The scale of the immediate volume gains was beyond anything previously seen in this market and surprised even Walkers.[3]

So, even though growth through distribution gains might have been about to plateau, Walkers felt that in 'Instant Win' promotions it had discovered another engine for dynamic growth. However, even here there were two concerns. First of all, it was unclear how important the novelty factor of these promotions was to their success, and hence whether repetition would result in declining effectiveness over time.[4] Second, it seemed inevitable that the competition would try to copy such a successful idea.

---

2. 'Grocery', as defined by the retail audit, comprises the large supermarket chains, minor multiples (such as Budgen's) and Co-op. 'Impulse' comprises independent grocers, CTNs, garages, off-licences, etc. In the Impulse channel, strong regional brands and the sheer variety of smaller outlets severely restricts the distribution of national brands.
3. The reasons for its dramatic success can be found in the nature of the promotions themselves, which in a number of ways represented something entirely new in the market. The prize fund was beyond anything previously offered. The promotional mechanic, which was varied slightly each time to maintain consumer interest, was unique – on discovering a blue sachet in your packet of crisps, you knew instantly that you had won. In addition, each of the promotions was supported by national TV advertising.
4. In fact, of the three Instant Win promotions run between March 1993 and August 1994, the first had been very clearly more successful than the second, which was in turn more successful than the third.

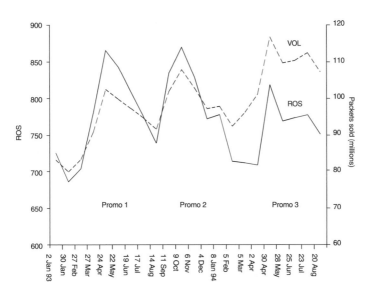

Figure 1: *Walkers volume and ROS pre-BMP*
Source: IRI Infoscan

Advertising

There was little doubt that the promotional advertising had been successful in boosting the sales effect of each promotion. However, in order to protect the salience of Walkers' own promotions in the face of almost inevitable copying by competitors, stronger branding of the 'Instant Win' promotions through advertising was felt to be desirable. It was felt that this could best be achieved by bringing the promotional and theme advertising together under a single brand umbrella.

There had been Walkers brand advertising on television at substantial weights both in the pre-promotional period and during 1994. Unfortunately, it had failed to increase brand awareness significantly. The feeling within the company at this time was that the brand was 'universal in size but not in perception' and that the advertising had to shoulder a large part of the blame. In addition, it appeared to have had little effect on sales.[5]

So, when Walkers put the advertising account out to pitch in mid-1994, it was with the intention of developing an integrated brand campaign incorporating new theme and promotional advertising.

THE PITCH BRIEFING

The brief recognised that distribution-derived growth was coming to an end, but asked for an advertising campaign that would maintain volume growth on a par

---

5. In fact, recent econometric modelling (see Appendix) has confirmed these suspicions. The pre-BMP advertising was indeed ineffective on sales performance.

with that achieved in the previous two years, primarily through ROS growth. In particular it needed to do this in two ways:

— Through theme advertising that would work harder than before and would generate ROS increases in its own right.

— Through promotional advertising which would be part of the same campaign and hence more strongly branded than before, and which would generate even more pronounced short-term ROS uplifts than the previous promotional advertising.

Because Walkers was already dominant in Impulse, and Grocery was becoming a larger component of the market, it was clear that strong volume growth could only be maintained if Walkers grew significantly in Grocery. Walkers had 22% brand share in this channel, versus 29% share in Impulse (year to August 1994) and Grocery was growing, Impulse declining, relatively – as shown in Table 1.

TABLE 1: WALKERS' SHARE OF MARKET

Share of market	Year to August 1992 %	Year to August 1993 %	Year to August 1994 %
Grocery	57	60	63
Impulse	43	40	37

So these objectives really implied the need to ensure strong rate of sale and volume growth in Grocery, while we could expect less of a volume increase from our already high share in Impulse.

With these aims in mind, BMP was appointed to handle the Walkers' business in August 1994.

DEVELOPING AN ADVERTISING STRATEGY

We knew that any advertising for the brand would have to appeal to children, who were heavy consumers of snacks, as well as purchasers in their own right in the Impulse channel. Much of the snack volume that they ate, however, was being purchased for them by their parents in the burgeoning Grocery channel. Here, 80% of purchases were made by adults. Adults were also becoming increasingly important as *consumers* of snacks – having grown up eating them they failed to desist from the habit in adulthood. It was clear that both children and adults were important to us.

We thus set out to create advertising that would genuinely and powerfully appeal to a mass audience of adults as well as children – no small task when the category advertising at this time was typified by short-term tactical approaches, irrelevant product claims, self-consciously zany imagery – and very few famous or talked-about campaigns.

From qualitative research conducted among crisp-lovers of all ages, we identified 'irresistibility' as the quality that embodied everything they most enjoyed about snacking. It followed that, whichever crisp could lay claim to being the most irresistible would, inevitably, also be the freshest, the tastiest, and so on: it was shorthand for the perfect crisp.

However, they also saw crisps as part of everyday life. As a result, it became clear that people were unlikely to empathise with any brand that took itself too seriously, and that any grandiose claims about irresistibility had to be treated with tongue firmly in cheek.

THE CREATIVE BRIEF

The creative brief thus called for advertising that would appeal to a mass audience, by owning the category high ground of irresistibility. The brief can be summarised as follows:

Target audience:	Adults and children
Proposition:	No one can resist Walkers Crisps
Support:	Product quality or Instant Win promotions
Tonal values:	Fun, unpretentious, informal, classless, social

THE WALKERS DUCK

The occasion for the launch of the new advertising was, in fact, a promotion, 'Moneybags II', which was to be launched in September 1994. The first advertising we produced featured the 'Walkers Duck', a talking duck from Leicester who was lucky enough to win £20 in his packet of Walkers. The endline 'There's Only One Walkers, Duck' worked both as a way of asserting the primacy of Walkers and as a colloquial nod to the brand's East-Midland roots. This execution proved to be very successful in supporting the promotion.

A subsequent series of 'Duck' executions, celebrating the irresistibility of Walkers crisps, had researched well in rough and the duck showed potential as a long-term spokesman for the brand. However, despite its success in boosting sales during the promotion, Walkers remained unsure about whether the subsequent executions really would have the necessary stature to make the Walkers brand famous. In October the difficult decision was made not to progress with the 'Duck' campaign, and to create another brand campaign for both theme and promotional advertising.

THE NEW CREATIVE BRIEFING

We wanted a creative vehicle that would generate PR and media coverage, but the revised creative brief was identical on all other critical dimensions. Given the importance of fame and the fact that we were aiming at a mass audience, we chose TV as the main medium.

In addition, this time the event that would occasion the new advertising was not a promotion, but the launch of an improved Cheese & Onion variety. It was felt that this much simpler piece of product news was a more appropriate place to start to establish a brand vehicle than a promotion, as had been the case with the duck.

THE CAMPAIGN IDEA

The idea for the campaign can be summarised as 'Walkers are so irresistible they make even nice guys turn nasty when it comes to crisps'.

What set the idea apart was the thought of casting ex-England and Leicester footballer Gary Lineker[6] as the nice guy turned nasty. Gary had appeared in Walkers advertising ten years earlier, and in the intervening period had gone from local hero to national institution.

While of the world of football, he was not confined to it; as the ambassador and genuine 'nice guy' of the game, Gary was as attractive to mums as to kids. His well-publicised return from playing in Japan offered us unique PR opportunities. Most important of all, his down-to-earth personality and roots in Walkers' Leicester heartland provided a seamless fit with our desired brand personality and the unpretentious values we wished to establish.

To date, five TV executions have been produced in the series, including two for further 'Instant Win' promotions (see Table 2).

TABLE 2: GARY LINEKER EXECUTIONS

Execution	Airdate	Objective
'Welcome Home'	Jan 95	Launch improved Cheese & Onion flavour
'Nun'	Mar 95	Support 'Instant Cheque' promotion
'Garymania'	May 95	Launch new Crinkles range
'Dial-a-Prize'	Sep 95	Support 'Dial-a-Prize' promotion
'Salt 'n Lineker'	Jan 96	Launch improved Salt & Vinegar flavour

MEDIA PLAN

The timing of the campaign and weights have been as shown in Figure 2:[7]

---

6. Whose great uncle, incidentally, used to supply potatoes to Walkers.
7. In addition to the main TV campaign, which was weighted towards mums and children, with special emphasis on programmes they might view together, a small portion of the budget (less than 9%) was allocated for tactical tasks and other media.

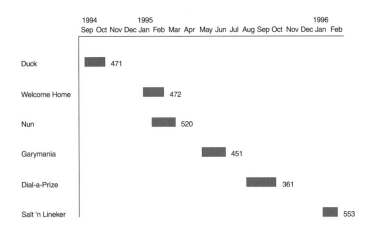

Figure 2: *Media plan (all figures in GRPs)*
Source: BARB

WALKERS' PERFORMANCE SINCE AUGUST 1994

Overall Volume Growth

Walkers' volume has risen strikingly since BMP's appointment in August 1994 and
the rate of growth has actually improved upon that of the previous two years.

TABLE 3: WALKERS VOLUME AND RATE OF GROWTH

	Walkers volume (millions of packs)	Annual growth %
MAT to Aug 1993	1152	+ 11.2
MAT to Aug 1994	1354	+17.5
MAT to Aug 1995	1659	+22.5

Source: IRI Infoscan

This growth has also been maintained since August 1995: volume to February
1996 (the last period of available data) is 19.3% up on the same period 12 months
earlier.

Since Walkers has continued to grow faster than the market over this period, its
share has also risen (Figure 3).

In addition, the peaks in Figure 3 equate to promotions and it can be seen that
the BMP-advertised promotions generated greater uplift (per TVR) compared with
those that came before. We can also see that, in contrast to the past, share between
the promotional periods settles to higher 'base levels', leading to higher sustained
growth levels.

'WELCOME HOME' 60 SECONDS

MVO: When a crisp as irresistible as Walkers introduces a new Cheese & Onion flavour...

...there's no more Mr Nice Guy.

'STAND' 30 SECONDS

MVO: To introduce Walkers new, tastier Salt & Vinegar flavour...

...they're calling them Salt 'n Lineker

(Music plays: 'Nessun Dorma')

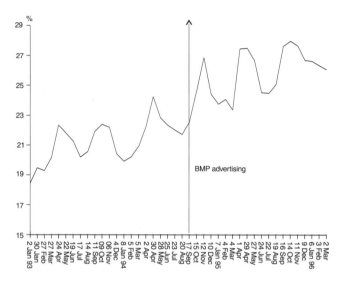

Figure 3: *Walkers' share of total salty snacks market*
Source: IRI Infoscan

Performance in Grocery

Walkers volume in Grocery grew by 44% between September 1994 and February 1996 (MATs), resulting in a growth in brand share which continues to trend upwards (Figure 4).

In addition this growth is, unlike that prior to September 1994, almost entirely the result of rate-of-sale growth rather than distribution gain.

Average rate of sale in Grocery over the first 12 months of BMP advertising was 23% higher than that during the previous year.

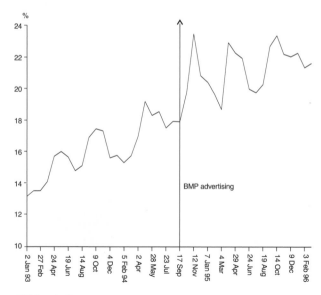

Figure 4: *Volume share of Walkers in Grocery*
Source: IRI Infoscan

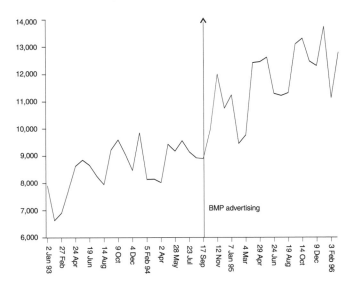

Figure 5: £ weighted ROS of Walkers in Grocery
Source: IRI Infoscan

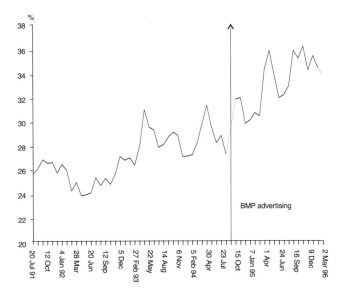

Figure 6: Volume share of Walkers in Impulse
Source: IRI Infoscan

The pattern of peaks and troughs occasioned by promotional activity is still evident, as we would expect. But from January, following the peak coinciding with the 'Duck' promotion, a significant change to the pattern commences. In each case following a promotion, rate of sale settles to a new, and higher, base level.

Performance in Impulse

Walkers has also performed fantastically well within Impulse. Here volume grew by 21% between September 1994 and February 1996, taking MAT share from 28.6% to 34.2%.

This meant that the brand actually grew more vigorously in Impulse than expected. These increases were largely caused by an unexpected growth in distribution over the Lineker advertising period, while ROS grew only slightly. The econometric modelling has been able to directly link this unexpected distribution growth with the advertising.

Performance: Conclusions

The marketing objectives of sustaining volume and share growth were successfully exceeded. This was achieved by:

— dramatically increasing rate of sale in Grocery;

— increasing volume in Impulse through advertising-fuelled distribution growth.

The Contribution of the Advertising

We believe that the BMP advertising was a significant cause of this continued success and that, without it, growth would have been far less significant. We aim to prove this by showing that the advertising worked exactly as planned, and can be related directly to the newly found fame of the brand:

— by an analysis of share-gain variation across regions with different levels of TVRs, showing that the advertising was causal in brand growth;

— by analysing the growth in different advertised varieties of Walkers crisps, showing that the advertising clearly influences consumer behaviour;

— by two econometric models showing directly that the advertising was responsible for a large proportion of the brand's growth;

— and finally by examining the part played by other variables, showing that no other activity could have been responsible for the effect we claim for our advertising.

HOW THE ADVERTISING WORKED

We have said that we set out to make advertising that would make the brand famous by appealing powerfully and equally to adults and children. The evidence suggests that, with the Lineker campaign, we succeeded beyond expectation.

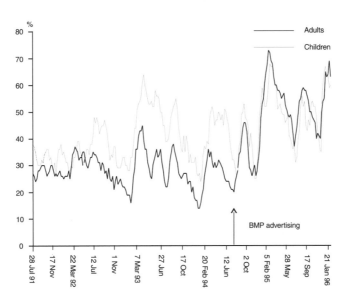

Figure 7: *Walkers – 'seen on TV recently'*
Source: Millward Brown

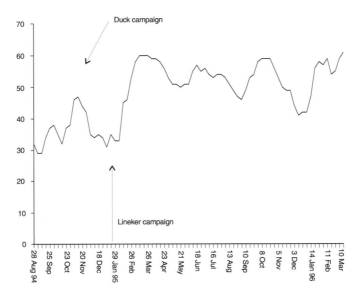

Figure 8: *'Have really good advertising' (Adult sample)*
Source: Millward Brown

Fame

From the outset, the Lineker campaign has generated an amount of TV and press coverage wildly in excess of anything previously seen in this market.

TV coverage has ranged from *News at Ten* to *Fantasy Football League*, *The Big Breakfast* and *How Do They Do That?*

It has also included coverage in *all* national press, from the *Times*, *Independent* and *Telegraph*, to the *Daily Mail*, *Mirror* and the front page of the *Sun* twice. Over time, as the public has become more familiar with the campaign theme, the tabloid newspapers have begun to vie with each other to be the first to release the news of 'What Gary is up to now'. Even in the 'grown-up' world of the business press, it has become standard practice for financial journalists to mention the Lineker campaign, and to link the success of the Walkers brand with it.

Such interest has, of course, been reflected in the awareness scores picked up by the Millward Brown tracking survey. In the past, Walkers' advertising was noticed much more by children than by adults. In contrast, the Lineker campaign has resulted in both *children's* awareness rising to new highs, and adult awareness being transformed, so that it has caught up with, and at times even overtaken, that of children. It is therefore the first Walkers campaign that has managed to attract the attention of the broad audience of all crisp eaters *and* buyers.

This appears to be true, albeit to a lesser degree, for the 'Duck' advertising. These higher overall levels of awareness are accompanied by greater *efficiency* of the advertising, as measured by the Awareness Index (AI). Immediately prior to BMP's advertising, the AI for children had fallen away to only 6 (category average 10), but over the course of the campaign it has risen to 15. Among adults the rise is much more remarkable, leaping first from 8 to 14, then to 16 for 'Nun', and 24 for Dial-a-Prize (category average 8).

Millward Brown's view of the Lineker campaign is that it:

> 'has generated the highest AI of any Walkers Crisps campaign (in the current survey) well above the market average, indeed, it is amongst the highest we have tracked across all markets'.

Appeal

Such awareness measures and such media attention appears to be a reflection of the extent to which the Lineker campaign has entered the hearts of the public.[8] In *Campaign*'s survey to find 'the nation's best-loved ads', Walkers took joint first place with Safeway's 'Harry'. Independently, a survey published in *Marketing* found Gary to be equal 'best-remembered face' in British TV advertising, with 77% branded recall, alongside BT's Bob Hoskins.[9]

Qualitative research groups across the country confirmed the popularity of the advertising and the appropriateness of using Gary Lineker as our 'crisp thief':

> 'I'd been told all about that ad before I saw it. Very funny.'

22-year-old lad

---

8.   Indeed, the public outcry surrounding the story of the banning of 'Welcome Home', led to the unusual step of the ITC reversing its decision.
9.   The latter campaign supported by approximately 20 times the spend of the Walkers advertising.

'There's not many people who could appeal across the board like him.'

Mum

'He's an idol, but because Walkers are so good, he pinches them.'

Mum

'He can steal my crisps anytime!'

13-year-old girl.

Source: Qualitative Research Groups

The Millward Brown attitudinal measures concerning the advertising are unfortunately not consistent pre and post the BMP advertising; however, the 'Have good advertising' statement clearly confirms that the duck to some extent, and Lineker to a great extent, not only cut through to, but were also highly appreciated by, our audience.

Millward Brown assessed the Lineker campaign as:

'extraordinarily successful, it has, in our view, contributed significantly to Walkers' ambition to become the definitive crisp brand – part of the fabric of British life'.

THE ADVERTISING CONTRIBUTION TO SALES

Regional Analysis

If, as we claim, the advertising was the major stimulant to the brand's recent growth, then we would expect growth to be more significant in areas exposed to heavier weights of the advertising. This is indeed the case.

It is best seen in the Grocery channel, where distribution growth was relatively small over the BMP-advertised period – distribution was already over 90% before BMP's appointment – and so correlation between growth and TVR levels might be expected to be seen fairly easily.

To illustrate this, we have compared Walkers' brand-share performance regionally across two periods:

Period 1 – the last 12 weeks immediately prior to BMP's first advertising for Walkers (June to August 1994)

Period 2 – the most recent 12 weeks of data available (approximately the first three months of 1996).

The country (excluding the Midlands)[10] breaks down naturally into three areas, defined by the amount of TV support over the whole BMP-advertised period – the time between our two test periods.

Area 1 – Scotland

Scotland received heavyweight support with 5,965 TVRs, as it was the area into which Walkers had most recently rolled out. The roll-out period, however, can fairly be said to have finished by the time we start our analysis in Period 1, given that the brand had already achieved 91% distribution in Grocery.

Area 2 – the rest of England and Wales (Excluding Anglia and Midlands)

These regions received very similar, higher levels of support – averaging 2,709 TVRs.

Area 3 – Anglia

This region received less advertising support than the rest of the country, with only 1,704 TVRs. This was because the price deal inherited by the new media agency in summer 1994 was considered too expensive, and the region was downweighted accordingly.

TABLE 4: CHANGES IN WALKERS' SHARE BETWEEN PERIODS 1 AND 2

Region	TVRs	Share Period 1	Share Period 2	% change
Scotland – high	5,965	8.18	15.95	95.0
Mid-weight areas	2,709	15.55	20.92	34.6
Anglia – low	1,704	23.80	27.58	15.9

We can see that higher levels of advertising support do indeed correlate with higher brand share growth rates. We do, however, need to eliminate the effects of (slightly) fluctuating distribution levels over the period, as in the following table:

---

10. We have not included the Midlands, Walkers' heartland, because there the brand is a well-loved local institution with nearly 50 years of history behind it. In the Midlands, Walkers dominates with a share of approximately 30% of the total crisps and snacks market, and the advertising was expected to, and did, work differently. The task was the more defensive one of holding onto existing loyal consumers, and maintaining the already high levels of share and rate of sale. Though even in the Midlands share increased by 8.6% between the two periods.

TABLE 5: EFFECTS OF DISTRIBUTION LEVELS

| | Period 1 | | Period 2 | | Share divided by £dist | | |
	% share	£dist	% share	£dist	P1	P2	% change
Scotland	8.18	90.7	15.95	99.3	9.02	16.06	78.1
Mid-weight	15.55	96.4	20.92	97.6	16.13	21.44	32.9
Anglia	23.80	100.0	27.58	100.0	23.80	27.58	15.9

Source: BARB, IRI Infoscan

It is clear from this that share growth is still higher in regions with more advertising, and this is not the result of distribution.

This fairly 'blunt' kind of analysis is less appropriate in the Impulse channel, because distribution over the BMP-advertised period actually continued to grow quite significantly and rather unexpectedly, thereby making the correlation between share growth and advertising more difficult to isolate. Trying to eliminate the distribution effect by looking at rate of sale is not sufficient because it appears that the BMP advertising drives distribution gains in Impulse as well as rate of sale.

In order to be able to determine what was really happening to the brand in the Impulse channel as a result of our advertising (as well as to produce a more detailed quantification of the advertising contribution in Grocery), we needed to construct a series of econometric models, on which we will focus shortly. Before that, however, there is another piece of evidence that clearly links sales performance with our advertising.

Variety Analysis

Each of the 'theme' advertising executions focused on a particular variety of Walkers crisps – Cheese & Onion flavour for 'Welcome Home', Crinkles for 'Garymania', and Salt & Vinegar flavour for 'Salt 'n Lineker'. In each case the performance of the advertised variety is boosted substantially at the time of the advertising.

Cheese & Onion share of the Walkers brand rose from 22.9% prior to the 'Welcome Home' advertising, to a peak of 25.7% immediately following it; Salt & Vinegar share shot up from 14.5% to 17.8%; and Crinkles nearly doubled its contribution to total Walkers crisps volume from 3.6% to 6.2% during the advertised month.

Hence it is clear that our adverts are powerful at driving consumer behaviour. While this does not prove that it has caused brand growth, it is highly indicative of the power of the campaign to influence consumer behaviour. We suggest that this is indicative of the effects it has on consumer purchasing of the brand.

Evidence from Econometric Analysis

We have constructed two econometric models – one for each trade channel. This has enabled us to quantify the contribution of advertising directly to sales increases in each channel, and has also revealed that, in line with our objectives, this contribution is a combination of more effective promotional *and,* for the first time in many years, effective theme advertising.

Grocery

As the insertion rate of winning coupons remained constant throughout all of the promotions, their scale naturally increased over time as overall brand volume grew. Yet despite this, prior to BMP involvement, each successive promotion had been generating less volume per TVR, as perhaps the novelty of the mechanic wore off. The model shows that the drop in effect per TVR between the first and second promotions, pre-BMP, was of the order of 50%, and between the second and third promotions of the order of 30%. 'Duck', the first BMP promotional ad, managed to reverse this trend, and achieved 10% more effect per TVR than the previous promotion, whilst the two Lineker-supported promotions have improved upon even this achievement (Table 6).

TABLE 6: EFFECT OF THE PROMOTIONS

	Millions of packs generated	TVRs	Millions of packs per 100 TVRs	% change versus previous promotion
Promo1	93.4	309	30.2	
Promo2	47.8	316	15.1	-50%
Promo3	76.7	734	10.5	-31%
'Duck'	54.0	471	11.5	+10%
'Nun'	66.4	520	12.8	+11%
'Dial-a-Prize'	65.1	361	18.0	+41%

Source: BARB, Econometric model

In addition to this, the Lineker promotional advertising has worked in a way in which the previous ones had not, generating not only a short-term effect on share, but also a longer-term step-change increase in share. 'Nun' seems to have generated a long-term (ie well beyond the end of the promotion) increase in share of 0.5% points, and 'Dial-a-Prize' a gain of 1% point. By integrating the promotional and theme advertising into one very successful vehicle, we have been able to create promotional advertising which has not only increased the success of the promotions themselves, but has also continued to work hard as brand advertising after the promotion has finished.

The theme advertising itself is also having a strong effect on share, which was not the case prior to the development of the Lineker campaign. The model shows that 'Welcome Home' generated an uplift of over 6 million bags of crisps in Grocery. The very first effects of 'Salt 'n Lineker' are just coming through in our data sample and it appears to be generating a similar effect per TVR, whilst the 'Garymania' ad for Crinkles generated extra sales for Walkers in Grocery of 3.5 million packets.

Impulse

The model has, surprisingly, revealed that the decline in the effectiveness of advertising each subsequent promotion pre-BMP was not so apparent in the Impulse channel.[11] It is not clear why this is the case, although it is possible that there was less of a wear-out effect for the novelty of the 'Instant Win' idea among children (who dominate purchase in the Impulse channel), than among adults (who dominate in Grocery). Whatever the reason, the model shows clearly that the promotion advertised by the duck reversed this decline and that the two Lineker-supported promotions have been much more successful at generating sales per TVR than any previous promotions.

TABLE 7: SALES GENERATED PER TVR

	Millions of packs generated	TVRs	Millions of packs per TVRs
Promo1	15.8	309	5.11
Promo2	16.2	316	5.13
Promo3	22.4	734	3.05
'Duck'	20.9	471	4.44
'Nun'	33.4	520	6.43
'Dial-a-Prize'	25.4	361	7.04

Source: BARB, Econometric model

Again, the model confirms that the Lineker theme advertising has worked, and has had a positive and significant effect on sales, unlike pre-Lineker theme advertising. In Impulse alone, 'Garymania' generated extra sales of 0.8 million packets of Crinkles, while 'Welcome Home' and 'Salt 'n Lineker' have produced sales of an extra million packs each so far – and the effect of 'Salt 'n Lineker' continues.

ELIMINATION OF OTHER VARIABLES

We have exhaustively examined the effect of other variables, both independently and in the econometric modelling. None of these other variables can explain the tremendous growth of Walkers since August 1994.

WALKERS – OVERALL PROFITABILITY OF THE CAMPAIGN

The econometric models show a very substantial sales gain resulting from advertising, as the advertising has not only driven share directly but has helped to increase share of front stocks in Grocery and overall distribution levels in Impulse.

In Impulse the contribution has been 67 million packs (5.1% of Impulse sales between the four weeks ending 15 October 1994 (Duck) and 2 March 1996).

---

11. Given the relative size of Impulse to Grocery, in the overall market this trend is still true.

In Grocery, if we take the whole period, and simply add the individual effect of all the pieces of advertising activity, then the total advertising effect has been 169 million packs, equivalent to approximately 13% of all sales over that period. However, in terms of looking at overall payback, the models show that their total effect is actually multiplicative rather than additive, in which case the total contribution becomes 276 million packs or 20% of total sales.

For every 1p profit margin per bag, the additional bags sold generate £3.4 million. BMP's total advertising spend over the whole period was £8.94 million. The exact margin is confidential but is in excess of 2p. Table 8 shows examples of how only small levels of profit margin provide substantial advertising 'profits'.

TABLE 8: EFFECT OF INCREASED PROFIT MARGIN

Profit margin per bag (pence)	Extra profit (£m)	Advertising cost (£m)	Profit net of ads (£m)
1	3.4	8.94	-5.54
2	6.8	8.94	-2.14
5	17.0	8.94	8.06
10	34.0	8.94	25.06

Source: Register Meal, Econometric modelling

Importantly though, this does not take into account the value for future sales of having appropriated in Grocery such a large share of front stocks, or in Impulse, of having ousted the competition. It is almost impossible to put a meaningful figure on this. However, there is no doubt that in their respective sectors, front stocks and distribution are key determinants of overall volume.

In addition, Hill & Knowlton, Walkers' PR company, believes that, to date, the campaign has generated over £1.6 million (advertising equivalent spend) in additional unpaid-for editorial coverage.

CONCLUSION

When Walkers Crisps came to BMP in 1994 the brand was undeniably successful already. But success generates its own problems, chief among them for Walkers being how to sustain the growth of the brand into the future.

We believe we have shown that it was advertising that played the critical role in stimulating Walkers' amazing success since appointment. But it is remarkable in two other ways which lend the case a wider application.

— As an example of genuinely effective targeting of a mass market. The Walkers advertising was aimed squarely at a mass audience, yet appealed as powerfully and effectually to each sector of that audience as could any advertising aimed at a particular niche within it.

— As an example of how advertising can provide a focus for other forms of consumer communication. The Walkers advertising was used to powerfully enhance other forms of marketing activity (particularly promotions, PR and product innovation), which had previously operated independently and with less success.

Thus the advertising dealt with the problems of success by transforming Walkers from a big brand into a genuinely strong one for the first time.

APPENDIX

Elimination of Variables

Product Quality
Walker's consistent ability to innovate has enabled it to maintain significant levels of unbranded preference throughout the 1990s.

However, this has been true throughout the BMP period, and before and hence cannot explain the increased rise in ROS since BMP's advertising started.

It is possible that our variety analysis could be explained by increases in product qualities of the specified flavour featured in the analysis. However, this is not the case for Crinkles/'Garymania', where the variant remained the same in terms of quality/taste appeal. It is possible that the Salt 'n Lineker name change had an effect but, if so, this could not have happened without the Lineker advertising.

Finally, if flavour improvements were the primary factor affecting sales then we would expect to see a sizeable *step change* in share at their introduction. There is no evidence from the models that this occurred, instead, a short-term *'spike'* in share coinciding only with the timing of the advertising is visible.

Price Reductions and Advertising Effects
Walkers' price has actually been fractionally reduced in real terms over the last few years. This has helped to boost Walkers' sales in both Grocery and Impulse. However, the econometric models present the advertising effects which we have previously claimed for the advertising net of the impacts from all other variables, including price and distribution, so this has no effect on our conclusions.

Tactical Promotion
Regional tactical activity supported by advertising has taken place for Walkers. For four weeks in February and March 1995, the 'Walkerman' promotion ran in the Tyne Tees area only. This involved a 'Walkerman' walking around the towns of the area. Spotting him and answering a question correctly resulted in winning a small cash prize. This was supported by a 10-second TV ad, produced by BMP.

While this promotion was believed to be successful, it only ran in Tyne Tees during the period discussed in this paper (it subsequently rolled out into Scotland and Lancashire in April 1996).

Hence it can only have affected sales in Tyne Tees. Given the enormous effects we claim for the advertising, and the fact that they occur nationally, we can see that 'Walkerman' can only have affected national sales over the BMP period slightly.

Effects of Walkers Increased Size

It is possible that Walkers' growth and hence increased volume at the start of each promotion, has in some way determined the size of success of the subsequent promotion. This is actually not the case.[12]

Nature of Instant Win Promotions

The nature of each promotion was similar although, as mentioned earlier, the number of (smaller) prizes increased as the brand grew – but the top prize did not. Hence the increasing success of the promotions cannot be attributed to increases in the top prize.

Competitive Expenditure

Levels of competitive spend actually increased significantly over the advertised period.

TABLE 9: COMPETITIVE SPEND

	£m	Index
1993	20.5	96
1994	23.1	108
1995	28.0	131

Thus, Walkers' success cannot be explained by reduction in competitive activity.

PR and Media Coverage

We would suggest that the PR coverage that Walkers has achieved since the advent of the Lineker campaign (and hence any related sales), ultimately resulted from the advertising. This was the main reason we dispensed with the otherwise promising Walkers 'Duck' campaign. In addition, practically all the coverage features the campaign itself, suggesting strongly that it would not have occurred without Lineker.

Hence, rather than eliminating effects of PR, we see them as effects of the advertising.

Point Of Sale

It is true that, since the Lineker campaign started, Walkers has been able to increase its POS presence. However, the vast majority of this is Lineker-related material – from 'Gary' shelf-wobblers to life-size cut-outs – and it is clear that willing acceptance of this material by the trade is in fact a result of the popularity and

---

12. We would contend that a) if this were true, then advertising, as we have shown, has played its part in growing the brand and hence creating these effects, and b) these effects can be eliminated by looking at percentage increase in share per TVR rather than just volume increase per TVR for each promotion. If we do this, we see similar trends to those illustrated earlier with the percentage increase in share per TVR actually increasing with each promotion, not decreasing. In fact, in Grocery 'Duck' produced 2.23% uplift in share per 100 TVRs, 'Nun' 2.25% and 'Dial-A-Prize' 3.05%.

success of the Lineker advertising. So rather than *eliminate* its effect, we claim it is another *consequence* of the campaign.

ECONOMETRIC MODELLING

Walker's Econometric Analysis: Explaining and Validating the Models

The models for both channels, particularly Grocery, are actually fairly complex, both having two equations. In Grocery these equations form a simultaneous system where share of volume and share of front stocks are jointly determined. In Impulse the equations explain the performance of Walkers' total volume and of its aggregate pack distribution. (Aggregate distribution is the sum of the sterling distribution across all available pack sizes and is a way of taking account of both the 'width' and 'depth' of distribution.)

Grocery – Theoretical Background

If a brand achieved an increased share of shelf space and thus greater in-store visibility, all else remaining equal, then one would expect this to lead to a higher level of share.

However, in today's hard-nosed Grocery environment the only way a brand can ever get a permanent increase in shelf space (front stocks) is to permanently raise the level of its share through some other mechanism. This will be rewarded with a greater share of shelf space, which could then generate some further share gains. If the effort to raise share is relatively short term then the brand will fairly quickly settle at a newer higher share/front stocks equilibrium. However, if the share building momentum can be maintained, a virtuous circle can be set up where share increases merit front stocks increases, which generate further share increases then further front stocks increases etc.

Modelling this type of process requires a simultaneous equation model with two equations, one for share of volume and one for share of front stocks (shelf space). These equations then capture the feedback mechanism whereby a rise in advertising pushes up share then front stocks, then share again (though less than initially) then front stocks again, then share, with the increments in share and front stocks reducing at each iteration until the overall levels are in equilibrium once again.

This type of structure is not simply imposed on the data, the data has to support it and the Walkers' grocery data had all the classic signs.

Firstly, the volume share and share of front stocks series are highly correlated (as in Figure 9). The correlation between the two is 97%, making it impossible to meaningfully build an ordinary least-squares model of share which could include any factors other than front stocks.

It is clear from studying the various data series at a graphical level that movements in front stocks are not independent of movements in those other series (like price relative to competitors), which theoretically should be included in a volume share model. The explanatory variables in a single equation model must be independent of one another, otherwise biased estimates of their individual contributions will result.

The modelling results show that the data does indeed support the hypothesis that the brand works as described above and that there is feedback between volume share and front stock share.

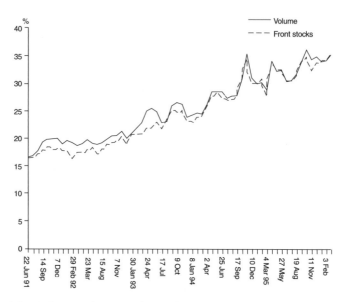

Figure 9: *Walkers' share in Grocery volume versus front stocks*
Source: IRI Infoscan

Grocery Simulation Results

It is interesting to see some of the results of the model simulations in order to appreciate the overall effect of the advertising. Figures 10 and 11 show the effects in Grocery of advertising on both volume share and share of front stocks.

Other results are:

— Pre-BMP brand advertising. There is no evidence from the econometric models that this was having a statistically significant effect on share.

— The step-change resulting from 'Nun' and 'Dial-A-Prize'. This resulted from a particularly strong increase in front stocks.

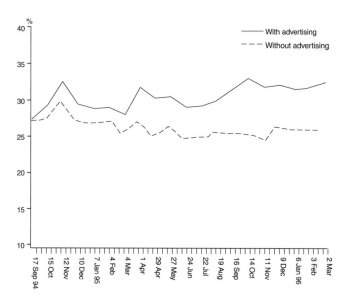

Figure 10: *Walkers volume share of crisps in Grocery, with and without advertising*

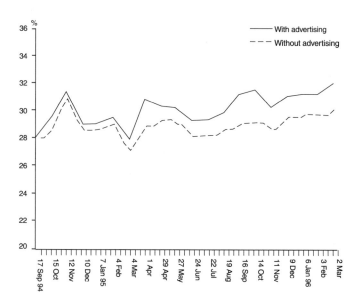

Figure 11: *Walkers volume share front stocks in Grocery, the effect of advertising*

Impulse – Theoretical Background

The environment in Impulse is clearly very different from that in Grocery. For a start, the Impulse sector has a tendency to stock only one brand of crisps with a smaller range of pack sizes. Changes in share of front stocks in Impulse are thus actually much more likely to be the result of distribution growth rather than increased visibility within any one store. (Things like gondola ends during promotional periods do not really exist in Impulse.) If wishing to investigate the influence of advertising on the trade it is thus much more appropriate in Impulse to look at the relationship between advertising and distribution rather than advertising and front stocks. In Impulse, it is much more plausible too, that the promise of advertising will have a direct influence on the number of stockists, particularly once the campaign has already attained a considerable degree of fame. It was also found that the implied average number of pack sizes available (aggregate pack distribution divided by brand distribution) varied over time. For that reason the most useful measure of distribution in Impulse appears to be aggregate pack distribution.

One would not really expect to see the feedback in Impulse that is evident in Grocery, mainly because a brand tends to be listed on its own. So, even if its sales improve in a particular outlet, it has no other brand to squeeze in order to set the virtuous circle in motion.

Impulse Simulation Results

Figures 12 and 13 show the total effects of advertising on sales and distribution in Impulse. The sales simulation includes the distribution effect.

Other results specifically mentioned are the promise of advertising. In Impulse, distribution rose considerably and permanently just prior to the third Lineker film ('Garymania') going on air in May 1995. There was also a further effect during airtime. The t-statistic on advertising prior to airtime was 2.1 and 4.8 during airtime.

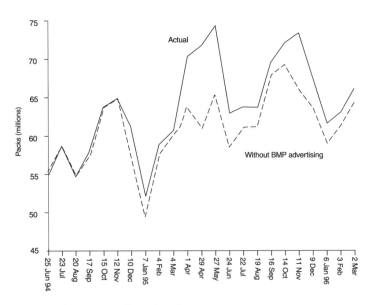

Figure 12: *Effect of BMP advertising on Walkers sales volume*

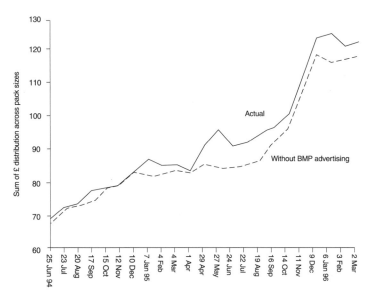

Figure 13: *Effect of BMP advertising on aggregate pack distribution*

Other Considerations

There are a number of features of the models which merit further explanation, most important of which is the treatment of promotions.

Promotions

In a market like this where the promotions and the advertising are so inextricably linked, it is a non-trivial task to separate the effect that the promotions themselves generate from that of the advertising. However, we are helped a great deal by the fact that different promotions have had different weights of advertising and that all the promotions in our sample have been relatively similar in terms of mechanic.

The model incorporates promotional uplifts in terms of two variables:

1. a promotional on-off switch which runs for the length of the production run (six weeks) but is lagged in the models to allow for the product to get from production line to shelf (the models are multiplicative in structure so they allow a larger promotional volume to occur as a result of promotion (rather than advertising) as the brand grows);

2. an advertising effect proportional to the weight of TVRs behind the promotion.

In addition, two promotions have a third component (an additional advertising variable specific to that promotion), as they experienced particularly strong responses proportional to the pattern of advertising activity behind them. One of these, 'Duck' ('Moneybags II') was a repeat of one of the earlier promotions, the other was 'Dial-A-Prize'.

There is no pre-determined production run for a promotion. The factory produces promotional packs for a period of six weeks and will produce more if a promotion seems to be doing particularly well. The number of promotional packs produced has increased in line with the size of the brand as a whole so that it is always roughly the same as a proportion of base sales levels but, as mentioned above, the multiplicative nature of the models takes this into account.

For example, the grocery model estimates that the promotions themselves add approximately 12% to volume (expressed as a percentage of four-weekly sales). Their initial contribution to share was 2.8 share points. This has risen as the brand has grown to 4.1 (on a four-weekly basis).

'Nun'

One of the promotions, that advertised by the 'Nun' film, does require special consideration and more complex analysis. The main reason for this is that the advertising continued to run for much longer than normal for a promotion in order to capitalise on the media interest in the brand. Promotional advertising normally runs for four to six weeks. 'Nun' was on air for considerably longer than this.

Although there was a limited number of promotional packs still lurking in the trade, the latter part of the 'Nun' activity was, therefore, really theme advertising and was not doing a genuine promotional job. The econometrics shows us that, after discounting the effects of the promotion itself, promotional advertising during Lineker generated approximately four times the volume per 100 TVRs that theme generates. In order to properly evaluate the effects of 'Nun', therefore, we must take this into account.

In order to realistically estimate what the 'Nun' promotional activity has contributed, we need to assume that the 520 TVRs originally allocated to the promotion were promotional and the rest were theme. The results presented earlier have taken this into account.

New Regions, Variants and Pack Sizes

Dummy variables were constructed for all these events, included in the analysis and tested for statistical significance.

Crisps Versus Salty Snacks

All the share data is expressed as share of salty snacks, as that is the market in which Walkers' considers it competes and thus the one whose trends are of most interest to it. Crisps are however the largest sector within this market and most of the competitive interaction is with them.

The econometric models all analyse Walkers' sales in the context of the crisp rather than the total salty snacks market. Obviously, from time to time, there are some effects on crisps from other products (eg Hula Hoops). However, evidence from the Grocery share model indicates that Walkers is only affected by these in line with its share of the market and therefore that it is unnecessary to include them in a share model. Although the Impulse model is of volume rather than share, there is no evidence that any systematic component is missing from the model and thus the concentration on crisps does seem to be valid.

10

AA

No more Mr Nice Guy

Dear Roger

Please find attached the script for the next Overdrive programme.
The main point that we producers want you to get across is as follows.
Advertising can be more than clever slogans, charming entertainment or persuasive sales messages. On occasions it can change the whole way an organisation thinks, behaves and is perceived.
In this case the AA's new advertising contained an idea so powerful that it had an impact throughout their business by:

— boosting internal morale;

— fundamentally changing the perception of what the AA is;

— winning the respect of a new peer group;

— scaring the competition;

— reassuring existing members;

— attracting new personal members;

— helping win big new commercial contracts;

— preventing price cuts.

Hope you like the script.
Cameron

PS. We've scripted your witty off-the-cuff comments as per usual.

OVERDRIVE – PROGRAMME NO. 135
WORKING TITLE: THE AA – NO MORE MR NICE GUY

(Open on Roger Maclean walking through motorway service station car park)

Roger: Tonight, *Overdrive* takes a look at what happens when that shiny second-hand Mondeo you bought from a bloke in Stretford says 'sorry mate, you've been done' and conks out at the side of the M6.

Yes, we're looking at the world of breakdown assistance.

And while we normally enjoy asking a Porsche a few difficult questions on a fast fourth-gear corner, tonight we'll be grilling the Porsche's bespectacled, besuited drivers. Yes, tonight we'll be asking the ad men why Britain's largest club spent millions of pounds on a new advertising campaign claiming to be Britain's '4th Emergency Service'.

(Camera pulls back to reveal 4th ES poster)

Tonight *Overdrive* asks the AA – why 'No More Mr Nice Guy'?

(Roll title credits and music)

(Roger, talking while driving)

Roger: Almost a third of all motorists are, like me, a member of the Automobile Association. Over 8 million people in one way or another pay their membership fees to one of Britain's largest non-profit making organisations. We think the man on the hard shoulder deserves some answers.

The first question is, why did anything need to change? Was there a problem in the first place? What was wrong with being a 'very nice man'?

Related to this is, *has* anything changed at the AA? Are they any more successful than they were in the past?

And if their fortunes changed, when did they change, *was it* when the new advertising message was introduced?

(Pulls up outside the AA HQ)

From reading their press releases, these are the soft questions. But Maclean has got some tough ones too. Firstly, even if sales perked up when the new advertising was introduced, is there any evidence that the advertising caused this improvement? In particular if a number of *other* things changed at the AA at around the same time – for example, the new livery – were those the real heroes?

You see I reckon that this '4th Emergency Service' thing is just a snappy slogan. I don't think it means anything more than a play on words.

And finally, the really tough question. I'm a member of this club and apparently they've spent something like £16 million pounds over the last three years on advertising. And that buys a lot of Tiger Tokens. Was it commercially justified? Let's ask.

Caption: The Problem

(Interview with Bob Sinclair, Sales and Marketing Director, AA Membership)

Roger: Bob – so tell me, you were responsible for changing the advertising – why did you feel you needed to change?

Bob: Quite simply, we knew that the AA provided the best breakdown service but the market wasn't agreeing with us!

Our advertising was not getting the message across and so we were finding it harder to recruit new members and harder to retain existing members.

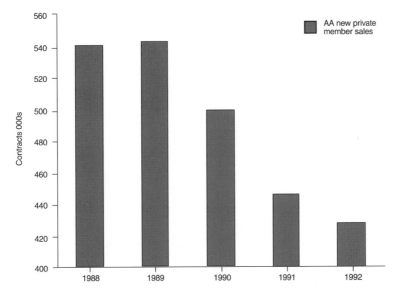

Figure 1: *AA new private member sales in decline*
Source: AA

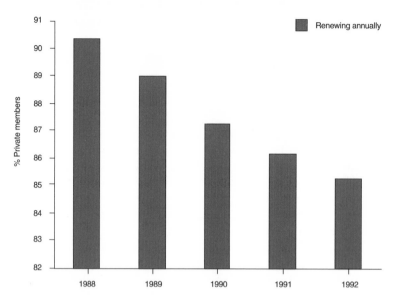

Figure 2: *Retention of existing private members also declining*
Source: AA

This was not only true with individual motorists but also in the fleet and manufacturer markets – this is where large companies or car manufacturers provide breakdown cover with all their cars – where deals were being done almost entirely on price. Unfortunately, I can't reveal the actual sales here but it is a substantial market for us and we weren't doing as well as we wanted to.

The net result was that we were losing members and their fees. And when you're a non-profit making organisation with fixed costs that is an uncomfortable feeling! If we couldn't reverse this decline we would have had to cut costs and/or the service and change the nature of the AA.

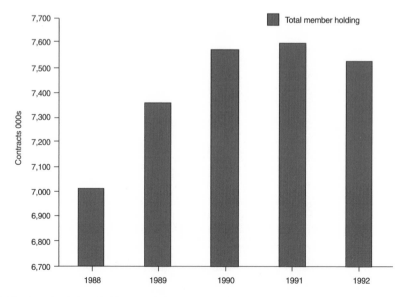

Figure 3: *Total member holding had begun to decline*
Source: AA

Roger: So what was causing this?

Bob: A number of things. Firstly, the recession of the early '90s was having an effect. Secondly, there seemed to be a long-term decline in the perceived value of our offering, as shown by the steady decline in our retention rate.

And in addition to that there was the competition. The RAC had aggressively promoted themselves as 'The New Knights of the Road' and people were increasingly seeing them as a more modern, dynamic and effective organisation. Now *we* knew that we were as good as if not better than them but they had the better image.

Perhaps, most of all, a new set of competitors – best represented by National Breakdown – had increasingly persuaded people that they provided just as good a service but much more cheaply.

Roger: How so?

Bob: Well, rather than have a fleet of mechanics directly employed by the people you call (like the AA and RAC do), they pass on calls to local garages which attend the breakdown. And because they don't have to carry the cost of the people on permanent standby they can charge people less.

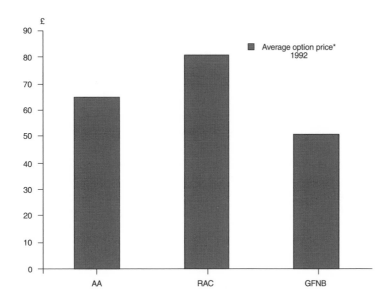

Figure 4: *Green Flag undercut both AA and RAC*
* Average option price is the average price of the membership options for the AA's Option 100, 200, 300 and 400 and the RAC's and Green Flag's equivalent options.
Source: AA

Roger: Sounds like a better deal to me.

Bob: Well, it does at a superficial level, but like all cut-price deals – especially when it comes to forms of insurance – there are hidden dangers.

Often people don't realise that they might have just bought cover that will tow them to the nearest garage where they will have to pay for repairs.

Then there is the issue of the garage's motivation – they can't make much from the call out fee, so perhaps they have to make money from charging for repairs.

Now most garages are straight but with the AA you can *guarantee* that all our patrols want to do is get you sorted out. They're not on commission.

And finally, there is the issue of standards. All our people are trained and monitored in a highly professional way – for example, our philosophy is 'driver first, car second' ie make sure the people are alright before you have a look at their motor. There is just no way that you can guarantee the same standards among a loose affiliation of garage mechanics spread across the country.

So who would you prefer to come out on a cold winter's night when you've got granny and the kids in the back?

Roger: So, despite granny and the kids, membership was declining?

Bob: Yes, it was very frustrating. In marketing terms we felt we had a superior service that deserved its price premium but the market was becoming commoditised. And because we believed in the value of what we did for our members we didn't want to reduce the 'spec' of our service to match the price of our competitors.

Roger: So what did you do?

Bob: The commercial objectives were very simple – to maintain (and ideally grow) membership and hence revenue without compromising margins. As I have implied before it is not market share *per se* that matters to us but the absolute numbers of fee-paying members we must attract. Thus if we could grow membership and revenue we could carry on providing our members with a high level of service.

So we set out to get people to look at what we did in a new light: to get them to see that we were in a different class to the competition.

We had been running a very successful advertising campaign that showed how friendly and helpful our patrols were – they were 'very nice men' and our customers were told that they 'knew a man who can'.

We wanted to keep the friendliness but raise the professionalism. Thus we started presenting ourselves not as just 'nice men' but as a highly professional emergency organisation. But, more importantly, we used our size to put ourselves into a premier league of emergency organisations, hopefully leaving all the other breakdown organisations languishing, metaphorically, in the Endsleigh First Division.

At the core of the idea was bringing out people's latent beliefs about the AA and putting them across in a dramatic but believable fashion.

(Run 'Big Four' commercial)

Caption: The Change

(Roger walking down a corridor)

Roger: And blow me down with an ad man's hot air but it does seem that you lot noticed this catchy little slogan.

'4TH EMERGENCY SERVICE'

The AA is the biggest breakdown patrol force in Britain.

So why aren't we No.1?

The AA is twice as big as our nearest competitor.

But we're not No. 2.

We deal with 13,000 calls for help a day.

But we're not even No. 3.

In fact the AA gets someone out of trouble every eight seconds.

We're proud to be No. 4.

To our members we're the 4th Emergency Service.

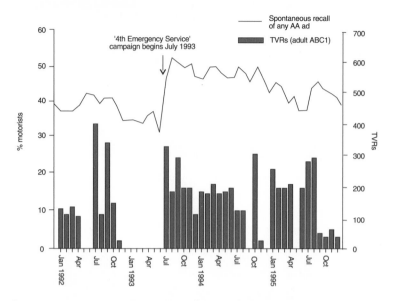

Figure 5: *'4th Emergency Service' campaign creates a step change in advertising awareness*
Source: Omnicar Tracking Survey

Not only that, most of you lot seem to agree with this '4th Emergency Service' claim – especially if you're an AA member.

Now if I'd answered that questionnaire I would have said 'what about the coastguard, matey' which you lot missed.

But the point is, does this mean anything, is this just a clever advertising slogan? I turned to Bob again.

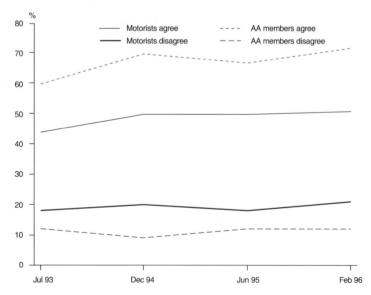

Figure 6: *Message is credible, especially to AA members and credibility increases over time*
Base: AA members/All motorists
Source: Omnicar Tracking Survey

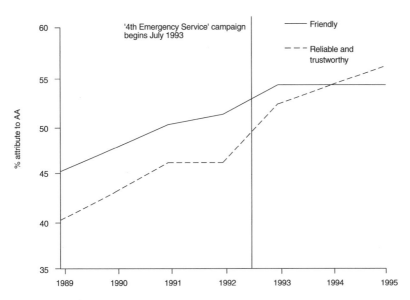

Figure 7: *AA message begins to reflect advertising message*
Base: All motorists
Source: Omnicar Tracking Survey

(Bob and Roger)

Roger: Nice slogan, where's the beef?

Bob: Let's look at people's perception of the AA. Over the years we have been measuring a number of attributes that people seem to want a breakdown service to have. On the two key measures of 'friendliness of service' and 'trustworthiness/ reliability of service' we have seen the latter surge and overtake the former, in synchrony with the new message.

Roger: But why do you think this is due to being called the 4th Emergency Service? Maybe you *are* providing a better service?

Bob: Well, we have also seen people's perception of our 'fix rate' rise by 12% while our internal data shows that, in reality, this has remained constant.

Additionally, we have made no changes in the way we ask the patrols to treat people. People may believe that they are being, or will be, treated better but it really is all in the eyes of the beholder.

Roger: Aha! So they are deceiving themselves?

Bob: Well not really. Our qualitative research seems to show that they have been looking at the same thing from two perspectives: AA patrol people as 'very nice men' or as 'members of one of the four emergency services'; and the latter is a more desirable image.

Roger: And you believe that this comes from the advertising?

Bob: Well of course nowadays they see this message all over the place. But initially it was *only* the advertising that was offering this new perspective. Perhaps if you sat in on some of our qualitative research groups you would see what I mean.

(Cut to film of motorists from research groups)

Man: 'It is a bloody emergency when you break down and you don't want some spotty kid with a spanner trying to sort it out. You do want an emergency service – like that ad says.'

Man: 'The difference is that they don't save lives. But they do come out when ever you call them – just the same.'

Woman: 'I remember when they used to be very nice men – quite sweet really. Now what with the uniforms and everything they seem to have more authority. They are a bit more like the police.'

Man: 'And I bet they get let off their speeding fines too!'

HHCL Creative Development Research

Roger: OK, so the warm-hearted British public sees you for the fine body of men and women that you are. But what about the hard-headed business world? What has happened in the commercial sector?

Bob: Well, direct research is harder to come by in this area but at an anecdotal level it does seem that some contracts were won on more than price and that there was a perceived benefit to giving the AA the contract. Again, we did not change the way we sold ourselves to the commercial sector beyond the image we presented.

'We use the position of the 4th Emergency Service prominently in our credentials presentations to both existing and new business services clients. It supports our contention that the AA is the only organisation that can claim emergency service status and is therefore the greatest reassurance that manufacturers can give their customers, whether they actually use the service or not. Manufacturers who are eager to establish their brand or reposition it use the association with our brand heavily.'

Graham Gill, Director Business Services, AA

Roger: Staying at the anecdotal level, is there any other evidence that the advertising had a beneficial effect?

Bob: Well, if I may answer that in a different way, there is plenty of other evidence that the *idea* of 'to our members we are the 4th Emergency Service' has a beneficial effect. For example, we have been gradually changing the livery of our vehicles. While in itself it is a more modern, professional and purposeful design, it is the idea of the 4th Emergency Service that gives that design its most powerful meaning.

More directly we have used the line, the design and, most importantly, the philosophy of the 4th Emergency Service on our membership materials, on other marketing communications and in our shops. Again, constantly presenting ourselves as a modern, trustworthy, professional emergency service enhances all these interactions the motorist has with the AA.

And at a simple but very effective level we now answer the phone 'AA Emergency Service' and that really changes the way the phone operators think about their jobs. While we have no specific quantitative staff opinion surveys on this issue, we are pretty sure that our patrol's morale has improved:

'Patrols see themselves as basically doing the same job that they've always done – they don't feel they've changed their service to members at all.

OLD AND NEW VANS

But it's in the public's perception and recognition of what they do that the patrols have noticed a big change. They've seen the public's expectations raised by the change from being 'very nice men' to being patrols from the '4th Emergency Service'. The public now see them as more modern and professional, respecting them more as figures with a certain amount of authority.

Previously the public would frequently refer to them as 'very nice men' – something which they felt was condescending and a little mocking.'

Tim Shallcross, Manager Front-line Training

Bob: But to prove just how fundamentally this idea has changed how people perceive and treat the AA, I'll give you two anecdotes.

Firstly, it would seem that there has been an effect on the AA's relations with the police, fire and ambulance. At a golf tournament between the emergency services the AA was invited to make up a four ball!

Roger: Were they polite enough to come 4th?

Bob: Quite. But my favourite anecdote though is the story a primary school teacher told us. She was teaching her class about the emergency services and talking about fireman, policemen and ambulances and some little kid said, 'miss, you've forgotten one – what about AA breakdown men?' Sounds silly, but this is just one indication of how far-reaching the idea has been.

(Presenter standing between an old and a new AA van)

Roger: Now, as those of us who have tried explaining to the policeman that it was our new ultra-loud Kenwood CD player that made us drive at 90mph know, you can never prove causation.

But it does seem that the advertising made people look at the AA in a new light, and in a light that makes it look like the best service available. So did it actually work – did sales go up?

Caption: The Sales Results

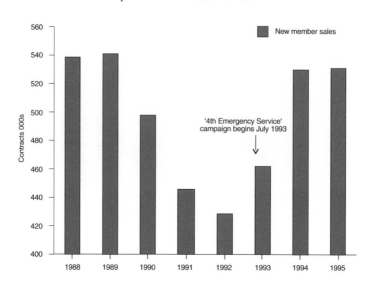

Figure 8: *AA new member sales recover*
Source: AA

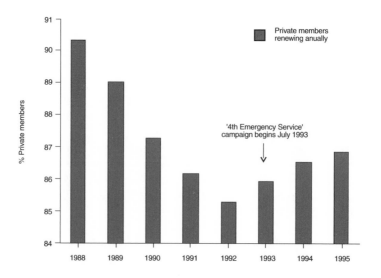

Figure 9: *Annual retention also improves*
Source: AA

Business sales are, and I quote, 'at a healthy level' – it's no secret that since 1992 the agency has won the Vauxhall, Daewoo and Skoda accounts. So add it all up and what do you get?

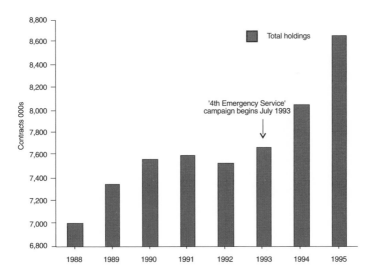

Figure 10: *Total holdings reach highest ever level*
Source: AA

They do seem to have stopped the decline in membership and indeed started growing again. And it all happens in synchrony with the new advertising message.

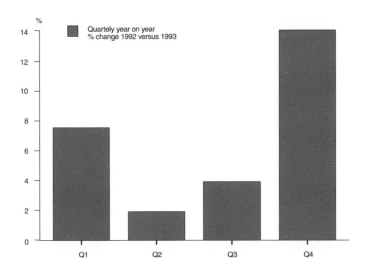

Figure 11: *New private member sales pick up strongly in second half of 1993*
Source: AA

To make the point even more strongly, just looking at 1993, they have a better second half than first.

Convincing stuff you might think. And what's more, here come their smug answers to the tough questions prepared by our Department of Cynicism. Some of you may want to nip out and make a cup of tea at this point as this is going to get a bit technical...

Did the AA outspend the competition?
Competitive adspends increased in line with the AA's.

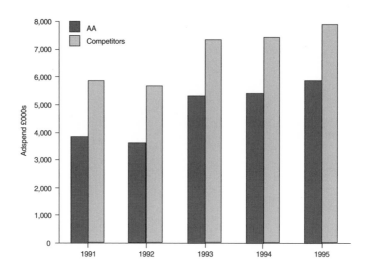

Figure 12: *AA advertising increases in line with competitive spend*
Source: Register/MEAL

Were there changes in the relative prices of the different organisations?
Relative to National Breakdown/Green Flag the price differential was unchanged.

Although we have no data for the average member transaction price of the RAC we can track the average price of a basket of their products that match the AA's portfolio. This shows that, in 1993, the AA's relative price was actually slightly worse than prior to the new advertising but sales improved. In 1994, the AA does become significantly cheaper and has an excellent sales performance. However when, in 1995, the more normal price differentials are restored, sales and retention continue to rise (Figure 13).

Once the advertising has 'done its job' and told people that the AA is the 4th Emergency Service isn't all the money spent after that wasted?
The role of the ongoing advertising is to introduce different expressions of the same core idea to further improve the AA's reputation. After all, by the very fact that other people are choosing other breakdown organisations there is still a lot of persuading to be done.

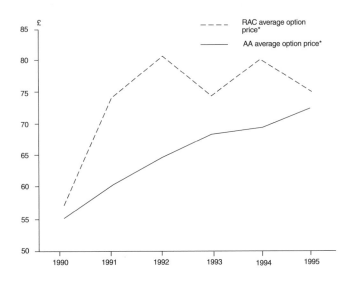

Figure 13: *Price differential narrows between AA and RAC*
* Average option price is the average price of the membership options for the AA's Option 100, 200, 300 and 400 and
the RAC's equivalent options
Source: Register/MEAL

To pick just one example, we have used the 4th Emergency Service vehicle (if you'll excuse the pun) to talk about how 'you're the member not the car', a feature unique to the AA at the time. This 'people first' attitude is exactly the sort of thing you would expect and want an emergency service to have.

And, looking at the tracking study, the advertising has brought to people's attention a benefit they were not aware of.

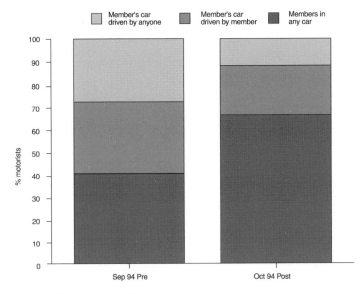

Figure 14: *Personal membership now more widely understood*
Base: All motorists
Source: Omnicar Tracking Survey

So the continuing role and value of advertising is to introduce new dimensions of the 4th Emergency Service idea both to attract as broad a membership as possible and to keep building the AA brand.

Roger: You can all come back now – *I'm* asking this one. Bob – you keep talking as if you've won the war. But haven't you been losing share?

Bob: Well we believe we're winning the battles which will allow us to go on to win the war. I say 'the war goes on' because the market is still being infested by more and more low-cost operators. They are both penetrating the private sector and serving the demands of car manufacturers who want cheap cover to bolt onto their cars. The net result is that the market is expanding but driven by low-cost operators – an economy sector is emerging if you like.

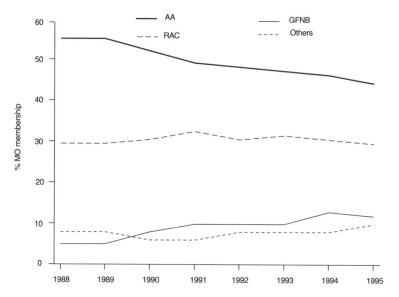

Figure 15: *AA share declines*
Base: All motoring organisation members
Source: AA

Now in share terms, if not in sale terms, the two premium service operators in this market have both been hit by this phenomenon. But, whereas the RAC responded in 1993 by introducing a new low-cost option (ie drastically slashing the price of their lowest-priced product), we responded by using advertising to re-present our whole offering to people. Price cutting versus brand building if you like.

Now we do not know a) what it cost the RAC to follow its strategy and b) whether it feels that the strategy has re-invigorated or weakened its business (have existing members demanded the new low-cost option for example?). Although from the company report we do know that its membership declined by 200,000 in 1995.

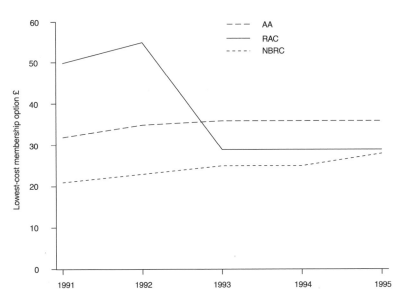

Figure 16: *RAC cut entry price in 1993*
Source: AA

But in the AA we know we have got ourselves back in shape to compete in this new environment. We say this because we have:

1. Got 'new member sales' back to pre-recessionary levels without having to match the cheapies' prices.

2. Stopped, and indeed reversed, our existing members' drift away from us to these new cheaper deals.

3. Started winning big commercial deals again by successfully selling a premium product in a highly price-sensitive market.

4. Restored pride to a whole company who instead of seeing themselves as a beleaguered market leader see themselves as leading the industry.

5. Quite simply, risen above the economy sector to have more members than ever before while maintaining margin.

Share is all very well, but you can buy share, and we believe that is what our competitors have done. At the end of the day it's how much money you're making that counts.

Caption: Does It All Add Up?

Roger: Well it's no use sulking in the pits, maybe it has had an effect. But, as I said at the start of the programme, the advertising has cost more than £16 million or around £5 million a year. Was it worth it?

Us boys that sat at the back of the maths class reading *Motor Sport* are not looking forward to the next bit. It's time to get out the back of the old Marlboro packet. Bob – help!

Bob: The first point is, in a non-profit making organisation run for the mutual benefit of its members, it's not as simple as calculating the additional profits for which the advertising expenditure was accountable.

Second, we always talk about the effect of the *idea* of the 4th Emergency Service rather than the 'advertising effect'.

However – to give some idea of the commercial effect of this idea we need to know what a new member is worth to the AA. I've told you that the average fee is around £75 but unfortunately I can't tell you what is left after deducting costs of servicing a new member. Sorry, can't reveal my gross margin.

Roger: Stalemate!

Bob: Not quite. You see I can *disguise* my margin by telling you what the 'lifetime' value of a member is. When a set of new members join we can fairly accurately predict how many will renew in year two, how many in year three and so on. With a bit of maths we can get to a figure of £55, which is the average five-year cumulative contribution for a new member after deducting servicing costs and other direct costs.

Roger: So £55 is a sort of 'lifetime value'.

Bob: Well, hopefully they stay longer than five years, but yes.

So let's get some numbers out. Using 1992 as a base line for when the 4th Emergency Service idea came in to play we find the following:

TABLE 1: ADDITIONAL MEMBERS SINCE 1992

	1993 (000s)	1994 (000s)	1995 (000s)	Total 1993–95 (000s)
New member sales versus 1992	34	102	103	239
Extra retained members versus 1992	27	51	64	142

And then multiplying by £55:

TABLE 2: VALUE OF NEW AND RETAINED MEMBERS.

	1993 (£million	1994 (£million)	1995 (£million)	Total 1993–95 £million
Value of new member sales	1.9	5.6	5.7	13.1
Value of extra retained members	1.5	2.8	3.5	7.8
Total value	3.4	8.4	9.2	20.9

Roger: Phew – big numbers Bob.

Bob: Yes and remember those don't include any extra revenue from the commercial sector. Let's just do one other calculation.

You see, maybe taking 1992 as a base year is optimistic. Maybe, with the RAC's low-priced product and all the other cheapies out there, our sales would have carried on down. Similarly, given that retention rates had been declining for several years in a very predictable way, is there any evidence that it would have bottomed out in 1992?

What this means is that you can do a 'best case' calculation by projecting the sales line down:

TABLE 3: ADDITIONAL MEMBERS SINCE 1992 – BEST CASE

	1993 (000s)	1994 (000s)	1995 (000s)	Total 1993–95 (000s)
New member sales	34	102	103	239
Projected down trend in sales	38	76	114	228
Hence incremental new member sales	72	178	217	467
Extra retained members	27	51	64	142
Projected down trend in member retention	49	98	147	294
Hence incremental retained members	76	149	211	436

Hence 'best case' value is:

TABLE 4: VALUE OF NEW AND RETAINED MEMBERS – BEST CASE

	1993 (£ million)	1994 (£ million)	1995 (£ million)	Total 1993–95 (£ million)
Value of new member sales	4.0	9.8	11.9	25.7
Value of extra retained members	4.2	8.2	11.6	*24.0
Total value	8.2	18.0	23.5	49.7

Bob: So, again excluding commercial sales, the *maximum* possible effect could be around £50 million. How much of this comes from the 4th Emergency Service idea is impossible to say.

But, as you can see, quite considerable amounts of extra cash have been generated in various parts of the business and just *one* of those could repay an advertising investment of around £5 million a year.

So, as I've asterisked above – reversing the decline in retention; or restoring new member sales to pre-recessionary levels; or even helping to secure a big commercial contract – any *one* of these repays the investment.

The other way of looking at it is, what else could we have spent the advertising money on? As you may recall, the RAC chose to cut its prices in response to competitive pressures.

Now our advertising expenditure works out at approximately £1 spent per year per member. So instead we could have dropped our prices by £1 across the board. Given how much the RAC seemed to need to drop the price of their entry-level product and given the £12 discount offered by the cheapies, it seems unlikely that £1 would have had much impact.

Or, put the other way round, if the advertising has justified only £1 of an average fee of £75 then it has paid for itself.

And given that we are still to reap the full long-term rewards of our new positioning we're pretty confident that we spent wisely!

(Roger, who is back on the road)

Roger: OK, I'm sold. Maybe I'm even tempted to believe that the new advertising caused so much competitive alarm that not only did the RAC very quickly change their advertising agency, but the whole of the marketing department left as well. And following this way of thinking, are we to assume that the National Breakdown Recovery Club was so put out that it changed its name to Green Flag so as to start all over again? Who knows?

On a less flippant note, the idea of the 4th Emergency Service has re-invigorated an organisation and, in a sense, rewritten its mission statement. Often advertising reflects the change in an organisation; here, in a sense, it led it.

'The 4th Emergency Service positioning has re-invigorated the AA and given us a new sense of purpose. I have no doubt that it has played a major part in the current success of our business.'

Frank Thackwray, MD, AA Membership

(Maclean carries on driving through heavy rain talking to camera)

Roger: Well, normally with these *Overdrive* investigations, someone ends up with a red face. Maybe this time it's me and here's why.

I think I've found that change was desperately needed at the AA and that the advertising was the catalyst for change.

I've found that the people who work at the AA, its members and its peers all now see it in a new and better light even though nothing has fundamentally changed about what it does.

And it was the idea of the 4th Emergency Service projected by the advertising that gave people this new perspective to see the AA in all its glory.

And, finally, we've seen that, with the increases in sales and retention, the advertising was a highly cost-effective way of stimulating this change, that ultimately went on to affect the whole organisation.

It brings a tear to my eye!

So maybe if Jeffrey Archer were here he would forgive me for saying that this advertising campaign has surely made the AA 'fourth amongst equals'.

Now where did I put my membership renewal form?

(Roll end credits and music)

11

How BT Made Advertising Work Smarter, Not Just Harder

INTRODUCTION

Question: How do you convince businessmen that a company deemed to have little interest in them, is now the expert in a market it has no obvious credentials in, while simultaneously bolstering share in the company's increasingly competitive core market?

Answer: You get your advertising to work smarter.

This paper demonstrates how Butterfield Day Devito Hockney, BT's Business Communications advertising agency for the past four years, helped BT establish itself among businesses, in markets more usually associated with information technology companies, while concurrently defending and growing its presence in the business telecommunications market. This lead to a +66% return on advertising investment for BT.

THE BT BUSINESS MARKETPLACE – A THREAT TO BT'S CORE BUSINESS

Businesses are faced with an increasing choice in the telecommunications market. Today, over 114 companies have licences to provide a service.

These companies target businesses, because they use the telephone more frequently than domestic consumers, and at the most expensive times of the day.

With BT seemingly focusing on the domestic consumer (it spent £23 million on TV in 1995 alone on Bob Hoskins' domestic consumer advertising), there is a great temptation for businesses to switch to another supplier who promises to give a more business-orientated service and better prices.

Add the fact that, in the interests of fair competition, BT is restricted in the types of business it can operate in, and in the prices it can charge, and it is not surprising that BT's market share is under severe threat.

BT's share is measured by revenue received from businesses using the Public Switched Telecommunication Network (PSTN), which is the telephone network we all use.

For reasons of confidentiality, we cannot quantify BT's current market share. But to give an indication of its size, its 1995 reports and accounts estimated that BT had an 83% share of the 'business market for telephone calls and provision of exchange lines'. This had been steadily declining over a number of years.

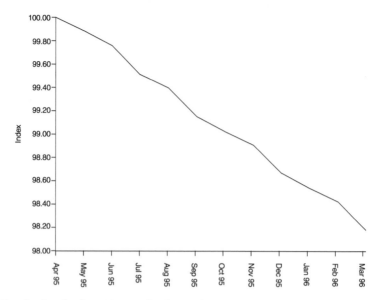

Figure 1: *BT predicted market share 1995/6 – indexed on April 1995*
Source: BT (projections are based on three-month rolling data; data excludes line rental)

At the beginning of its 1995/96 financial year, BT's share of calls made by businesses over the PSTN was predicted to continue its long-term decline.

While the indices may suggest that share was only expected to fall gradually, this nevertheless equates to a significant amount of money. A 1% decline in share equates to a loss in revenue of approximately £36 million over one year.

THE BT BUSINESS MARKETPLACE – A NEED TO EXPAND INTO NEW MARKETS

Apart from new telecommunications competitors, BT's position is threatened by companies better associated with computing, who are starting to offer *new* types of communication for businesses – communication that involves computers sending and receiving information down the phone line.

Over the next five years, it is 'calls made by computers' that will drive increased usage of the PSTN and thus revenue. Hence, BT must have a presence in this marketplace and, indeed, BT already has the necessary products and services to compete.

Unfortunately, there is a popular misconception that BT runs the telephone network, and little else. And, consequently, if a business is venturing into new technology, such as linking computers, then it is likely to go to a computer specialist for advice on how to do so.

THE CHALLENGE FOR BT

Thus, by the end of 1994, it was clear that, if BT was to defend its market share, it needed to fight a battle on two fronts to:

— defend its position as the leader in business telecommunications;

— establish a significant presence as an expert in PC-based communications.

Defending BT's Position in the Telecommunications Market

With telecommunications, customers make purchase decisions based on who can offer the best *Value for Money*, where VfM = price + quality of service.

Indeed, statistical analysis conducted by BT in 1992 demonstrated a direct correlation between BT's VfM perceptions and market share. This relationship is summarised in Figure 2, and shows an R^2 of 0.72.

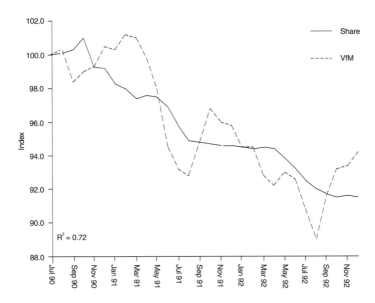

Figure 2: *BT PSTN share index versus Value for Money rating*
Source: BT/NOP

But how can VfM perceptions be influenced ?

BT looked at the effect of both price advertising and service-based advertising against VfM perceptions over a two-year period (August 1992–94). The work showed that service-based messages have the greatest potential to have an impact on VfM perceptions in both the short and the long term.

Thus it was decided to look to quality of service for a way to influence perceptions of VfM and thus defend brand share. But how?

BT measures the relationship it has with businesses via ten brand value statements. These statements are grouped into three categories:

BT's Brand Value Statements

Quality of Involvement

Friendly: BT employees are friendly and approachable
Interested: BT is clearly interested in doing business with you
Empathetic: BT understands communications needs from the customer's point
                of view

Quality of Response

Accessible: It is easy to find someone at BT who will ensure your needs are met
Inspirational: BT regularly comes up with good ideas
Intelligent: BT provides intelligent solutions to customers' problems
                BT has a flexible approach to meeting customers' needs
Empowering: BT helps customers get the most out of communications

Core Beliefs

Genuine: BT is a company you feel you can trust
                BT charges fairly

Source : BT

These values were developed through quantitative and qualitative studies, and measured monthly via quantitative tracking.

Table 1 below shows how BT performed on the ten values.

TABLE 1 : AVERAGE RATINGS SEPT 1994 TO AUG 1995
(MEAN SCORES OF RATINGS ON A TEN-POINT SCALE)

Quality of Involvement	Friendly	7.34
	Empathetic	6.92
	Interested	6.67
Quality of Response	Empowering	6.58
	Intelligent (Flexible)	6.47
	Intelligent (Solutions)	6.46
	Accessible	6.45
	Inspirational	6.34
Core Beliefs	Genuine (Trust)	6.99
	Genuine (Charges Fairly)	5.41

The tracking study showed that, in 1994/5, BT's main competitive assets were the basic values of friendliness, empathy and trust.

However, in order to build upon perceptions of VfM, BT needed to develop and strengthen differentiation on all dimensions of its 'Quality of Response' to businesses.

This is because, not only are these among BT's weakest rated values, but also 'Quality of Response' is the most *tangible* measure of the service that BT gives to its customers, because it relates directly to interaction between the customer and BT.

Figure 3 illustrates that, when combined, these measures act as excellent predictors of VfM ratings for BT.

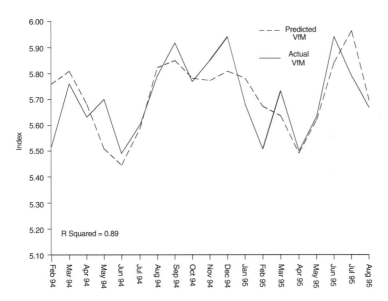

Figure 3: *VfM actual ratings versus those predicted by 'Quality of Response' brand value scores*
Source: NOP/BDDH

Thus, because of the strong correlation, in order to defend market share, BT needed to improve its VfM perceptions. And to do that, BT first needed to improve its 'Quality of Response' brand values.

Establishing a Presence in PC-Based Communications

While businesses were aware of, and anxious to benefit from, new communications technologies (they recognised that better communications equal better business efficiencies), they were not taking any action to find out more.

As telecommunications and computer companies begin to encroach on each others' areas, it is difficult for the average businessman to know who to go to for what service.

This is particularly confusing for the 1.8 million small to medium-sized businesses in the UK. These are typically businesses with less than 100 employees, who probably do not have specialist IT departments or communications managers.

Qualitative research conducted by BDDH in January 1995 among 'Business Decision Makers' (BDMs), typically chairmen, MDs and FDs of small to medium-sized businesses, showed that confusion over the supply structure was part of a much bigger picture of barriers to market entry.

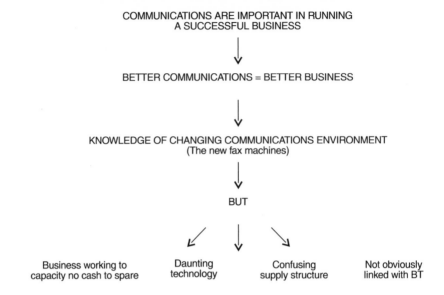

The research found that the technology was felt to have little relevance to this audience. It was seen as daunting and complicated information technology, more for larger companies, who had both the time and the specialist knowledge to implement it.

Consequently, as an overworked, small to medium-sized business, with little time or money to spare, there was little incentive to find out more.

But this same research identified an opportunity for BT.

One of the main tools a business uses to *communicate* is the telephone. Thus BT is, in the eyes of small to medium businesses, an expert in the field of communication.

Furthermore, this research confirmed BT's brand value strengths of 'trustworthy' and 'friendly'.

So, when it was put to the respondents that enabling computers to share information was actually a new and *better* form of communication (and not complicated IT equipment), three previously unthought-of facts became apparent:

— These new ways of communicating may be something they could use in their business.

— BT would be a significant player in this marketplace.

— BT would be a natural place to go to for help and advice on these matters.

THE OBJECTIVES FOR ADVERTISING

The broad marketing objective therefore, was to defend BT's market share. There were two ways in which advertising could contribute to this:

— By improving BT's VfM by differentiating on service;

— By creating a desire for new communications technology among small to medium- sized businesses.

The Role for Advertising

Advertising's role was to inspire businesses to explore all communications opportunities with BT, by positioning BT as the expert source for advice and help, and demonstrating to businesses just what can be achieved.

The key message for customer's to take out was that 'BT is the guide to help you realise the potential of communications to enable you and your business to work more effectively'.

This was quite a step change from the previous business-to-business advertising activity from BT, 'We Want Your Business' ('WWYB'), which ran in autumn 1993. This campaign was designed to convince businesses that BT was *interested* in them. Whereas 'WWYB' spoke of problems and solutions, our new campaign needed to talk about possibilities and opportunities, it needed to inspire as well as inform.

However, we could not lose touch with reality. Businessmen were recession-beaten, they could see light at the end of the tunnel, but were not yet ready to be whisked away by visionary theories of what was possible.

THE CREATIVE STRATEGY

A fine balance was needed between:

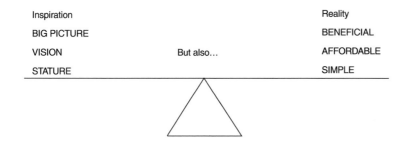

In the aftermath of the recession, people were working harder. Improved communications technology offered a solution, because better communications led to time-saving efficiencies.

In short, communications offered a smarter way of working. And, because saving time enabled businesses to get even more work done, the campaign theme became: 'Work Smarter, Not Just Harder' ('WSNJH').

THE CREATIVE VEHICLE

In order to further enhance 'reality', and make the message as relevant as possible, BDDH created a fictional company for TV and radio, and launched the UK's first business drama.

This creative solution had a number of benefits:

— It allowed us to demonstrate the use for, and benefit of, communications applications, thus create a desire for new and better ways to communicate.

— It allowed us to show all levels of employee, at different stages of understanding, benefiting from the technology, which helped to make it less daunting.

— It allowed us to be inspiring but at the same time realistic, by showing what was possible for a business our audience could relate to.

We used captions on the TV to help the audience understand how the company was benefiting from the use of communications.

In the press, we took the captions from the TV as the point of integration. We also continued (from previous campaigns) to use the *FT* pink as the execution's main feature, a well-known and recognised cipher for 'business'.

THE CAMPAIGN

Overall, nine TV executions were produced. After four ten-second executions teasing on, and introducing, the drama, a 60-second introductory commercial ran for two weeks, setting the scene for what was to follow. (In fact the first time this execution ran, the 60-second execution was preceded by 30-second of TV drama style 'titles' that introduced each of the characters.)

Following the introductory commercial, three executions ran consecutively, each featuring a communications application.

The applications were: PC Videophone, (the product for your PC that enables you to see who you are talking to on the phone), sending and receiving documents by PC (Officelink), and Freefone 0800 numbers. This latter application, a telecommunications product, was included in the campaign to demonstrate how the traditional and new communications technologies work together. Each of these applications was supported in the press.

'WORK SMARTER, NOT JUST HARDER'

Thus, the media schedule was as shown in Table 2.

TABLE 2: MEDIA SCHEDULE 1995 (£)

		28/8	4/9	11/9	18/9	25/9	2/10	9/10	16/10	23/10	Total TV	Total press	Total spend
Teasers	TV	64,000									64,000		
	Press	59,825										59,825	
90" Introduction	TV		167,000								167,000		
60" The First Step	TV		1,183,000								1,183,00		
PC Videophone	TV				1,300,000						1,300,000		
	Press				491,205							491,205	
Freefone 0800	TV						1,111,000				1,111,000		
	Press						488,942					488,942	
Officelink	TV								689,000		689,000		
	Press								468,515			468,515	
Totals		123,825	1,350,000		1,791,205		1,599,942	1,157,515			4,514,000	1,508,487	6,022,487

(Officelink is the package that enables you to send and receive data by PC)

EVALUATING THE CAMPAIGN

In order to defend market share the advertising had two main objectives:

— to improve BT's VfM by differentiating on service;

— to create a desire for new communications technology amongst small to medium-sized businesses.

Creating a Desire for New Communications Technology

Most of the targets for 'Work Smarter Not Just Harder' were set against the performance of the autumn 1993 'We Want Your Business' campaign, with an allowance made for the difference between the two campaigns' media spend.

The autumn 1993 campaign was the previously significant above-the-line campaign by BT targeted at the business audience, a campaign which overachieved on all targets, stabilising market share, improving businessmen's attitudes towards BT and increasing product sales. Within BT, the campaign was generally regarded as the most successful business-to-business work it had produced to date. Indeed, the campaign received a commendation in the 1994 IPA Advertising Effectiveness Awards.

Accounting for media inflation, 'WSNJH' received only 70% of the spend of the autumn 1993 campaign. Initially, targets were downweighted accordingly. However, BT expected and needed this campaign to work harder, and so all targets were then inflated by 20%.

The campaign performance was measured by an Advertising Tracking (ADTRACK) study conducted by NOP, among the target audience.

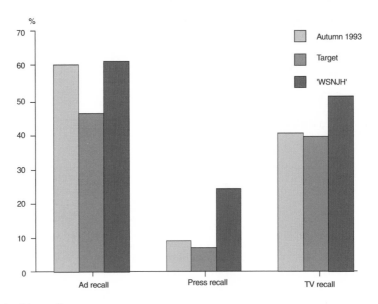

Figure 4: *Advertising recall*
Source: NOP ADTRACK

In trying to create a desire for new communications technology through advertising, the creative work needed to have impact and involvement.

Advertising recall exceeded both the targets set for it and the recall figures of the autumn 1993 campaign, despite the lower media spend.

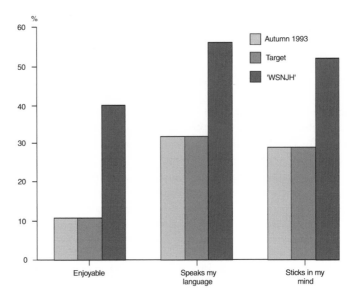

Figure 5: *Campaign reactions*
Source: NOP ADTRACK

More importantly, the advertising was positively received. Respondents found the advertising far more involving than the autumn 1993 campaign.

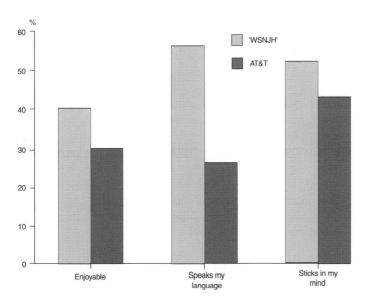

Figure 6: *Campaign reactions – BT versus AT&T*
Source: NOP ADTRACK

Even more significant, AT&T ran a campaign over the same period, focusing on similar issues to BT's campaign. BT's business drama on TV managed to capture the imaginations of the business audience better, as Figure 6 illustrates.

Figure 7 shows how well the impact and involvement then translated into desired communication.

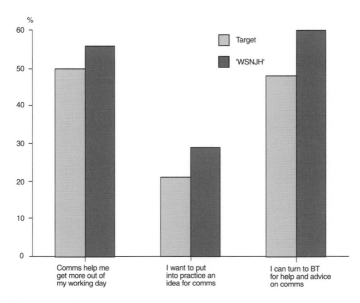

Figure 7: *Campaign communication*
Source: NOP ADTRACK

The primary objective of inspiring businesses to explore communications opportunities with BT, by positioning BT as the expert source for advice and help, was achieved.

The results were that 56% of the business audience felt that communications could help them to get more out of their working day, exceeding the 50% target set by BT. This in turn inspired 29% of businessmen to want to put into practice an idea for communications in their business. Further, 60% felt that they could turn to BT for help and advice on these issues.

The figures from research are encouraging, but what impact did the campaign have in practice?

Table 3 shows the response received over the duration of campaign. We would expect to receive enquiries after the campaign had finished. However, these would be difficult to attribute to the advertising, and so this section concentrates on enquiries received during the campaign period only.

TABLE 3 : CAMPAIGN RESPONSES

	Target	'WSNJH'	% Difference
Enquiries	30,000	51,448	71
PC Videophone leads	3300	5094	54
Freefone 0800 leads	3100	3252	5
Officelink leads	3100	3917	26
Other/general leads	-	4,714	
Total leads	9500	16,977	79

Source : BT CCC

'Enquiries' relates to the number of calls made to the campaign phoneline, on any subject matter relating to BT, not just specific to the focus of the campaign.

This is a measure of how much the advertising encourages people to talk to someone at BT. Given that one of the desired improvements in brand value is accessibility, this measure is an important one.

The campaign generated 51,448 enquiries over the advertised period, exceeding the autumn 1993 campaign's achievement (38,500) by 34% and the set target by 71%.

This in turn led to an overachievement on all *lead* targets by 79%, where leads are defined as a caller requesting information or advice specific to the product featured in the advertising.

Equating these leads to product sales is difficult. There are two reasons for this.

First, the objective of the campaign was to encourage businesses to call BT for advice, not to buy directly. Consequently, the call handling procedure within BT reflected this objective. Fulfilment literature was prepared to provide advice and, from that literature, one could then make a purchase if desired.

Unfortunately, the way BT measures sales provides no means of attributing the ultimate sale to the initial lead generated. This is because, once the lead comes in, it is passed on to the relevant sales division. That division also handles leads derived from other avenues, but it does not record the source. Thus, once the lead is passed on, it is lost for analysis purposes.

Second, the nature of the products being sold to customers is such that a sale can take months to complete. Consequently, it would be impossible to measure revenue generated over the campaign period.

Nevertheless, Table 4 attempts to give value to the leads, by relating the cost of the products featured to those leads, and comparing the potential income against that desired from the targets set.

TABLE 4 : POTENTIAL VALUE OF LEADS GENERATED

	Average price £	Target income £	Potential income £	Difference £
PC Videophone	2,335	7,705,500	11,894,490	+4,188,990
Freefone 0800	500	1,550,000	1,626,000	+76,000
Officelink	189	585,900	740,313	+154,413
Total		9,841,400	14,260,803	+4,419,403

Source : BT/BDDH

Potentially, the leads generated by the advertising were worth at least £14 million to BT because the products advertised tended to be the cheaper options in their respective ranges, and so there was an opportunity for BT to 'sell up'.

That said, no one ever converts all leads generated! However, we know from an analysis conducted by BT on a sample of leads generated by a campaign that ran in spring 1993, that 12% of leads generated were finally converted to sales. If we assume that this was the case in 1995, then the advertising would have generated £1.7 million in direct product sales.

But these products' real value to BT is that the businesses are less likely to approach a competitor for their communications requirements and thus, over time, the business's usage of the products will generate revenue from the PSTN for BT and not for somebody else.

Thus, overachieving on lead targets was the first step towards defending BT's market share of PSTN usage. Simultaneously improving BT's 'Quality of Response' perceptions achieved far more than that.

Improving BT's VfM by Differentiating on Service

In this section the tracking data is primarily taken from BT's ongoing monthly Brand Perception monitor, as opposed to the ADTRACK data quoted in the previous section.

The service targets for this campaign were defined by the five brand values concerning BT's 'Quality of Response' to the customer.

Figure 8 overleaf shows the achievement of the campaign on the five values, by comparing ratings taken at the end of the campaign period, against those achieved in the autumn 1993 campaign, and their position a year and a month previously.

This demonstrates that, over the campaign period, the brand value ratings exceeded everything achieved by BT to that point, in fact, they were at a statistically significant all-time high.

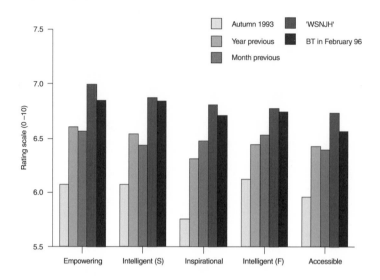

Figure 8: *Quality of Response brand value ratings*
Source: BT Monthly Business Brand, Attitudes and Price Perceptions

Better still, the campaign helped *sustain* higher ratings, hence the inclusion of the February 1996 data, although those ratings may eventually fall back without further advertising support.

Furthermore, the tracking also monitors BT's current key competitor in business telecommunications, Mercury. It is shown that, over the campaign period, there was not only a significant positive shift in BT's perceptions but also negative movements in Mercury's, further strengthening BT's competitive positioning.

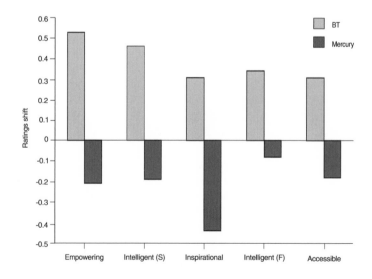

Figure 9: *Ratings shift over campaign period – BT versus Mercury*
Source: BT Monthly Business Brand, Attitudes and Price Perceptions

The combined effect of these shifts had an equally significant effect on BT's VfM.

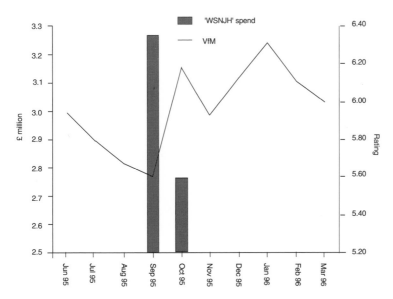

Figure 10: *Trend in monthly VfM ratings*
Source: BT Monthly Business Brand, Attitudes and Price Perceptions/IDK/Zenith

Again, the perception of BT providing VfM reached an all-time high over the campaign period, and was maintained thereafter into 1996.

Thus, the campaign had achieved its objective of improving the 'Quality of Response' values of BT and thus its Value for Money perceptions.

Furthermore, the model developed at the end of 1992 correlating VfM perceptions with market share performance held true in 1995. The model had an R^2 value of 0.85.

We can isolate the contribution of the 'WSNJH' advertising to this overall growth, using econometric modelling. The model does not use the market share data calculated from research but, instead, uses income received by BT from businesses over the PSTN.

The model shows that the direct contribution of the two-month 'WSNJH' campaign to BT call revenues from businesses was £10 million. This equates to a return of +66% on total media spend.

LOOKING AT OTHER POSSIBLE CONTRIBUTORS TO SHARE GROWTH

There are a number of other factors that could have played roles in BT's business market success in the autumn of 1995.

Other BT Advertising Activity

BT had two other campaigns running over the same period.

TABLE 5 : OTHER BT ADVERTISING ACTIVITY

	September £	October £	Total £
'WSNJH'	3,265,030 (TV/Press)	2,757,457 (TV/Press)	6,022,487
BT Corporate	1,202,000 (TV)	788,000 (TV)	1,990,000
BT Personal	1,107,000 (TV)	—	1,107,000

Source : IDK/Zenith Media

The BT Personal Communications advertising was for Call Minder, a new service for domestic consumers. The advertising ran only in the Central and Meridian areas. Consequently, it is reasonable to assume that this activity did not contribute to the market share growth among businesses.

The BT Corporate campaign was targeted at opinion formers in the large financial institutions and Government, a different audience to the 'WSNJH' campaign.

However, the campaign did run nationally on TV, in similar time slots, and so would be seen by our target audience. Hence, one would expect the Corporate campaign to have some effect on BT's business performance.

The econometric model used to assess the contribution of the 'WSNJH' campaign, also calculated the contribution of the Corporate campaign.

Over the same period, the direct contribution of the BT Corporate campaign to BT's PSTN revenues was £2.1 million. Thus, the 'WSNJH' campaign contributed five times the revenue on three times the spend of the Corporate campaign. Or, in other words, as Figure 11 shows, the 'WSNJH' campaign achieved a 67% return on media spend, against a return of just 5% from the Corporate campaign.

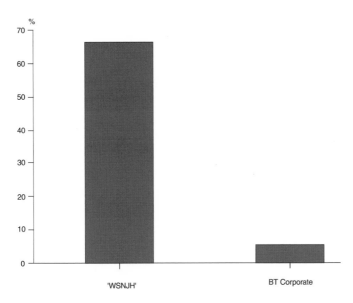

Figure 11: *Return on media spend comparison*
Source: BT/IDK/Zenith

Other BT Promotional Activity

There was no other promotional activity throughout the campaign. There was, however, PR about the campaign itself, and PR about the concept of working smarter.

It is impossible to judge the effect that PR had on the campaign, except to say that, without the advertising and the advertising strategy, there would have been no PR.

Price

There was no change to BT's pricing over the course of the campaign. There had been considerable pricing activity earlier on in the year, when BT launched by-the-second charging. But the effect of that had diminished by the time 'WSNJH' began.

Product

BT's product had not changed. For some time, BT had been providing computer-based communications. All that changed over the course of the campaign was businesses' awareness of BT's offer, and that was driven by the advertising.

APPENDIX

Relationship between VfM and Brand Share

It is reasonable to assume that brand share is affected by the following.

1. The spread of competition: obviously, customers first have to have a choice and, over the last few years, the competition has made itself available to an increasing number of BT customers. Most customers now have a choice of more than two suppliers.

2. The strength of the competition: once customers have a choice, they can then decide which supplier to use based on their perceived respective merits, ie which one offers the best VfM.

The model was developed between 1990 and 1992, when it was found that BT's business communications VfM rating moved closely in line with its brand share.

A deterioration in brand share can be seen after bad news (eg record profits for BT), and amelioration after good news (eg the introduction of pricing discounts). Over this time period, the R^2 between the two variables was 0.72.

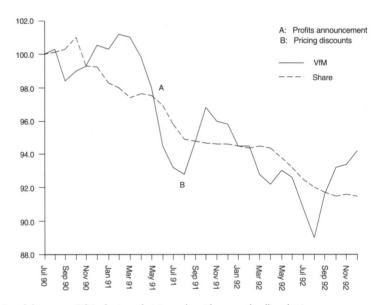

Figure 12: *Brand share versus VfM – business decision makers (three-month rolling data)*

The availability of competition also has to be taken into account when forecasting brand share. This is more difficult as, unlike VfM, there is no monthly tracking figure for this factor.

A crude proxy would be time and, indeed, the R^2 between time and VfM is 0.96. However, as can be seen, VfM and brand share have moved broadly in tandem and, if one regresses brand share against both time and VfM, the collinearity between the two independent variables prevents VfM from significantly contributing to the equation.

One way around this impasse is to combine the collinear variables into a new variable which is their weighted sum. This has been done by assigning approximately one-fifth of the weight to VfM and gradually increasing it over time. The R^2 is still 0.96, but this equation should perform better in the future rather than one based solely on time.

This modified equation is still not ideal, in that time is a less than satisfactory proxy for the availability of competition and the assignment of weights is necessarily somewhat arbitrary.

Ideally, one needs to track the percentage of customers who have a choice of suppliers, including how many, and whether they are aware of them and have evaluated them. The marketing efforts of the competition also need to be taken into account. This would then address the part of the brand share that is not affected by VfM.

Since the model was developed in 1992, the relationship has strengthened between VfM and brand share. The R^2 statistic now stands at 0.85.

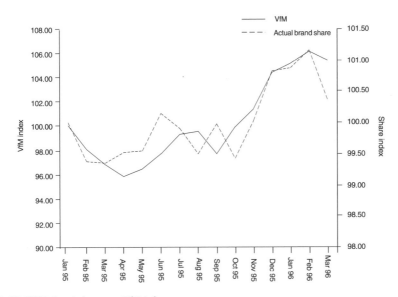

Figure 13: *BT PSTN share index versus VfM index*

VfM Drivers

Based on the Monthly Business Brand Attitudes and Price Perceptions report, there is a strong correlation between VfM and the 'Quality of Response' brand perceptions of 'accessible', 'inspirational', 'empowering' and 'intelligent'. This is illustrated by Figure 14 which shows VfM moving in line with the average of the 'Quality of Response' brand perception ratings (Source: BT).

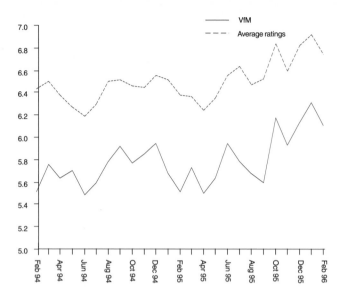

Figure 14: *BT 'Quality of Response' average ratings versus VfM*
Source: BT Monthly Business Brand Attitudes and Price Perceptions

12

Murphy's Irish Stout
One brand's weakness, another brand's strength

INTRODUCTION

Guinness is one of the UK's most famous and most successful brands.

With many great advertising campaigns to support it over the years, almost ubiquitous distribution and a huge market share of 80%, Guinness had created what might be called a 'consumer monopoly' in drinkers' minds.

This paper aims to demonstrate how, with clear strategic thinking, Murphy's advertising was able to identify Guinness' hidden weaknesses and exploit them with Murphy's relative and potential strengths.

This resulted in a fresh segmentation of the stout market that allowed Murphy's to create space in consumers' minds as the alternative stout.

In doing this, Murphy's was able to reverse a slight decline, and re-ignite significant growth both in the on- and off-trade.

But, maybe even more significantly, Murphy's was also able to establish with the consumer, the press and, indeed, even the Irish, that there are two stout brands in this world, Guinness *and* Murphy's, and thereby break that consumer monopoly.

DEVELOPING A BRAND AND ADVERTISING STRATEGY

Only a small number of brands compete in the UK stout market. Apart from Guinness and Murphy's, only Beamish, at half Murphy's size, represents any significant volume. This paper concentrates on the key battle between Guinness and Murphy's.

Murphy's Irish Stout is owned by Heineken Worldwide. Whitbread has been the sole licensee to brew, market and sell Murphy's in the UK since it bought the licence in 1987.

Murphy's is a stout, a 'black beer', thicker and heavier than lager or bitter, and brewed using burnt barley which gives it its dark colour.

Between 1987 and 1993 the brand had achieved a reasonable degree of success.

Supported with advertising, Murphy's had gained nearly 10% of the stout market, a relatively small base of distribution and some awareness and credibility among consumers.

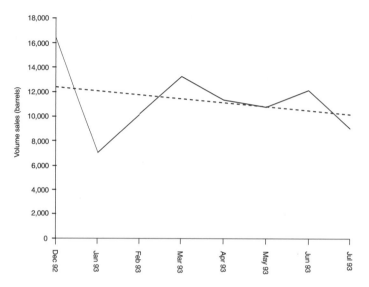

Figure 1: *Murphy's on-trade volume 1993 (pre-'Not Bitter' campaign)*
Source: BMS

However, by 1993, Murphy's future success was looking uncertain. In the on-trade, Murphy's volume was, at best, flat, as Figure 1 illustrates. And indeed share overall had slipped into decline.

TABLE 1: MURPHY'S SHARE OF THE TOTAL STOUT MARKET

1992	1993
%	%
10.6	9.6

Source: Whitbread Marketing Information

Whitbread's salesforce was finding it increasingly difficult to drive distribution and, indeed, there was some evidence that the brand was beginning to face delisting. We suspected that, if this decline was allowed to continue, the brand's fortunes would begin to spiral down.

Murphy's survival as a brand depended on finding a way forward to re-ignite growth. A daunting task given that, in order to do this, we had to take on the awesome power of Guinness.

Guinness: King of Stout

Truly, Guinness could be said in 1993 to be the King of Stout in every way – sales, distribution, promotional spend, advertising history and, of course, 'consumer allegiance'.

Sales

Guinness was the 'King of Stout', holding over 80% share.

TABLE 2: STOUT MARKET BRAND SHARES – 1993

	Volume share %
Murphy's	9.6
Guinness	80.1
Others	10.3

Source: Whitbread Marketing Information

Distribution

Guinness enjoyed the highest distribution of any beer (90%). This gave it enormous ubiquity and presence. You could go into almost any pub in the country and be able to order a Guinness.

A Heavily Supported Brand

Guinness has enjoyed many famous advertising campaigns over the years – from 'Toucans' to 'Guinless'. Many consumers today can even remember the line 'Guinness is good for you'.

The campaign that ran between 1987 and 1994 was equally famous. That campaign featured Rutger Hauer as brand cipher, and was backed by a huge media spend of over £45 million.

TABLE 3: GUINNESS ADVERTISING SPEND (£000s)

1988	1989	1990	1991	1992	1993	1994
5,167	6,896	6,495	6,970	7,840	5,444	9,370

Source: MEAL

A Growing Brand

The Rutger Hauer campaign had helped revitalise the market (albeit in the generic name of Guinness), and had successfully recruited new drinkers by focusing on the uniqueness of Guinness' acquired taste. It had built a highly aspirational image for the brand, based on the values of individuality and discernment. Consequently, Guinness had become a 'graduation beer': a beer which drinkers aspired to.

TABLE 4: PENETRATION OF DRINKERS WHO HAVE DRUNK STOUT IN THE PAST SEVEN DAYS

	1988	1989	1990	1991	1992	1993
Base:	10,513	10,580	10,629	10,667	10,681	10,707
% Drinkers	*3.9	*4.1	*4.1	4.7	4.9	5.2

Source: PAS Drinks Survey
* = Includes Draught Guinness only as Murphy's/Beamish at very low levels

A Consumer Monopoly

'It's just natural to order Guinness…Guinness is to stout as Kellogg's is to cornflakes.'

Source: The Research Business, June 1993

Guinness did not represent the stout market. It *was* the stout market.

'There is really no such thing as a British *stout* market. What there is is a *Guinness* market.'

Source: Research Perspectives – Qual. February 1988

In effect, Guinness enjoyed a consumer monopoly which it had successfully nurtured and grown over the years to the point where consumers had no need for another stout brand.

While one might expect the trade to want some healthy competition for Guinness, the practicalities of bar space in a market which only represented 5.5% of total beer volume, meant that they needed a strong argument to persuade them to give up this valuable space.

The Challenge

Trying to pick a fight with Guinness, whose marketing clout and budget just about matched its brand share, and which was showing no obvious signs of weakness, in a market where no-one wanted or needed another stout brand, seemed a daunting task.

The challenge for Murphy's within this setting was to find a way of breaking Guinness' consumer monopoly and opening the market (and the minds of drinkers) to a competitive stout brand.

TAKING ON GUINNESS

We embarked, therefore, on a process of identifying Guinness' relative strengths and weaknesses that we could exploit to the benefit of Murphy's.

In looking for a 'way in' we used both qualitative and quantitative research, to fully interrogate Guinness' product and image in the context of the entire stout-drinking experience.

Were there any stout values Guinness had not occupied? Had it left any values unattended? Were there any Guinness brand values that were relatively weak, particularly in relation to Murphy's brand strengths?

These were the questions we held in our minds as we went searching for a way of breaking Guinness' consumer monopoly.

First, we looked at the product.

Product

Guinness had made an enormous virtue of its acquired taste for years. Its taste delivery was the key to its highly aspirational image of being 'the thinking man's pint'. Despite consumer belief that this was an enormous benefit of the brand, we reminded ourselves that 'an acquired taste' can be simply another way of saying that it is *'difficult to drink'*.

Our research, conducted among both Guinness drinkers and non-drinkers, confirmed that its taste was, in fact, a barrier to both increased consumption for some, and to entering the market for others.

Knowing that Murphy's was easier to drink than Guinness, presented a very considerable opportunity for Murphy's to position itself as a more accessible product.

> 'Murphy's was felt to be particularly palatable and easy to drink, especially in comparison with Guinness.'

> Source: The Research Business, 1992

For the first time, the stout market might begin to segment on a taste dimension for some consumers, and in so doing create space in people's minds for Murphy's.

Next we looked at image.

Image

Many stout drinkers found Guinness' mysterious and individualistic brand personality very appealing. However, qualitative research had revealed that this imagery was being re-interpreted by some as aloof and pretentious.

> 'Guinness is a bit bizarre and weird...it's elitist and intellectual and a bit intense.'

> Source: Occasional Guinness Drinker, 1992

Indeed our advertising research showed that 18% of those aware of Guinness advertising believed it to be 'pretentious'. (Source: MRSL.)

While this was a minority view, it demonstrated to us that there was an image chink in the Guinness armour that Murphy's could exploit.

Stout Values versus Guinness

The more we spoke to consumers about how they drank stout, the more it seemed to us that Guinness, especially in its pretentious guise, did not represent the core values of the market.

Stout has a certain role within consumers' drinking repertoire. It tends to be a leisurely pint rather than a 'getting drunk' pint. By virtue of the slow, relaxed manner in which it is commonly consumed, stout is associated with sociable, laid-back values, typified by a rural Irish community pub. It became clear in research that consumers have a warm and romantic view of stout.

> 'The perfect place for stout is always a distant somewhere else that is imbued with romanticism ...most typically an old-fashioned Dublin bar.'

> Source: The Research Business, June 1993

These values stem directly from stout's Irish heritage. They had been neglected by Guinness in its attempt to appeal to new, younger drinkers. While Guinness may be well known as a brand that comes from Ireland, it had moved away from the emotional values of 'Irishness'.

This, we believed, represented a big opportunity for Murphy's to occupy an area of stout imagery that Guinness had left unattended and, in so doing, we could draw further attention to Guinness' aloof personality.

Perhaps we would also create a new segmentation of the market in terms of emotional reward (a 'relaxed' occasion versus a 'style' occasion) and in terms of the attitude of the drinker ('laid-back' and 'sociable' versus 'pretentious' and 'distant').

Our Brand Vision for Murphy's

We felt confident that Murphy's had the potential to become the accessible and easy-going stout brand with an easy drinking taste. We hoped this would enable us to reframe Guinness in consumers' minds and highlight the weaknesses that we had identified, a harsh taste and an aloof personality.

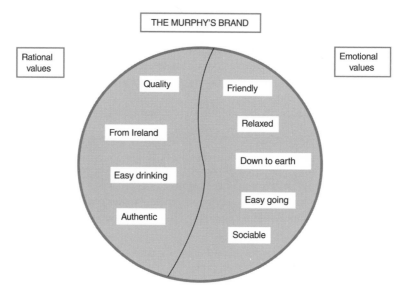

Figure 2: *Murphy's brand values*

TARGETING

We needed to apply our strategic thinking carefully among the right target audience.

We knew that this would not be an easy task, as not all drinkers found Guinness inaccessible. So we targeted the groups most likely to need help accessing stout.

Regular Guinness drinkers were the least likely group of drinkers to switch brands, as they were already members of the 'stout club'.

We discovered, however, that many occasional Guinness drinkers were inhibited by the Guinness taste. This group was far more likely to be appreciative of an easy drinking offering; the likelihood being that these drinkers would actually increase their consumption to the benefit of Murphy's.

Non-stout drinkers also represented an enormous opportunity. Many non-drinkers were 'stout-wannabes': beer drinkers who aspired to Guinness but were put off by its taste and intimidating imagery. Murphy's was best placed to take advantage of their desire to drink stout.

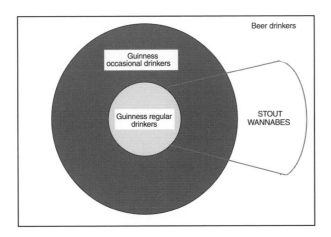

Figure 3: *Murphy's target audience*

MURPHY'S CREATIVE BRIEF

Client: Whitbread.

Product: Murphy's Irish Stout.

THE PRODUCT IS?

Draught stout brewed in Cork and the UK.

THE BRAND IS?

The easy-going stout from mythical Ireland.

WHY ARE WE ADVERTISING?

To develop Murphy's as the stout brand that people would prefer to drink instead of Guinness.

WHO ARE WE TALKING TO?

Men, not lads, who drink Guinness now and then or who would like to drink it but do not like the taste (stout wannabes).

WHAT DO WE WANT PEOPLE TO THINK AND FEEL?

Murphy's is the easy-drinking stout.

WHAT JUSTIFICATION ARE WE PROVIDING AS SUPPORT?

Murphy's is an extremely palatable and accessible drink. It is less bitter and lighter than Guinness.

MEDIA STRATEGY

Role for Television

We needed to select media that could powerfully convey the emotions of our brand positioning, which meant that TV was a prerequisite.

It was imperative that programmes reflected the easy-going, Irish personality as much as possible, and were seen at a time when our target was in 'relaxed mode', conducive to Murphy's drinking occasions.

TV buying revolved around programming that our target audience specifically chose to watch, thus the audience repeatedly hit our target while actively choosing to watch its favourite programmes. We also 'cherry-picked' programmes particularly relevant to our positioning – for example, *The Commitments*, *Gaelic Games* and whenever Ireland played rugby.

As Murphy's, like Guinness, is drunk occasionally, and therefore prone to slip the consumers' mental list of drinks, our media selection had to keep the brand front of mind continuously. We therefore maintained as continuous a presence as we could throughout the year using TV. However, our media budgets meant that there would be some gaps.

The Role for Press

The role for press was to 'fill-in' at those times of year when there was no television advertising.

The press executions were developed to be as different as possible from Guinness. When Guinness was running small-space, black-and-white ads, we opted for full-colour double-page spreads. For added impact and interest, we inserted our press ads into publications sideways.

THE ADVERTISING IDEA

The advertising idea associated the easy drinking nature of Murphy's (versus Guinness) with the easy-going, emotional values of Ireland.

The endline: 'Like the Murphy's, I'm not bitter' worked, we hoped, by linking the brand with an aspirational state of mind and further confirming the product's palatability.

The campaign has run from August 1993 to date.

'NOVICE'

SOUND: (MVO) That's it! I took O'Brian's advice on the seventh horse in the Accumulator, and it came in – seventh.

SOUND: (MVO) But like the Murphy's…I'm not bitter.

SOUND: (MVO) Especially as I had a side bet on the St Barnabus steeplechase.

Like the Murphy's, they're not bitter.

'SOME NECK'

SOUND: (MVO) My Granda always told me it wasn't worth going to his local dance. Firstly, it's one hell of a walk.

SOUND: (MVO) Secondly, it was really dangerous.

SOUND: (MVO) All the girls were looking for a husband.

SOUND: (MVO) But worst of all, no-one could carry the barrels of Draught Murphy's over here.

SOUND: (MVO) But like the Murphy's...

SOUND: (MVO) ..me and my Granda, we're not bitter.

Like the Murphy's, they're not bitter.

POSTER ADS

Gerard had the bottle to jump for charity,
but like the Murphy's he wasn't bitter.

THANKS TO A WIDGET MURPHY'S IS THE FIRST DRAUGHT STOUT IN A BOTTLE

Finbar needed the hair of the dog,
but like the Murphy's he wasn't bitter.

Maria's blind date didn't measure up to expectations
but like the Murphy's she wasn't bitter.

SO, WHAT HAPPENED FOLLOWING THE ADVERTISING?

Since the Murphy's advertising campaign broke in August 1993, the brand has achieved significant and consistent growth in both the on- and off-trade.

This section aims to demonstrate the overall brand achievements of the period of advertising from September 1993 to date, before going on to dissect the contribution of advertising to sales.

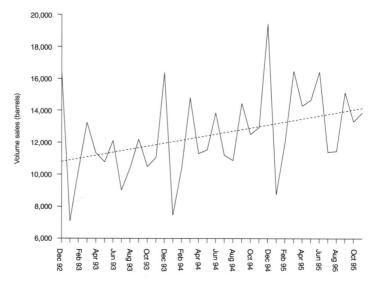

Figure 4: *Murphy's on-trade volume*
Source: BMS

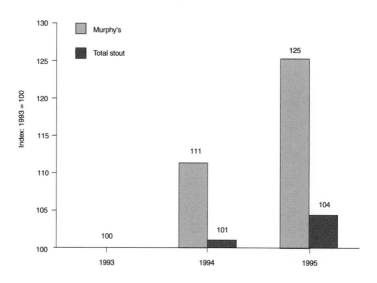

Figure 5: *Murphy's versus market-on-trade*
Source: BMS

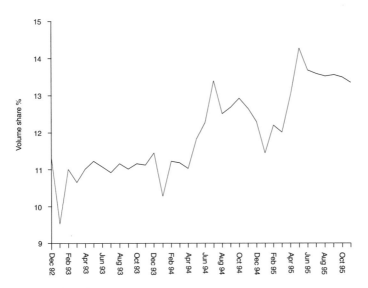

Figure 6: *Murphy's on-trade share of stout*
Source: BMS

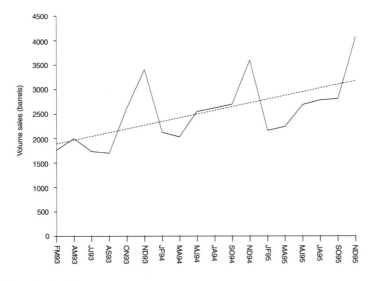

Figure 7: *Murphy's off-trade volume*
Source: Stats MR

On-Trade (Pubs)

In the on-trade, Murphy's volume has shown a significant increase from approximately 9,000 barrels per month to approximately 14,000 barrels per month by the autumn of 1995.

We can compare this volume growth to growth in the total market (Figure 5).

Consequently, Murphy's volume share of stout has grown from around 11% to 13%. This is a very significant increase in the beer market. It equates to an increase in revenue of £16.9 million.

Off-Trade (Take-Home)

Murphy's volume in the off-trade has grown from less than 2,000 barrels per bi-month at the beginning of 1993, to nearly 3,000 barrels by the end of 1995.
We can compare this performance to the market in Figure 8.

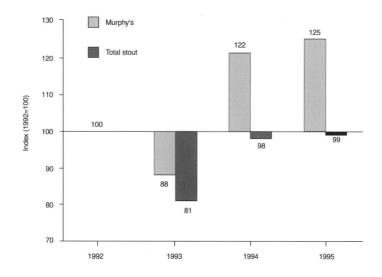

Figure 8: *Murphy's versus market-off-trade*
Source: Stats MR

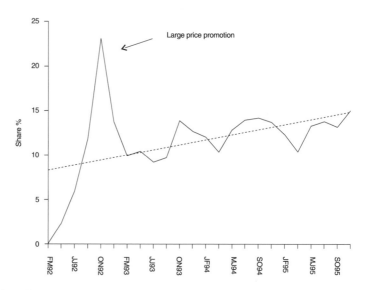

Figure 9: *Murphy's off-trade share of stout*
Source: Stats MR (October/November 1992 saw an extraordinary price-based promotion which significantly boosted share in the short term).

Over the same period, there has been a continuous increase in Murphy's volume share from around 10% to 13%. This increase is equivalent to £5.1 million revenue.

ADVERTISING CONTRIBUTION

As the characteristics and behaviour of the on- and off-trade beer market show very different patterns, we have treated them separately in isolating the advertising effects on each.

Off-Trade

As might be expected, many factors have varied in the off-trade sector during the period 1993–95.

Some of these factors will have affected the stout market overall, for example, seasonality and disposable consumer income. We established that these factors affected Murphy's and Guinness equally and therefore they have been eliminated from our models.

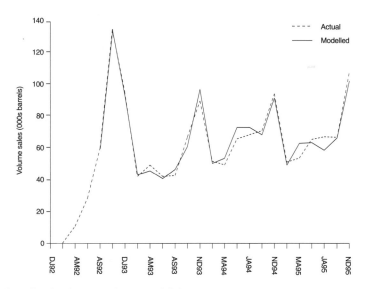

Figure 10: *Murphy's off-trade volume, actual versus modelled*
Source: Stats MR
NB: Data periods change November 1993

Other factors could be expected to have affected individual brands – distribution, pricing and, of course, advertising. We have therefore constructed a model which allows us to isolate, and estimate the size of, the advertising effect.

By plotting the ratio of Murphy's rate of sale to that of Guinness, we removed the effect of any distribution changes.

A relative pricing variable was explicitly entered into the model.

Finally, the advertising spends for Guinness and Murphy's were entered as adstocks to estimate the size of the advertising effect. The resulting model gives a very close fit between the model and the actual data, with all relevant quantifications being significant from zero at the 99% confidence level.

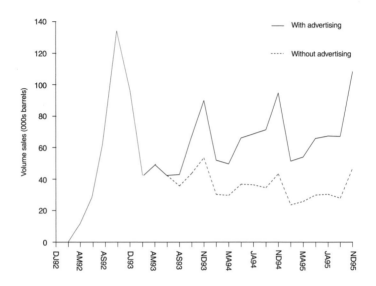

Figure 11: *Murphy's off-trade volume, with and without advertising*
Source: Stats MR

Figure 11 shows a simulation of the model, setting the Murphy's 'I'm not bitter' campaign to zero (ie showing what would have happened had we not advertised).

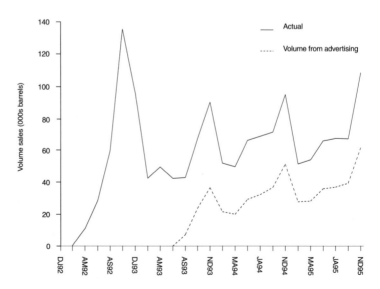

Figure 12: *Murphy's off-trade volume from advertising*
Source: Stats MR

The difference between the simulation and the actual volume shows the contribution of the advertising to Murphy's sales.

The model shows that Murphy's advertising contributed a 97% sales increase over the advertised period. *This equates to 60,130 barrels.*

Figure 12 shows the advertising contribution to sales more clearly.

This, however, is not the full extent of the payback. Figure 13 shows the continued contribution of the advertising, by projecting the carry-over effect from the current campaign (if we were to stop advertising from now) into the future.

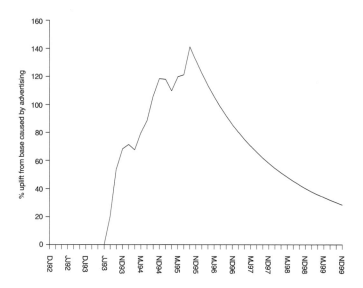

Figure 13: *Carry-over effect from Murphy's advertising in the off-trade*
Source: Model Simulation

On-Trade

It is very unusual to be able to model the on-trade market, due to the unreliability of data in the public domain and, as a result, this has never before been attempted in an IPA paper.

Instead we have taken a sample of Whitbread Inns (which although owned by Whitbread, operates as a separate company and profit centre).

As Figure 14 shows, it is reasonable to take this sample as representative of UK pubs as a whole, since the two groups behave in exactly the same way.

It is also the case that Murphy's is given no special treatment simply because these pubs are Whitbread pubs.

By taking the sample which has stocked both Murphy's and Guinness continuously over the advertising period, we have eliminated the effect of distribution, and the *quality* of distribution for the two brands is obviously the same since they are in exactly the same pubs.

Finally, relative pricing of the two brands was constant over the period.

The only remaining variables that could be expected to affect the sales levels of Guinness and Murphy's are advertising for the two brands, and the model has been constructed to examine this. This is again a close fit between the models and the actual data, with all relevant quantifications being significantly different from zero at the 99% confidence level (see Appendix 1 and 2).

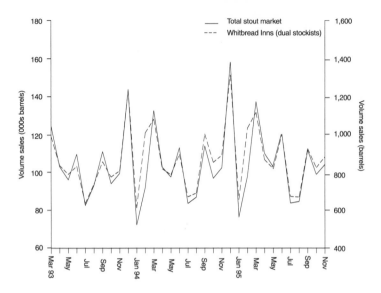

Figure 14: *Comparison of Whitbread Inns versus market*
Source: BMS/Whitbread Marketing Information

As can be seen in Figure 15, the on-trade model achieves exactly the same fit as that of the off-trade.

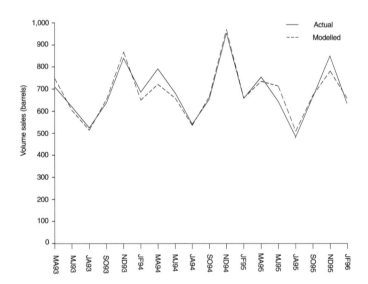

Figure 15: *Murphy's on-trade volume, actual and modelled*
Source: Whitbread Marketing Information

Figure 16 shows a simulation of the model, setting the Murphy's 'I'm not bitter' campaign to zero (ie showing what would have happened had we not advertised).

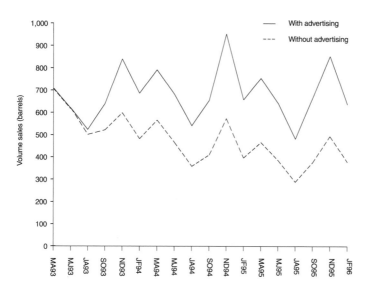

Figure 16: *Murphy's on-trade volume, with and without advertising*
Source: Whitbread Marketing Information

Figure 17 shows the advertising contribution to sales over the advertised period more clearly.

The advertising accounted for a 51% uplift in Murphy's volume sales. This equates to 131,542 additional barrels nationally.

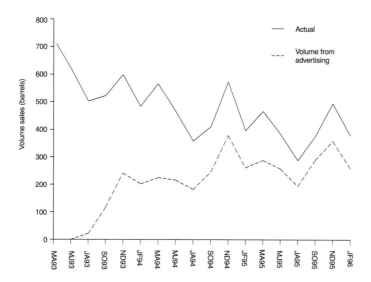

Figure 17: *Murphy's on-trade volume from advertising*
Source: Whitbread Marketing Information

Again, the advertising has a carry-over effect on Murphy's volume as shown in Figure 18 (assuming advertising stops from now). The advertising decay rate is the same in both the on- and off-trade.

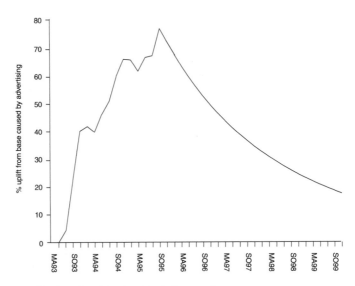

Figure 18: *Carry-over effect from Murphy's advertising in the on-trade*
Source: Model Simulation

Summary of the Advertising Effect

The contribution of advertising is equivalent to an increase of 51% in on-trade volume and 97% in off-trade volume.

These figures are calculated on the basis of what would have happened if there had been no advertising, compared to what would have happened when there was advertising.

During this period, actual share for Murphy's increased by +2% in the on-trade and +3% in the off-trade (this represents an 18% and 27% volume increase respectively).

Clearly, these actual movements in Murphy's share masked what was a very significant advertising effect.

So, what is stopping this advertising effect from manifesting itself in a greater actual share uplift for Murphy's?

The answer is Guinness advertising. As one would expect (and Figures 19 and 20 show), Guinness advertising has a negative effect on Murphy's sales. What is surprising is that, in spite of Guinness' very effective advertising at very heavy weights, Murphy's advertising more than compensates for that loss.

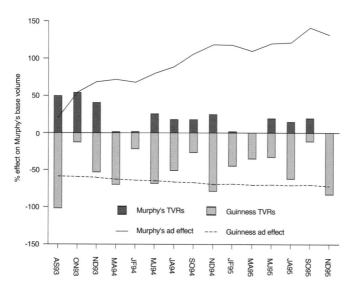

Figure 19: *Murphy's and Guinness advertising effect in the off-trade*
Source: Model Simulation

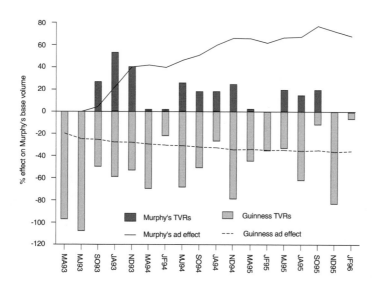

Figure 20: *Murphy's and Guinness advertising effect in the on-trade*
Source: Model Simulation

TVR for TVR, Murphy's advertising has a greater effect than Guinness advertising.

This relationship between Guinness and Murphy's advertising suggests an interesting theory about how Murphy's advertising is working. Murphy's advertising is defending the Murphy's brand from attack by Guinness advertising.

We believe that it is doing this by creating exclusive properties for Murphy's in the minds of consumers that Guinness advertising cannot reach.

This is a significant first step in the direction of breaking down Guinness' monopoly status.

There are now aspects of stout that Guinness does not own and cannot alter, despite a very popular advertising campaign.

Murphy's is an example of how misleading it can be to rely upon increases in raw sales or share data to demonstrate an advertising effect. Advertising can have a very significant effect on sales without that effect being immediately obvious.

HOW THE ADVERTISING WORKED

Our intermediate advertising and brand measures indicate that the advertising worked exactly as we intended.

Advertising Awareness

First, the advertising cut through and was seen by the vast majority of beer drinkers. Spontaneous advertising awareness doubled over the period (from 23% in July 1993 to 54% in October 1995), as did total (prompted) awareness (from 39% to 70%).

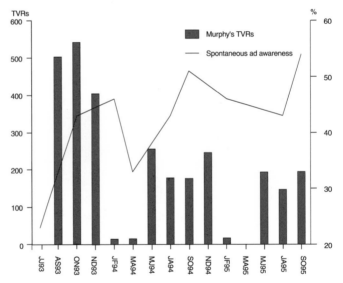

Figure 21: *Spontaneous advertising awareness*
Base: Beer drinkers
Source: MRSL

Advertising impact is confirmed by the fact that over 60% of those people claiming to have seen any Murphy's advertising can repeat the endline word-for-word without prompting. We believe that this level of playback is reached only by such famous examples as: 'The World's Favourite Airline', or '...helps you work, rest and play'.

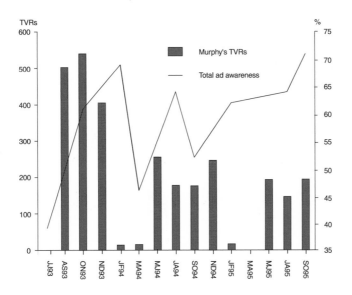

Figure 22: *Total advertising awareness (spontaneous and prompted)*
Base: Beer drinkers
Source: MRSL

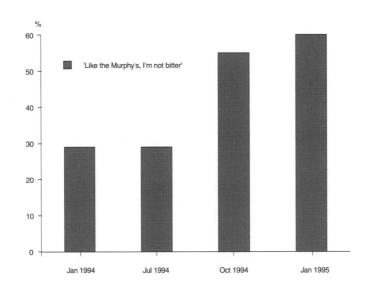

Figure 23: *Awareness of Murphy's slogan*
Base: All those claiming to have seen any advertising for Murphy's
Source: MRSL

Advertising Communication

The advertising is clearly communicating (at a spontaneous level) that Murphy's 'is not bitter' and that it is 'smooth' and 'Irish'.

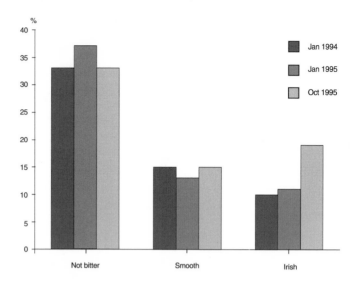

Figure 24: *Spontaneous advertising communication*
Base: All those claiming to have seen advertising for Murphy's
Source: MRSL

By comparison to Guinness, we have successfully carved out a segment within the market, as we intended. Murphy's has achieved a distinct personality versus Guinness of being sociable, friendly, relaxed and down to earth, whereas Guinness performs at low levels against these attributes in preference for remaining 'individualistic', 'fashionable' and 'stylish'.

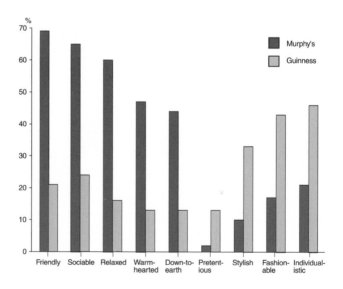

Figure 25: *Murphy's personality conveyed via the advertising versus Guinness*
Base: All those claiming to have seen any advertising for Murphy's
Source: MRSL

Murphy's personality is also consonant with the roots of stout, implying that, again, we are communicating brand values as desired.

Effect on Perceptions of the Brand

Importantly, when put head to head against Guinness, the Murphy's brand holds an overwhelming lead over Guinness as 'less bitter tasting' and 'easier to drink', and, most spectacularly given Guinness's heritage, 37% of beer drinkers see no difference between the two brands as 'authentically Irish'; a further 20% believing that Murphy's is *more* authentically Irish compared to Guinness.

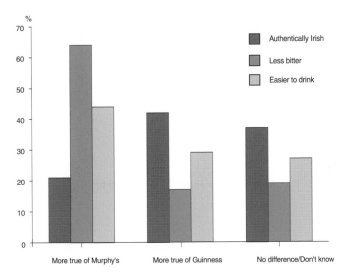

Figure 26: *Statements more true of Murphy's or Guinness brands*
Base: All those aware of Murphy's and Guinness brands – January 1995
Source: MRSL

In our qualitative research consumers could talk about this new brand image for Murphy's.

'Murphy's is friendlier than Guinness...more like your mate.'

'They're [Murphy's] going for a more down-to-earth feel...a laid-back, Irish sort of thing.'

Source: Murphy's Occasional Drinker

Liking the Advertising

As an additional point, Murphy's advertising is increasingly liked by beer drinkers: surely a sign that emotional empathy with the brand was likely to increase.

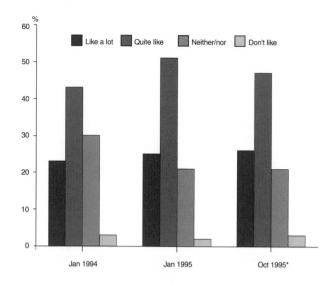

Figure 27: *Liking of Murphy's advertising*
Base: All those claiming to have seen any advertising for Murphy's
Source: MRSL

AMONGST WHOM HAS THE ADVERTISING WORKED

Total Drinkers

There has been a significant increase in claimed drinking of Murphy's. Over the two years of this advertising campaign, an additional 386,000 drinkers have adopted the brand. This represents about a 23% increase in the number of Murphy's drinkers over the two-year period – four times as many as Guinness which, by comparison, has only increased its drinker franchise by 94,000 over the same period.

TABLE 5: MURPHY'S PENETRATION OF DRINKERS

	1993	1995
Total population (million)	45,300	45,650
All drinkers of either canned or draught Murphy's	1,648	2,034
% of total population	3.6	4.5
All drinkers of either canned or draught Murphy's	5,185	5,279
% of total population	11.4	11.5

Source: TGI

New Drinkers

TGI reveals that 147,000 Guinness occasional drinkers have added Murphy's to their repertoire. This accounts for a 25% increase in the number of Guinness occasional drinkers who ever drink Murphy's.

TABLE 6: GUINNESS OCCASIONAL DRINKERS WHO ALSO
DRINK MURPHY'S

	1993	1995
000s of drinkers	608	755
% of drinkers	31	35

Source: TGI

Murphy's has only attracted 1,000 regular Guinness drinkers. The remaining 238,000 new Murphy's drinkers are most likely to have come from outside the stout category.

We seem to have been successful at leveraging Murphy's accessible brand values among those who needed it most.

SECONDARY BENEFITS OF ADVERTISING AND PAYBACK

As well as the achievements outlined above in terms of numbers of drinkers and extra barrels, we have achieved an enormous amount of publicity around the advertising for Murphy's, and have helped the brand in other markets.

In Ireland, the success of the brand in the UK sparked increased sales in Dublin via the tourist industry. Tourists, expecting to find Murphy's in its homeland, created a strong selling point for the Murphy's Ireland brewery salesforce, as well as an unexpected uplift in sales.

'Over the last couple of years, we've found publicans increasingly asking for Murphy's during the summer season. The success of the brand in the UK has certainly given an unexpected boost to sales here.'

Patrick Conway, Murphy's Brewery Ireland Marketing Director

Payback

The contribution of advertising comes from both Murphy's on-trade draught and off-trade cans.

Advertising's Contribution to Murphy's Irish Stout
The volume sales uplift for total Murphy's volume sales estimated from the models for the period August 1993 to December 1995 is:

On-trade	131,542 barrels
Off-trade	60,130 barrels
Total	191,672 barrels

Note: This underestimates the effects of the advertising beyond December 1995, thereby seriously underestimating the total effect.

Since August 1993, total media and production costs have come to £7.9 million (BBH actual billing).

In order for the advertising to have recouped this cost, given the volume uplift above, Whitbread would need to make a minimum average net profit of £41.30 per barrel. We can confirm that Whitbread does achieve this minimum level of profit and more. Therefore, the advertising has, at the very least, paid for all the costs of creating and showing it.

CONCLUSIONS

There has also been press comment, in trade and consumer media, relating to the Murphy's brand and, specifically, to the battle for share between Murphy's and Guinness. Although this cannot be directly attributable to the advertising, much of this comment implies that the press believe that Murphy's is a far bigger brand than it actually is.

We believe that the advertising played a large part in building a general belief that the Murphy's brand is bigger in the minds of our drinkers, the trade and the press world than it represents in actual share terms. Consumer demand for Murphy's now far outweighs its actual brand share – 32% of beer drinkers now see us as their first choice stout. This leaves us only 20 points behind Guinness.

TABLE 7: FIRST CHOICE STOUT BRAND
AMONG BEER DRINKERS

Murphy's %	Guinness %
32	53

Source: MRSL – October 1995

Maybe we have finally begun to break the Guinness consumer monopoly.

TECHNICAL APPENDIX 1

This Appendix quantifies the sales effects of the Murphy's 'I'm not bitter' advertising campaign for both the on- and off-trade and describes the methodology employed to approximate the sales effects of advertising contained in the figures of the main text.

Although the on- and off-trade were modelled separately, the general methodology for both was very similar. A discussion of the similarities are followed by details of the data, quantifications and statistical validation diagnostics for the on- and off-trade.

Common Features

Regression analysis was used to model the advertising effects. Because of data limitations the models needed to be parsimonious while still capturing the important influences (variables).

A number of variables influence this market. Distribution and seasonality are key. Modelling volume sales directly would require the inclusion of seasonal factors, Murphy's distribution, competitive distribution, and a variety of other factors that drive the market, thereby using up valuable degrees of freedom.

However, in general, if a brand's volume moves in line with market, seasonality and the other macro influences, modelling *share* can reduce the number of explicit influences (explanatory variables) needed to be taken into account. This approach would still require the inclusion of distribution variables (ie the 'micro' variables).

Modelling share would have been an option given that Murphy's seasonality is identical to that of Guinness. However, to reduce the number of explanatory variables still further, the ratio of Murphy's rate of sale to Guinness rate of sale was modelled, thereby discounting for both Guinness and Murphy's distribution, seasonality and other factors influencing the total market.

Modelling the ratio of rates of sale does represent (in technical parlance) a restriction on the parameters of the model. These restrictions were tested and validated. Thus the model equation can be solved for volume sales as follows:

RoS(M)/RoS(G) = the model

Note: RoS(M)/RoS(G) = (Volume(M)/Distribution(M))/(Volume(G)/Distribution(G))

Thus

Volume(M) = (the model) x Distribution(M) x Volume(G)/Distribution(G)

This is the general principal used to calculate volume movements. In the case of the off-trade Murphy's model, the volume solution is slightly more complex because Stats MR weighted rate of sale data was used.

For the on-trade model the volume solution was more straightforward because distribution for Murphy's and Guinness was identical (ie all pubs in the sample were dual stockists selling both Murphy's and Guinness continuously throughout the three-year period).

Murphy's – Off-Trade

Source data: Stats MR bi-monthly volume, value, price and weighted rate of sale data from January 1992 (the launch of the take-home product) to December 1995. Advertising data from BARB (via DDS).

Four key explanatory variables were required to construct the model.

1.   Price enters the equation as the natural log of the relative price (ie Murphy's to Guinness). The estimated price elasticity was approximately 2 which is typical of what would be expected from a canned beer.

2. & 3. Murphy's and Guinness advertising enters the regression equation as 2.5% decay per month adstocks. These variables were not log transformed. This means that, technically, the volume solution to the advertising variables has an exponential mathematical form. However, the exponent is so small that the adverting effects are linear across the historical ranges.

4. The October to November 1992 bi-monthly data shows a large and untypical uplift in sales. Two unique events occurred in this period. First there was a burst of Murphy's TV advertising from the previous campaign and second there was a unprecedented 'four for one' promotion. In essence two unique events in one period means that it is impossible to quantify the individual influences. Therefore a dummy variable was used to capture the joint effect of the advertising and the promotion.

Note that the advertising in this particular bi-month is not included in any of the advertising effect calculations.

Stats MR changed the data reporting periodicity in November 1993. This was taken into account by appropriately changing the periodicity of the explanatory variables (including the adstock variables). Furthermore, statistical tests were carried out to validate the consistency of the data in terms of constant variance and the absence of a proportional shift in the data (parameter stability tests and split sample variance ratio test).

Regression Equation Parameter Values and Statistical Diagnostics

Method: Ordinary Least Squares. Observations 21

Dependent variable: Natural log of the ratio of Murphy's weighted RoS to Guinness canned draught weight RoS.

Variable	Coefficient	Standard error	t-ratio
Constant	-0.265	0.127	2.08
Price	-1.967	0.446	4.40
Guinness ads	-0.0000864	0.0000172	5.03
Murphy's ads	0.000243	0.0000383	6.35
Promotion	0.767	0.092	8.30

All of the variables have small standard errors in relation to their parameters with 2-tailed p-values of 0.0004, 0.0001, 0.00004, 0.000002 respectively, ie all explanatory variables are significantly different from zero at the 99.9% confidence level (excluding the constant term which has no interpretation within the context of this analysis).

Fit diagnostics

R-Squared = 0.91, R-bar Squared = 0.89, estimated regression standard error = 0.081 (approximately 8%), SSR = 0.103844.

Tests for failure of the Gauss-Markov conditions

Normality of residuals: Jarque-Bera (distributed chi-squared 2) = 0.7 indicating normally distributed errors.

Absence of residual autocorrelation: DWS = 2.21.

Tests for higher order autocorrelation

LM(1) Chi-squared 1 = 0.4 f-test analog (1,24) = 0.3
LM(2) Chi-squared 2 = 0.6 f-test analog (2,23) = 0.2
LM(3) Chi-squared 3 = 0.9 f-test analog (3,22) = 0.2
LM(4) Chi-squared 4 = 1.4 f-test analog (4,21) = 0.2
LM(5) Chi-squared 5 = 1.6 f-test analog (5,20) = 0.3
LM(6) Chi-squared 6 = 3.9 f-test analog (6,19) = 0.4
   All tests fall well below the 95% critical values, indicating the absence of residual autocorrelation.

Absence of ARCH errors

LM(1) Chi-squared 1 = 0.9 f-test analog (1,20) = 0.8
LM(2) Chi-squared 2 = 1.8 f-test analog (2,19) = 0.9
   All tests fall well below the 95% critical values, indicating the absence of ARCH error.
   Chow forecasting tests for parameter stability and variance ratio test for constant variance:
   $f(4,12) = 1.6, f(6,6)=1.13$

   The tests fall well below the 95% critical values, indicating homoscedastic residuals and stable parameters.

Murphy's – On-Trade

Source data: All Whitbread public houses continually stocking both draught Murphy's and draught Guinness for the bi-month periods March/April 1993 to January/February 1996. Advertising data from BARB (via DDS).
   Three key explanatory variables were required to construct the model.

1.& 2. Murphy's and Guinness advertising enters the regression equation as 2.5% decay per month adstocks. These variables were not log transformed. This means that, technically, the volume solution to the advertising variables has an exponential mathematical form. However, the exponent is so small that the advertising effects are linear across the historical ranges.

3.   There is a recording anomaly in the data which caused an understatement of Guinness sales in one period and an overstatement in the following period, thereby distorting the true Murphy's-to-Guinness ratio. The exact correction required to adjust the data is unknown. Therefore, rather than tamper with the raw data, this anomaly was adjusted by introducing a dummy variable of the form ... 0 0 0 1 -1 0 0 ... which in effect estimates and compensates for this anomaly.
   Price does not enter the on-trade model. The reason is that the relative price of draught Murphy's to draught Guinness has remained constant over the period in

the data set supplied by Whitbread Limited. Thus there is no variation in the ratio of Murphy's to Guinness RoS attributable to relative price changes.

Regression Equation Parameter Values and Statistical Diagnostics

Method: Ordinary Least Squares. Observations 18

Dependent variable: Natural log of the ratio of Murphy's RoS to Guinness RoS.

Variable	Coefficient	Standard error	t-ratio
Constant	-0.881	0.687	1.28
Guinness ads	-0.0000303	0.00000769	3.99
Murphy's ads	0.0001581	0.00003659	4.33
Data adjustment	-0.176	0.040	4.37

All of the variables have small standard errors in relation to their parameters with 2-tailed p-values of 0.0015, 0.0008, 0.00008 respectively, ie all explanatory variables are significantly different from zero at the 99.9% confidence level (excluding the constant term which has no interpretation within the context of this analysis).

Fit diagnostics

R-Squared = 0.92, R-bar Squared = 0.89, estimated regression standard error = 0.0546 (approximately 5.5%), SSR = 0.041774.

Tests for failure of the Gauss-Markov conditions

Normality of residuals: Jarque-Bera (distributed chi-squared 2) = 0.1 indicating normally distributed errors.
    Absence of residual autocorrelation: DWS = 1.61

Tests for higher order autocorrelation

LM(1) Chi-squared 1 = 0.4 f-test analog (1,17) = 0.3
LM(2) Chi-squared 2 = 2.5 f-test analog (2,16) = 0.9
LM(3) Chi-squared 3 = 6.1 f-test analog (3,15) = 1.2
LM(4) Chi-squared 4 = 7.2 f-test analog (4,14) = 1.6
LM(5) Chi-squared 5 = 8.6 f-test analog (5,13) = 1.8
LM(6) Chi-squared 6 = 8.9 f-test analog (6,12) = 1.8
    All tests fall well below the 95% critical values, indicating the absence of residual autocorrelation.

Absence of ARCH errors

LM(1) Chi-squared 1 = 0.1 f-test analog (1,20) = 0.1
LM(2) Chi-squared 2 = 0.8 f-test analog (2,19) = 0.3

All tests fall well below the 95% critical values, indicating the absence of ARCH error.

Chow forecasting tests for parameter stability and variance ratio test for constant variance:

$f(4,11) = 2.7$, $f(5,6)=1.1$

The tests fall well below the 95% critical values, indicating homoscedastic errors and stable parameters.

TECHNICAL APPENDIX 2: ON-TRADE DATA USED FOR MODELLING

This Appendix describes and discusses the on-trade data supplied by Whitbread Inns Limited used for the modelling.

Data availability in the public domain for the on-trade is notoriously incomplete. One of the major difficulties is the measurement of distribution and rate of sale. Potentially this presented a fundamental difficulty to the analysis of Murphy's on-trade sales/RoS.

However, Whitbread Inns Limited has a very large estate of public houses for which it has accurate recorded sales volume date for the period March 1993 to February 1996. This data was made available and comprised:

— Solus Guinness pubs;

— Solus Murphy's pubs;

— Dual stockists of Guinness and Murphy's.

The *solus* Murphy's and Guinness volume data was not used for modelling, for the general reasons outlined in Technical Appendix 1. However, this 'solus' data was used to validate the fact that Murphy's and Guinness sales exhibited identical seasonality, and that the dual stockists exhibited the same sales pattern as the solus outlets.

For the modelling all of the data for the 216 public houses with continual dual stocking over the full period March 1993 to February 1996 were used (ie the raw sample was not edited in any way).

The advantages of using the dual stockists were:

a) Comparison of like with like where Guinness and Murphy's compete head to head (the acid test).

b) Distribution was obviously identical and therefore simplified the analysis.

There are a number of issues that need to be aired regarding the validity of using this data to represent Murphy's rate of sale for the country as a whole.

It would be erroneous to claim that the 216 dual stockists was a perfect sample, and representative across *all dimensions* of the total UK off-trade. It is, however, reasonable that this *census* of Whitbread dual stockists is a useful/valid first approximation of the on-trade.

This sample is likely to underestimate the advertising effect on the total market for Murphy's draft for the following reasons:

— The 'sample' has pubs from most TV regions, but not all. Given that the regional advertising weights were almost identical to the national picture the 'sample' is representative in terms of the advertising effect.

— The south of England is over-represented in the 'sample'. However, the regional differences in the consumption of stout are small (excluding Northern Ireland).

— The sample comprises 'mature' Murphy's stockists in that they have stocked it for at least three years, and most of the pubs much longer. Thus it is reasonable to suppose that Murphy's volume growth in this sample would be lower than in the country as a whole.

— Finally, plotting the sample stout volume against national stout volume shows a very high correlation. Thus, even though the sample is not totally representative on all dimensions, the sample does, and therefore can, be used as a strong indicator and proxy for the Guinness and Murphy's volume movements.

13

De Beers

'Hard times: selling diamonds in a recession'
(how a great British idea worked across
Europe and beyond)

INTRODUCTION

There are several reasons why this case is uniquely interesting: there is no brand *per se* and every product is a one-off over whose finished form, design, price, packaging and distribution system the client has no control.

There is a dual target audience with differing needs and motivations in 23 culturally and historically disparate countries.

Nor is this a case of a demonstrable link between advertising effectiveness and client profitability, but rather one where advertising has worked to maintain *viability* for its sponsor and *stability* for an entire industry worldwide.

We will demonstrate how a change in advertising deployment, unifying all countries under a single approach (in spite of their idiosyncrasies), during one of the worst economic recessions worldwide, worked to build shareholder and trade confidence and maintain a healthy balance between short-term sales and long-term image exclusivity among consumers.

BACKGROUND – HOW DE BEERS OPERATES

It helps to understand the process by which diamonds get to the consumer in order to appreciate the problem De Beers has in trying to influence it.

Diamonds are mined in Australia, Zaire, Botswana, Russia, South Africa, South America and Namibia. On average, 250 tons of ore have to be dug out in order to produce one carat of polished gem diamond. Mining is a long-term project, and diamond producers are not in the business of short-term profits.

Gem diamonds have no functional value whatsoever, and because they are not an essential commodity like oil, demand can be erratic. During the Great Depression, the diamond market shrank rapidly and volatility was fuelled by fear of oversupply and falling prices. Thousands of diamond miners in Southern Africa lost their jobs.

It was at this time that De Beers founded the Central Selling Organisation (CSO), which has contractual agreements with the major diamond-producing nations to purchase and value all their annual production of rough diamonds at controlled prices. This amounts to 80% of world production.

The benefits of selling their rough diamond production through De Beers gives the diamond-producing nations greater financial stability to underpin the cost of mining. The liability for De Beers is that, unless there is consumer demand for diamond jewellery (DJ), the rising cost of its stockpile could, arguably, bankrupt the company. Feeding rough diamonds into the pipeline is the start; the commercial necessity is to keep the polished product going out.

In order to generate this consumer 'pull-through', De Beers undertakes the advertising and promotion of diamond jewellery around the globe on behalf of the entire diamond industry, in close co-operation with the jewellery trade, whose representatives cut, polish, design, set and retail the finished product. It is against this imperative that we shall see how successful the advertising has been.

GLOBAL SLUMP

Hard Times Ahead

The diamond business has traditionally been inextricably tied to the economy. History shows that there is a close relationship between GDP and consumer confidence, and between consumer confidence and sales of diamond jewellery. Figure 1 shows the correlation for the world's biggest diamond market, America, which accounted for around a third of the world's gem diamond retail value, during 1979–89, just before the recession began to bite. Details are in Appendix 1, but our model shows an excellent fit of 0.97894 (a perfect fit being 1.0).

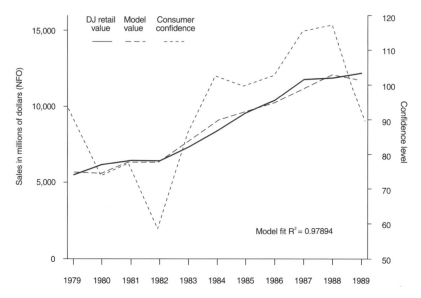

Figure 1: *Consumer confidence effect on diamond retail value USA, 1979–89*

The drop in GDP in eight markets from 1988 onwards outlined in Figure 2 typifies the widespread and severe recession.

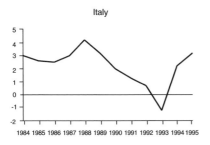

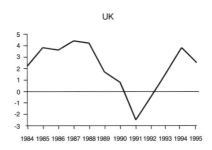

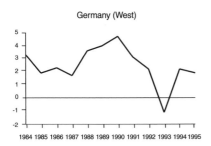

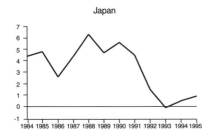

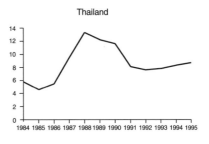

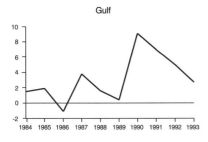

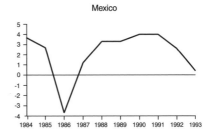

Figure 2: *Global slump – % change in GDP*
Source: International Financial Statistics Yearbook
(No data after 1993 for Mexico and Gulf)

Unlike its predecessors, this recession was not part of a regular cycle, the indications were that recovery would be slow and post-recession growth would be weak for years.

After the borrow-and-spend boom of the '80s, investors, producers and consumers strove to reduce their liabilities, and tightened their belts as the '90s began.

As Figure 3 illustrates, in 1992, Europeans were more likely to be hanging onto their savings and discretionary income. This applied to other markets also as they entered recession. People changed into more hesitant, sober purchasers, reluctant to allocate their discretionary income to anything other than essential goods and services.

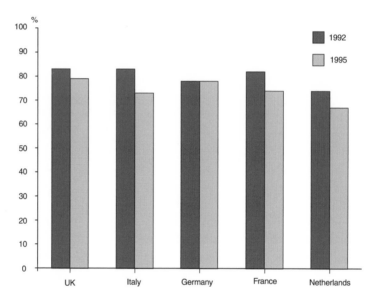

Figure 3: *Agreement with statement 'I think it is really important to save for the future'*
Source: Frontiers, Henley Centre 1995/6

As Figures 4 and 5 show, UK sales of watches and expensive cars were certainly suffering. This pattern was reflected elsewhere in the developed world.

Diamond jewellery is clearly a luxury product, by its very definition 'non-essential to one's lifestyle'. Nor is its competitive set limited to a grouping of 'other luxury goods'.

In Europe, competition ranges from the temporal (holidays), the practical (fridge freezers), the necessary (mortgage), investments, the children, social pressure (throwing a party) as well as watches (which do have 'functional alibis'), and other precious coloured stone jewellery. In the US, cubic zirconium, which looks the same to the untrained eye at a fraction of the price, is added to the list. In the East, there is major competition from gold, which serves many purposes beyond social display, both as an investment and a form of currency.

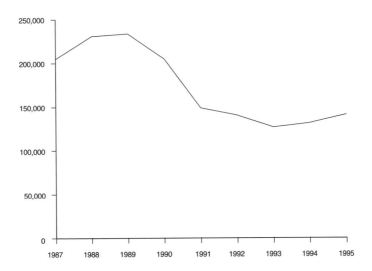

Figure 4: *UK luxury/executive car sales*
Source: Society of Motor Manufacturers and Traders

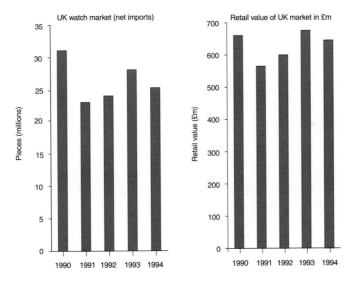

Figure 5: *Watch sales (pieces and value)*
Source: Board of Trade

There were other warning signs. Figure 6 shows the close correlation between rough diamond sales and retail sales worldwide. In 1993, rough sales fell while retail sales remained constant. This reflects the loss of confidence among industry members who started to reduce inventory. Jewellers continued to sell, but de-stocked in order to save money and reduce their liability. Had this trend continued, it would have led to reduced sales in the long term due to a combination of a reduced saliency of diamond jewellery with a more limited choice of jewellery on offer to the customer.

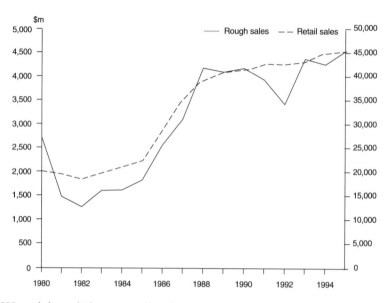

Figure 6: CSO *rough diamond sales versus world retail sales (£m) 1980–95*
Source: De Beers

De Beers therefore had to take steps to prevent the potential dramatic erosion of diamond jewellery sales and avert the long-term damage of the pipeline filling up, an ensuing oversupply and price drop, which would then affect stock prices, mining and cutting industries, jewellers' businesses and the image saliency of diamonds.

Limited Funds

De Beers spends around 0.4% of the value of world diamond jewellery sales (which includes labour costs, setting value and retail mark up) on marketing. This equates to around 4% of CSO turnover (ie rough diamond sales).

This is a considerably smaller percentage than other luxury goods advertisers, who assign 10–15% of revenue to marketing, and perfume advertisers whose budgets go as high as 25% (Source: *Economist*, January 1993).

As Figure 7 shows, there was no significant budget increase to help address the task. A cost-effective way of doing this might be to adopt Marshall MacCluhan's 'one world, one ad' policy. But could we pull it off, given the variety of cultures and religions within our market scope?

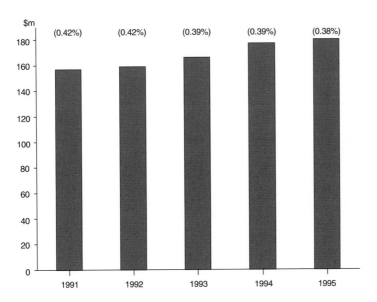

Figure 7: *De Beers worldwide marketing budget/% retail value*
Source: De Beers

BUSINESS AND ADVERTISING OBJECTIVES

The role for advertising by the CSO is to manage effectively the esteem (and value) with which diamonds are perceived around the world. It has succeeded in taking something with no functional worth, appreciated by a small minority of the elite, and turning it into something that can be enjoyed by the majority, amid the proliferation of other luxury goods. Historically, this has been achieved via the 'gift of love' positioning, and the development of diamond traditions or occasions, such as the 'Sweet Ten' anniversary ring in Japan.

The challenge is for diamonds to 'own' these occasions, to the extent that consumers believe the cash investment to be *emotionally*, rather than financially, rewarding.

Advertising is used to present the core values of diamonds (beauty, rarity, uniqueness, brilliance, purity, everlasting durability) via their emotional specialness (gift of love).

The 1992–93 business objective for De Beers' consumer marketing division was to protect sales related to core 'occasions' business segments in the face of deepening worldwide recession.

This could be achieved by one of two routes according to market development.

1. By maximising the return from the *mature* markets via consumers 'trading up' to more expensive pieces. This definition includes the UK, US and Italy, where diamond ownership is around 70%. (It is important to note that the higher the retail price, the higher the percentage of diamond content within the retail price paid. Thus, higher priced jewellery is of disproportionate importance to the diamond industry. You cannot add much more gold to a ring; you can add a lot more diamond.)

2. By growing *developing* markets via increased penetration of diamond jewellery ownership, resulting in a growth in the number of pieces sold. This 'acquisition' definition (Figure 8) includes markets like Thailand, Mexico and the Gulf where gold is strong but diamond traditions are less well established. In Thailand, for instance, penetration is a mere 5.5%, and concentrated in cities.

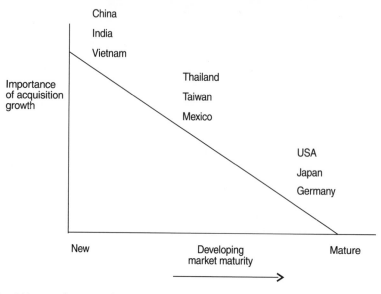

Figure 8: *Acquisition growth versus trade-up strategy definition*

CENTRAL ADVERTISING OBJECTIVES

1. To strengthen diamond jewellery's position as the ultimate gift of love in the face of a continued recession and increased competition.

2. To translate those positive attitudes into purchase behaviour.

The task ahead was huge and other factors had to be considered as we strove to identify a universal strategy.

Historical, Cultural and Religious Differences

A few examples illustrate this diversity.

Engagement
Within Europe, practices differ widely; 70% of UK couples currently buy diamond engagement rings whereas, in Germany, there is no engagement ring tradition; couples simply get married.

Marriage
In Islamic circles, bridal sets (comprising necklace, earrings, bracelet and ring) symbolise parental care and are given by both sets of parents as a nest egg for the bride.

Other Occasions
US traditions include the 'Sweet Sixteen' diamond for fathers to give their daughters in recognition of their transition to womanhood. The birth of a child is often commemorated with diamond jewellery.

Other Jewels
Japan has historically had a pearl-based jewel tradition. There was no Japanese word for diamond until the 1960s.

Other Precious Metals
In Eastern cultures, from Turkey to the Far East, everything revolves around gold as a form of security or portable wealth.

Social Changes

Diamond sales have historical links with the social traditions of marriage and celebrations, which not only vary in their significance between countries and cultures, but are themselves undergoing change. In the West, for example, family structures have loosened as marriage rates have fallen from 10 per 1,000 population in 1970 to 7 per 1,000 population in 1993. The divorce rate increased by 50% in the same period. Even the average age of the first marriage has risen from 23 to 25 years, which in turn delays childbirth.

'DIAMOND ENGAGEMENT RING' – UK

SUMMARY OF ADVERTISING CHALLENGES

— To unify all the important mature and developing countries under a single approach, flexible enough to recognise local needs.

— To identify a single powerful consumer motivation out of a turmoil of national differences, among markets as culturally, religiously, historically and economically diverse as Europe and Asia, the Gulf and the USA, Australia and South America.

— To provide executional guidance to enhance the creative idea rather than unpick it as it traversed those boundaries.

LOVE CONQUERS ALL

Developing the Creative Brief

Diamonds hold a special place in history: they have been thought to possess magical powers, fought over, even worshipped. The word 'diamond' comes from the Greek *adamas*, meaning unconquerable. The indestructibility of sparkling diamonds makes them the perfect symbol for an enduring relationship. The line 'A diamond is forever' was first penned in the US in 1947. Well established in the West, the line was being taken for granted, and without revitalisation would not stop our recession-conscious customers from putting off the purchase or trading down to a coloured (eg sapphire or ruby) stone piece. In the East, where diamond jewellery is less well established as a love symbol, the line is imbued with less romantic meaning.

Whatever the individual market idiosyncrasies, the role of diamond jewellery still came down to just one thing – that the giver wanted to express the enduring love they felt for the recipient and the joy they would feel receiving and wearing such a gift.

The universal truth that 'Love Conquers All' really is apposite for De Beers' worldwide strategy. However, we still had to find a way of expressing this in a much more powerful way.

Strategically, we had to lift diamonds above the effects of recession and put love onto a higher plane. Research indicated that if the emotion in our advertising could be 'turbo-charged', and diamonds be positioned as the *ultimate* gift of love, we could win over people's hearts before their recession-conscious minds stepped in and rationally dissuaded or 'downgraded' them.

'ANNIVERSARY RING' – SPAIN

Para un aniversario especial, sorpréndala con un diamante que supere el de sus deseos.

Un diamante es para siempre.
De Beers

Consequently, the creative teams were asked to focus on the moment of giving rather than wearing as this seemed to be the most emotionally charged (and rewarding) moment for our dual audience of giver and receiver (Figure 9). Diamonds may be ice-cold and hard but they engender a fiery passion.

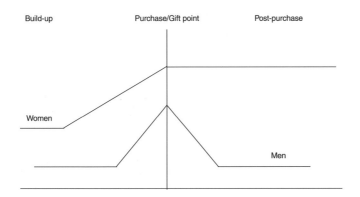

Figure 9: *The experience curve*
Source: The Qualitative Consultancy, 4 Country European Research

A Change in Media

Historically, De Beers ran predominantly women's print campaigns displaying a variety of jewellery to suit different markets' needs and budgets.

Now, the recession demanded more aggressive consumer media to successfully ratchet up the emotional response to the 'ultimate gift of love' message. We chose TV and cinema to:

— reach a broader target audience, watching 'together' as couples, and evoke a strong emotional response between them simultaneously;

— exploit the added power of moving images and sound.

The media target audience was primarily adults aged 25+, although engagement ring cinema audiences were slightly younger. Due to the length of the purchase cycle, we deployed a drip-buying policy of quality programming, where joint viewing was anticipated. This would enable us to reach high saliency levels and then maintain them.

Added (Production) Value

Each market used to produce its own print campaigns of between two and ten different executions. Photographing diamonds, especially against skin, is notoriously difficult, because they are relatively small and technically very difficult to light. Each diamond is individual and reacts to light in its own way. Print production quality was always an expensive challenge.

'BRIDAL SET' – GULF STATES

Diamonds – The gift of a lifetime.

The night of a lifetime.

Diamonds – A unique brilliance.

The everlasting symbol of happiness.

A diamond is forever.

Historically, the estimated *annual* worldwide print production budget for De Beers had been in excess of US$1.5 million.

For the switch to television, the use of new techniques with lasers and fibre-optic lighting combined with the stark contrast of shadows provided the ideal backdrop to display the scintillation of each individual stone. The production costs for the first three TV executions which ran for *over three years* were US$700,000.

Not only was the advertising more effective in communicating the appeal of diamond jewellery to a wide audience, it was also more cost effective to produce, enabling markets that would not normally warrant TV advertising to share its benefits.

The Brilliant Creative Idea – Intimate Anonymity

The power of the resultant 'Shadows' idea lies in the anonymity of the people and the setting, and the prominent showcasing of the jewellery at the musically climactic moment of giving.

This apparently simple device carries a complex raft of messages and associations. Consumer feedback about the worth, desirability and suitability of diamond jewellery emanated from a breadth of elements within the campaign, building to a whole greater than the sum of the parts.

— *The powerful music track* captured the attention, communicated drama, emotion and romance. It had all the sophistication that diamond advertising must aspire to.

— *The visual intrigue of the shadows* was involving; something to decipher and imagine.

— *The anonymity of the shadows*, while they were evidently human in form, was also mysterious, romantic and potentially ME! Race, colour, class, age are all irrelevant when you are a shadow. This was key to the cross-cultural acceptance of the communication.

— *The sophistication of black and white* stood out amidst colour commercials.

— *The story* encapsulated a relationship. Consumers wanted it to happen to them; it was simultaneously involving and aspirational.

The production technique was a *dramatic showcase* for the product; big, beautiful and highly desirable.

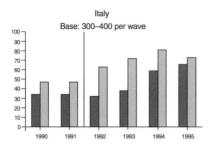

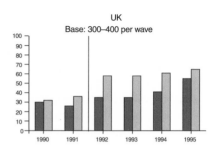

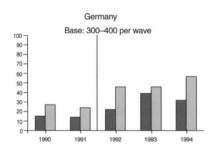

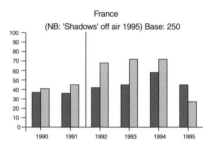

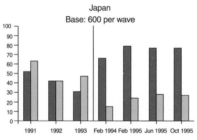

* 'Shadows' run in rotation with other copy

*Recall not asked in Thailand

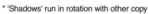

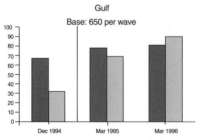

* Significant jewellers' own advertising in Gulf

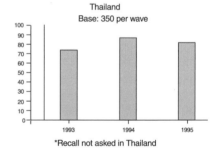

■ Advertising recall

▫ Advertising recognition

── 'Shadows' launch

Figure 10: *Advertising awareness*
Source: BTS (RI, RSL, Merac, SRG, Infoplan)

EVALUATION OF THE CAMPAIGN

Positive Consumer Response

For several years, De Beers has commissioned regular Brand Tracking Surveys (BTS), to investigate advertising awareness, diamond jewellery imagery and desirability among adult consumers in key markets.

The timing of these studies varies by market and the questionnaires are not precisely comparable. Image parameters measured in one market may differ from another. Inevitably, the perfect continuous tracking study worldwide is an unaffordable option. In order to strike the right balance between affordability, accuracy and what is needed for national marketing purposes, certain data collection adaptations are necessary.

The annual BTS ignores market seasonality and is unable to read the short-term impact of advertising. It does, however, allow rolling year-on-year data accumulation for comparison, as well being fairly sensitive to cross-border similarities and differences.

Figure 10 shows how both spontaneous advertising recall and prompted recognition of the 'Shadows' campaign has continued to build in all markets surveyed while the campaign has been on air.

Figure 11 overleaf shows the universally high 'likeability' rating of the advertising. While some marketers believe that this is a less important measurement, De Beers feels that it is a cost of entry in creating advertising to enhance the desirability of diamond jewellery, especially when you are talking about a very intimate moment in people's lives.

More evocative than these are perhaps the following quotes from a US wear-out survey by the BRS Group Inc, (March 1996):

'It's a different approach than loud, obnoxious advertising. It has good music, mysterious. I like the shadows, it tells a nice story, it's classy.'

Chicago Male, 25–39 years

'I like this advertising because my sons (aged 22 and 15) ask about diamonds and how women feel and it starts a nice discussion. My younger son is 15 and he'll come and get me and say "Look, mom, it's the diamond commercial".'

New Jersey Female, 40–54 years

Given that it takes time to effect attitude shifts, Table 1 overleaf shows how comparable attitude statements about diamond jewellery, tracked over time, by market, have remained constant or improved since 'Shadows' started.

The 'gift of love' significance has been particularly strengthened in Japan and the US, and diamonds' suitability to mark important occasions has grown in the UK, Italy and the US. Diamonds' position versus gold in the Gulf has also improved significantly.

As pointed out earlier, ownership penetration varies greatly by market, and the number of people who buy diamond jewellery in a given year is actually very small, the vast majority are simply at various stages of the buying process.

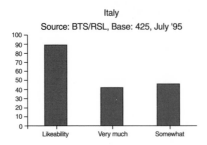

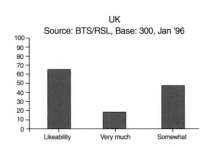

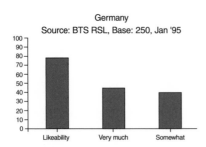

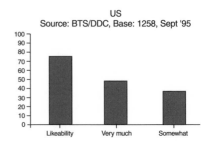

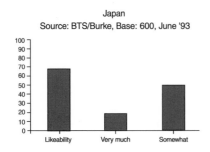

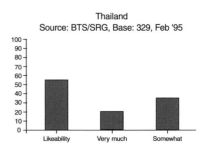

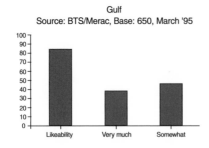

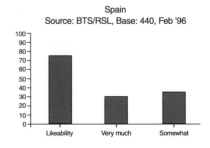

Figure 11: *Advertising likeability*

TABLE 1: ATTITUDES TO DIAMOND JEWELLERY

Germany**

% agreeing	'91 %	'92 %	'93 %	'94 %	'95 %
Ultimate gift of love	59	51	55	53	54
Best way of marking an important occasion in one's life	50	45	43	45	46
King of all precious stones	77	73	74	73	81
Worth the expense	61	62	62	69	77
Contemporary	n/a	n/a	n/a	n/a	65

Base: 300–400 per wave
Source: BTS/RSL/RI

UK**

% agreeing	'91 %	'92 %	'93 %	'94 %	'95 %
Ultimate gift of love	59	61	61	67	64
Best way of marking an important occasion in one's life	54	51	52	55	79
King of all precious stones	61	56	63	63	65
Worth the expense	66	67	65	67	67
Contemporary	n/a	n/a	n/a	n/a	52

Base: 300–400 per wave
Source: BTS/RI/RSL

Italy**

% agreeing	'91 %	'92 %	'93 %	'94 %	'95 %
Ultimate gift of love	48	47	49	50	49
Best way of marking an important occasion in one's life	54	55	58	59	74
King of all precious stones	75	74	71	76	76
Worth the expense	63	64	64	63	66
Contemporary	n/a	n/a	n/a	n/a	26

Base: 300–400 per wave
Source: BTS/RI/RSL

USA

% agreeing	'91 %	'92 %	'93 %	'94 %	'95 %
Expression of love	69	70	70	76	81
Diamonds are more beautiful than any other stone	53	56	55	59	58
Best way of marking an important occasion in one's life	52	52	47	55	61
Worth the expense	65	60	61	65	65

Base: 1,300 per year
Source: BTS, BTS/DDC

Japan*

% agreeing	'91 %	'92 %	'93 %	'94 %	'95 %
Ultimate gift of love	32	33	26	34	39
Best way of marking an important occasion in one's life	n/a	44	44	45	48
Diamonds are more beautiful than any other stone	n/a	49	49	45	61

Base: 600 per wave
Source: BTS, Infoplan

Gulf

Five point scale	Dec '94	March '95	March '96
Ultimate gift of love	3.5	3.7	n/a
Worth the expense	3.8	3.7	3.6
Every woman should have diamond jewellery	3.0	3.3	3.8
I would consider diamond jewellery over gold	2.3	3.2	4.0

Base: 650 per wave
Source: BTS/Merac

n/a   not asked
*   change in sample in 1995
**   change in research agency in 1995

Thailand

% agreeing	'94 %	'95 %	'96 %
Ultimate gift of love	57	49	57
Worth the expense	63	57	56
Contemporary	86	84	85

Base: 350 per wave
Source: BTS SRG

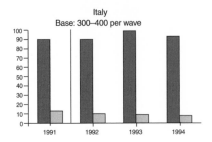

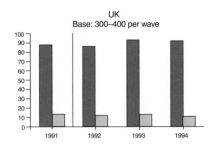

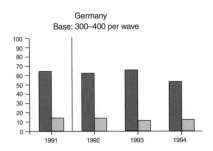

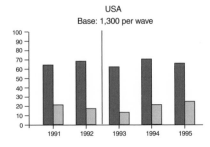

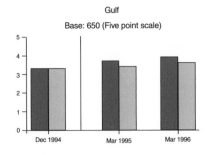

* Desirability not asked in Thailand

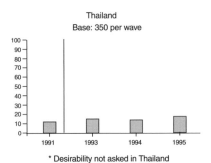

Figure 12: *Desirability of diamond jewellery*
Source: BTS (RI/RSI/Merac/Infoplan/SRG/DDC)

The challenge is to keep the 'pipeline' emptying, hence the gulf illustrated in Figure 12 between diamond desirability and likely purchase within the next 12 months.

Nonetheless, the desirability of diamond jewellery has been maintained over time and, while the incidence of people saying they are likely to acquire diamond jewellery in the next 12 months has never been large, it has suffered very little in Europe as a result of belt-tightening or postponement, and not at all in the international markets.

Diamond Acquisition Rates/Trading up

The Diamond Acquisition Survey (DAS) is also conducted regularly to monitor the acquisition of diamond jewellery and penetration of diamond jewellery ownership.

Figure 13 compares diamond jewellery acquisition rates with the average price paid, by market, over time. Since 'Shadows', acquisition decline has been arrested and average price has increased. Increased average price confirms the success of the trade-up strategy. An exception is Italy, where the research methodology changed in 1994 (which may explain the drop), and the dollar exchange has been punitive. In lira, average price has increased since the advertising began.

It should also be noted that, in Thailand, acquisition among our key target segment of women aged 25–44, rose from 6.6% to 8.05%.

Figure 14 further confirms the success of the trade-up strategy. It shows the relationship between retail value and average price. When retail value appears to have declined, but the average price has increased (or decreased to a lesser degree), this indicates that the consumer has increased the diamond content of their jewellery. Noteworthy countries are the UK, Italy, Germany and Spain.

Comparative Competitive Performance – Gold Jewellery

The World Gold Council (WGC) conducts (broadly) comparable consumer acquisition studies into the gold jewellery market, to identify shifts in purchasing behaviour and measure the volume and value of gold jewellery purchases. The data points straddle the launch of the 'Shadows' advertising in Europe.

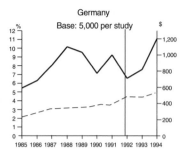

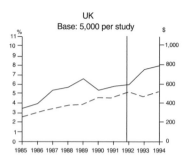

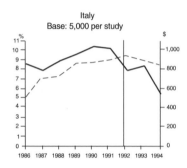

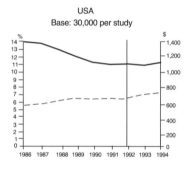

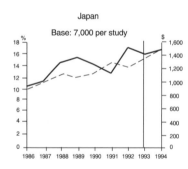

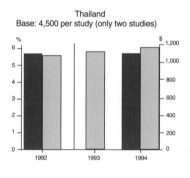

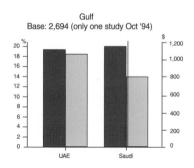

Figure 13: *Diamond acquisition rates, (past 12 months) and average price US$*
Source: DAS/BMRB

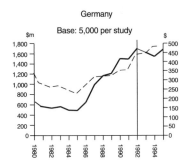

Germany

Base: 5,000 per study

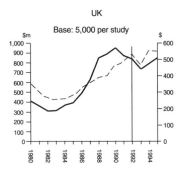

UK

Base: 5,000 per study

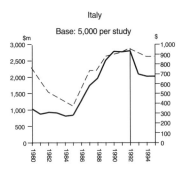

Italy

Base: 5,000 per study

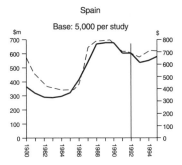

Spain

Base: 5,000 per study

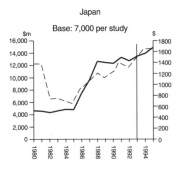

Japan

Base: 7,000 per study

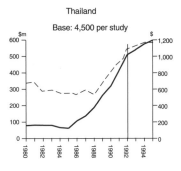

Thailand

Base: 4,500 per study

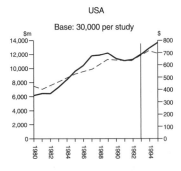

USA

Base: 30,000 per study

Start of 'Shadows'

Average price

Retail value

Figure 14: *Average price paid/total retail value US$*
Source: De Beers/DAS/BMRB

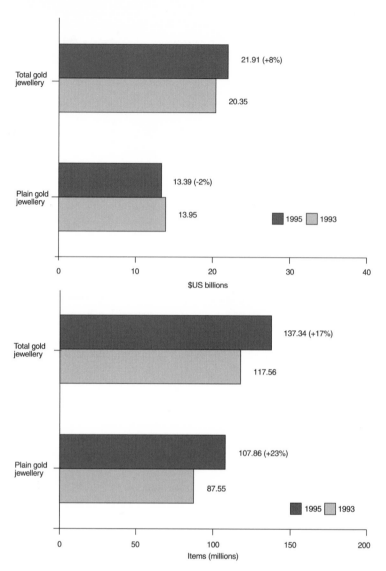

Figure 15: *European jewellery market volume and value*
Source: WGC/Research International, Gold Jewellery Consumer Acquisition Survey

Figure 15 shows the European results for total gold jewellery (plain gold and gem-set) and plain gold jewellery by market value and market volume (pieces sold).

The value of plain gold jewellery sales fell by 2% while total gold jewellery rose by 8%. In terms of pieces sold, both segments saw increases of 23% and 17% respectively. This implies that European consumers were buying more, but less expensive, plain gold pieces, while increasing their purchase of more expensive gem-set jewellery items. While WGC does not extract the diamond content within the gem-set gold jewellery, our own trade panel data tells us that four-fifths of value sales contain diamonds, and two-fifths of the pieces (Source: European Data and Research Retailer Panel, 1992–94).

Figure 16 shows that in Saudi Arabia, which accounts for 60% of Gulf gold consumption, the gold market (including bars), has grown since 1992. For gold jewellery, value growth has been in gem-set gold. Similar dramatic increases are shown for the number of pieces bought containing gems since the campaign started.

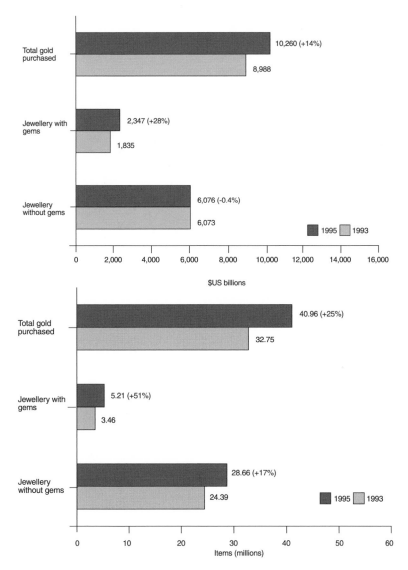

Figure 16: *Saudi Arabia gold jewellery market value and volume*
Source: WGC/Research International

The trend in the United States illustrated in Figure 17 shows that, while the campaign has been on air, total gold jewellery value (containing gems) has increased, while the number of pieces has declined, indicating trade up.

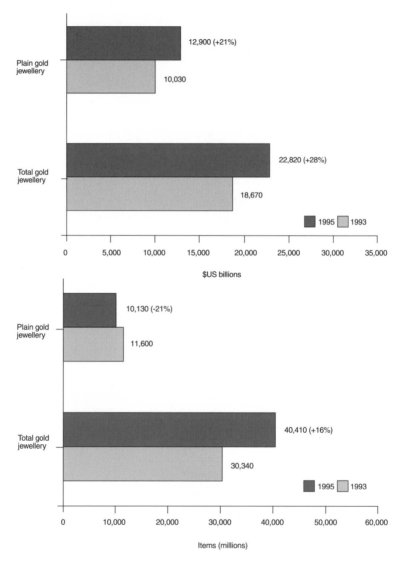

Figure 17: *USA gold jewellery market value and volume*
Source: WGC/Research International
('Shadows' started in the US in 1993)

Trade Enthusiasm and Support

As an integral part of its 'pull' marketing strategy, De Beers runs a trade association in key markets, called the 'Carat Club'. Invited members are from the leaders in the local diamond industry; retailers, designers and wholesalers.

The latest membership survey conducted at the end of 1995/early 1996, illustrates their enthusiasm for the 'Shadows' campaign, an acknowledgement from a normally grudging audience of its positive effective on their business.

UK

'It is the best campaign De Beers has ever done, with enormous benefit to the retailers. It has created an awareness for diamonds we have never seen before.'

Edward Fischgrund, Owner, County Classics, Designer/Manufacturer

'The market was in the doldrums, and people were buying on price. Ratners had created this market of "flash for cash" and the "Shadows" campaign has lifted the caratage sales quite considerably.'

Kjeld Jacobsen, MD of Argenta Design, Jeweller/Manufacturer

'We get very strong pull-through. Our diamond sales have increased and we do a broader range of designs now – the fact that consumers come up to you and ask for what they have seen on TV is evidence enough.'

Eric Smith, Designer and Retailer, 'A' store

'Had the advertising not run it would have had a negative effect on my business; the quality of the brand image has been improved and has brought in more clients.'

Nigel Salloway, Owner, Salloways Jewellers, 'B' store

GERMANY

'The De Beers campaign reaches the soul of the consumer. This is only way of selling more high-quality diamond jewellery in Germany.'

Dr Andreas Freisfeld, Owner, Cadoro Jeweller Group, 'B' store

'Right from the start, I realised that the De Beers campaign would be convincing as a concept. But I also thought that the producers would find it difficult to sell the pieces to our partner jewellers. The success of the campaign was also the success of our sales of jewellery. I am glad that I have been proved wrong.'

Dr Breuer, Managing Director, Laudier, Manufacturer

'The new campaign harmonises completely with our Classic New Designs and is especially suitable for sales of high-quality diamond jewellery. In co-operation with the trade we do everything to make the campaign a success for jewellers.'

Jurgen Leuz, Owner, Schaffrath Bros., Manufacturer

ITALY

'We have seen a 20–25% boost in sales. [Without the campaign] we would surely have seen a drop in business because the jewellery market in Italy is generally going through a tough period.'

Armando Tappa, Direttore Marketing, Blue White, Manufacturer

'The campaign has been important to us. Without it we would not have seen the increases over the years in requests for diamond jewellery – particularly "verette" anniversary rings.'

Bernadotti Bibigi, Manufacturer

'It helped to keep diamonds top-of-mind against the growing competition of other consumer goods, which would have progressively taken slices of the cake away from our market.'

Lamperti, Owner, Lamperti Jewellers, 'A' store

AUSTRALIA

'This campaign has been very noticeable and the jewellery stands out well, so much that we have received consumer enquiries and subsequent sales.'

Julian Farren Price, Owner, J Farren Price, 'A' store

'A high-class, elegant campaign that does a lot to raise the image of diamonds among consumers and gives them a range of occasions and reasons to buy.'

Cameron Marks, Percy Marks, 'A' store

USA

'We have even had people ask if we would send them the music so they could play it while proposing marriage. If that does not show impact on the consumer market I don't know what does.'

Thomas P Dorman, Executive Director of the American Gem Society

'I feel the "Shadows" campaign has increased diamond jewellery sales quite dramatically. For example, not only did our diamond engagement rings increase by 15% but the sell-through at the retail level increased a dramatic 25%. This campaign has also helped in the sale of larger centre stones which, in turn, has created higher price point sales.'

Arthur D'Annunzio, D'Annunzio and Co., Diamond Jewellery Manufacturer

'This is hard to measure but our consumer enquiries doubled between 1994 and 1995. I am sure it had to do with increased consumer interest in diamond jewellery after seeing the advertising.'

Barry Sullivan, President, Art Carved Bridal, approx 5,200 retail jewellers

'Diamond jewellery sales have grown steadily, despite the slow economy. The campaign has succeeded in underscoring the emotional and romantic symbolism of the diamond, reinforcing the reasons people buy diamond jewellery – love!'

Lynn Ramsay, President/CEO Jewellery Information Centre

MEXICO

'De Beers' advertising has influenced highly our diamond sales, since the beauty of the advertising converts the diamond jewellery piece into something more desirable. Obviously it increases sales. It makes us want to become better in our diamond inventories, in our diamond quality and our knowledge, because it gives us the security that we will sell more diamonds.'

Gloria Ceballos, Owner/Manager, Daniel e Hijos, 'A' store

'It has given prestige and image to my business, and has positioned us on the same level as all other countries.'

Javier Garcia Yturriai, Owner/Manager, Garcia Yturriai Joyeria, 'A' store

'Diamond awareness and prestige would not have been increased so strongly. It has created the need among consumers to give a diamond as a symbol of love.'

GULF

'It has created awareness among the non-believers in investing or even buying diamond jewellery. They realise that the stones are worth the money and that they are getting good value.'

Usama Alawazir, Marketing Manager, Mo'awad, Jeweller to the Royal Family, Saudi Arabia and Gulf Countries

'De Beers' "Shadows" advertising came at the right time. People were spending more money on other luxury goods and diamond jewellery sales were going down. Since the campaign, our sales of diamond jewellery have stabilised and we are now going to do a campaign on solitaires ourselves.'

Ahmed Al Mussali, Manufacturer, UAE

'The advertising has raised consumers' curiosity about diamonds. They are now more interested to come into the shop to enquire about diamonds. In the past it used to be all about gold, now more ask about diamond jewellery.'

Baksh, 'A' store, Saudi Arabia

Quantitative evidence from the US (Figure 18) shows how in 1996 De Beers' advertising took the number one slot *ahead of the economy* for the first time, in trade acknowledgement of its role as a positive influence over diamond jewellery sales.

Sales Maintained in Spite of Confidence Levels

As explained earlier, one of the key measures affecting sales of luxury goods in a recession (and diamond jewellery in particular), is consumer confidence.

Prior to and during the campaign period, consumer confidence was affected by international economic issues (like the Gulf conflict), as well as domestic ones, such as the cost of unification in Germany, or Japan's biggest companies posting their first losses combined with the effects of the Kobe earthquake.

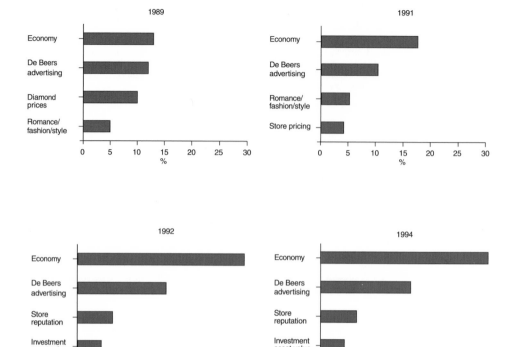

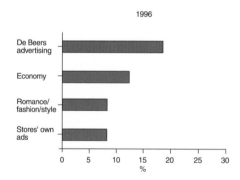

Figure 18: *Top four factors affecting US market for diamonds and diamond jewellery*
Base: 100 per wave
Sample: Independent and small chain jewellers in US
Source: De Beers/Meyers Research

Self-evident to the eye, Figure 19 shows how diamond retail value responded to the 'Shadows' advertising run during the recession in the respective countries, by bucking the despondent consumer confidence trend levels and maintaining a steady growth. The markets shown are those for which consumer confidence figures are available (ie developed markets).

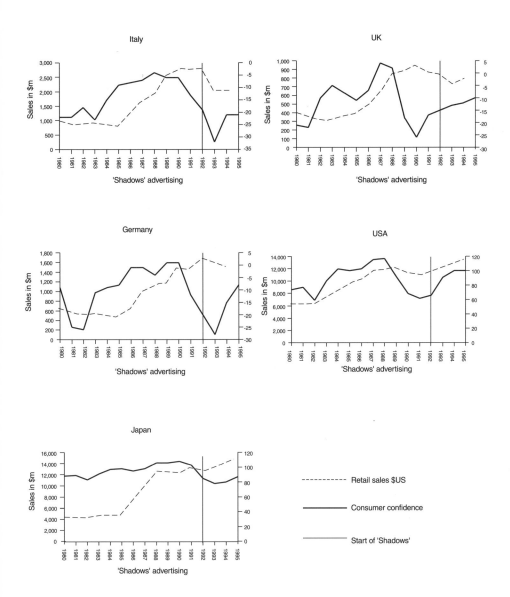

Figure 19: *Diamond jewellery sales and consumer confidence*
Sources: Sales – De Beers/RID/BMRB
Confidence: Nikkei Consumption Forecast Index (Japan), The Conference Board (US), GFK Index Konsumklima (Europe)

We then ran the model (shown in Figure 1) developed for the US forward in time to the end of 1995. Figure 20 shows that the advertising improved sales by 2% above expected levels in the first year, rising to 14% by the end of 1995. This gives us a three-year campaign average of +8% in sales, accounting for $2,715 million additional retail sales in the US for that period. As the US advertising budget for the period was $113 million, this represents a phenomenal return on investment.

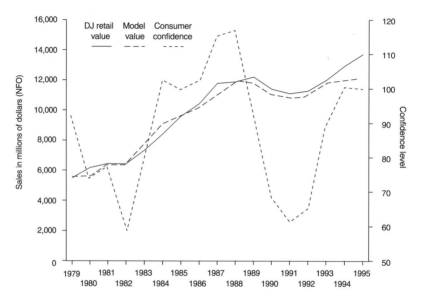

Figure 20: *US consumer confidence/diamond retail value model*

The US is too large and too mature a market to assume that the same sales response to the advertising would necessarily apply across the rest of the world. Nevertheless, the worldwide marketing spend of $558 million (80% on 'Shadows' advertising), is felt to have been well invested.

De Beers' Management Perspective

The Crisis Averted

'Despite the sluggish performance of the global economy in 1993...the combined profits of De Beers (Group) recovered by 21% to US$595 million. This satisfactory outcome owed something to the beginnings of renewed growth in retail sales. It owed far more, however, to the successful (marketing) measures taken by the CSO to restore stability and confidence to the market. The crisis that had threatened in 1992 was averted.'

Chairman's Statement, Annual Report 1993

Sales Reach New Peak

'Consumer and retail jewellery surveys suggest that the value of diamond jewellery sales worldwide increased by 5% in 1995 to a new peak. More people acquired more diamond jewellery, spent more money and bought more polished carats than ever before.'

Chairman's Statement, Annual report 1995

Advertising Does Pay

'Whatever short-term shocks we have absorbed, the long-term trend has been one of ever-increasing demand for polished diamonds...The diamond market did not "just grow". We have been involved in its development through careful and targeted stimulation by our consumer marketing division. This year we will spend about 4% of our turnover on nurturing demand for the product you sell – the polished diamond – and we think this is money well spent.'

Nicholas Oppenheimer, World Diamond Congress, Tel Aviv, 28 May 1996

Business Results

Figure 21 overleaf and Table 2 illustrate the upward trend of De Beers' business results over the period of the campaign.

TABLE 2: DE BEERS' BUSINESS RESULTS

	1992	1993	1994	1995
Rand m	1,656	2,012	2,332	2,665

De Beers consolidated mines company balance sheet

	1992	1993	1994	1995
US$m	5,685	5,839	5,886	5,879

Whole De Beers Group balance sheet

We are not arguing that advertising was the only thing affecting De Beers' business success over the last four years. There are other major factors to consider:

— the arrival of democracy in South Africa;

— the renewed trade agreement with the Russians after some period of speculation;

— the proportion of De Beers' own rough diamonds sold versus those mined by others;

— leakage of rough diamonds from Russian mines not sold through the CSO.

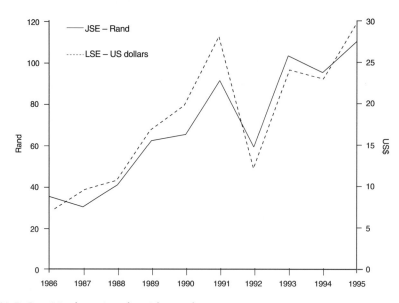

Figure 21: *De Beers joint share price at financial year end*
Source: De Beers 1995 Annual Report

It is, of course, difficult to extrapolate and quantify the impact of these economic and political factors on De Beers' business results in order to then isolate the effect of the advertising.

We believe, however, the preceding evidence from De Beers' management, global economic trends, comparative competitive performance, the jewellery retail trade and, importantly, the consumer, enable us to justify the impact that the campaign had on the diamond industry as a whole, both as a confidence builder and a sales builder, all over the world.

WHAT ELSE COULD IT HAVE BEEN?

The Sceptic's View

'Come off it. Diamonds are closely linked to the commemoration of engagements, wedding anniversaries and the birth of a child. People do not stop getting married and having children just because there is a recession on. De Beers would have sold just as many diamonds anyway.'

The close links between these 'rites of passage' have been successfully created by De Beers' advertising in the first place. But outside of the mature western markets of Europe and the US, these 'rites of passage' occasions are *not* well established, and in all markets, gold, coloured stones and cubic zirconium can represent a very viable consumer jewellery alternative.

'Own up. It's a monopoly and they control everything. Outside forces are irrelevant.'

Not so. Nobody *needs* diamonds. They serve no useful function. Diamond jewellery is not bought as an investment. The marketing challenge is to make people want it. Creating a 'pull' strategy is tough, especially during a recession. Comparable advertised items, such as watches and gold jewellery with genuine functional worth or investment value, did not fare as well.

'It's all in the exchange rate. The weak US dollar makes the whole thing look much healthier than it really is. If you did it in yen or Deutschmarks they wouldn't have made nearly so much money.'

The use of the US$ at constant exchange rates ensures better comparability, and, most importantly, diamonds are traded in US$. The domestic exchange rate in each country does vary considerably in how it fared versus the US dollar during the period reported.

A market that was particularly hit by the exchange rate was Italy, where lira sales did improve while dollar sales did not (as demonstrated in Figure 19).

'Retail sales were strong before the advertising broke, they weren't going down and they would have kept going anyway despite the drop in consumer confidence.'

De Beers was still advertising using local creative work at that time, which was presumably having some impact. However, there is usually a lag between consumer confidence and sales, both in terms of decline and recovery. The power of the 'Shadows' campaign meant that sales did not follow the decline of consumer confidence but instead remained steady. This in turn encouraged the trade to stop de-stocking, start building up inventory again and offer the consumer more enticing jewellery pieces.

'So what's the payback? They spent $560 million, what did they get?'

It is impossible to calculate the exact financial impact the advertising has had on the health of the diamond industry as a whole, and De Beers' profitability in particular. However, failure to increase sales in this instance was simply not an option. While diamonds are not brands, the evidence is that the advertising has had a positive attitudinal and emotional impact against all audiences, and this in turn has been reflected in sales stability.

'The Asian economy never went into recession, in fact, the reverse. Those markets kept the whole thing buoyant.'

Japan had a deep recession. Hong Kong has 1997 to worry about. Other Asian markets are not strong diamond markets but are emerging.

In 1994, the East Asia region accounted for only 17% of rough sales and, while this has almost doubled since 1980 (see Figure 22 overleaf), its growth has been gradual over the entire period.

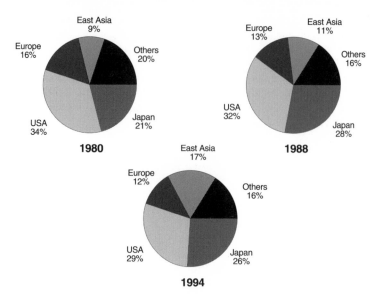

Figure 22: *Advertised markets diamond value share*

ESTIMATING ADVERTISING CONTRIBUTION

Short Term – Linking Advertising to Retail Sales

The advertising has helped to separate the diamond industry's fortunes from the vicissitudes of consumer confidence levels, and maintain overall diamond jewellery market value stability (Figure 23). It has done this by:

— causing 'trade up' (in mature markets) by raising the average price paid, due to increased diamond content within the jewellery;

— building penetration in developing markets;

— creating/reinforcing diamond occasions;

— making strong partners of the jewellery trade;

— reassuring investors of the potential of the diamond market.

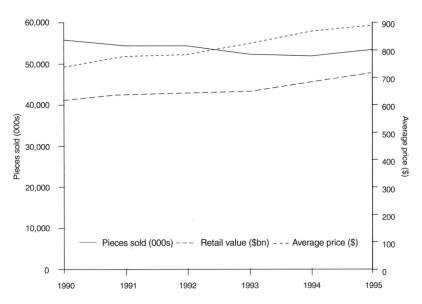

Figure 23: *World market for diamond jewellery*
Source: De Beers/DAS/BMRB

Long Term – Maintaining Image Saliency

The campaign has maintained (in some markets increased) the desirability of diamonds among consumers. The benefits of this will be manifest in future sales as they pass along the 'purchase pipeline'.

In image terms, we have made diamonds more special than gold and other precious gems, and reinforced their role as the ultimate gift of love, to help ensure that 'it' really is forever.

Overall, the campaign has scored highest-ever advertising awareness, recall and likeability for any campaign De Beers has ever run. The finished films have achieved extremely high McCollum Spielman pre-test scores in the US (Table 3) and strong stand-out in Europe (Table 4).

TABLE 3: McCOLLUM SPIELMAN TESTS,
'SHADOWS' CAMPAIGN AVERAGE

	Normative data %	Previous highest %	'Shadows' %
Clutter/awareness	40	44	46
Main idea	29	33	36
Purchase interest	46	50	55

TABLE 4: ADVERTISING IMPACT IN EUROPE

% agreeing	UK (498)	Germany (401)	Italy (508)
It's different from other ads	73	74	84
It is attention grabbing	66	70	71
It is one of the best ads I have seen recently	32	38	49

THE FUTURE

Given the success to date, we are actively looking at a number of potential developing diamond markets – Vietnam, Argentina and Colombia – and the suitability of 'Shadows' to run there. We have launched 'Shadows' in Turkey this year, and continue to investigate other Middle Eastern markets such as Lebanon, Syria and Egypt. We are currently conducting a pilot advertising programme in Russia.

Thus, the De Beers 'Shadows' campaign continues to demonstrate its flexibility and adaptability to be effective in a wide variety of very different cultures, while promoting a range of diamond products in just about every market in the world.

APPENDIX 1

Countries where 'Shadows' has Run

EUROPE

Germany	Austria
Holland	Belgium
France	Italy
UK	Spain
Turkey	

INTERNATIONAL

USA	Canada
Thailand	Mexico
Kuwait	Japan
Brazil	UAE
South Africa	Saudi Arabia
Philippines	Australia
Russia	Oman

APPENDIX 2

Technical Model

In order to isolate the effect of consumer confidence on retail value we have run a regression analysis over the period 1979–89, taking retail value as the dependent and consumer confidence as the independent, and taking out the underlying trend of market growth over the decade. The model shows an almost perfect fit of 0.97894. We then ran the model forward in time to the end of 1995.

Date	Confidence	Retail value $	Model prediction of retail value	Difference (Index)
1979	91.9	5,485	5,583	
1980	73.8	6,174	5,622	
1981	77.4	6,450	6,361	
1982	59.0	6,426	6,390	
1983	85.7	7,330	7,873	
1984	102.3	8,400	9,030	
1985	100.0	9,577	9,578	
1986	102.6	10,407	10,284	
1987	115.2	11,773	11,313	
1988	116.8	11,877	11,987	
1989	91.5	12,194	11,794	
1990	68.5	11,397	11,053	
1991	61.6	11,101	10,831	
1992	65.9	11,274	10,969	
1993	90.6	11,984	11,765	102
1994	100.0	12,928	12,068	107
1995	100.0	13,704	12,068	114
		38,616	35,901	108

14

Ross Harper
Creating a legal precedent

IN A NUTSHELL

This is a simple story of bravery and rewards. It is about the initiative taken by our client, Ross Harper, to be the first in Scotland to advertise Legal Aid on television; and to make commercials of a kind that were revolutionary for the legal sector.

And it is about the returns that followed: £600,000+ of fee income, representing a payback on advertising investment in excess of 700%.

WE PLEAD POVERTY

Almost all of the modest budget (£82,500) was needed to air the campaign, so we could afford only a limited amount of consumer research to develop and evaluate it. We made the most of published information and opinion to make the case for advertising. We filmed our own advertising demo using agency staff which we then explored in creative development research to help us understand how best to exploit the opportunity. Evaluation relies mostly on the direct response results themselves and on the elimination of other possible factors, and is supported by a qualitative analysis of the advertising.

BUT FIRST THINGS FIRST

What is Ross Harper?

Ross Harper is a legal firm operating out of 11 branches in high streets throughout West Central Scotland. It is market leader with £3.3 million of Legal Aid business. The firm deals almost exclusively in the private (ie consumer) sector, with no interest in corporate or company law.

STARTING OUT IN ADVERTISING

In 1988 the legal profession in Scotland was allowed to advertise its services for the first time. Ross Harper was one of the first firms to do so, running 'limited' campaigns in the consumer press to raise name awareness.

While possessed of a marketing and advertising mindset, Ross Harper did not and does not have dedicated marketing personnel. The advertising budget is fought for each year and is only available from the business generated by the previous year's marketing activity.

Yet in 1994 – the period on which this case study is based – the firm had the bravery to almost double its advertising spend and to dedicate it to TV. What lay behind this decision?

BECOMING A 'FULL-ON' ADVERTISER

As the 'original legal advertiser', Ross Harper had always, arguably, had a propensity to believe in the power of advertising. It led the company to consider if becoming a serious advertiser could accelerate its growth. More specifically, could advertising help it meet its stated business objective: to achieve £500,000 of fee income from the advertising budget – essentially a six-fold return on investment.

CHECKING OUT THE OPPORTUNITY

Legal Aid was becoming an increasingly significant sector, growing from approximately £59 million in 1989/90 to approximately £109.5 million in 1992/93 and predicted to reach £139.6 million in 1996/97. (Source: Scottish Legal Aid Board.)

The firm already had a meaningful share of that sector.

If any legal firm were in pole position to dominate the sector, it was surely Ross Harper.

Its distribution network was consistent with the socio-economic profile of Legal Aid users. Not only that, just under 10% of the male population of West Central Scotland corresponded to the Legal Aid user profile. (Source: TGI.)

It was the only player to have consistently, albeit modestly, advertised and its branch network was the largest against the intended target audience.

So, there was a good fit between market opportunity and client expertise, between audience availability and branch accessibility.

COULD ADVERTISING HELP EXPLOIT THE OPPORTUNITY?

It seemed likely. The potential universe was already sufficiently large and getting larger; the competition seemed unlikely or unable to outspend us; and there were no 'product' or service problems that could undermine any advertising communications.

So, the role for our advertising would be to steal share away from competitors by raising our voice above theirs and communicating the right message. We decided to explore if and how we could motivate a) new users and b) repeat users of Legal Aid, to use Ross Harper instead of the competition.

To this end we conducted research with people who had used or might use Legal Aid for one or both of its two principal uses: cases of divorce/domestic violence and criminal cases.

DEVELOPING THE ADVERTISING STRATEGY

Research showed that consumer understanding of what Legal Aid is and whom it is for, needed to be improved. Most of our potential *new users* perceived that Legal Aid was for criminal cases only and not civil (eg divorce); that it was not free but subsidised; that it was complicated to access; and that it was intended for extreme cases/hardened criminals – ie 'not for me'. These misperceptions meant that many potential users of 'civil' Legal Aid – ie people who could choose whether or not to use a lawyer – were staying out of the market.

Thus it was vital to communicate the range (not just criminal but also civil) of Legal Aid applications; that it is free; that it is easy to access; and that it is relevant to 'people like you'.

Our potential *repeat users*, who tend to be 'criminal' users, were already initiated into the system and knew that it was both free and easy to access. They tended to be less aware, however, that it could also be used for civil cases. But the real advertising task against this group of people was to differentiate Ross Harper from the plethora of competition and position the firm as 'the best help you can get when you're in a tough spot'.

Many repeat users have long-established relationships with their lawyers, and often invest him/her with totemic values; that is, they perceive most lawyers as competent but perceive their own particular lawyer as having a special gift, being a lucky mascot, someone who understands and empathises with them while also playing the role of legal heavy hitter.

We knew that it would be difficult to break this bond. However, research gave us the key. Many repeat users perceive that they are lucrative for their lawyers and that they are just as important to their lawyer as their lawyer is to them. Some of them believe that their lawyers begin to take them for granted and do not try as hard as they once did to 'get a result'. While some did not want to rock the boat, others sensed their own power and seemed willing to use it.

'My previous solicitor would have thrown me to the wolves, he wasn't interested anymore.'

Male, Criminal Legal Aid user

'I'd made him too much money, my file was getting thicker and thicker, he sort of went through the motions.'

Male, Criminal Legal Aid user
Source: The Morgan Partnership Qualitative, 1993

We knew that they prized 'trying harder' and 'pulling out all the stops' very highly and, if they felt this had deteriorated in their own lawyer, then this was the way in for the advertising.

The potential user of advice regarding divorce or protection from domestic violence is in some ways a different kettle of fish. S/he is not afraid of the system but of another individual. But s/he too needs a champion.

We argued that we could address first-time and repeat users of Legal Aid within the same campaign, as well as civil and criminal users. We had learned that, while different emphases were appropriate for different people, a commonality of emotional experience unified them. They all felt extremely anxious and vulnerable at the critical moment, and above all wanted to be rescued and protected by the most dedicated and 'sussed' lawyer.

> 'They've got to keep chasing things up, hounding people – they're all you've got, you're in their hands.'
>
> Female, Civil Legal Aid user

> 'Often they don't tell you what's going on, you're wondering what's happening, it can go on for months. You want to feel he's right on top of it, he knows what to do.'
>
> Male, Criminal Legal Aid user
> Source: The Morgan Partnership Qualitative, 1993

The anxiety and vulnerability surrounding the situation were exactly the leverage we needed to demonstrate Ross Harper as the antidote: the firm to call on when you need your anxiety to be alleviated and your vulnerability defended.

Moreover, by rooting the creative idea in the emotional drama experienced by the individual, we would create compelling identification between the individual who was experiencing difficulties at that time and the advertising. We would also set up powerful emotional memories that could be triggered if an individual found him- or herself in difficulties in the future. In both cases the Ross Harper name would have to be inextricably linked with the resolution, or implied resolution, of those difficulties.

COULD ROSS HARPER AFFORD TO EXPLOIT THE OPPORTUNITY?

The available annual budget for 1994 was £82,500. Prior use of television in 1993 had been encouraging, and further analysis supported the recommendation that TV become the lead medium:

— We could buy exactly the audience we were seeking to target.

— We could do so with sufficient impact and weight on the available budget.

— We could own the medium since it was, and seemed likely to remain, competitor-free.

— This was the medium best suited to dramatising the highly charged situations in which Legal Aid services are often required.

— The medium's 'living room' domain would help our audience perceive Ross Harper as an accessible legal firm.

— The medium's status and credibility would help reassure people in an anxious state of mind that Ross Harper was good enough to represent them.

So, we had satisfied ourselves that we could afford to exploit the market opportunity with the right medium.

At this stage 'bravery' metamorphosed into 'courage of conviction': we took the entire budget and invested every single pound in television.

SUMMARY OF OBJECTIVES AND STRATEGY

The Marketing Objective

— To increase fee income by £500,000.

The Advertising Objectives

— To increase new users of Ross Harper Legal Aid by a) stealing repeat users from other Legal Aid providers and b) gaining first-time users.

— To increase new users for both civil and criminal business.

— To stimulate calls to Ross Harper via its freephone number.

The Advertising Strategy

— Position Ross Harper as the Legal Aid Gold Standard by demonstrating the firm's ability and determination to provide help that works when you need it most.

The Proposition

'Ross Harper: The helping hand for a drowning man (or woman)'

'GET YOURSELF A GOOD LAWYER'

You're under arrest...

In here, Sir...

We're going to charge you...

Is there anyone you would like us to contact?

I can't stand it anymore...

You better get yourself a good lawyer...

THE COMMERCIALS

Three 10-second commercials were developed. Each cameo focused on the critical moment when the need for legal help becomes urgent:

— when a woman has had 'enough' and wants to start divorce proceedings;

— when someone is 'lifted' doing the (criminal) deed;

— when someone is asked by a police officer, 'Is there anyone you want us to contact for you?'

A 30-second composite of the above was also developed.

Cinema Verité was the genre: the commercials were duotone videos shot with a hand-held camera. The sense of intimidation and anxiety is palpable. The need for help and protection is all too real.

Law Society regulations forbid claims of superiority. We managed, nevertheless, to secure approval for the strapline, *'You better get yourself a good lawyer'*, for the 30-second commercial.

The freephone number (0800 11 12 13) appeared at the end of each commercial, as did the line, *'Legal Advice is Free'*.

The commercials cost £24,000 to produce but were financed from the 1993 budget. Scotland had never before seen such dramatic and hard-hitting advertising for a firm of lawyers.

THE 0800 NUMBER

This service is staffed 24 hours a day, seven days a week, 365 days a year. This means that potential clients can have access to help literally whenever they need it.

It also means that we can get a clear reading of the effects of the campaign by comparing call levels (that result in appointments) in and out of campaign periods.

THE MEDIA STRATEGY

We have already made the case for television: powerful messages on a powerful medium. Here we shall consider the media buying strategy.

Our strategy was to use the force of the opponent against himself. The way in which we were obliged to buy our television airtime was actually in our best interests. So, we were able to get the price, and hence the volume, as well as the profile that we wanted.

The demographics of applicants for Legal Aid have been defined as outlined in Table 1.

TABLE 1: TARGET AUDIENCE

	%
Male	89
16–30 years old	76
Single	84
Unemployed	76
Earnings below £135.00 p/w	92

Source: The Scottish Office Central Research Unit, 1994

The best translation of this definition into television research data (BARB) produced a primary audience of C2DE Men Not in Full-Time Employment (MNFT).

For television buying purposes it was to our advantage to declare an audience of all adults. While this covered off women (and men) in matrimonial disputes, we were also able to exploit the viewing levels and patterns of C2DE MNFT.

Exploiting the Suitability of Television

STV is watched by the vast majority of Ross Harper's potential clients, and the Strathclyde region, which makes up about 75% of the STV transmission area, recorded the highest number of crimes and offences in Scotland in 1994. (Source: The Scottish Office, 1995.)

The profile of viewers in the STV area, compared to the rest of the UK, shows high indices for C2DE MNFT.

TABLE 2: PROFILE OF STV VERSUS NETWORK

Men	Network %	STV %	Index
AB	20.0	16.0	80
C1	26.9	26.0	97
C2	25.9	23.6	91
D	15.9	19.5	123
E	11.4	14.9	131
Working	62.6	59.2	95
Not working	37.4	40.8	109

Source: BARB

What is more, the weight of viewing by our audience is 4% above the average for all adults, and the actual airtime for the campaign then outperformed this natural bias by a further 11%.

TABLE 3: ACTUAL RATING CONVERSION STV C2DE MNFT
TVRS VERSUS ALL ADULT TVRS INDICES

All brands	Ross Harper
104	115

Source: BARB/DDS

Exploiting the Local Rate Card

The STV local rate card works in Ross Harper's favour, in that certain daypart segments, ie night- and daytime, are not heavily demanded by all adult brands, but can be used to target C2DE MNFT.

On the local rate card the agency should have less control over exactly where the spots are transmitted in a daypart segment. However, certain programmes were identified as having a high rating conversion for C2DE MNFT, and this influenced the approach the agency used to exploit airtime to its fullest potential.

Programming

Despite the fact that the local rate card is designed to afford us almost no control over our precise airtime allocation, the agency achieved transmissions in programmes which would not only be complementary to the Ross Harper commercials, but which also had above average conversions to the C2DE MNFT target audience. The appropriateness of these programmes, both in terms of their content and audience, was an important part of maximising the impact of the campaign. A selection of these programmes is as follows:

— *The Bill*;

— *The Chief*;

— *Prisoner Cell Block H*;

— *The Knock*;

— *Police Stop*.

In addition, spots were bought in the *Early Evening News*, *News at Ten* and *Scotland Today*, all of which converted well, quite possibly due to the fact that Ross Harper clients were checking to see whether they were personally mentioned!

HOW MUCH WE SPENT, WHEN

It was decided to concentrate resources in four intense bursts: one in February, one in April, one in September and one in November. These timings were chosen to coincide with historical business peaks.

TABLE 4: CAMPAIGN BURSTS

Month	Period of advertising 1994	Spend (£)	Adult TVRs
February	27 Jan– 20 Feb	28,026	626
March			
April	15–30 April	16,742	313
May			
June			
July			
August			
September	1–18 Sept	22,297	338
October			
November	1 –15 Nov	15,811	276
Total		82,876	1553

Sources: BARB/DDS, The Morgan Partnership

AUDIENCE DELIVERY

The campaign delivery exceeded forecast, converting very well indeed against our primary audience of C2DE MNFT.

TABLE 5: TELEVISION CAMPAIGN VERSUS ALL TIME, STV, 1994

Segment	All time daypart delivery			Ross Harper daypart delivery		
	Adults %	C2DE MNFT %	Index conversion on TVRs	Adults %	C2DE MNFT %	Index conversion on TVRs
Coffee	5	4	86	6	6	103
Daytime	10	8	86	16	15	104
Pre-peak	10	11	113	12	15	140
Early peak	29	30	107	28	31	130
Late peak	34	35	106	33	29	103
Post-peak	9	9	105	3	2	80
Night-time	3	3	106	2	2	129
Total			104			115

Source: BARB/DDS

WHAT THE CAMPAIGN ACHIEVED

Our key method of evaluation is measuring calls (that resulted in appointments) made to Ross Harper on the 0800 number, as its exposure is confined to television activity and local *Yellow Pages* directories. The 0800 number had no other advertising exposure.

We would ask the reader to bear in mind our earlier plea of poverty, which meant that other quantitative measures were simply not affordable.

But, is there actually any more valid an evaluation of advertising response levels than data collected in this way?

During the period 1 January–30 December 1994, the total number of appointments made on the 0800 number was 2,320, representing an average cost of

£35.56 per appointment. Of all appointments made, 75% were actually executed and 95% of these executed appointments actually converted to business.

We feel justified in including appointments made outside the four TV bursts as the 'gestation period' (from seeing the advertising to finding oneself in a situation that requires Legal Aid), can take some time.

The high conversion rate of appointments to actual business means that the audience targeted by the TV advertising was the audience responding; people outside that audience would probably not have qualified for Legal Aid and Legal Aid business would not have been generated.

Even if we confine ourselves to appointments generated in TV-advertised months alone, we can see from Figure 1 that the pattern of response mirrors exactly the pattern of advertising spend.

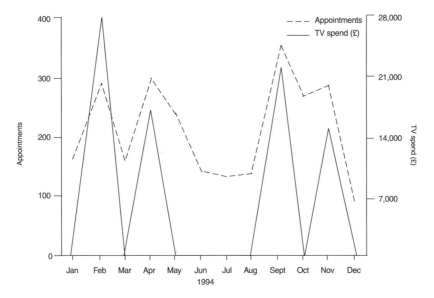

Figure 1: *Appointments generated versus TV spend*
Sources: Ross Harper; The Morgan Partnership

A total of 1,228 appointments was generated by the four TV bursts, distributed as shown in Table 6.

TABLE 6: APPOINTMENTS GENERATED

Month of TV burst	Appointments
February	293
April	297
September	351
November	287

Source: Ross Harper

The 1,228 appointments generated in the TV-advertised months February, April, September and November, represent 53% of the total 2,320 appointments generated over the year. In other words, a third of the year yielded just over half the annual appointments.

What is more, the average number of appointments generated in a TV-advertised month was 307, compared with an average of 136 for each non-advertised month. So, each TV-advertised month was on average 125% more productive than its non-advertised counterpart.

Assessment undertaken by our client reveals that the aggregate fee income for all the cases generated by the 0800 number during 1994 was in excess of £600,000 (or £350 per case), representing a payback factor of over 7.2.

Although this case history is restricted to results that we have been able to measure, it is reasonable to hypothesise that:

1. The advertising activity generates business from non-Legal Aid clients.

2. The advertising activity stimulates contact with Ross Harper by means other than the 0800 number.

WHAT ELSE, APART FROM ADVERTISING, COULD HAVE PRODUCED THESE RESULTS?

We will look at each of the likely candidates in turn.

1. *Yellow Pages.*

2. Price.

3. Distribution.

4. Seasonality.

5. Competitor advertising.

6. Growth in crime and Legal Aid applications.

Yellow Pages

This is a theoretical but unlikely factor. The 0800 number did appear in *Yellow Pages* as well as on TV. Appointments that were driven by *Yellow Pages* were not monitored and we cannot therefore separate these out from TV advertising-driven appointments. However, given the sharp increases in appointments at the exact times of the TV advertising, people who may have found the number in *Yellow Pages* were almost certainly prompted to do so by the TV advertising.

Price

This was not a factor. Price is, by definition, irrelevant to Legal Aid users. Moreover, it was not easier in 1994 to qualify for Legal Aid than in previous years, so there were not more people suddenly in the market. (Source: Scottish Legal Aid Board.) Legal Aid rates were frozen at this time (1993–94). (Source: Scottish Legal Aid Board.) In other words, Ross Harper Legal Aid income did not increase due to an increase in hourly rates.

Distribution

This was not a factor either. Ross Harper had the same number of 'shops' throughout 1994 as it had in 1993.

Seasonality

We have looked at seasonality of recorded crime over three years (1993, 1994 and 1995). The peak months are April/May/June and the trough months are October/November/December. We can see from Table 7 that appointments generated for Ross Harper during the corresponding months outperformed the market.

TABLE 7: SEASONALITY OF RECORDED CRIME VERSUS ROSS HARPER APPOINTMENTS, % VARIANCES VERSUS ANNUAL AVERAGES

	April/May/June	October/November/December
Recorded crime	+3.1	-1.6
Appointments for Ross Harper	+5.7	+1.2

Sources: The Scottish Office, Ross Harper

Competitor Advertising

Ross Harper was the only West Central Scotland firm of solicitors to advertise on TV during 1994:

TABLE 8: SOLICITORS ADVERTISING ON TV IN 1994

Firm	£ spend	Adult TVRs
Ross Harper	93,702	1,553
Gordon Thomson (Edinburgh)	19,017	210

Source: BARB/DDS

As far as press advertising is concerned, we can see that this was of a very small volume indeed.

TABLE 9: SOLICITORS ADVERTISING IN SCOTTISH PRESS IN 1994

Firm	£ spend
Digby Brown & Co	1,977
Neill Clerk Solicitors	590

Source: Register MEAL

Growth in Recorded Crime and Legal Aid Applications

We can see from Table 10 below that recorded crime in Scotland actually decreased by 3% during 1993 and 1994.

TABLE 10: RECORDED CRIME IN SCOTLAND

1990	1991	1992	1993	1994
535,864	592,774	589,562	543,013	527,064

Source: The Scottish Office, 1995

This is inconclusive evidence, however. While cases of recorded crime decreased, it is not known whether numbers of charges brought by the police actually increased or decreased.

If we turn to Criminal Legal Aid applications, we see an increase of 7% during 1993/4–1994/95.

TABLE 11: APPLICATIONS FOR CRIMINAL LEGAL AID IN SCOTLAND

1990/1	1991/2	1992/3	1993/4	1994/5
70,885	78,437	69,714	66,529	71,401

Source: The Scottish Legal Aid Board, 1995

However, while the Legal Aid applications market grew by 7%, Ross Harper's Legal Aid business grew by a greater factor.

Indeed, Ross Harper is far and away the top Legal Aid earner. Over £1.5 million separates the firm from its nearest competitor.

TABLE 12: THE TOP TEN EARNERS

Position	Firm	1995/96 £	1994/95 £
1	Ross Harper	3,342,356	3,316,806
2	Bruce Short & Co	1,379,641	1,622,307
3	Ian McCarry	1,233,680	1,385,988
4	George Mathers & Co	1,191,577	1,184,485
5	More & Co	1,154,260	1,707,959
6	Drummond Miller	1,145,386	992,831
7	Blair & Bryden	1,101,305	1,222,292
8	Gilfedder McInnes	1,093,197	1,123,296
9	Adams	1,064,015	998,055
10	Robert Kerr	1,036,861	974,405

Source: The Scottish Legal Aid Board

HOW DID THE ADVERTISING WORK?

We had intended that the advertising should work by persuading people that Ross Harper was their best hope of effective legal help. We conducted qualitative post-campaign research to explore if and how the target audience's take-out from, and attitudes to, the commercials were in line with our intentions.

These comments from the research speak for themselves:

'I've seen Ross Harper advertising. It's saying, "Are you in trouble? Help is at hand". '

Female, Civil Legal Aid user

'They're good (the commercials), they're true, that's what like it is (in a police station). You're happier knowing that your solicitor knows where you are and is trying to get you out.'

Female, Civil Legal Aid user

'You just want to get out – that ad on the telly's got it right.'

Male, Criminal Legal Aid user

'Ross Harper is one of the best, you need a lawyer who's tough – 'cos the situation you're in can be intimidating...on the TV they're saying "Don't worry, we're coming".'

Male, Criminal Legal Aid user
Source: The Morgan Partnership Qualitative, 1995

CONCLUSION

Ross Harper created a legal precedent by being the first in Scotland to advertise Legal Aid on television and by making commercials of a kind that were revolutionary for the legal sector.

The total budget of £82,500 was spent on TV.

The campaign generated fee income in excess of £600,000 which was more than 20% greater than the ambitious objective set, and represents a payback factor of 7.2 on the advertising investment.

The story that started in bravery ended with rewards.

The Defence rests.

We have sought to prove beyond reasonable doubt that it was not the butler, but the advertising that done it!

Section Three

Advertising over the longer term

15

Barclaycard

'Put it away Bough'

THE ARGUMENT

In 1990, important changes were taking place in the UK credit card market, threatening the position of the two dominant brands. This story is of how Barclaycard survived, and profited from, these upheavals – unlike Access which, without decisive management and effective advertising support, significantly declined.

Barclaycard reversed a declining share trend, achieved brand leadership, enhanced profitability, and established itself as a premium brand in an increasingly commoditised market. While a number of marketing activities together contributed to this success, the new advertising campaign, started in 1991, has been crucial in strengthening the brand's position. Also, a model shows that the advertising has already paid for itself in revenue from increased card turnover.

CREDIT CARDS IN THE UK BEFORE 1990

To understand how the market was changing by 1990, we first review briefly some earlier history.

Barclaycard was launched in 1966, the UK's first credit card. It was followed seven years later by Access, managed by a consortium of four other banks. For many years, these two brands dominated the market[1] between them.

Originally, Barclaycard and Access created their own retailer networks. After a few years, however, in order to extend their coverage abroad, each became part of a global network: Barclaycard with VISA, Access with MasterCard.

While this was a necessary move, it also helped open the market to competition. Now retailers would accept any VISA or MasterCard, new entrants to the market did not have to create their own networks; they simply made an agreement with VISA or MasterCard. Other VISA cards, like TSB Trustcard, began to appear.

---

1. An alternative product, the charge card, was available from American Express and Diner's Club. Charge cards were targeted at high earners who would pay off all charges each month, as well as a significant annual fee. Credit cards offered extended credit, and were free (before 1990); credit card issuers made their money primarily from the interest on outstanding balances.

Nevertheless, Barclaycard and Access continued to dominate the market during the 1970s and 1980s, supported by famous, heavyweight advertising campaigns.[2] Meanwhile, the total UK credit card market continued to grow:[3]

TABLE 1: CREDIT CARD GROWTH 1974–88

Index 1974 = 100	1974	1977	1980	1983	1986	1989
Number of cards	100	110	200	260	370	410
Real turnover	100	120	210	430	920	1,520

Source: Barclaycard

THE SITUATION IN 1990

By 1990, elements of this picture were changing in ways which threatened both Barclaycard and Access.

Market Growth Plateaued

Card penetration levelled at around 32% – most of those whom card issuers regarded as sound credit risks had now got a card (or had decided they did not want one).

The Number of Visa Cards Available in the UK Increased

By 1989 there were more than 30 cards available. Meanwhile, a potential threat to the whole credit card category emerged in 1987 – the debit card.[4] And, despite the talk of a 'cashless society', ATMs (cash machines) mean cash is now easier to get hold of than ever – it still accounts for 90% of transactions.

The Beginning of the Recession

Not only was money tight, but people were conscious of financial difficulties associated with 'credit'.

---

2. Barclaycard used Dudley Moore and then, for nine years, Alan Whicker, who demonstrated the card's global acceptability. Access created the animated card, the well known 'flexible friend'.
3. Market growth was driven by increasing overall card penetration, and later by increasing retailer acceptability, which stimulated greater usage.
4. With a debit card, funds are immediately transferred electronically to the payee's bank account. While this has the disadvantage, relative to credit cards, of no interest-free period before payment is required, it appeals to people who prefer to make payments immediately in order to feel more in control of their finances. So, although debit cards have positioned themselves as a replacement for cheques, the fact that it is a plastic card, and works in a similar way to a credit card at the point of sale, makes it attractive to those customers who are reluctant to use credit cards because of the temptation of taking extended credit.

Profitability Became Harder to Achieve

— More credit card holders were 'full payers' (ie paying their account in full each month). This meant that they paid no interest to the card issuer, who effectively managed their account for nothing.

— Credit card fraud increased steadily – the costs of this are largely borne by card issuers.

— Meanwhile, the cost of funds (interest rates) was increasing, without a corresponding increase in the rates charged to customers, thus squeezing margins.

As a result, Barclaycard's card issuing operation made a loss in 1990.

THE BARCLAYCARD RELAUNCH 1990

In response to the profitability problem, by 1990, all the major card issuers were preparing to introduce an annual fee, to create a profit stream independent of the amount of extended credit and fluctuations in interest rates. Although the sums proposed were not large (around £10 a year), there was considerable customer resistance to paying anything for a service they traditionally regarded as free.

Given the increased competition and the onset of recession, card issuers were extremely apprehensive about being the first to move, fearing a large number of defections to 'free' cards.

At Barclaycard a great deal of thought and research went into managing this process. The fee was introduced as one element in a major product relaunch, code-named K2. The package finally chosen was as follows:

— an annual fee of £8;

— a small reduction in interest rate (from 29.8% to 27.8%);

— new cardholder benefits – Purchase Cover (100-day insurance on any item over £50 bought with a Barclaycard), and International Rescue (assistance and advice when travelling abroad). These were benefits that had previously only been available from exclusive, high-fee charge cards such as American Express;

— the opportunity for Barclaycard VISA holders to apply for a new Barclaycard MasterCard (included in the same annual fee).

As it turned out, Barclaycard was not the first: in January 1990 Lloyd's introduced a £12 fee on its Access card.[5] In May 1990, Barclaycard wrote to all customers with a brochure explaining the new package, supported by extensive telephone contact to answer queries and persuade immediate 'rejecters' to reconsider.

Customers were also assured that, if they decided to cancel their card within the next 12 months, their fee would be refunded.

As a result, Barclaycard lost about a million 'dormant' customers and a much smaller number of active customers – fewer, in fact, than anticipated.[6]

The relaunch was, effectively, handled without advertising support. Since 1981, the advertising had featured Alan Whicker in a variety of exotic locations, demonstrating that Barclaycard was accepted in many more places worldwide than 'certain other cards'.[7] This campaign was under review at the time of the relaunch for two reasons:

1. All the market changes described above, together with the enhanced product benefits, meant that 'international acceptability' on its own was no longer an adequate competitive positioning.[8]

2. Whicker himself, though still popular and closely associated with Barclaycard, was getting older, with declining appeal to younger consumers. The campaign itself was running out of steam after nine years and looking a little tired.

BMP DDB was appointed as Barclaycard's new advertising agency in May 1990, with the following brief.

ADVERTISING OBJECTIVES POST-RELAUNCH – GETTING, KEEPING, AND USING BARCLAYCARD

The relaunch had successfully negotiated the introduction of a fee and upgraded the product relative to competitors. This was a necessary step towards addressing the brand's longer-term objectives, but not enough on its own to achieve them. The advertising goals set in 1990 were as follows:

---

5. As a result Lloyd's lost some 30% of its Access customers.
6. Historically, Barclaycards had been issued to Barclays Bank current account customers for use as a cheque guarantee card. A proportion of users had therefore never wanted a credit card and in many cases never used it as such. Barclaycard were happy to convert these 'dormant' users to a simple cheque guarantee card – dormant cards are a source of cost, not revenue. So although the total user base went down from 8 million to 6.5 million, about a million of these were dormant users who represented no loss to the brand's income. 485,000 active users had been lost by December 1990, which was within the confidence limits of research predictions but towards the lower end of this range.
7. This was meant as a comparison with American Express, but frequently interpreted as a comparison with Access – a misunderstanding Barclaycard was happy to live with.
8. International acceptability was, in reality, a VISA property rather than a Barclaycard property.

Customer Retention

Although attrition at the relaunch had been minimised, we could not assume there would be no delayed reaction – customers had an increasing choice of cards with no fee. In particular, it was important to hold on to customers who, at least sometimes, took advantage of extended credit; customers with existing credit outstanding might only be waiting to repay this before moving.

Increasing Turnover

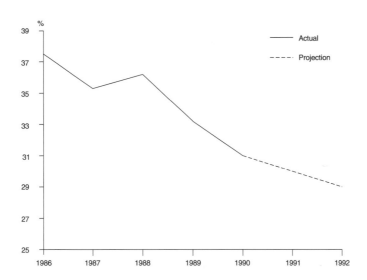

Figure 1: *Barclaycard share of turnover 1986–92 (including projection)*
Source: BBA

Barclaycard's share of turnover had been in decline during the late '80s as more competitors came into the market (Figure 1). Projections, if this continued, were a turnover share of 30% in 1991 and 29% by the end of 1992.[9] The target was to reverse this trend and be at 31% by the end of 1992.

Increasing Share of New Cardholders

While total penetration of credit cards was no longer expected to grow, there is always a need to attract new market entrants, primarily younger people (18–35). Barclaycard's share of new cardholders had declined as competitors such as TSB

---

9. This may not sound much, but 1% turnover share was worth about £280 million in 1990, and turnover is the main short-term determinant of extended credit which remained the main source of income.

Trustcard targeted younger audiences; in 1990 it was 15%, well below share of existing users. The task of reversing this decline would be addressed through direct response as well as media advertising;[10] the role of advertising was supportive, to increase the brand's attractiveness, especially to younger people.

In short, we wanted people to *get* the card, *keep* the card and *use* the card. These are linked: research shows that the more often people use a credit card, the more likely they are to keep it.

ADVERTISING STRATEGY

Research showed that, in 1990, most people saw all credit cards as very similar, with hardly any measurable image differences between Barclaycard and Access. The enhanced services offered by the card were potential differentiators. They also offered incentives to *get, keep,* and – especially in the case of Purchase Cover – *use* the card.

The new card benefits had already been communicated at relaunch via a mailed brochure (and a good deal of editorial coverage). As a result, research showed fairly high prompted awareness that Barclaycard offered these services.

However, there seemed to be an important difference between being aware of the benefits and valuing them, regarding them as personally relevant, or even believing them to be differentiating. Negative attitudes to credit cards generally led many customers to be suspicious – 'where's the catch?' or to find other ways of denying their significance – 'I expect they all do that, don't they?'. So neither general perceptions of Barclaycard nor turnover increased in the months following the relaunch.

TABLE 2: PROMPTED AWARENESS OF PRODUCT CHANGES

	October 1990 %
Annual fee	93
Purchase Cover	58
International Rescue	55
Free MasterCard	53

Base: Barclaycard holders
Source: Barclaycard Internal Research

---

10. The main mechanisms for recruiting new Barclaycard users are leaflets in Barclays branches (primarily targeted at Barclays customers); inserts in magazines; and direct mail, targeted at young people and others.

TABLE 3: ATTITUDES AND TURNOVER NOT IMPROVED
BY AWARENESS OF PRODUCT CHANGES

(a) % agreeing that Barclaycard	Pre-April 1990	Post-October 1990
Provides special benefits and services for cardholders	40	39
Provides a high quality customer service	44	45
cares for its customers' needs	40	36
(b) Share of credit card turnover	31.8	31.6

(a) Base: Barclaycard holders
Source: Millward Brown
(b) Source: BBA

The role for advertising was to make these product benefits real, believable, relevant, and closely associated to Barclaycard, and so use them to develop a new overall positioning for the brand as a premium quality card, differentiated from the plethora of 'ordinary' credit cards available.

As a secondary communication, we wanted to continue to associate Barclaycard with worldwide acceptability, its one existing image difference from Access.[11]

The primary target audience was existing Barclaycard holders, and an important secondary audience was considered to be potential new entrants to the market, with the emphasis on younger people aged 18 to 34.

The creative challenge was to follow the Alan Whicker campaign. Although it was beginning to tire, it was still well liked by many, and almost synonymous with Barclaycard. Its scores for branded awareness and enjoyment were expected to be hard to match. Another 'personality' was only one way of replacing Whicker and this was the route eventually chosen. It had to be someone who appealed across a wide range of target groups, from the wealthy older users to 20-year-olds choosing their first credit card. We were fortunate to get Rowan Atkinson.

THE CAMPAIGN 1991–95

Although featuring a well known actor, the new campaign moved from Whicker's 'presenter' format to a dramatic mode. Rowan Atkinson appears as a bungling secret agent called Richard Latham. Although equipped with a Barclaycard, Latham is always dismissive about its usefulness and as a result is repeatedly without support or protection when things go wrong. In contrast his assistant, Bough, demonstrates the benefits of Barclaycard usage and provides a mouthpiece for information about it.

This formula has proved extremely effective. It is flexible enough to communicate a number of different messages and its intelligent humour, where the

---

11. Access, existing only in the UK and weakly associated in consumers' minds with MasterCard, was not believed to be as internationally acceptable as Barclaycard. This worked to Barclaycard's advantage, there were many cases of Access consumers applying for a Barclaycard when they had to make a trip abroad. In the long term, however, we realised that this was not necessarily a sustainable advantage.

cynical Latham always ends up a figure of fun, wins people over in a way that a more rational, straight approach would not.

Between 1991 and the end of 1995, 14 films were made featuring eight different benefits.

Media planning has focused advertising at peak times of user activity in order to stimulate usage:

January/February: sales, holiday booking;

June/July: holiday spending;

November/December: pre-Christmas.

From 1991 to 1995 £41.8 million was spent on the TV campaign, a total of 15,410 TVRs.[12]

THE RESULTS 1991–95

We can look at the results of the campaign at three levels.

First, responses to the advertising itself. The campaign has become extremely famous and well liked, exceeding the high standards set by Whicker. Besides being well branded and entertaining, it is also highly efficient in communicating specific product messages.

Second, we look at consumers' perceptions of the brand. Barclaycard has distanced itself from Access, and has got closer to (even overtaken) American Express. These changes in image are directly related to the themes of the advertising. The attractiveness of the brand to younger people has been improved.

Third, and most importantly, we estimate the contribution of the advertising to meeting Barclaycard's business objectives:

— Getting the card – increasing share of new acquirers.

— Keeping the card – ownership has held up in the face of ever-increasing competition. In particular the GM Card, despite a successful launch, took relatively little business from Barclaycard.

— Using the card – share of turnover and of outstandings[13] has increased, and an econometric model relates the increase in Barclaycard turnover to advertising.

---

12. Other media have been used at very low levels: posters on Purchase Cover in 1993 (£688,000), press in 1992 (£486,000) and radio in 1993 (£49,000). The TV films have also been shown in cinemas with a total spend of £822,000 between 1992 and 1995.
13. Outstandings = the total amount of extended credit outstanding at any point in time. In terms of business performance, share of outstandings is even more important than share of turnover.

'TEAPOT' 60 SECONDS

Latham: Excuse me, Sir Brian.

Bough: Got the present, sir?
Latham: Of course Bough.

Bough: Enough in the whip round then?
Latham: 75 pounds and 14p.
Bough: 14p! Who put that in? I don't
suppose you bought it with your...

Latham: With my Barclaycard. Oh yes
obviously Bough. I had a manilla envelope
stuffed with cash so naturally I used
Barclaycard.
Bough: It would have been insured against
loss or damage.

Latham: Bough! This is the wedding of the
daughter of the head of MI7. There are four
men on the roof, two in the choir and the
vicar has no previous convictions. I think
that's ample insurance for a china teapot.

Sound: Breaking teapot.

'MOLE' 60 SECONDS

Latham: Thank you ladies and gentlemen, a very impressive turnout. In fact the only person I can't see here is the ambassador.

Latham: Ah, that's better.
Sir Wilfred: What the devil do you think you're playing at, Latham?
Latham: I was about to ask you the same question.

Latham: Yesterday you collected rather a lot of money from this man and today we hear you are to meet a courier in this very Embassy.

Latham: That ambassador has the behaviour pattern of a mole!
Bough: That is the behaviour pattern of a man who has lost his Barclaycard. First they send cash then a replacement card.

Latham: Oh come on Mr Moley. Yes Bough let him in, the more the merrier. A Barclaycard? To Moscow? And how do they do that, pray? By motorcycle messen... ger?

Latham: Thank you Sir Wilfred for taking part in our training exercise. Realism is obviously of paramount importance.

Latham: Come on Bough, untie Sir Wilfred.

'SNAKEBITE' 60 SECONDS

Bough: There's still no answer sir.
Latham: Right Bough, we're going in.

Latham: Wendy! Right Bough, you loosen his clothing, I'll get the local doctor.

Latham: Blast!
Bough: What is it sir?
Latham: Apparently he is the local doctor.

Latham: That's enough loosening for now Bough.
Bough: I'm looking for his Barclaycard sir.
Latham: His Barclaycard! This man's in no state to go shopping.

Bough: I'm going to phone them up for medical advice sir.
Latham: You're going to phone Barclaycard for medical advice?
Bough: Barclaycard International Rescue sir, they can send doctors…

Latham: We're wasting our time here Bough. This man has a serious case of snakebite and there's only one thing that's going to save him. I'm going to have to locate the wound and suck out the poison. Yes, I actually think perhaps you should phone Barclaycard Bough, I'm not sure I've got the… you know, my lips are a little…

Latham: Well, I thought I had a solution but then…

For full written details of Barclaycard services and conditions, dial 100 Freefone Barclaycard.

RESULTS: RESPONSE TO THE ADVERTISING ITSELF

Awareness of Barclaycard TV advertising grew steadily from 28% at the beginning of 1991 throughout 1992 and 1993 and, since then, has remained very high at around 50%, well above American Express and Access. The Millward Brown model of this trend calculates an Awareness Index of between 4 and 8 for the various executions; more significantly, it also shows a base level of ad awareness rising from 14% at the start of the campaign to 21% by 1994.[14]

Barclaycard anticipated that it might take two or three years before memories of the new campaign supplanted Alan Whicker. In fact, this happened much more quickly. By the end of the first year, identified recall of Atkinson was far higher than that of Whicker and, within two years, mentions of Whicker had virtually disappeared from the research.

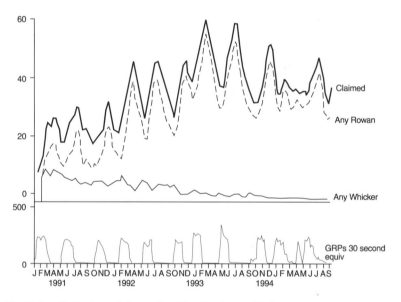

Figure 2: *Identified recall – Barclaycard (first recall only), rolling four-weekly data*

Opinions of the advertising are also strongly positive, both absolutely and relative to other credit card advertising. From the start, around 60% of those recalling the campaign claimed to enjoy watching it. The figures shown in Table 4 are totals for 1995:

---

14. Millward Brown's 'Awareness Index' indicates the amount of extra advertising recall generated by 100 TVRs. The base level is what advertising recall declines to when all short-term advertising memories have decayed. As the base can move over time it can be regarded as an indication of longer-term advertising effect. The all-category average is 4.

TABLE 4: OPINIONS OF THE ADVERTISING

1995	Barclaycard %	Amex %	Access %	GM Card %
Any positive	89	55	55	59
I like the people in it	63	11	28	9
I enjoy watching it	59	11	28	9
Any negative	12	29	26	32
I'm getting fed up with seeing it	9	20	15	18

Base: Definite recallers
Source: Millward Brown

Although some of the more popular films have now had very high ratings, viewers are not getting tired of them.[15] The Latham campaign has now had more than twice as many ratings in five years as Whicker had in nine, but enjoyment scores are far higher and wear-out much lower than they were for the last burst of Whicker.

TABLE 5: COMPARISON OF WHICKER AND LATHAM CAMPAIGNS

	Last burst of Whicker (May 1990) %	Latham burst (December 1995) %
I enjoy watching it	25	59
I'm getting fed up with seeing it	20	6
Total campaign TVRs to date	c 7,000	15,410

Respondents also agree that the advertising gives *positive impressions* of the brand.

TABLE 6: IMPRESSIONS GIVEN BY ADVERTISING: HOW STRONGLY DO YOU AGREE THAT THIS AD GIVES THE IMPRESSION THAT [BRAND]...?

% agree strongly	Barclaycard	Access	Amex
Is continuously looking at ways to update/improve service	23	12	8
Is in touch with the general public	22	9	12
Is offering you something different	19	5	12
Is the sort of card for you	12	4	6
Can always be relied on	28	17	32

Base: Definite recallers, 1994 total
NB: More recent data cannot be used for confidentiality reasons
Source: Millward Brown

---

15. 'Cairo' has had 2,262 TVRs, which means that, on average, everyone in the country has seen it 20 times! The most successful films therefore continue to be shown in the repertoire. We believe this contributes to the interest and variety of the campaign when on air.

Also:

— In a Campaign poll in 1996 among the general public, Barclaycard was voted the third best-liked advertising campaign in the UK.

— Of 1,200 ads tested using the Millward Brown Link Test, 'Teapot' and 'Cairo' have the fourth and sixth highest 'enjoyment' scores.

— In a survey conducted for Marketing magazine into personality advertising, 60% correctly associated Rowan Atkinson with Barclaycard (the third highest result).

Enjoyment and memorability do not themselves prove effectiveness, but given the traditional suspicion and even hostility with which many consumers regard credit cards, we believe that these positive responses to the advertising have been a crucial mechanism in increasing the positive perceptions and increased usage of Barclaycard.

Moreover, the ads clearly do more than entertain – the tracking study shows that they communicate specific product messages in an impactful way.

Table 7, for example, shows the percentage of definite recallers mentioning purchase insurance cover spontaneously when recalling each of four ads about that benefit.

TABLE 7: MESSAGE COMMUNICATION

	Cairo %	Dinghy %	Shopping %	Teapot %
Mentioning purchase insurance	81	91	78	89

Base: Definite recallers 1991–95[16]
Source: Millward Brown

These responses to the advertising have also influenced beliefs and feelings about the brand itself.

RESULTS: BRAND PERCEPTIONS

Before the current campaign, perceptions of Access and Barclaycard were virtually identical on all the quantitative measures taken, Barclaycard only having a higher score than Access on 'international acceptability'. Amex, on the other hand, had a more distinct image than either, and was found desirable and aspirational by many more consumers than were likely to own one.

---

16. The fact that Access scores also increase (though by much less) is best explained as a halo effect from Barclaycard, a legacy of the traditional belief that 'all credit cards are the same'. In fact Access (unlike some competitors) did not introduce any similar services.

Since 1991, Barclaycard has moved away from Access on a number of dimensions, and closer to Amex (though Amex remains a strong brand).

TABLE 8: CHANGES IN BRAND PERCEPTIONS 1990–94

	1990			1994		
	Barclaycard %	Access %	Amex %	Barclaycard %	Access %	Amex %
Provides special benefits and services for cardholders	22	22	38	45	34	37
Provides special emergency assistance anywhere in the world	17	17	45	59	29	47
Provides insurance cover on goods bought with the card	15	14	37	65	38	32
Provides high-quality customer service	21	23	33	45	38	33

Base: All adults
Source: Millward Brown

There is a clear relationship between the content of the commercials shown and movements on specific attributes such as 'insurance cover'; this can be shown by modelling trends in these attributes in a very similar way to modelling awareness (Figure 3).

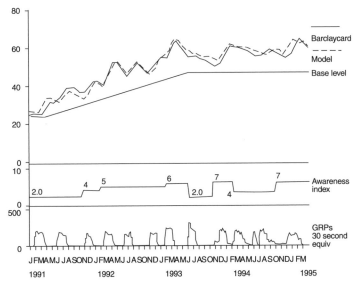

Figure 3: *Image – provides insurance cover on goods with the card. Rolling eight-weekly data*

Other image attributes show clearly that Barclaycard has established itself as the perceived leader and innovator in the market.

TABLE 9: BRAND PERCEPTIONS

	Barclaycard %	Access %	Amex %
Ahead of competition	40	21	21
Doing well these days	53	36	32
Among first to introduce new ideas	33	15	8
Is market leader	50	36	40
Wealth of experience	61	46	45

Base: All adults 1994
Source: Millward Brown

RESULTS: BUSINESS

Getting Cards

Since 1990 Barclaycard's share of new cardholders has risen substantially:

TABLE 10: SHARE OF NEW CARDHOLDERS

6 m/e September	1990 %	1991 %	1992 %	1993 %	1994 %	1995 %
Barclaycard VISA share	15	15	19	23	24	25

Source: FRS

Since 1993 Barclaycard (along with other card issuers), has increased its direct marketing effort targeted at card recruitment, so advertising alone cannot claim responsibility for this improvement. We do know, however, from many indications in the tracking study and in qualitative research, that Barclaycard's relative attractiveness to younger people has increased since the days of Whicker, even among those who have not responded to the direct marketing. It seems likely therefore that advertising has helped to make Barclaycard more generally attractive and has hence made recruitment activity more effective.

Keeping Cards

Since 1990, the credit card market has become ever more competitive. In 1990, there were 30 different VISA cards; today there are probably over 500. Many of these charge no fee. Some have copied Purchase Cover, and some now offer significantly reduced interest rates (whereas in 1990 all cards offered similar rates). Many are affinity cards, which incentivise acquisition and use by making contributions to charities or clubs.

Under these circumstances, it is a considerable achievement for Barclaycard to have increased its share of cards from 29% just after the relaunch to 32%, and then maintained this share in the face of competition – including the GM launch. In contrast, Access has declined from 37% to 25%, so that for some time now Barclaycard has overtaken Access (Figure 4).

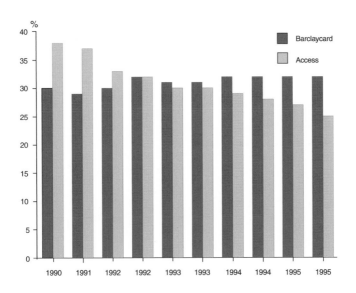

Figure 4: *Share of credit cards*
Source: FRS

While the numbers of cards are to some extent inflated by the issue of Barclaycard MasterCards, the same pattern holds if we look at the number of cardholders (Figure 5).

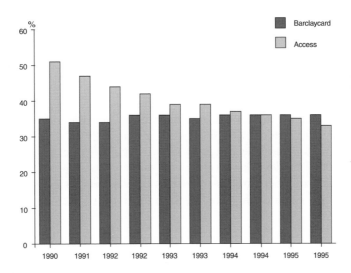

Figure 5: *Share of cardholders*
Source: FRS

A further indication of loyalty is given by the question (see Table 11), asked of dual brand users until 1993. This shows a marked increase for Barclaycard, against a static picture for Access.

TABLE 11: DUAL USERS' PREFERENCE – WHICH PAYMENT CARD WOULD YOU KEEP
IF YOU COULD ONLY KEEP ONE?

	Dec 1990 (pre ads) %	1991 %	1992 %	1993 %
Barclaycard	40	44	49	51
Access	26	25	27	27

Base: Dual holders
Source: Millward Brown

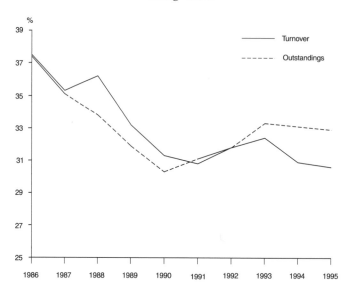

Using Cards

Figure 6: *Barclaycard share*
Source: BBA

Figure 6 shows how the decline in both share of turnover and share of outstandings was reversed after the start of the new campaign in 1991.[17]

The most conclusive evidence of advertising's effect on card usage comes from an econometric model. This measures the effects of advertising on average turnover per Barclaycard VISA card. (Any effects of MasterCard are therefore excluded.) Unfortunately, much of the detail of this model must remain confidential but, since

---

17. The dip in share of turnover in 1994 is caused mainly by the launch of the GM card. This was a new credit card offering holders collector points which could be redeemed for a discount against any new GM (Vauxhall) car. This launch increased total market turnover as GM cardholders began to use their cards whenever they could in order to save points towards their new Vauxhall. Most of this extra turnover did not translate into extended credit, which explains why Barclaycard's share of outstandings held up. Both turnover and outstandings for Barclaycard, however, increased strongly in 1994 and 1995 in absolute terms (in fact growth rates were higher than in the previous three years), despite the loss in share. Despite heavy TV advertising, the GM card has taken less than 3% of the market. In fact Barclaycard lost far fewer cardholders to the GM card than would be predicted from its market share.

1991, it shows that advertising increased total turnover per Barclaycard VISA by approximately 3% each year.[18]

OTHER POSSIBLE FACTORS THAT MIGHT HAVE EXPLAINED BARCLAYCARD'S PERFORMANCE

We believe that advertising for Barclaycard works in synergy with other parts of the marketing programme. But no other initiative taken since 1990 is enough to explain away the brand's improved position. Some other possibilities, however, deserve discussion.

The Launch of Barclaycard MasterCard

This has added to the number of Barclaycards issued, provided a useful additional service to some cardholders, and encouraged dual users to drop their Access cards.

However, total penetration of Barclaycard MasterCard has never been more than 10% of all Barclaycard cardholders and, as all MasterCards have been issued to existing Barclaycard VISA holders, it has had no effect on penetration. MasterCard has not been featured in media advertising. The model shows that advertising affects VISA turnover quite independently of MasterCard.

The Decline of Access

It seems, though we have no privileged information, that throughout this period there were differences between the Access banks on credit card policy.[19] As a result Access did not improve its product, and its advertising was inconsistent and lightweight. So is Barclaycard's success simply a reflection of the weakness of its major competitor?

The answer is no. Access declined partly because the Access banks were promoting their own VISA cards; the natural action for Access customers to take would be to stay with their own bank[20] or to defect to one of the other *free* cards on offer. So Barclaycard would not automatically benefit from the decline of Access.

Instead, it could be argued that the decline of Access was not particularly helpful to Barclaycard. It reinforced perceptions of the market as fragmented and commoditised, where cards were chosen on price or as a service provided by a

---

18. Bear in mind that total market turnover is now over £30 billion a year.
19. The strength of the Access brand was also seen as a barrier by the MasterCard network. In April 1996, the Access brand was sold to MasterCard by the four Access banks. It is believed that MasterCard will cease to use the name in the UK and replace it with the MasterCard brand.
20. Access customers nearly all banked with one of the Access banks. It is worth mentioning that the relative fortunes of Barclaycard and Access over this period were not influenced by any shift in patterns of current account holding.

current account bank. And the lack of effective Access advertising meant that the task of supporting credit card usage fell largely onto Barclaycard.

We suggest that Access is best seen as an indicator of what might have happened to Barclaycard. Access was originally, if anything, a larger and stronger brand but, without effective support, succumbed to competitive pressure.

Other Parts of the Marketing Mix

There is no point in trying to 'eliminate' the effects of other marketing activities since 1990 in the traditional 'effectiveness awards' style. The one thing that we can claim is that, despite price-led competition, Barclaycard's success is not due to reduction in price. In fact, the £8 fee was increased two years later to £10, with no adverse effects.

Barclaycard's success is a result of an *integrated* marketing programme:

— A successful points collection scheme, Profiles, has existed to encourage card use since 1988.

— In response to the GM Card, Barclaycard moved swiftly to tie up a parallel deal with Ford.

— Barclaycard makes extensive use of direct mail, both included in monthly statements and separately; a magazine is also mailed to cardholders.

— Telephone contact staff have been extensively trained in customer care.

It would therefore be meaningless to claim that advertising is responsible for any particular 'share' of the brand's success, which is due to the efforts of an extensive marketing programme. We can, however, point to some evidence that advertising has made a distinctive contribution: the modelling that relates awareness of product benefits to advertising, and the model that links advertising expenditure to turnover, as well as the extremely high profile and popularity the campaign has enjoyed. What we can also do, based on research evidence, is build a picture of how the advertising works, and why it is complementary to other marketing activities, doing specific things that they do not.

HOW DO WE BELIEVE THE ADVERTISING WORKS?

What are the particular mechanisms by which Barclaycard TV advertising assists the overall objectives of getting, keeping, and using the card?

Empathy/Involvement

Many consumers have traditionally regarded credit card issuers with some suspicion or even dislike – partly a fear of getting into debt, partly an understandable feeling about a company whose primary contact with the customer consists of a bill at the end of the month (and an occasional phone call, which may well only happen because some problem has occurred). The advertising provides Barclaycard with a continuous presence, a human face, and an effective way of communicating with an initially unsympathetic audience. We know from tracking and qualitative research that it also positions the brand as younger, more friendly and having a sense of humour. It therefore creates a more receptive atmosphere for other types of communication such as direct mail or telephone contact.

Relevance

The unique ability of television to 'dramatise' product claims makes these more interesting and relevant to the consumer – the lost binoculars, the burning rug, the police cell all create powerful visual demonstrations of what can go wrong. By doing this, advertising stimulates usage and gives rational reasons for choosing to get, or keep, the card.

Leadership

Having the most famous and best-liked advertising in the sector helps to position Barclaycard as perceived market leader (as does the use of 60-second time lengths and high production values). People want to be with 'the leader' – it offers both reassurance and a positive self image.

Positioning

Both the content of the advertising, and its sophisticated style, differentiate the brand from rival credit cards, particularly Access, and have moved it much closer in perceptual terms to American Express. In 1990, Amex was the only brand in the payment card area with a strongly distinguished brand image. For most credit card customers it was aspirational, but out of reach. Barclaycard now shares this position, while its humour also differentiates it from Amex's much more serious persona.

PUTTING A VALUE ON THE ADVERTISING

Looking purely at the short-term effects of Barclaycard advertising on turnover, the model shows that £40 million of advertising from 1991 to 1995 stimulated turnover per Barclaycard VISA card by an average of around 3% each year. We are unable to reveal precise turnover figures or financial calculations but, if this extra turnover is assumed in turn to create extra extended credit (and this is fair because in this market the two are closely correlated), it is not difficult to produce figures, even on conservative estimates, suggesting that this extra card usage has been sufficient in itself to pay for the cost of the advertising.

The real object of the advertising, however, was to help defend and strengthen the brand's competitive position. We have argued that it did this successfully. The financial benefits of this are far harder to quantify, but also considerably greater. If Barclaycard's share decline had continued, or if it had followed the pattern of Access, many more billions of turnover would have been progressively lost, as well as the fee income from lost cardholders, to say nothing of the future profit streams which the brand may now expect to earn in the future.

The market continues to become ever more competitive, with new American contenders now offering extremely low introductory rates in order to attract custom. (Low rates are not necessarily in the long-term interest of the consumer, as there are often hidden costs or reductions in service level involved.) With no signs of wear-out yet in the Latham campaign, we and Barclaycard feel confident that the brand will continue to withstand these pressures and to satisfy its six million customers.

16

Love Over Gold

The untold story of TV's greatest romance

IN THE BEGINNING

Gold Blend was launched by Nestlé in the mid-1960s. It used the new freeze-dried technology to provide a smoother, richer taste, and was sold at a price premium to Nescafé of around 25%.

It was an excellent product, outperforming its rivals in taste tests, and was very successful in its early years. It reached a peak brand share of 7.8% in 1969, but thereafter drifted away slightly until, by the mid-1980s, the share was around 6.5%.

THE STRATEGIC INSIGHT

Up to 1987, advertising had concentrated on the product itself, using the mnemonic of a gold bean to suggest product superiority. The problem was that, although Gold Blend performed well as a product, and was seen as upmarket and high quality, it was not accessible for the bulk of coffee buyers. The rational product message was only interesting to a minority of upmarket coffee drinkers. The brand's appeal was therefore limited to upmarket coffee connoisseurs. However, given the broad acceptability of the product, we, here at McCann-Erickson, believed there was a bigger opportunity.

Realising this, we determined to create advertising which, through its popular appeal, would make the brand more accessible to the mass market while still maintaining its quality, upmarket image and premium positioning. We therefore moved from product claims to a more emotional approach which involved the consumer more – Gold Blend would be the coffee you drank to demonstrate your sophistication. We did this by creating a sophisticated world you could become involved in and be part of. As such it could become a powerful brand to which anyone could relate.

There was also a change in tonality. The previous advertising had featured Fiona Fullerton as a spokesperson. While aspirational, she reflected a strident feminism, which many women found unappealing. The brief for the new ads was for a softer form of feminism; a woman who was an equal in lifestyle, success and intellect, without being aggressive – a switch from material to more human values.

In summary, what we wanted to do was to use populist advertising to increase the accessibility of the brand without changing its positioning.

THE CREATIVE INSIGHT

The task the creative team set itself was to produce a campaign that was talked about as much as the programmes. Unusually for most advertising ideas the stimulus for the creative idea came from the media plan. The size of the advertising budget for Gold Blend meant that we needed to produce two or three TV commercials a year. The team realised that, rather than have individual executions, we could present them sequentially as a series.

And what were people talking about at the time on television? It was the upmarket series like *Dallas*, *Dynasty* and, most interesting to us, *Moonlighting*. This last programme featured two combative protagonists, who were clearly meant for each other. However, something always conspired to keep them apart. It was a sophisticated romance, and the theme appealed immensely to the women who were our target. This 'sophisticated romance' became the campaign theme.

The other original element was the idea of acting like a programme maker. Thus each episode ended with a cliffhanger, leaving the viewer wanting to know what happened next. And just as TV companies advertise future episodes with trailers and press ads, so did we. In the days before the second episode was due to appear, small-space black-and-white press ads appeared in the TV listings pages. Just as TV companies try to create added publicity and momentum for their programmes by encouraging coverage in the popular press, and by creating merchandise based on the programme, so, as we will show later, did we.

The media strategy complemented this approach, building on the drama of the romance rather than simply chasing cost per thousand. The bulk of the budget was spent on TV, using a burst strategy to emphasise the cliffhanger endings. Each burst began with a brief reminder of the previous episode. In the second week the new episode was launched, buying into high-rating programmes to build cover and impact for the new episode. In the early stages of each series we moved the story on more quickly with a faster production of episodes to get people involved in the story.

ADVERTISING STRATEGY SUMMARY

Target

Women of any class, who saw themselves as slightly more discriminating than the norm, but who were not coffee connoisseurs. For the second series a greater emphasis was put on younger women.

Objective

To position Gold Blend as an upmarket coffee, in a class of its own, worth every penny, but which anyone could drink.

THE FIRST SERIES

THE SECOND SERIES

To build an emotional bond between the target and the brand through the shared Gold Blend world of sophistication and romance.

And hence to broaden the appeal of the brand to new, less overtly upmarket, users.

Strategy

To involve the target in the world of Gold Blend where 'Classy women drink Gold Blend'.

Brand Image

Stylish good taste.

CAMPAIGN STRUCTURE/MEDIA PLAN

The campaign broke in November 1987 with a burst of 700 TVRs. The second episode appeared in June 1988. Thereafter it has generally had four bursts a year with about three executions per year.

The weight of the campaign has been relatively consistent, receiving between 2,500 and 3,000 TVRs per year, declining slightly over the years, as the fame of the campaign has allowed us to run at lower weights without losing impact. This weight is lower than that of the previous campaign, which received around 3,500 TVRs per year. The success the current campaign has achieved is therefore due to its creative impact rather than its media weight.

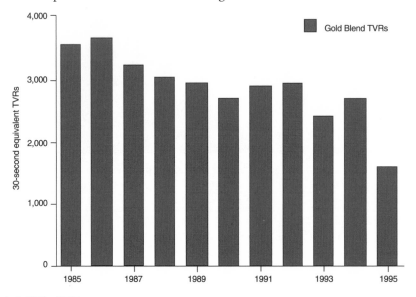

Figure 1: *Gold Blend TVRs*

Originally the first series was intended to run for six episodes. In the end, because it was so successful, it ran for twelve episodes over five and a half years.

However, all stories must end, and in early 1993 it climaxed with the 'I love you' ad; the screening of a compilation of all 11 episodes to date; and a final commercial where the happy couple disappeared into the sunset.

As we will see, the first campaign drove penetration, but the bulk of this was among over-45s. For the second series we determined to extend our success to younger women. A core objective of the new series therefore was to appeal to a younger target. We deliberately made the protagonists younger, with lifestyles more relevant to this target, and more lively.

We also had a different storyline while keeping the core property – the 'Sophisticated Romance'. Instead of a story of a couple brought together through the coffee but kept apart by events, it was the classic battle between romance (and Gold Blend) on the one hand and material wealth on the other, represented by two male suitors. The first commercial in the second series broke in November 1993, but not before we took another leaf from the programme-makers' book, and ran a trailer ad for the new campaign in the summer of 1993. By early 1996 the second series had run for six episodes, and has proved on all key measures – awareness, liking, involvement, brand awareness and sales – to be building on the success of the first. We now feel confident that we have a territory – 'Sophisticated Romance' – which can run and run.

SALES EFFECTIVENESS

The campaign has been a great success in sales terms, with sales now over 60% higher in volume terms than before the campaign started. This is despite no growth in the market as a whole, and means that Gold Blend now has a sterling share of 13%, making it clearly the second-biggest brand in the market behind Nescafé granules.

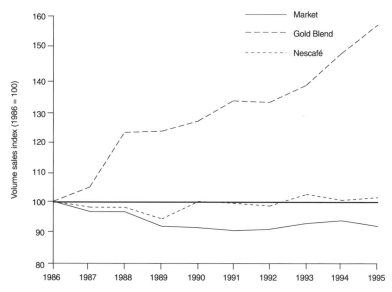

Figure 2: *Gold Blend volume sales*
Source: Nielsen

This sales increase comprises three clear periods. Firstly, Gold Blend grew rapidly immediately after the start of the campaign. This growth continued thereafter but seemed to hit a plateau in 1992. At this point we took action and, in 1993, introduced the second series with a revised target. Following this, sales growth recommenced, and continues to date, despite the fact the market declined in 1995. In retrospect, we probably should have changed campaigns earlier. All in all Gold Blend is a success story and continues to be so. Indeed, only last year it was one of *Marketing* magazine's 'fastest growing brands of the year' in its annual survey. This was seven years into the current campaign.

On top of this, the campaign is one that has really captured the public's imagination. How many other campaigns have managed to make the front page of the *Sun*, displacing the news that Princess Anne was having a romance with Tim Lawrence to second place, and to be the feature of a *Times* editorial? How many other campaigns have had the nerve to advertise themselves in the TV listings pages, and actually get people to tune in to watch the spot? When the first episode of the second series was shown in the centre break of *Brookside* and advertised in the listings pages, BARB saw a 67% increase in the number of people switching into the break compared to the week before. How many other campaigns are famous enough in themselves to spawn a CD and cassette compilation that went gold? So far the campaign has spawned a book, two CD/cassettes and a video, each successful and profitable in their own right for Nestlé and, at the same time, increasing the power of the campaign.

The *Love Over Gold* CD:	Straight into the Top 10 album charts
The *Love Over Gold* book:	Straight into the Top 10 bestsellers
Best of Gold Blend video:	Sold 1,500 copies (people actually bought copies of our ads!)

What we need to demonstrate is not that Gold Blend is a market success, nor that the advertising was a popular success, but that the two were linked.

WHAT ELSE COULD IT HAVE BEEN?

Price

What matters in this market is price relative to the competition. Nescafé as brand leader with 40% of the market sets the prices. While actual prices have varied with commodity prices, Gold Blend's relative price versus Nescafé and Kenco has remained unchanged, except for short-term variations which reflect promotional activity or phasing of price increases.

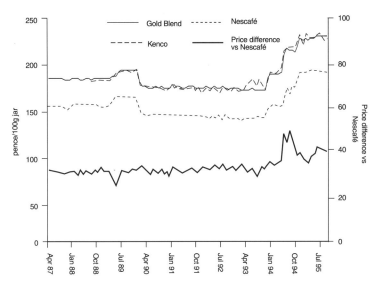

Figure 3: *Gold Blend pricing*
Source: Nielsen

Distribution

Distribution for Gold Blend was good even in 1986/7 at 90% sterling. Distribution has not been a significant factor in the brand's success.

Competitive Activity

Like any successful brand, Gold Blend's success has encouraged rivals. Most, for example Maxwell House Master Blend and Maxwell House Classic, failed. The most successful were Kenco and supermarkets' own-brand freeze-dried.

Kenco was launched in 1988 at the same price as Gold Blend. It rapidly reached a brand share of just under 3%, growing to 3.7% with the launch of the Cherie Lunghi campaign, with a further 2.7% coming from line extensions. Despite what was undoubtedly a successful competitive launch, Gold Blend continued to grow through this period, only plateauing in 1992. Moreover, with the introduction of the second series in 1993, Gold Blend's growth has resumed and Kenco's has been halted.

Own-label activity has mostly concentrated on price promotions, and in this context most of the supermarkets have been pursuing a policy of selling direct equivalents to Gold Blend, some of which look very like Gold Blend. This activity has been an almost constant factor during the period and, if anything, has increased in recent years.

Since 1987 then, the competitive context for Gold Blend has got tougher rather than easier, at least partially as a result of Gold Blend's success. However, the strength of Gold Blend as a brand is seeing off the threat presented by these rivals.

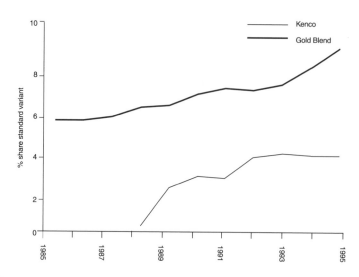

Figure 4: *The effect of Kenco*
Source: Nielsen

Product Improvements

Nestlé takes great pride in the quality of its products, and undoubtedly the quality of Gold Blend has been a major factor in its success. Indeed it is a basic theme of this paper that it was the combination of a good product and powerful and appropriate brand advertising from 1987 that has created Gold Blend's success.

Gold Blend has existed since the mid-1960s and has always done well in product tests. It regularly outperforms its major competitors in blind product tests. However, it was only when the new advertising was introduced in 1987 that sales started to take off.

Since 1987 the product has seen a number of improvements – the most recent being improved in-jar aroma in 1994. However, what these have done is to maintain the brand's lead over its competition, who have also been improving their products. This is shown in two product-preference tests conducted between Kenco and Gold Blend in 1989 and 1993 (the latter involving the in-jar aroma product pre-launch).

TABLE 1: PREFERENCE TESTS

	1989 %	1993 %
Prefer Gold Blend	55	57
Prefer Kenco	33	36
No Preference	12	7

Source: Nestlé paired-comparison consumer-preference tests

Certainly all the most significant improvements, including the improved aroma mentioned above, were also introduced on Nescafé, which has not seen comparable growth levels. Across the period Nescafé has held its own in volume terms, marginally outperforming the market, but has not seen any growth.

Packaging

Whilst Gold Blend was the first brand to move to a square jar, this packaging format has since been copied, particularly by private label, and is not seen by consumers as a major part of its appeal. Gold Blend's packaging has not changed significantly during the period of this campaign.

TABLE 2: MOST APPEALING PACKAGING

'Has packaging you like'	% agreeing
Kenco	24
Nescafé	20
Gold Blend	14
Maxwell House	9

Source: Tracking Study, November 1995
(Base: Those aware of each brand)

If anything, then, the pack has been a restraining factor on the brand's success.

Media Coverage

There has been a vast increase in media coverage of Gold Blend since 1987, virtually all revolving around the campaign itself. We estimate the value of this if translated into advertising terms to be, on average, £1 million a year (source: Allan Allbeury Communications/Universal McCann). While this has helped the success of the campaign, it is something we deliberately sought to stage-manage; looking for stories around each episode (eg the dress Louise wore in the first episode of the new series became a fashion piece linked to a competition), timing the release of information, and controlling which papers received which story. The situation was so extreme towards the climax of the first series that Nestlé and McCann's employees were being offered substantial sums to reveal what happened next. We continue to use the fame of the campaign both through PR, sponsorship and promotions. For example, on Valentine's Day 1995, we sponsored the *Evening Standard* 'Guide for Lovers' and, during Euro 96, promoted a romantic film festival with UCI.

We have managed to create a virtuous circle, where famous advertising has spawned media coverage, which in turn has enhanced the fame of the advertising. While we planned for this at the start of the campaign, in the event we succeeded beyond our wildest dreams.

CAN WE DEMONSTRATE A DIRECT LINK BETWEEN THE ADVERTISING AND SALES?

Unfortunately regional testing was ruled out at an early stage, both because of Nestlé's desire to build on its success nationally, but also because of the nature of the contracts with the TV contractors. Similarly, because of the success of the campaign there was no prolonged period off air.

However, two special analyses were conducted – AGB's MediaSpan and an econometric analysis of sales.

MediaSpan

AGB's MediaSpan provides a link between an individual's viewing of advertising and their purchasing, and is available for the period from 1993 to 1995 (ie the period covering the second series). This allows us to quantify advertising's short-term contribution to sales. Specifically it answers the question 'are people who have seen our advertising in the last two weeks more likely to buy Gold Blend than those who have not?' This shows:

— there is a strong correlation between exposure to advertising and purchase. People who had seen one or more ad in the last two weeks bought 4% more Gold Blend than those who had not;

— the advertising works more strongly when combined with favourable pricing. With low pricing it increases volume by up to 20%. When it is higher the advertising still works, but needs more exposures (three) and even then has a smaller effect (+7%).

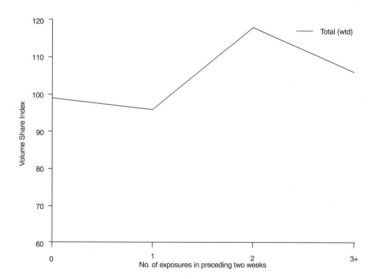

Figure 5: *Nescafé Gold Blend – short-term response to advertising exposure, low relative price weeks*
Source: MediaSpan

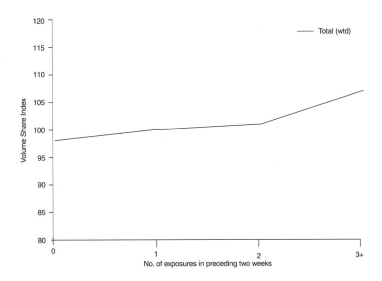

Figure 6: *Nescafé Gold Blend – short-term response to advertising exposure, high relative price weeks*
Source: MediaSpan

As well as these short-term effects, MediaSpan can also give us some insight into longer-term effects. We can look at those people who have a high weight of viewing. These people will have been more exposed to more Gold Blend advertising over the years and, if it is effective, their probability of buying Gold Blend should increase. In fact this has happened, as we can see from the divergence of the two lines in Figures 7 and 8. The effect is strongest among the 16–44 group, who became a particular target for the second series, which started in November 1993.

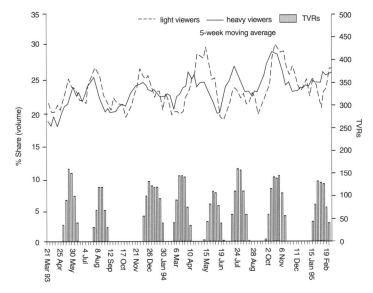

Figure 7: *Nescafé Gold Blend – brand share within weight of viewing groups*
Source: MediaSpan

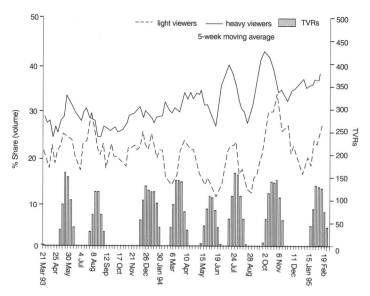

Figure 8: *Nescafé Gold Blend – age 16–44, brand share within weight of viewing groups*
Source: MediaSpan

Econometric Analysis

An econometric analysis of Gold Blend's sales shows a similar picture, with advertising being one of the main drivers of sales share, along with price and promotions. The effect is such that 835 TVRs of advertising create a short-term increase of 25 tonnes, about a 9% increase in monthly sales.

BUSINESS EFFECT

In the short term the advertising is not cost-effective. At a simple level sales growth has averaged around £6 million a year, little more than the advertising spend at £5 million. However, this growth has been compound and consistent. New buyers brought in through the advertising have become loyal buyers; 45% of new buyers of Gold Blend in 1994 and 1995 went on to become repeat buyers (source: AGB). This compound effect means that Gold Blend sales are now worth £50 million a year in real terms more than they were prior to the start of the campaign in 1987. Average advertising expenditure on Gold Blend across the period was £5 million a year.

HOW DID THE ADVERTISING WORK?

The advertising was highly memorable, with 63% aware of the advertising at its peak and 48% able to recall details of the campaign (source: Tracking Study). This peak occurred in 1995 when the fourth episode of the second series was on air – the episode when the couple shared a bedroom. In 1989, 1990 and 1991 it was the second most memorable campaign on *Marketing*'s Adwatch survey of all brands in all categories, and has been consistently in the top ten in other years.

Qualitative research showed the advertising worked by portraying an upmarket, sophisticated image for Gold Blend that, because of the populist nature of the advertising, was accessible to everyone. This appeals because the image is aspirational for our target and, at a rational level, communicates quality: 'If people like that drink it it must be good'. The popular appeal of the advertising means that people accept these messages, even though they know the characters are advertising inventions. They seem to be conspiring with us to go along with the fantasy because they are enjoying it.

Quantitatively we find people say that Gold Blend is an 'upmarket' coffee, and say it has advertising they like.

TABLE 3: % AGREEING 'IT IS AN UPMARKET COFFEE'

	ABC1 %	C2DE %	Total %
Gold Blend	31	28	30
Kenco	30	32	31
Nescafé	12	22	18
Maxwell House	3	7	5

Source: Tracking Study 1995

TABLE 4: % AGREEING 'IT HAS ADVERTISING YOU LIKE'

	ABC1 %	C2DE %	Total %
Gold Blend	37	34	35
Kenco	19	18	19
Nescafé	21	28	25
Maxwell House	10	12	11

Source: Tracking Study 1995

This is true particularly of ABC1s, but is also true to quite a large extent among C2DEs. The result is that Gold Blend now appeals to a broad range of people, while still maintaining its upmarket image. This can be seen in brand penetration which has expanded most among C2DEs, who previously found the product appealing but the brand inaccessible (see Figure 9 overleaf).

As previously stated, a secondary aim of the second series, which started in November 1993, was to create more appeal among younger people. As well as the MediaSpan analysis this is shown in penetration growth. Between 1986 and 1993, penetration (drinking yesterday, source: NDS) grew by 46% among over 45s, but only by 4% among under 45s. Since 1993 the pattern has changed. From 1993 to 1996 penetration grew by 15% among under 45s and 14% among over 45s.

Also this has been confirmed in the tracking study data, where the advertising, while liked by everyone, has stronger appeal to younger respondents and, in particular, is the only advertising in this market to generate real involvement.

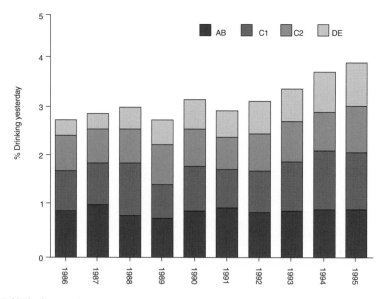

Figure 9: *Gold Blend penetrations*
Source: National Drinks Survey

TABLE 5: % AGREEING 'HAS ADVERTISING YOU LIKE'

	16–44 %	45+ %
Gold Blend	39	30
Kenco	19	18
Nescafé	26	24
Maxwell House	13	10

Base: All aware of brand
Source: Tracking Study 1995

TABLE 6: % AGREEING 'I FOUND MYSELF GETTING CAUGHT UP
IN WHAT WAS HAPPENING'

	16–44 %	45+ %
Gold Blend	28	22
Kenco	6	10
Nescafé	10	10
Maxwell House	7	7

Base: those recognising a storyboard of each ad
Source: Tracking Study 1995

HOW DID IT AFFECT THE REST OF THE PORTFOLIO?

During the period of Gold Blend's success Nescafé as a brand performed roughly in line with the market, while some of the other new Nestlé brands, Alta Rica, Cap Colombie and Cappuccino actually increased share. Thus the growth in Gold Blend's share was all incremental for Nestlé, and was achieved without cannibalising the other brands in the portfolio. This is despite advertising weights which were lower (eg Nescafé averaged 6,000 TVRs pre-1987 and 5,000 since).

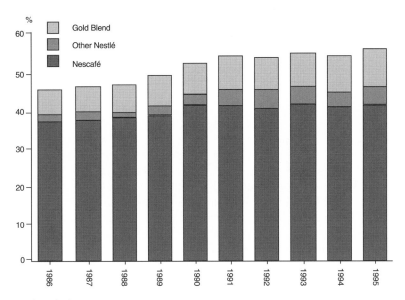

Figure 10: *Total Nestlé share*
Source: Nielsen

INTERNATIONAL SUCCESS

Although Nestlé believe in local advertising solutions, the Gold Blend campaign has proved capable of crossing borders. In most cases, reshot using local actors, it has run successfully in the US, Canada, Denmark, Norway, Sweden, Finland and Chile. However, it is not always identical; in the US, Sharon Maughan (from our first series) has a son. Still other countries, such as France and Australia, have used the basic theme of a series of ads charting the story of a sophisticated romance.

SUMMARY

The Gold Blend story may be the story of a love affair, but it is also a story of success. It is advertising the public loves. But it is also advertising that has resulted in sales success. It has grown from a minor player to the second-biggest coffee brand and one of the country's top 50 brands. And that success is no fly by night. It has been sustained over nearly ten years, with each year building on the previous one.

Moreover this was not chance, but came from the aim of creating an accessible 'upmarket' brand, and the ambition to be more like the programmes between which the advertising appeared.

The increased size of the brand is worth £50 million each year in sales, at a cost on average of £5 million a year in advertising spend. Furthermore this does not represent increased advertising spend, merely a more effective use of that money.

All in all a great success. To quote David Hudson, Communications Director of Nestlé UK:

> 'It is a campaign I take real pride in. Sometimes people ask me if the amount we spend on advertising is worth it. I tell them to look at the Gold Blend campaign.'

The one question we have left unanswered is 'what will happen next?'. We're not saying!

TECHNICAL APPENDIX

MediaSpan

MediaSpan is a way of looking at AGB's Superpanel households and comparing their buying of coffee brands and their viewing of television.

It works by 'fusing' the Superpanel and the BARB viewing panel. It does this by matching respondents on the BARB panel with those on the Superpanel. Information is collected about each Superpanel housewife's claimed usual viewing behaviour and matched to the usual (metered) behaviour of the BARB housewives. Thus the two panels are fused in terms of the viewing behaviour of each. The process has been validated by a series of holdout tests. BARB members living in the London TV area were excluded from the test and their viewing behaviour predicted by matching them with donors from the remainder of the panel. The correlation between the two was excellent ($r = 0.91$), and the pattern of prediction errors is unbiased.

The result of this is that, for each individual housewife, we know both their viewing history and their purchasing. For each individual purchase we can see what exposure they have had to our advertising. This allows us to construct a simple contingency table with four cells, depending on whether the housewife has been exposed to our advertising in the period immediately prior to her making a purchase, and whether she bought our brand or a competitor's. If advertising has had an effect then our brand share among those who have recently seen our advertising will be higher than among those who have not. This is the basis of the simple claim that 'seeing one ad or more in the last two weeks increases the volume of Gold Blend bought by 4%'.

In doing this it is important to ensure that there are no other factors which could cause this effect. Most other factors are automatically excluded. Housewives who have seen our advertising are generally no more likely to have been exposed to promotion, pricing or distribution changes than those who have not (at least with a well-distributed, well-established brand like Gold Blend). The main potential confounding factor is overall weight of viewing. Those who watch a lot of TV are more likely to have seen a Gold Blend ad recently than those who have not. This is a particular problem if the brand is naturally strong (or weak) among heavy viewers. This is certainly the case for Nescafé itself but is not a particular problem for Gold Blend. However, it is possible to remove this effect by looking at the effect of advertising separately for each weight of viewing group. Without doing this the effect on Gold Blend is that advertising increases sales by 4.3%. When this is controlled for, the effect is 4.0%, with no clear relationship between overall weight of viewing and advertising effect.

Similarly the effect can be assessed for all purchases made during periods when Gold Blend's price as measured on the AGB Superpanel was low compared to the competition (Kenco and 'Gold' own-label) and when it was high. It can also be broken out between those who have seen the ad once in the two weeks prior to purchase, those who have seen it twice and so on. Thus the effect of advertising is greatest among those who have seen the ad twice or more in the preceding two weeks and when the pricing is favourable.

All this analysis is based on viewing behaviour over the previous two weeks (ie a very short-term effect). The consideration of long-term effects is simpler. The Superpanel is split into those who are light viewers of TV and those who are heavier. If the advertising is having an effect, then we would expect the purchasing patterns of these to diverge over time as those who have seen more of the advertising increase their purchasing of the brand. This is unlikely to be dramatic for Gold Blend overall, over the period (1993–1995) that AGB has fused the panels since the campaign started six years before. However, as is shown in Figure 8, the effect comes through clearly with the new target.

Econometric Model

An Ordinary Least Squares Model of Gold Blend was constructed for Nestlé by Connections. Actually the reason for this model was to look at price but, in order to do so realistically, advertising was included as a variable.

Eight variables were found to be significant:

— Four separate price variables relating Gold Blend's price to that of its competition.

— Gift packs (eg free After Eight banded to pack).

— Two other promotional factors.

— Advertising.

Together these accounted for 82% of the variation in share of Gold Blend across the period 1990 to 1994.

$R^2 = 0.82$
F statistic $(8,46) = 30.8$
Number of observations = 55
Standard error of estimate = 0.27

Advertising was modelled by TVRs weighted by share of voice, ie TVRs without competitive activity were assumed to be more effective than those with. The co-efficient for advertising was 0.0012, which means that 835 TVRs will generate approximately an extra 25 tonnes of sales. The effect of advertising was highly significant (t = 3.95).

17

Kraft Philadelphia
The Philadelphia Story

A WORD FROM OUR CLIENT

'Over the last decade, the Philly girls have become one of the great advertising properties in the UK food business. They have created a strong bond with the British public while proving a flexible communication vehicle for developing and growing the Philadelphia brand.

The campaign effect has built the brand consistently year in, year out. The brand and the girls have moved with the times – new situations, brand innovations, line extensions, new usage have all been handled in a light-hearted, witty, humorous and effective fashion.

Most importantly, ten years on, the Philly girls continue to grow brand volume strongly, despite private-label and a huge explosion of choice in the chiller cabinet. The contribution made by the campaign to the value of the brand is, we estimate, more than double the advertising investment we made over the same period.'

Ronnie Bell, Managing Director, Kraft Jacobs Suchard UK

INTRODUCTION

The last ten years have seen classic fmcg brands facing unheralded pressures. Philadelphia confronted the challenges of a changing retail environment, increasingly powerful competition from retailers' own brands and changing consumer eating habits and attitudes to food, yet still grew by +2.6 times in retail sales value.

This case history involves textbook brand management incorporating extensions, promotions and, as this paper will demonstrate above all, the support of a consistent, long-running, popular and powerful TV campaign. It did this by:

— developing a wider role for the brand in people's everyday food repertoire by repositioning it from the special occasion luxury product that it was for a few up to the mid-1980s, to the 'everyday indulgence' enjoyed by many more that it is today;

— building a powerful set of images and associations for Philadelphia, capable of sustaining the brand over time, maintaining relevance to consumers and defending it against increasing competition;

— protecting its +50% market share and justifying its +20% price premium over own-label soft white cheeses despite their improving product quality and growing consumer acceptance;

— improving the financial health of the brand by nearly trebling its retail sales value over nine and a half years.

A STAR IS BORN

Cream cheese was invented in 1872 in Chester, New York. As the name suggests, it was a blend of cream and hard cheese. Philadelphia cream cheese was born eight years later in 1880. Kraft purchased the brand in 1928, and Philadelphia was introduced to the British public in 1963. It was the first premium soft white cheese to be available in the UK.

To that generation, Philadelphia was the premium soft white cheese – a position it held unchallenged for the next 20 years. It looked and tasted like nothing else on the market – justifying a charmingly simple launch advertising claim, *'At last, something quite new!'* (if only things were as simple today). We pick up the story in 1984 – two years before the launch of the advertising campaign with which we are concerned here.

PHILADELPHIA UNWRAPPED

Product

Philadelphia is a soft white cheese with a cool, fresh taste and a luxurious, creamy texture. Its core product attributes can best be summed up as cool, creamy and pure, providing unique eating enjoyment on a number of different levels (Figure 1).

Product Benefit

Rationally and emotionally, Philadelphia delivers 'permissible indulgence' – permissible because it is a natural, healthy, savoury food (it is not chocolate after all), and indulgent because of its sensory characteristics (ie creaminess). This case history demonstrates how a nearly ten-year-old advertising campaign rooted in this key benefit has helped to make this indulgence even more permissible and more widely accessible.

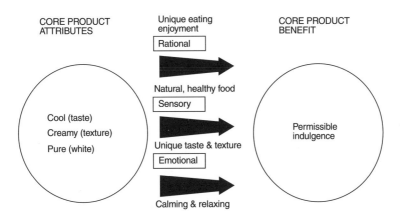

Figure 1: *Core product attributes*

THE PHILADELPHIA STORY

There have been four distinct phases of brand strategy within which important short-term advertising-driven achievements can be demonstrated (Figure 2). We have used these to tell the 'Philadelphia Story'.

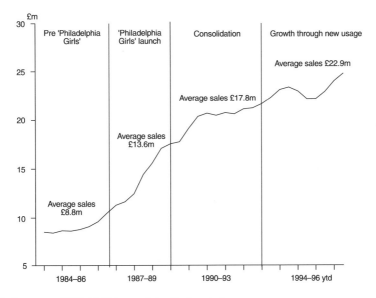

Figure 2: *The four stages of Philadelphia's growth (retail sales value)*
Source: IRI/JWT

(A)	Pre 'Philadelphia Girls'	1984–86
(B)	'Philadelphia Girls' launch	1987–89
(C)	Consolidation	1990–93
(D)	Growth through new usage	1994–96

PRE 'PHILADELPHIA GIRLS' (1984–86)

Having created the soft white cheese sector, by the mid-1980s, Philadelphia still had over half the market and was still the only branded, advertised player. To achieve further volume we did not have the option therefore of expanding by stealing share from rival brands. Philadelphia had to grow the market, while maintaining brand share at this high level. Although the only sensible decision at the time, it subsequently led to problems.

There were three challenges facing the brand.

'Everyone's Concerned About Fat'

By the mid-1980s fat had become a general health concern. Calories and fat were becoming an increasingly important issue for women (our core Philadelphia consumers).

The clearest way to demonstrate this is to look at their buying behaviour. Throughout the 1980s, high-fat products were in decline, while new, ultra low-fat products came onto the market and grew extraordinarily rapidly.

TABLE 1: GROWTH OF LOW-FAT PRODUCTS

Market value (£m)	1984	1986	Change +/-
Butter (80% fat)	412	346	-66
Margarine (80% fat)	299	303	+4
Low-fat spreads (40% fat or less)	43	89	+46
Very low-fat yoghurt	0	30	+30

Source: Mintel/LFRA estimates

Unfortunately for Philadelphia, it was seen as a high-fat product; consumers wrongly believed it was higher in fat than both butter and peanut butter.

TABLE 2: % OF PEOPLE WHO THINK THE BRAND IS 'FULL FAT'

	%	Actual fat content per 100g
Philadelphia	35	30g
Kerrygold	27	82g
Sunpat	17	51g

Base: 852 housewives
Source: Millward Brown, 1986

'You Can Have too Much of a Good Thing'

True to the core positioning of a 'permissible indulgence', Philadelphia was largely used on the cheeseboard, with crackers, for special occasions.

TABLE 3: PHILADELPHIA IMAGE STATEMENTS,
DEVIATIONS FROM EXPECTED NORMS

Good for special occasions	+27
Particularly creamy	+26
Mild and creamy taste	+16
Tastes delicious	+14

Source: Millward Brown Analysis, 1986

Philadelphia's advertising at the time set the brand on a pedestal as an occasional indulgence to be appreciated and savoured like wine. It positioned the brand firmly within a context of refinement and sophistication.

This meant that the brand tended to be purchased infrequently and had not attempted to establish itself as part of people's everyday eating habits.

'It's not for the Likes of You and Me'

Philadelphia has always been a 'female' brand, both in terms of its users and its personality.

In 1986, the brand had a penetration of only 15% of the population. Its core consumer was typically female, socially upscale and 25–45 years old (Figure 3).

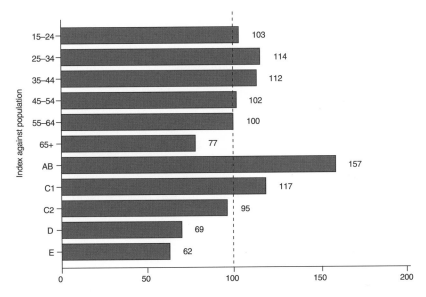

Figure 3: *Philadelphia consumer profile (1986)*
Base: 19,349 adults 15+ years
Brand Penetration: 15.1%
Source: BMRB/TGI

Philadelphia was personified by Penelope Keith, but we would have preferred the mainstream appeal of Felicity Kendal.

In response to consumer concerns over high-fat products, Kraft Jacobs Suchard developed a 'light' version of Philadelphia. It was half the fat of 'regular' and was every bit as cool, creamy, pure and delicious. It set a new quality standard for light products, and one that private-label struggled to match. Consumers looking for a lower-fat product needed to sacrifice little, if any, taste.

Philadelphia consumers found it hard to tell the difference between regular and light Philadelphia.

Quotes from Research among Loyal Philadelphia Buyers
Regarding the Light Variant

'It tastes really cool and creamy...'

'Oh, I thought this wouldn't taste nearly as good, but it's not bad really.'

'They taste the same don't they!'

Source: JWT Qualitative Research, 1987

The launch of Light Philadelphia posed massive new challenges for the portfolio management and advertising strategy of Philadelphia cream cheese.

The light variant was judged to need its own discrete advertising vehicle in order to communicate best its unique product benefits. Therefore, at the launch of Light Philadelphia in 1986, a twin-track advertising campaign was pursued – one introduced the new low-fat variant, the other continued to support the regular product.

The 'Light' execution reflected the prevailing health trends at the time. It balanced images of the pleasure of eating Philadelphia with a low-fat message.

This firmly positioned it in reduced-calorie territory, and thus limited the appeal of the new variant, as the following illustrates:

'The "light" launch commercial was a little too "diety"...taste was communicated but the onus was on its low calorie content – she's something of an earnest weight-watching type.'

Source: DRSM Qualitative Research Report

In practice, the launch of Light Philadelphia was rather a damp squib – we saw no major sales uplift until the end of the following year when a new creative vehicle had been introduced.

We had to find a way to communicate the 'light' message in a way that strongly linked it to the core parent brand benefit of a cool, creamy, pure indulgence, a way of linking this core of 'permissible indulgence' to both variants.

The creative solution was a campaign that has become known as the 'Philadelphia Girls'.

'PHILADELPHIA GIRLS' LAUNCH' (1987–89)

The central creative property of the 'Philadelphia Girls' is two talkative secretaries – Sarah and Anne. Sarah (the blonde one) is the wide-eyed, innocent, naïve brand novice and Anne (the dark one) is the East-End sophisticate brand expert. Although we name them here, to TV viewers, they are just the 'Philadelphia Girls'.

Anne introduces Sarah to the exciting, 'sophisticated' world of Philadelphia. Sarah watches wide-eyed and only wishes that she was as up-to-the-minute as her friend. Philadelphia is at the heart of Anne's office chatter, she loves to indulge herself with its cool, rich creaminess.

What sounds like a highly indulgent and still 'special occasion' scenario was brought down to earth by humour. This juxtaposition of humour and indulgent product values allowed Anne to adopt the role of 'brand advocate', speaking about the brand in a way that would have otherwise defied credibility.

With this campaign, we believed we had found a way of remaining true to our core product values – 'cool, creamy, pure' – while making them relevant to a wider audience in a more everyday context. The first advertisement in the campaign in the autumn of 1987 could not have been more down-to-earth – two secretaries comparing their sandwiches over lunch at their desks, and agreeing that the one with the Philadelphia was more interesting than the wilting 'ordinary sandwich'.

IMMEDIATE SUCCESSES

Campaign Awareness

The launch of the 'Philadelphia Girls' saw a step change in claimed advertising recall for Philadelphia.

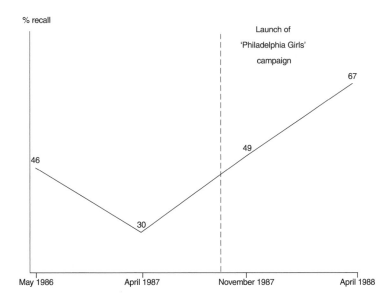

Figure 4: *Claimed recall of Philadelphia advertising (campaign launch period)*
Source: Millward Brown

The Millward Brown Awareness Index is the average level of advertising recall generated by 100 TVRs. While the comparable average for all food advertising is 5, the 'Philadelphia Girls' scored more than three times this average at 17, nine points higher than the previous Philadelphia campaign.

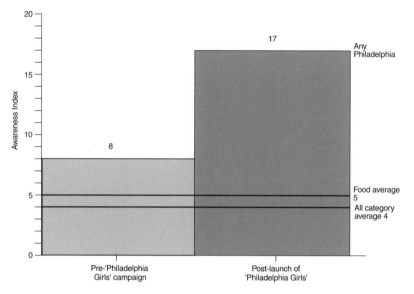

Figure 5: *Philadelphia Awareness Index (1986–88)*
Source: Millward Brown

Increasing Sales

The 'Philadelphia Girls' had an almost immediate sales effect on both the packaged soft white cheese market and on Philadelphia's share within it (Figures 6 and 7). Again, we can see a step change in the brand's performance.

Figure 6: *The soft white cheese market (retail sales value 1985–89)*
Source: IRI

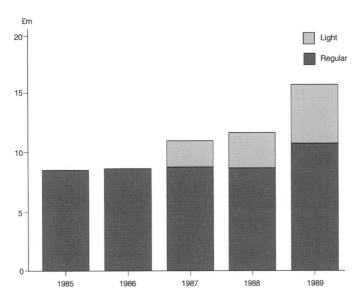

Figure 7: *Regular and Light Philadelphia (retail sales value 1985–89)*
Source: IRI

CONSOLIDATION (1990–93)

New Market Entrants

By both growing the soft white cheese market and making it more mainstream in appeal, Philadelphia had made a rod for its own back as all the major grocery multiples launched (and even relaunched with improved formulations) their own versions of Philadelphia.

Competition was not limited to own-label launches. There was also a flurry of branded launches at the same time, many of them continental soft cheeses at a significant premium to Philadelphia (Figure 8).

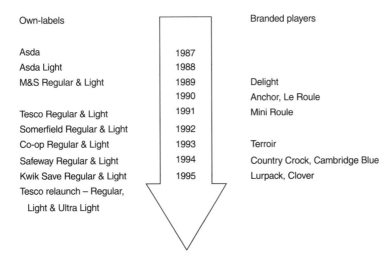

Figure 8: *Launches of packed soft white cheeses*
Source: IRI

Philadelphia found itself squeezed from the top end of the market, by premium, continental cheeses and, from the bottom, by own-label soft white cheeses.

It would be fair to expect that, in the face of this strong competitive onslaught, the Philadelphia brand would find both its share and its price premium being eroded significantly. In fact, neither occurred.

The brand was in a healthy state and ready to respond to meet new challenges – the consumer was possibly receptive to some new ideas from Philadelphia.

GROWTH THROUGH NEW USAGE 1994–96

Brand Strategy

Having successfully addressed the 'fat' issue via a light variant, and the rather exclusive positioning by making the brand more accessible, mainstream and everyday, Philadelphia faced another factor limiting its growth potential.

Philadelphia was most commonly eaten on crackers and bread (Figure 9). This was limiting the number of occasions on which the brand was taken out of the fridge.

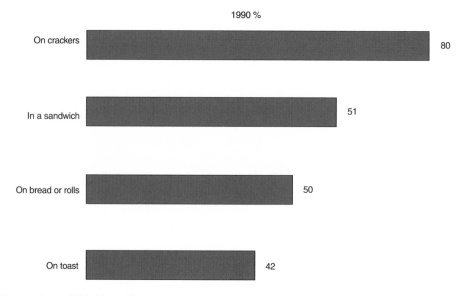

Figure 9: *Usage of Philadelphia (all users)*
Source: Millward Brown

The brand consumption profile had a large 'infrequent purchase' tail. Only a quarter (26%) of Philadelphia consumers were eating it more than once a week (Figure 10).

Frequent eaters of Philadelphia had invented all kinds of opportunities (excuses) to enjoy it more often.

The strategy we put in place was to show new serving suggestions to less frequent Philadelphia users, in order to expand their consumption of the brand.

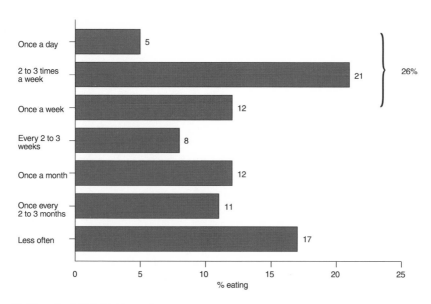

Figure 10: *How often is Philadelphia eaten?*
Source: MRBI

Over time, this 'extended usage' strategy has been executed in a number of different ways (Figure 11).

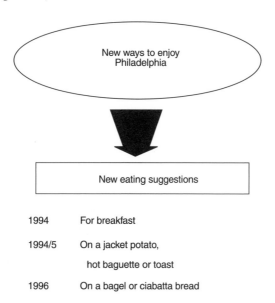

Figure 11: *New ways to enjoy Philadelphia*
Source: KJS/JWT

Quotes for Qualitative Research among Frequent Philadelphia Eaters

'You can experiment with it.'

'If you make a vegetable casserole, you can melt it across the top.'

'Jacket potato, biscuits, it's everyday for me.'

'My husband has it for breakfast on toast.'

Source: DRSM, 1995

Immediate Successes

The objective of the advertising became to effect a behavioural change – to get people to use Philadelphia in ways they might have not previously considered.

There were two strands to the advertising strategy: show people new ways to eat Philadelphia and show them new occasions to eat it.

We knew that our advertising still had to remain true to our core brand values – 'permissible indulgence' – while remaining flexible enough to communicate clearly a new usage message. Again, the 'Philadelphia Girls' proved the ideal vehicle to do this. Their mere presence in the advertising had become synonymous with the brand and its values, while their love for Philadelphia allowed them to talk directly about new eating suggestions without losing any of the charm of the long-running campaign idea.

In 1994 we decided to attempt a radical behavioural change by taking a cheese – Philadelphia – onto the British breakfast tray (very continental).

Millward Brown figures at the time showed a dramatic uplift in claimed usage at breakfast.

TABLE 4: CLAIMED USAGE OCCASIONS FOR PHILADELPHIA (ALL USERS)

	1993 %	1994 %	% +/-
Can be eaten for breakfast	8	36	+28
Can be eaten at any mealtime	14	50	+36

Source: Millward Brown 1995

In 1994/5, we also showed three new hot usage suggestions. All aimed to make Philadelphia more appropriate to eat in winter. In the commercials, Sarah invites Anne around to her flat to be treated with hot baguettes, toast and jacket potatoes all smothered in cool creamy Philadelphia.

Millward Brown data at the time showed the impact on people's behaviour.

TABLE 5: CLAIMED RECENT USAGE OF PHILADELPHIA (ALL USERS)

	Pre-burst %	Post-burst %	% +/-
On jacket potatoes	38	45	+7
On warm bread rolls	23	27	+4

Source: Millward Brown, 1995

1996 saw the 'Philadelphia Girls' introducing us to the delights of Philadelphia served on a ciabatta roll and on a bagel, while 'surfing the internet' and using an 'interactive language laboratory' – further evidence of the campaign's ability not only to introduce new serving suggestions but also to remain contemporary and abreast of current trends and eating habits, ensuring its continued relevance to consumers.

THE WHOLE STORY (1985–95)

Famous Well-Loved Advertising

One of the most graphic ways of demonstrating the impact and life of an advertising campaign is to see how long it remains in people's memories. It is a particularly important measure when the advertising is so inextricably linked with the brand's core values as is Philadelphia, so much so that longevity becomes a measure of depth and breadth of values added through advertising.

The Millward Brown 'Base Level' is a measure of the accumulated value that the advertising has over time: ie what percentage of people go on thinking that they have recently seen a commercial for the brand when, in fact, what they are recalling is not the last execution, but rather the cumulative effect of seeing the campaign over many years.

The 'Philadelphia Girls' campaign took the brand's Base Level from 7 to a massive 27. This is compared to an average for all brands of 9 – vivid testimony of the 'longer and broader' effect of the advertising (Figure 12).

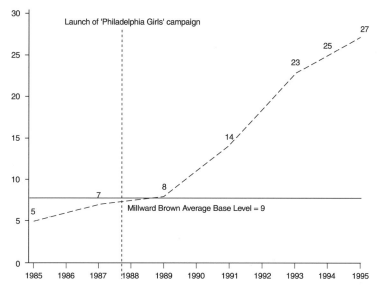

Figure 12: *Philadelphia base level, 1985–95*
Source: Millward Brown

'COOL & FRESH' 1986 (PRIOR TO 'PHILADELPHIA GIRLS')

'LAY IT ON THICK' 1987 (LAUNCH OF 'PHILADELPHIA GIRLS')

'ROOM SERVICE' 1994

'STARS IN HER EYES' 1994

'ON THE CARDS' 1994

'STORM IN A TEACUP' 1996

Qualitative advertising research illustrates how well loved the 'Philadelphia Girls' are and how effectively they have evolved over time:

> 'Most respondents identified with them [the girls]. They were acknowledged to be parodies of real people...silly/dizzy, friendly and occasionally competitive. Respondents suggested they would miss them if the campaign stopped.'

> 'Over time the girls have developed from being colleagues to being friends...now both can teach each other about Philly.'

Source: DRSM, April 1995

Brand Democratisation

Over a nine-year period, the brand lost its niche image, Philadelphia could be enjoyed at any time, not just on special occasions. This was achieved without diminishing any of Philadelphia's appetite appeal; perceptions of it as delicious, indulgent and creamy-tasting actually increased.

TABLE 6: CHANGING IMAGE PERCEPTIONS 1986–95

	1985 %	1990 %	1995 %	+/- % change
Good for special occasions	50	45	40	-10
Particularly creamy	47	43	48	+1
Mild and creamy taste	40	45	48	+8
Tastes delicious	39	36	41	+2
Is an indulgent snack	31	29	40	+9

Base: All agreeing with statement
Source: Millward Brown tracking study

Not only had Philadelphia succeeded in keeping its core consumers, who had moved with the brand and were now 35–45 years old (ie ten years older), it had also successfully attracted new, younger consumers into the brand – growing its consumer base to almost one-quarter of the population. It had also become more mainstream in its appeal, losing some of its over-dependence on socially upscale consumers.

TABLE 7: PHILADELPHIA DEMOGRAPHIC PROFILE

	1985	1995	+/- %
Base:	19,349	23,819	
Brand penetration:	15.1%	23.5%	+8.4%
	Index against population		
15–24 years	103	112	+9
25–34 years	114	109	-5
35–44 years	112	121	+9
45–54 years	102	112	+10
55–64 years	100	99	-1
65+ years	77	69	-8
AB	157	128	-29
C1	117	116	-1
C2	95	93	-2
D	69	76	+7
E	62	68	+6

Source: BMRB/TGI

Building Brand Stature

Philadelphia is not a large brand by packed grocery standards (one-fifth of the retail sales value of Tetley Tea bags, for example), but it feels like a big brand. It is a household name. It is not just media folk who love the 'Philadelphia Girls' – their fame lasts for longer than the time the commercials spend on air. They exist outside the commercials that created them, and the actresses have even been given their own TV show.

There is no risk of the messengers dwarfing the message as the 'Philadelphia Girls' are synonomous with the brand name and values. Their existence outside the commercials depends on the good humour, enjoyment and forgivable indulgence which characterises the Philadelphia advertising, which these other activities extend and complement.

Increasing the Market Value

Despite intense competition from own-label and new brand launches, Philadelphia has continued to grow more rapidly than the rest of the market.

When compared to overall market growth, it is clear that the soft white cheese sector has been driven by Philadelphia's growth for the last ten years (Figure 13).

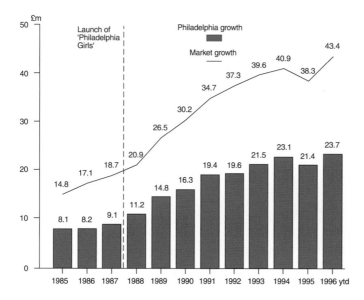

Figure 13: *Market and brand growth (discounting the effect of food inflation)*
Source: IRI

Increasing the Brand's Value

Since the launch of the 'Philadelphia Girls' campaign, the brand has performed the difficult balancing act of expanding the market as a whole and expanding Philadelphia's substantial share of that market. Sales of cream cheese in the 1996 year to date are 2.5 times greater by value then they were in 1987. Sales of Philadelphia have done even better – 2.9 times greater at the start of 1996 than they were at the start of 1987 (after discounting the effects of food inflation).

Protecting Brand Share

From the mid-1980s, Philadelphia has been faced with a whole raft of new own-label and branded competitors. Own-label offerings were considerably cheaper; new brands were priced, packaged and positioned as the more expensive alternatives.

The best demonstration of the entrenched values consistently reinforced by the advertising is that no other brand has ever captured more that 10% of the market. Shape (Philadelphia's main branded rival) now has value brand share of just 5% – slightly less than in 1985.

Despite this two-way squeeze, Philadelphia actually grew both its volume and value share of the total packaged soft white cheese market (Figures 14 and 15).

Rather than cannibalise sales of Regular, Light actually grew the Philadelphia brand (Figure 16). It was only in 1995 that sales of Light overtook Regular for the first time.

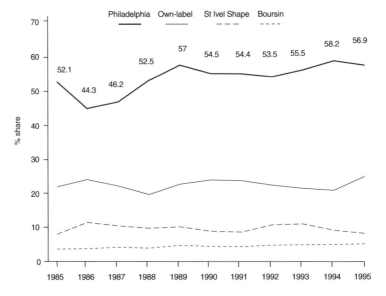

Figure 14: *Volume share 1985–95*
Source: IRI

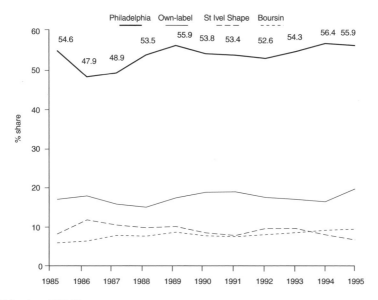

Figure 15: *Value share 1985–95*
Source: IRI

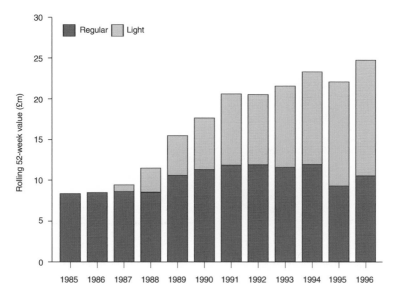

Figure 16: *Sales of Philadelphia by variant*
Source: IRI

Fighting off Own-Label

Looking at related product fields, it would have been reasonable to expect that, as the market grew, own-label would take an increasingly dominant share of sales. This was not the case. In fact, own-label penetration of the market is lower than any other related food product field (Figure 17).

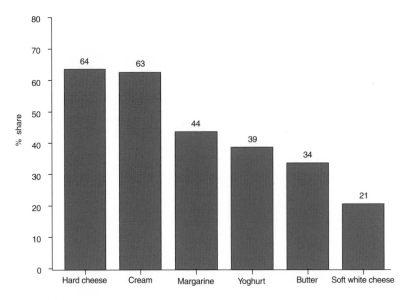

Figure 17: *Own-label shares of dairy products 1990–95*
Source: Datamonitor

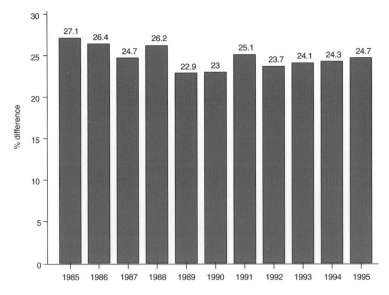

Figure 18: *Price differential versus own-label*
Source: IRI

The strength of Philadelphia brand values has not only maintained its share against all newcomers, but has continued to justify a price premium of +20% over own-label soft white cheeses (Figure 18).

HOW THE ADVERTISING HAS WORKED

Our media strategy has been very important to the way in which the advertising has achieved its objectives. The commercials have mainly been deployed on a four-weekly on-air/off-air cycle. This allowed us to maintain a year-round presence for the brand – always keeping Philadelphia front-of-mind.

The result was a Millward Brown Base Level for the advertising that not only climbed rapidly throughout the campaign but was also able to sustain high levels of year-in-year-out recall (Figure 19).

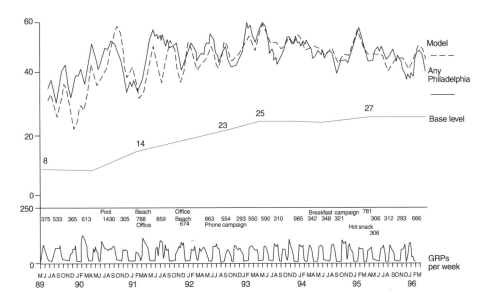

Figure 19: *Year-in year-out recall, rolling eight-weekly data*
Base: Main sample
Source: Millward Brown

In order to confirm the link between high advertising recall and growing sales, we used econometric modelling to compare four-weekly sales data with our four-weekly media cycle over the last ten years of the brand's history. This failed to identify any discernible short-term sales effect. We believe that this was due to the fact that the measuring points for sales coincided with each four-week burst of advertising – thereby masking the short-term kick-up in sales at the start of each advertising burst. By measuring the peaks of every sales cycle, the model inevitably produced a straight line.

Any long-term advertising effect is simply the aggregate of many short-term effects. We believe we have already proven the long-term effects of advertising Philadelphia in increasing people's consumption of the brand. We also wanted to demonstrate a short-term effect on people's purchase behaviour.

We decided, therefore, to use the more sensitive measure of plotting weekly sales figures against weekly TVR impacts, over an 18-month period, to determine our short-term advertising sales effect.

Our model has discounted pricing and promotional activities and has treated distribution as a constant. The model demonstrates a +8.4% short-term uplift in sales through multiples and co-ops as a direct result of the advertising (Figure 20). This is the equivalent of +623,000kg or 4.9 million standard (125g) packs of Philadelphia.

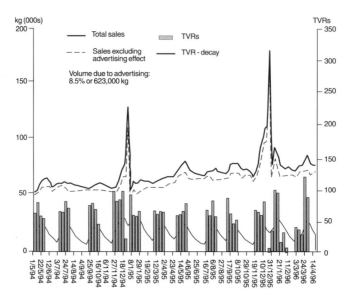

Figure 20: *Philadelphia cream cheese, volume sales – multiples and co-ops, May 1994–May 1996*

This short-term effect of advertising demonstrated is over and above the already considerable long-term contribution that advertising has already made to the brand's continuing success.

ISOLATING THE ADVERTISING EFFECT

In order to isolate the effect of Philadelphia advertising in maintaining and strengthening the brand over a near ten-year period we examined and eliminated other factors.

Distribution

Philadelphia enjoys near optimum distribution and has done since the early 1980s – moving from 92% of sterling weighted distribution in 1984 to 96% in 1995. Therefore, distribution cannot account for any substantial element of growth.

Product Formulation

Regular Philadelphia's product formulation has altered little over the last 30 years and Light Philadelphia has been unchanged since its launch in October 1987. There can be no doubt that a major contribution to the success of the Philadelphia brand, and its ability to justify its premium price, has come from the consistent product and the consistent communication of its cool, creamy and pure attributes.

Packaging

The Philadelphia pack design today very closely resembles the pack in which the brand was launched in 1963. Philadelphia established the rules of the category by which all new entrants to the market have had to conform.

The pack's bold use of silver, blue and white has come to symbolise the coolness, creaminess and purity of the product itself, and is a key component to the brand's fame.

In 1983 the brand became available in a tub as well as the traditional brick format while the foil front and pack graphics remained constant. Since this change occurred four years prior to the 'Philadelphia Girls' campaign, its effects have been discounted.

Promotions and Pricing

Promotions on Philadelphia have tended to give extra value to the consumer (eg 25% extra free). These have traditionally run at Christmas and have usually produced short-term gains in share, which can be monitored, and their long-term significance discounted by econometric modelling. The dramatic sales uplift that occurred in December 1995 was due to a 50% extra free promotion. Again this has been taken into consideration when modelling the effects of advertising. Since Philadelphia has sustained such a significant and consistent price premium over the entire period in question, it is unlikely that the strong performance of the brand was fuelled by value-led promotions.

Weight of Advertising Support

Since the launch of the 'Philadelphia Girls' campaign the brand has maintained a fairly consistent share of voice – never falling below 70% (Figure 21).

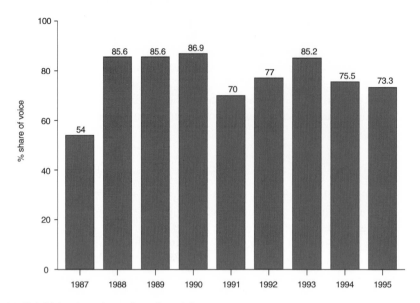

Figure 21: *Philadelphia share of voice (by media spend)*
Source: Media Register

No other branded player in this market has ever had a major advertising presence, and thus competitive media activity has been discounted as a possible contributor to market growth.

Flavour Variants

In the 1990s, Philadelphia has tactically used new flavour variants to add news at the point of purchase (ie in the chiller cabinet). In 1990 Pineapple, Garlic & Herbs and Salmon were launched as Light variants. In 1995, Pepper was launched, replacing Pineapple and, in 1996, Ham was launched, replacing Salmon.

These flavour variants have never accounted for more than 5% of Philadelphia's brand value and thus cannot be a key factor.

THE FUTURE

Presently, the 'Philadelphia Girls' will be on air to launch Philadelphia 'Handisnacks' – a new combination of whipped Philadelphia and breadsticks, ideal for 'permissible indulgence' whilst on the hoof. This is yet another demonstration of the flexibility of the campaign idea, allowing the brand to evolve with the changing eating habits of its consumers.

Although it is far too early to track this campaign, its incredibly high scores in an impact and communication pre-test led Millward Brown to describe it as 'the best Link Test result for a new product we've ever seen'. It seems only fair to allow the 'Girls' to sum up the current state of play in their own unique style – 'lovely'.

18

Seven Years In Provence

How a change in strategy helped Stella Artois retain market dominance

BACKGROUND

The Extent of Stella's Dominance

Stella is a classic example of the power of brands and, as a corollary, advertising. In its Belgian homeland, Stella is a swilling lager lacking in premium credentials; in blind taste tests in the UK the product regularly finishes bottom of the league (being too bitter for many).

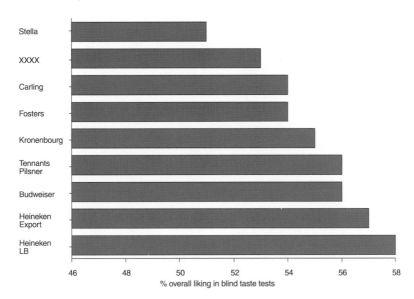

Figure 1: *Attitudes to the Stella product*
Source: Martin Hamblin

However, add the Stella name and the perspective of British lager drinkers changes radically.

'Stella is regarded as the epitome of full-flavoured lager, it is something to savour, a real drink of the highest quality…it is not so much established as positively timeless. It is, in short, a classic brand.'

Source: Nick Kenway, September 1995

This phenomenon, where brand potency overcomes product reality, is also seen quantitatively. Stella outperforms its key competitors on almost every image dimension.

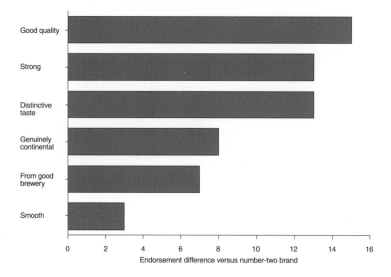

Figure 2: *Image differential versus number-two brand*
Source: Whitbread Market Research

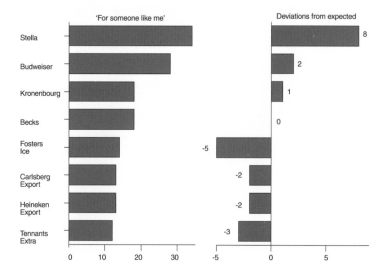

Figure 3: *Brand preference*
Source: Whitbread Market Research

It also has the greatest consumer preference of any premium lager brand.

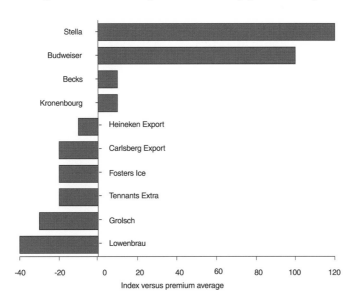

Figure 4: *Brands drunk regularly*
Source: Whitbread Market Research

As a result, Stella is clear market leader, selling nearly 900,000 barrels in 1995, enough to fill the Albert Hall twice over.

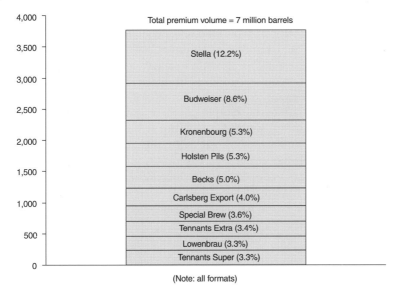

Figure 5: *Premium lager volume – top ten brands (1995)*
Source: Whitbread Corporate Information

How Stella Came to Dominance

Since 'standard' lager first revolutionised British beer drinking in the early '70s, there has been an ongoing 'lagerisation' of the country's pubs and supermarkets.

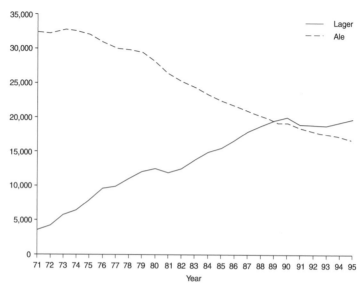

Figure 6: *Volume sales – lager versus ale*
Source: BMS/Whitbread

By 1980, lager had captured over 30% of beer volume, with 'standard' still the dominant variant (over 80% of total sales). But change was on the horizon. As the decade of badge-wearing unfolded, the more affluent and individualistic of consumers turned increasingly to premium lager; its lower penetration offered exclusivity, its price was an outward sign of affluence, and its strength an indication of quality and discernment.

And it was Stella that best exemplified these qualities. The brand had been advertised in the press on a quality/cost platform since the early '70s. However, both campaign and brand came of age with the addition of the 'Reassuringly Expensive' endline in 1982. In two words this captured the spirit of the times, positioning Stella drinkers as discerning and successful, with the cash to prove it.

From that point on the brand flourished. Its share of premium lager rose from 6% to 11%, while commanding a significant price premium over comparable brands.[1]

However, all good things come to an end and, towards the turn of the decade there were signs that the conditions under which the brand had thrived were changing.

---

1.   The 1992 Effectiveness Awards' winning paper 'Reassuringly Expensive' covers this period up to 1989 in detail (*Advertising Works 7*).

Changing Market Dynamics

The driving force behind these changes was the consistent growth premium lager has enjoyed since the mid '80s.

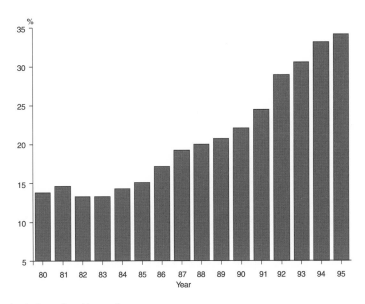

Figure 7: *Premium's share of total lager sales*
Source: BMS/Whitbread

Not simply a case of 'early adopters' drinking more, premium lager was instead following a classic adoption curve, with mainstream 'followers' entering the market as it matured (evidenced by growth in penetration).

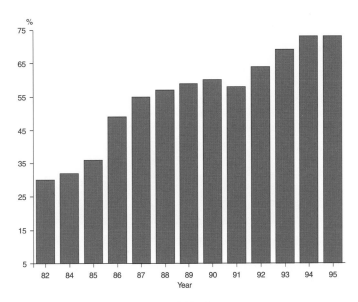

Figure 8: *Premium lager penetration among 18- to 34-year-old males*
Source: TGI

Unlike the experimental and individualistic core users, these new premium lager devotees were more likely to be younger 'ordinary blokes', trading up from standard lager as premium became better established. They brought with them different needs and motivations as a consequence.

Alongside this increased penetration, there was also massive growth in the number of brands consumers could choose from over this period (Figure 9).

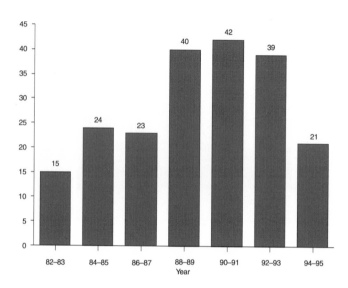

Figure 9: *Premium lager launches*
Source: Whitbread Take Home Annual Report

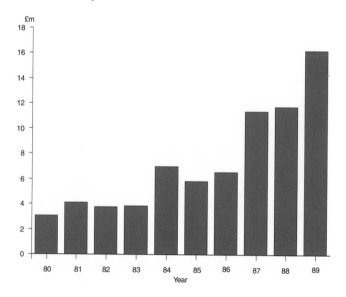

Figure 10: *Key competitor spend*
Source: Media Register

In turn, this brand explosion was mirrored by a big increase in media investment as the major players fought to be heard. In 1980 only five premium brands advertised, spending £3 million; by 1989 ten brands spent over five times this amount, mostly behind high-profile television campaigns (Figure 10).

The Implications for Stella

For Stella this market explosion was a double-edged sword. As market leader it benefited initially from the increase in penetration; distribution alone made it a default option for many. However, growth also presented the brand with problems it had not faced before.

To begin with, Stella's media investment had actually fallen as that of the competition increased; consequently, share of voice suffered dramatically, plummeting from 17% to 4%.

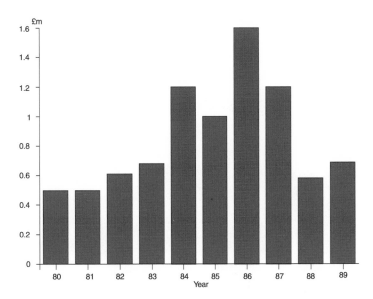

Figure 11: *Stella media spend*
Source: Media Register

In a repertoire market, this declining presence had potentially detrimental implications for Stella, despite its market-leader status.

Even among core users, there was danger of erosion in its share of repertoire consumption, while among new market entrants the situation was even more precarious.

Stella might have been attracting these younger, more mainstream drinkers, but they were not necessarily wedded to it in the same way early adopters were.

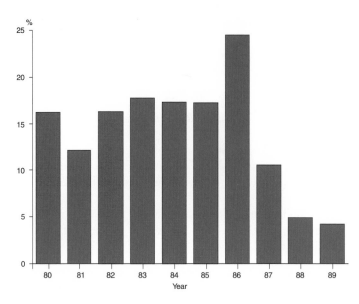

Figure 12: *Stella share of voice*
Source: Media Register

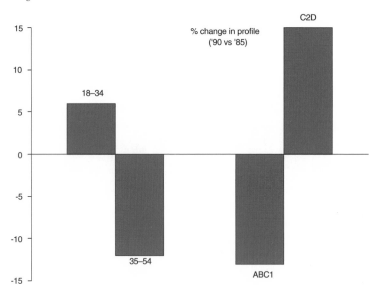

Figure 13: *The changing profile of Stella drinkers*
Source: TGI

The fact that the brand's media and creative strategy seemed unlikely to consummate the marriage only made matters worse. In an increasingly TV-orientated, mainstream market, Stella's press-only campaign and 'opinion former' buying strategy had the potential for invisibility. Moreover, even if the 'ordinary blokes' the brand now needed to appeal to did see a Stella execution it could easily pass them by; the shift from stylish bar to back-street boozer meant the price and exclusivity message was far less relevant than it had been previously.

This was exacerbated by the onset of recession, high interest rates and plummeting house prices, which had left consumer confidence at a low ebb; Stella's message actually had the potential to be salt in the wound for some. As a researcher concluded:

> 'The executions appealed to the more advertising literate and discerning, but were rejected by the majority as too verbose and sophisticated…[the focus on expense] touched a raw nerve for many.'

Source: MBL, July 1993

So, as the '90s beckoned, Stella found itself facing tougher competition, with a radically reduced share of voice, a new type of drinker to appeal to and a potentially less than relevant advertising message.

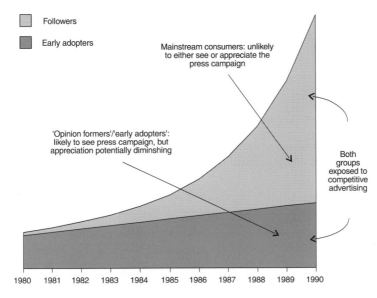

Figure 14: *The diminishing effectiveness of Stella's consumer communications*

There was no danger of absolute rejection. However, changing market dynamics and reduced advertising effectiveness meant that Stella's dominance of drinker repertoires was no longer unassailable; the threat of marginalisation was looming, even among core users.

Evidence of a Downturn in Stella's Fortunes

By the turn of the decade, this threat was fast becoming reality. First, Stella was becoming less salient, a worrying sign for a brand of its size.

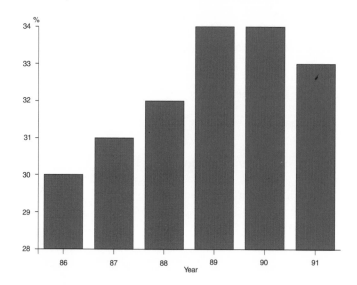

Figure 15: *Stella – Spontaneous brand awareness*
NB: Data go back no further than 1986
Source: Whitbread Market Research, lager U&A

This was mirrored by a decline in claimed usage; Stella's position in drinker repertoires was weakening as feared.

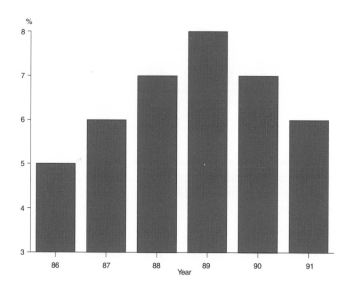

Figure 16: *Stella usage – drink most often*
NB: Data go back no further than 1986
Source: Whitbread Market Research, lager U&A

Also, as the more recent advertising tracking study shows, brand empathy was suffering.

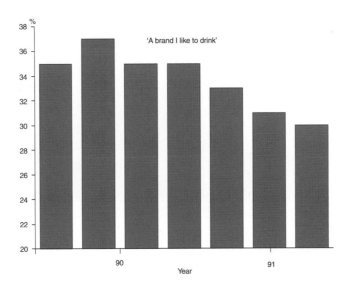

Figure 17: *Stella brand empathy*
Source: Millward Brown tracking study

As brand appeal and repertoire pre-eminence waned, Stella also suffered erosion of its previously fortress-like brand share (Figure 18).[2]

In two years, brand share declined by nearly 1% point. Arguably, this could be attributed to increased competition in a growing market. However, more worrying was the impact on volume (Figure 19).

2. NB: for the purposes of this paper we will concentrate specifically on Stella's performance in draught and cans. We recognise that bottles are a significant growth area. However, Stella has always been, and remains to this day, a minor player in that sector: 10% of volume versus 35% for the total market. It is more representative of brand performance, therefore, to concentrate on those formats which account for 90% of sales. The fact remains, though, that regardless of whether bottles are included or excluded, Stella is still a dominant market leader.

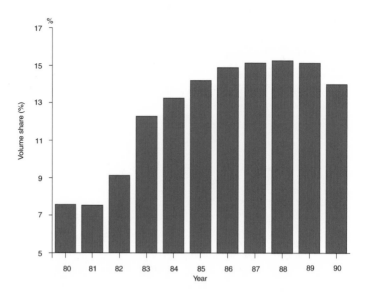

Figure 18: *Stella share*
Source: BMS/Whitbread

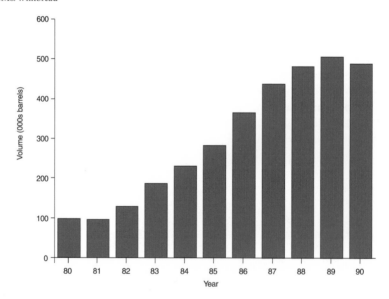

Figure 19: *Stella sales*
Source: BMS/Whitbread

It has since been calculated that, between 1988 and 1990, Stella effectively 'lost' over 56,000 barrels.[3] This may not seem much for a brand which was selling close

---

3. Lost volume calculated by estimating what Stella's sales would have been if it had grown in line with the market; ie if its share had remained constant at 1988 levels.

to 500,000 barrels a year. However, with a wholesale price averaging £200 a barrel, it was equivalent to a turnover loss of £11.3 million.

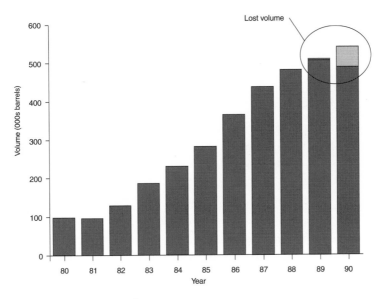

Figure 20: *Stella sales (actual versus expected)*
Source: BMS/Whitbread

Something had to be done. Even if Stella did not lose its number one position, Whitbread could not afford to haemorrhage this much money from one of its biggest brands.

Advertising clearly had a role to play in any remedial action; it was potentially a contributory factor to Stella's under-performance after all, but still arguably the most potent weapon in the brand's armoury when it came to rectifying the situation. At the start of 1990, therefore, an extensive review was prescribed.

THE ADVERTISING SOLUTION

What Advertising had to Achieve

The objective for Stella as the '90s unfolded was clear: to compete more effectively in the new mainstream premium lager market, to stop the decline in fortunes and to reassert its former dominance.

To produce advertising that helped deliver this clearly required two things: a creative strategy relevant to the new premium lager environment and a media strategy which would allow our message to be heard. To help inform these, strategic development research was conducted.

Strategic Development

Research confirmed that the Stella message needed to be updated; if the brand was to be relevant in the new decade it needed to be brought in line with a more mainstream audience and changing consumer attitudes ('credibility' and 'value' more than 'exclusivity' and 'high price').

At the same time though, we needed to tread carefully; research also showed that, in an abstract sense, Stella's 'gold standard' positioning and 'reassuringly expensive' line remained incredibly potent and valuable assets. While both needed to be reframed, especially Stella's now potentially alienating high price claim, we certainly did not want to throw the baby out with the bath water.

To tread this thin line effectively, the creative brief moved away from the realms of 'expensive' (so it must be good quality), asking instead for advertising that positioned Stella as:

'*The* lager of supreme quality and worth.'

This might seem an exercise in semantics. However, it proved fundamental in turning around the brand's fortunes, representing as it did a subtle but potent shift in emphasis away from the consumers' ability to pay, to their discernment as drinkers.

But this was only half the job done; the advertising also needed to be seen, which required a media decision.

Even with a new message, a press-only strategy was unlikely to be competitive in the new world of premium lager. In future, we would need to shout far louder. As a consequence, TV was the obvious choice. The stature it guaranteed made it the only medium commensurate with Stella's brand-leader status. Moreover, it would better enable Stella to communicate with the new, mainstream premium lager drinker.

Advertising Development – the Birth of a Great Campaign

The creative work which emerged was built around the simple idea that 'those people who appreciate good lager would give up anything for a pint of Stella Artois'.

The first execution, 'Jacques' (the template for subsequent films – 'Monet', 'Rainbow' and 'Good Samaritan'), took its inspiration from the acclaimed French film *Jean de Florette*.

In terms of looks, pace, tone and structure this broke all the rules of the day. Where most ads were deliberately complex and 'difficult' or firmly rooted in the frenetic world of '80s 'one-upmanship', Stella ploughed its own distinct furrow.

With its timeless Provençal setting and relaxed pace, 'Jacques' dripped with charm and quality connotations, perfectly reinterpreting the Stella positioning while remaining close to the heartbeat of the brand. Here was something both the Stella cognoscenti could appreciate, given the overt link with French cinema, as well as the majority of new drinkers, simply because it was a good yarn interestingly told.

However, trouble was on the horizon.

With echoes of the birth of Heineken's 'Refreshes the Parts' campaign in the early '70s, research painted a more ambiguous picture of the campaign's potential. Both qualitatively and quantitatively the idea was understood and was considered to be very different. However, many respondents criticised it as boring, slow, unmemorable and lacking in humour (the music, now one of the campaign trademarks), being a prime culprit:

'Brand-linked memorability is such that advertising awareness is likely to be below average. There is an indication that the commercial will not fuel a sense of exclusivity around the brand or communicate quality worth paying for.'

Source: Millward Brown Link Test, May 1990

'For most the storyline was felt to be uninteresting and boring, and the humour not strong enough. Though obviously very different, the execution was not felt to be particularly memorable.'

Source: BMRB, July 1990

Fortunately, both the agency and client had total confidence that 'Jacques' was right for Stella. As had been the case with the 'Refreshes the Parts' campaign in the early '70s, this lukewarm response was attributed to the 'shock of the new'. In a leap of faith everything proceeded as planned.

PUTTING THE CAMPAIGN ON AIR

To date, £12.8 million has been invested in supporting the 'Reassuringly Expensive' campaign on TV. With a combined production budget of £1.4 million, this equates to a total investment of £14.2 million since 1990.

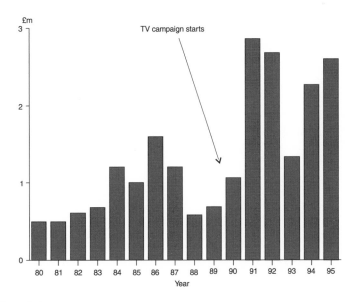

Figure 21: *Stella media investment*
Source: Media Register

Initially at least, this took the form of a regional test.[4] By the following year though, Stella had become a fully fledged, nationally advertised brand.

However, despite these big spend increases, investment across this period was actually relatively low for the market. Consequently, Stella's share of voice did not enjoy a similar enhancement, remaining below the levels achieved during the early '80s.

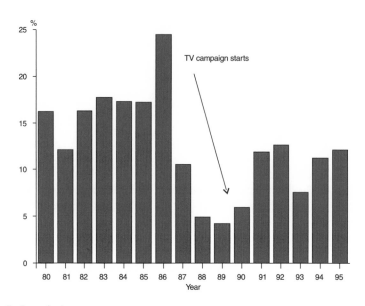

Figure 22: *Stella share of voice*
Source: Media Register

In fact, since going fully national, the brand has still been heavily outspent by some of its arch advertising rivals.

So, even with an increased spend and a shift to TV, Stella still had its work cut out when it came to competing in the new premium lager world.

---

4.   London only in June 1990, rolling out to TVS and HTV at the end of the year.

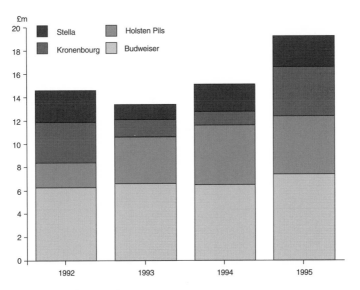

Figure 23: *Competitive premium lager spend*
Source: Media Register

'ON-AIR' PERFORMANCE OF 'REASSURINGLY EXPENSIVE'

Fortunately, the lukewarm response predicted by research did not materialise when the advertising was aired in the real world; the 'shock of the new' became a genuine and noticeable point of difference.

> 'The advertising is admirably different from the frenetic weirdness of the competition. It has great stand-out against its rivals, which all tend to plough the same furrow.'

Source: Graham Hall and Associates, 1993

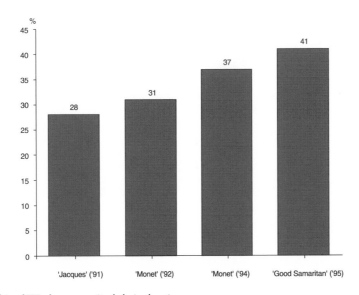

Figure 24: *Claimed TV ad awareness (peak during burst)*
Source: Millward Brown

Moreover, this impact has increased with each airing (despite the spend issues discussed earlier), culminating with the latest film, 'Good Samaritan'.

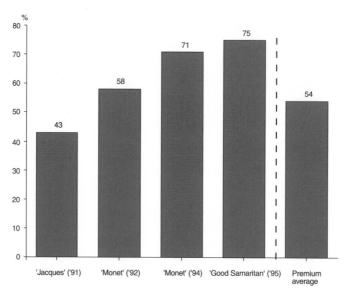

Figure 25: *Proportion correctly branding from stills*
Source: Millward Brown

The campaign has also proved to be very well liked, even among a mainstream audience.

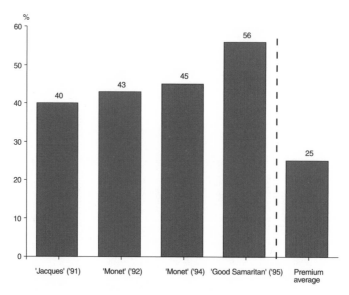

Figure 26: *Proportion who 'enjoy watching'*
Source: Millward Brown

Finally, the TV incarnation of 'Reassuringly Expensive' has clearly communicated the new Stella message of quality and worth.

'A popular campaign which communicates that Stella is a high-quality lager worth paying for. It is successful because its communication is effective, relevant and unique.'

Source: Okwell Associates, 1991

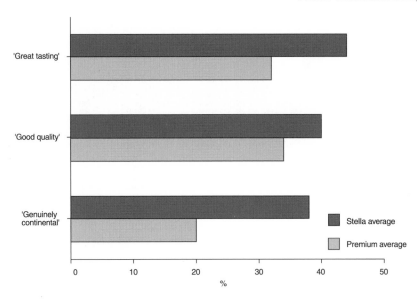

Figure 27: *Key communication from commercials*
Source: Millward Brown

And there appears to be no waning in the campaign's potency to this day.

'The advertising – like the beer – has a good reputation and is regarded as one of the best campaigns around. Distinctive, entertaining and appropriate for Stella, it is above and apart from the usual frenetic, humour-orientated offerings.'

Source: Alistair Burns, 1996

ADVERTISING'S EFFECT ON INTERMEDIARY MEASURES

Once the campaign became properly established after going national, goodwill towards the advertising soon translated into improved brand perceptions; Stella forced its way back into the hearts, minds and repertoires of drinkers.

In terms of consumer attitudes then, the advertising does seem to have achieved its objective; it has helped make Stella relevant, motivating and appealing to a new generation of premium lager drinkers, allowing the brand to reinforce its repertoire position and reassert its 'Gold Standard' positioning.

The real test, though, would come with sales; if advertising did not shift pints at the Dog & Duck the investment would have been to no avail.

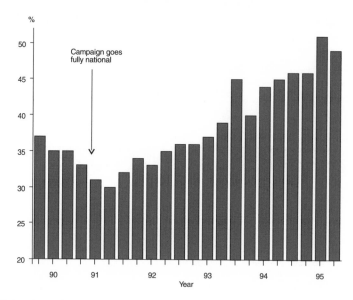

Figure 28: *Stella brand empathy*
Source: Millward Brown

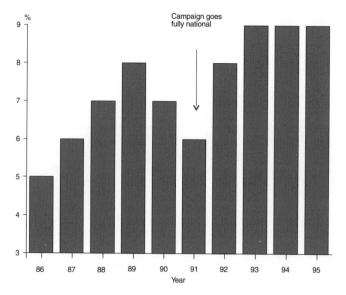

Figure 29: *Proportion claiming to drink Stella most often*
Source: Whitbread Market Research

SALES EFFECT

Setting the Scene

Before considering sales effect, there are two factors that should be taken into account.

First, the market conditions which contributed to Stella's downturn in fortunes still remain to a large extent. Without remedial action it is likely therefore that the brand's fall from grace would have continued.

Second, as with the downturn, which took the form of a gradual erosion as opposed to an immediate collapse, the effect of advertising was expected to be a gradual improvement rather than a step change.

Identifying a Sales Effect

Since the campaign went national in 1991, Stella's share performance has improved every year, with 1995 seeing the brand's greatest uplift since 1983 (and this in a market over 150% bigger), and a new peak of 18.2%.

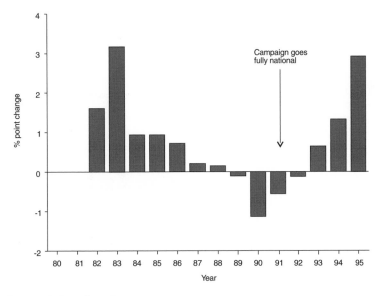

Figure 30: *Changes in Stella's volume share*
Source: BMS/Whitbread

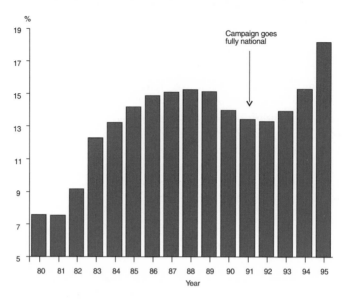

Figure 31: *Stella's share performance post-advertising*
Source: BMS/Whitbread

This share uplift in turn resulted in a volume surge. From a low in 1991 of 460,000 barrels, volume increased by 67% to a new record of 767,000 barrels in 1995. Over the same period the rest of the market grew by only 16%.

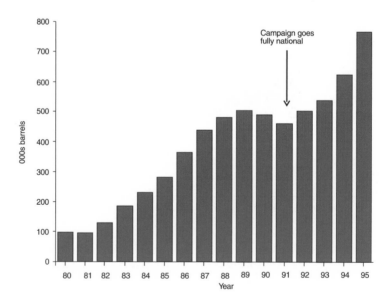

Figure 32: *Stella's volume performance post-advertising*
Source: BMS/Whitbread

Looking specifically at the off-trade, where more detailed information is available, confirms this performance. Mirroring overall share, Stella's rate of sale had been in decline pre-advertising. However, post-advertising, rate of sale has increased every year, with the 1995 peak some 80% higher.

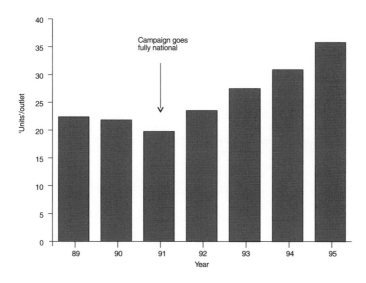

Figure 33: *Stella's off-trade rate of sale*
Source: Stats MR

And this was not just a market effect. Over the same period key competitors saw only limited improvements. In fact, from a ROS 22% higher than the number-two brand (Kronenbourg) in 1991, Stella's sales improved over the period such that ROS was 77% higher in 1995.

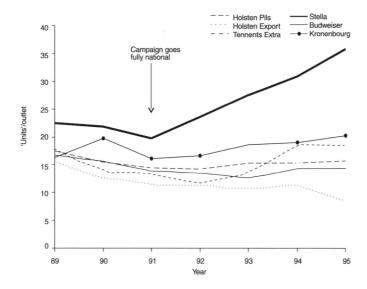

Figure 34: *Competitive off-trade rate of sale*
NB: Cans only
Source: Stats MR

As a final sign of effectiveness, it is worth considering Stella's competitive set. In the face of stiff competition, most of Stella's adversaries in 1990 have fallen down the pecking order as new players have emerged. Stella, in contrast, has strengthened its position at the top, despite the pre-advertising signs that it too was in decline.

TABLE 1: STELLA'S COMPETITIVE SET

Top five premium lager brands in 1990	Top five premium lager brands in 1995
Stella Artois (10%)	Stella Artois (12.2%)
Holsten Pils (7.7%)	Budweiser (8.6%)
Tennants Extra (6.8%)	Kronenbourg (5.3%)
Carlsberg Export (5.8%)	Holsten Pils (5.3%)
Carlsberg Special Brew (5.8%)	Becks (5.0%)

Discounting Other Factors

First, format can be discounted. A pint down the pub in 1991 was the same as a pint in 1995; similarly in the off-trade, Stella cans have always appeared in the main pack sizes.

Promotional spend (eg on extra-fill) was not a significant variable either. Stella's use of these weapons is no greater (and perhaps even less) than its competitors. Also, as their impact tends to be short-term and tactical, the relevance to 'longer and broader' cases is negligible.

Distribution is also relatively easy to discount. In the on-trade, 10,816 outlets stocked draught Stella in 1991. Though this had risen to 11,151 by 1995, the increase of 3% was far below the sales uplift of 70%. In the off-trade, distribution remained uncompromisingly high over the period.

Price can be excluded as well. In 1991, Stella's average wholesale price stood at £216 per barrel, a premium over key competitors of £5. In 1995, wholesale price had increased by 19% to £256, with a similar £5 premium. This does seem to discount price as a contributory factor in Stella's sales uplift. Unfortunately, due to unforeseen data unavailability, we do not know whether anything significant happened during the intervening period. However, Stella's performance in the off-trade sheds some light on what transpired.

During the brand's mid-'80s heyday it commanded a retail price premium. However, during its period of share decline at the turn of the decade, Stella actually traded at below the market average price.

Conversely, when Stella's share was improving post-advertising, its price premium actually reasserted itself. At worst, this discounts price as a variable[5] (if anything it was working *against* increased sales). At best, it is evidence of additional advertising effectiveness, the shift to TV allowing Stella to reclaim its 'Reassuringly Expensive' promise (although we will not attempt to prove this).

---

5.   Given that Stats MR takes into account money-off and extra-fill in its pricing data, this is further evidence that promotional activity was not an influencing factor.

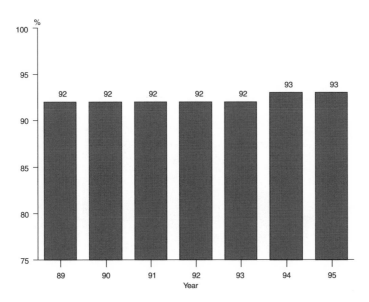

Figure 35: *Stella's off-trade £ distribution*
Source: Stats MR

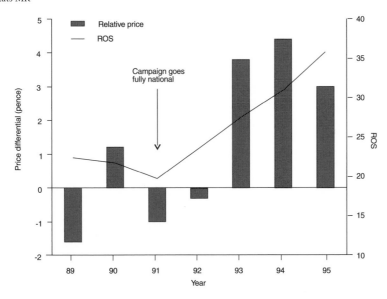

Figure 36: *Stella's off-trade price differential vs ROS*
Source: Stats MR

Quantifying a Volume Effect

So the upturn in Stella's sales fortunes does seem to be a function of advertising. But just how significant was it?

For sake of argument, we will assume that without advertising share erosion would have slowed anyway, bottoming out at the 1992 level of 13.3%.

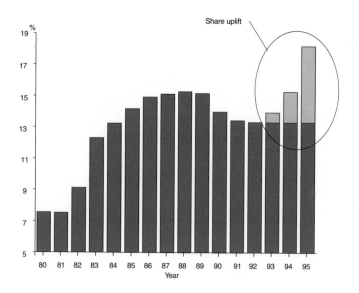

Figure 37: *Stella's share uplift due to advertising*
Source: BMS/Whitbread

In turn, this equates to incremental volume of nearly 280,000 barrels, an uplift of around 20%.

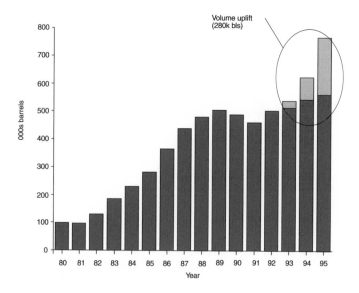

Figure 38: *Stella's volume uplift due to advertising*
Source: BMS/Whitbread

However, was this enough to pay back the initial £14.2 million investment?

PAYBACK

To err on the side of caution, we will attribute a proportion of the 280,000 barrel uplift, say 10%, to distribution.[6] Even with this possibly exaggerated assumption though, the revenue uplift attributable to advertising would still be in the region of £68 million.[7]

Whitbread will not allow exact margins to be revealed. However, taking a range of 25% to 30% equates to incremental gross profit of between £16.9 million and £20.3 million.

Given advertising investment of £14.2 million, this delivers incremental net returns on investment of between £2.7 million and £6.1 million.

And this is only the obvious effect of advertising in the here and now; there are other, less obvious, signs of effectiveness to also consider.

FURTHER EVIDENCE OF ADVERTISING EFFECTIVENESS

First, Stella is an 'account opener' for Whitbread. Any outlet wishing to stock it has to take other, potentially less appealing, brands as well. Stella's performance has implications therefore for the whole Whitbread portfolio. Even though distribution might not have increased significantly over the advertised period, the resurgence in appeal attributable to advertising (together with the natural 'churn' in outlets stocking that takes place in the on-trade), will have had an impact on sales of other brands. We will not attempt to quantify this, but the value to the company is likely to be significant.

Second, Stella's improved performance *now* also has implications for the future. This we will attempt to calculate, based on a number of (again conservative) assumptions.

---

6. This is to take into account both the 3% distribution increase and the fact that these new outlets may have been better 'quality' in terms of the volume they delivered (although this cannot be proved either way).
7. Based on an average wholesale price across the period of around £240 a barrel.

— Without the initial advertising Stella's share would have stabilised at the pre-advertising level of 13.3%;

— With continued support it will (at least) maintain its current peak of 18.2%;

— Support will increase from an average of £2.4 million a year (media and production) to an average of £4.7 million (in line with current expenditure);

— Wholesale price will remain at the 1996 level of £263 a barrel;

— Margin ranges already used will still hold good;

— All other factors will remain constant.

Applying these to Whitbread's latest estimates of market growth (17% between 1995 and 2000) suggests incremental volume due to advertising to the end of the decade of over 1.1 million barrels.

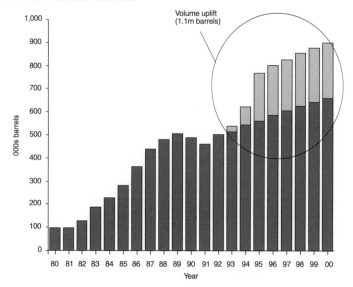

Figure 39: *Likely volume uplift generated by advertising to the end of the decade*
Source: BMS/Whitbread

In turn, this equates to total return on investment to the end of the decade of between £54.3 million and £72.7 million.

We believe this performance is perfect ammunition to rebuff those who doubt the value of advertising.

In a recent Campaign article ('How can advertising demonstrate that it works?') Hamish Pringle, Chairman of the IPA's Advertising Effectiveness committee, said that 'Financial Directors pay lip service to the value of advertising...they don't take it seriously as a long-term investment option'. These doubters should take note.

If Whitbread had invested in a bank rather than advertising, returns for the same period would be around £19 million;[8] even the stock market would return only £31 million.[9] Both are well below the likely return from advertising. We must conclude, therefore, that the investment has been a wise one.

CONCLUSIONS

Stella is a dominant market leader. However, even the strongest of brands can go through hard times. For Stella the turn of the decade was such a time; changing market dynamics resulted in erosion of share and volume.

However, as a consequence of the subsequent change in strategy and move to TV, Stella has more than reasserted its dominance. After its seven years in Provence, the brand's share and volume are now greater than ever before.

Moreover, the possible net returns on investment to the end of the decade could be in the region of £70 million. This would not have been achievable if advertising had not first turned around brand performance.

Along with Whitbread and Interbrew, we believe that this is conclusive evidence of advertising effectiveness.

---

8. Based on actual and yearly base rates.
9. Based on actual and forecast average yearly FTSE growth rates.

19

I Can't Believe It's Not Butter!

From extraordinary launch to long-term success

BEFORE LAUNCH

Van den Bergh Foods (VdBF) is the dominant force in the UK margarine and low-fat spreads market (MLF), with around 45% of market volume. In 1991, its strength lay with the more established health and baking sectors of the market, rather than the newer, premium-priced butter taste sector dominated by Clover and Golden Crown. The launch of ICBINB! was an attempt to break into this sector.

Before launch, ICBINB! was not intended to be a controversial brand. It was envisaged as an off-the-peg package which had been successful in the US and which could do well in the UK. The package included product, packaging and television advertising.

ICBINB! is positioned as a brand which offers a delicious buttery taste, but is a bit healthier to eat than butter.

Before launch, Research International carried out a full market mix test. This forecast volumes of 5,500 tonnes in year one, with an on-going volume of around 7,000 tonnes.

OUT OF ADVERSITY…

There was one major difference between the original plan and the actual launch. Just days before launch, the TV advertising was banned. This ban was based on an unresolved issue surrounding the legality of the use of the word 'butter' in the brand name of a margarine. A number of organisations – including West Sussex Trading Standards Office, MAFF and the Butter Council – were involved and there was a threat of legal action against the brand. Obviously this was potentially disastrous.

Despite the threat of legal action, the press was persuaded to run ICBINB! advertising. The proposed TV budget was shifted into a concentrated 11-day press blitz. In order to stir up as much controversy as possible, and thus to create maximum awareness, the TV ban became the core creative idea.

AN UNUSUAL PRESS LAUNCH

The campaign began on 29 October 1991, with an execution which featured the storyboard of the banned commercial. In so doing, it was simply transferring the TV advertising to press.

Further executions followed on 30 and 31 of October, 1, 3, 4, 7, 8 and 13 November. The advertising mapped out the unfolding story of the brand launch, until, on 13 November, it had to apologise for the out-of-stock situation in many supermarkets.

Not surprisingly, the advertising itself became news, to the extent that it was featured on BBC1, BBC2 and ITV news on 13 October. It is estimated that the combined audience for the afternoon and evening bulletins was around 19.4 million. In addition, the story also appeared on Channel 4's *The Word* on 1 November (audience four million).

All together, this 'illegal' brand and its stroppy advertising generated 90 minutes of free air-time.

DID IT SELL ANY MARGARINE?

Within a month of the advertising breaking, brand awareness had climbed to 38%, with advertising awareness at 26%. Nor was awareness limited to the fact that this was a 'banned' brand. 53% of consumers understood the advertising's main message to be that ICBINB! tastes like butter – very useful when the objective is to sell a delicious, buttery-tasting spread.

The notoriety also helped the trade. Originally, the 1991 distribution target was 50%. By the end of the year, however, it had reached 75% – everyone wanted to stock this brand that people were talking about. This feeling was reinforced by taking the advertising into trade publications such as *The Grocer*.

After only two months in the market, ICBINB! had already achieved 2% volume share. Expectations of its future success were upgraded accordingly.

The extent to which expectations were upgraded can be gauged by looking at the mix test forecasts which used the original US advertising, versus actual tonnage.

TABLE 1: PRE-LAUNCH ESTIMATE VERSUS ACTUAL TONNAGE

	Estimate tonnes	Actual tonnes
Year 1	5,500	8,000
Year 2	7,200	12,000

Source: RI, Microtest and VdBF

BUILDING ON SUCCESS

The launch had been an undoubted success and the pressure was on to sustain this. Obviously, the ban could not be news forever and, by December 1991, it was felt necessary to focus on ICBINB!'s product attributes.

Obviously the brand was being closely monitored in terms of quantitative data, such as penetration, trial, repeat rates, demographic data and rate of sale. In addition, qualitative research was carried out to explore consumer perceptions in more depth, in order to help us to continue to distinguish ICBINB! from its competitors.

Research by Burns Research Ltd confirmed that, largely because of its controversial advertising, ICBINB! was developing a distinctive personality which stood apart from the great mass of brands in this category. This personality was instrumental in capturing consumers' attention and stimulating trial. Thus the research concluded:

> 'The campaign was tonally appreciated for its non-conformism and sense of intrigue. It was seen to be slightly sensational and controversial which introduced a sense of presence for the brand...On the back of this, an embryonic personality was emerging, a personality which was cheeky, provocative and non-conformist.'

We took this as core learning for the development of future advertising. During the first half of 1992 new press work was developed. While focusing on conventional product attributes: taste, health and price, the advertising was set apart by its challenging, confident (one could almost say cocky) personality and the strong, clear art direction which had marked out the campaign from the very beginning.

With this support the brand continued to maintain the high levels of volume which had been stimulated by the launch.

In June 1992, a new 1kg size was launched. Initially supported by a price promotion and further press advertising, the brand share moved up a notch. However, it was only with the launch of the first TV advertising in August 1992, that share began to accelerate significantly. Figure 1 shows the major activities during the first year of ICBINB!'s life.

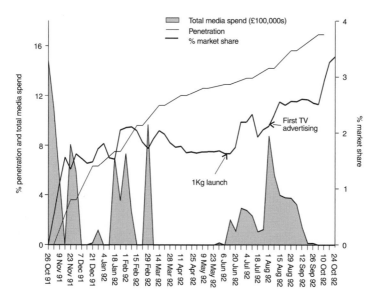

Figure 1: *Year 1 penetration and share*
Source: VdBF/ Register/MEAL

'LAUNDERETTE/SHY MALE COW'

SOUND: Music
Female: I haven't seen you here before.

Male: I'm new to the area.

Female: What do you think?

Male: Lovely.

Female: I see you're reading that shocking news about I Can't Believe It's Not Butter!

Male: Yes.

Female: Less than half the fat of saturated butter.

Male: And made with buttermilk for that fresh butter-like taste, I don't like it.

Female: I bet I know what you do like.

MVO: I Can't Believe It's Not Butter, can you?

Female: Ah, seems like there's less of everything these days.

'TWO COWS, VIDEO BOOTH'

Female: Is it on?
Female 2: Get on with it.

Female: Oh I can't, I'm shy.

Female 2: We want to complain
about these adverts for...

Female: I Can't Believe It's Not
Butter!

Female 2: They say it's made with
buttermilk for a fresh butter-like
taste.

Female: Yeah, but they also say it's
high in polyunsaturates.

Low in saturates with virtually no
cholesterol.

Female 2: Now does that sound like
butter to you? Does it!?

Female: Can I do my song now?

MVO: I Can't Believe It's Not
Butter!

Can you?

'STOCK BROKER/GOING THROUGH THE ROOF'

SOUND: Music and location effects.
Male: What! It's got to be a mistake.

Male 2: What's happened?

Male: You told me to put all my money in butter.
Female: Aargh!

Male 2: No, I said I Can't Believe It's Not Butter!

Male: Why would I want to do that?

Male 2: Because it contains less than half the saturated fat of butter.

Female: And it's made with buttermilk for that fresh butter-like taste.

Male 2: It's going through the roof.

Aargh!

MVO: I Can't Believe It's Not Butter, can you?

Male: Get me down, could you just get me down, get the ladder and get me down.

THE NEXT CHALLENGE: TV

After the success of the launch, the pressure was on to sustain the momentum. To do this it was felt that another high-profile push was needed to drive penetration – ideally this meant TV.

When, by December 1991, no legal action had been taken against the brand name, the TV advertising ban was lifted. The task now was to capture the impact and energy of the press work, within TV advertising.

Although the US advertising had originally been deemed appropriate, research showed that it was no longer suitable. Tonally it was dissonant with the personality that had been created by the press work. A new campaign was, therefore, needed for the UK.

This research also confirmed the value of ICBINB!'s distinctive personality in stimulating consumer interest and distinguishing ICBINB! from its competitors, in what consumers saw as a cluttered, confusing and rather boring market. In addition, this emotional appeal was underpinned by relevant functional benefits: buttery taste and health.

In product terms, ICBINB!'s health benefit was the same as overt health brands such as Flora. Like Flora it is 'high in polyunsaturates, low in saturates' and contains virtually no cholesterol. This descriptor is known as the 'pufa litany' and is the form of words used in advertising. BACC legislation at that time meant that it could not be tampered with. In the original brief, we tried to highlight the 'virtually no cholesterol' part of the litany but to no avail, it could not be communicated in a way consumers noticed.

Furthermore, in image terms health is less central to the ICBINB! franchise than its buttery taste and challenging persona. Health is a secondary reassurance rather than a primary motivator. It means that you do not need to feel guilty, because ICBINB! is healthier to eat than butter.

Thus, the proposition on the first TV brief was that 'ICBINB! is the ballsy brand that offers the taste of butter with virtually no cholesterol'.

The 'Cow World' campaign was developed from that brief and is still running successfully and helping to build brand share almost four years later.

Similarly the positioning has not changed. Every piece of advertising has revolved around the three key elements: ICBINB! has a brash, intrusive personality, a deliciously buttery taste and it is a bit better for you than butter.

'COW WORLD': SUCCESSFULLY BREAKING RULES

As with the original launch work, the TV advertising broke the 'rules' of the category, both written and unwritten. In using cows (albeit latex puppets) as the protagonists, the advertising was encroaching on butter's sacred turf: it was using dairy symbols, forbidden territory for non-butter spreads. This in itself was an invitation to controversy.

More subtly, the advertising confounded many of consumers' expectations of margarine/spread advertising. Its primary benefit is its butter-like taste, but the advertising does not feature the usual beautiful spreading shots. It has a health benefit, but no happy, healthy people are portrayed in the ads.

Even more significantly, the advertising dared to risk the dislike of consumers. It was intrusive and impactful, but it undoubtedly polarised, with high levels of dislikes as well as likes.

This polarisation was apparent from the first tracking study, which showed three times the average level of negative comment, much higher than would normally be tolerated.

TABLE 2: ADVERTISING DISLIKES

	'Video Box' %	'Outraged' %	VdB average %
Any negative comment	22	18	6
Don't like it	18	15	5
Might put people off	9	6	1

Source: Millward Brown Tracking, December 1992

However, we were not unduly worried by these results. This was partly because, by the time the tracking came through, the advertising had already performed well in 'real life'. It was also because we realised that this was not a brand that behaved in a conventional way. In fact, this tendency towards higher-than-average levels of dislikes is one that has continued. This is not advertising everyone feels warm about, just as the brand itself does not make everyone respond positively.

Accepting this, the advertising has not been softened in an attempt to achieve universal appeal. Rather, it continues to work strongly against a specific type of consumer. People either like it or they don't, but either way they notice it.

In a low-interest market like yellow fats, merely being noticed is in itself a real advantage. To be noticed and clearly associated with a distinct benefit such as butter-like taste is even better.

This is exactly what the advertising has done. It has consistently achieved extremely high levels of awareness, with Millward Brown awareness indices of around three times the market norm (12 vs 4).

The cows have become established as a distinctive branding device, as well as being central to the communication. As far as consumers are concerned, cows equals butter equals great taste. Marry this benefit with the levels of impact which the cows' antics generate, and it is not surprising that brand share has continued to grow.

THE ICBINB! CONSUMER

As has been said, ICBINB! advertising is not universally loved. This became apparent very early in the brand's life. Just watching people in research groups talking about ICBINB! advertising was very enlightening.

Obviously all potential ICBINB! users want buttery taste. What separates them however are their different emotional responses to ICBINB!'s brash personality. Three main groups emerged.

1. Desperately uncomfortable. These people completely rejected ICBINB! as 'gimmicky' and 'silly'. It would demean their status as grown-ups to be seen using such a ridiculous brand.

2. Uncomfortable – again they would describe the brand as 'gimmicky' and 'silly' – but at the same time admitted to a sneaking curiosity. They found it difficult to ignore the brand and its claims.

3. Cheerfully entertained. Even these people used the words 'silly' and 'gimmicky'. They happily acknowledged that everything about this brand, from its advertising and its name, to the 'funny bun on the pack' is 'a bit daft'. However, they also openly found it entertaining and challenging.

Throughout the brand's life, the advertising has been used to drive penetration. Obviously, Group 3 consumers tended to be first into the brand. However, as time has gone by, it has been necessary to bring in more Group 2 consumers, without losing our Group 3 people or diluting our distinctive image.

TGI Lifestyle was used to build on the qualitative learning. We were looking for shared consumer attitudes which could be harnessed to appeal to both groups. A distinctive ICBINB!-type person emerged.

The target ICBINB! user loves change and novelty; has an indulgent streak; likes to be entertained rather than informed; enjoys advertising; and loves to go in for competitions (with indices of 130 and 143 for 'I often enter competitions in magazines' and 'I often enter competitions on packets and labels').

This information helped us to understand how we might be vulnerable to new brands (and thus how to protect ourselves), as well as triggering ideas which helped us to use the advertising in new ways to strengthen ICBINB!'s franchise.

THE 1995/96 STRATEGY

ICBINB! started with relatively modest targets. However, each year's success led to an upgrading in our expectations of what might be achievable. In planning for 1996, therefore, we were more ambitious than ever before. We also knew more about the brand and its consumer.

Our core objective was to broaden our consumer base by bringing in more Group 2-type consumers. To do this, we needed to reassure them that ICBINB! is not merely hype with no substance. At the same time, we did not want to dilute the intrusive personality which was the very thing which set ICBINB! apart from the competition.

To meet our objectives therefore, we realised that we had to:

1. maintain our high profile by continuing to produce intrusive advertising which achieves high Millward Brown awareness indices;

2. continue to communicate our positioning: a buttery taste but a bit better for you than butter;

3. continually refresh the campaign with visibly different executions (some brands in this market have suffered through campaigns in which individual executions are not sufficiently differentiated);

4. build on consumer attitudinal triggers, to maintain a sense of novelty and freshness.

This fourth point has been central to the development of creative work during the last two years. One of the simplest examples of how this works comes from the development of the most recent executions.

FIGHTING OFF CHALLENGERS

The most recent executions, 'Launderette' and 'Wall Street' were developed at a crucial time for the brand. With the launch of Utterly Butterly in April 1995, we were facing our toughest challenge to date. Like ICBINB!, Utterly Butterly shares the same taste-with-a-bit-of-health benefit; has a quirky, yet explicitly benefit-focused name; bright yellow packaging; and high-impact advertising which is not afraid to polarise.

It very quickly built up high levels of awareness and trial. Therefore, it was imperative that we maintained our saliency and relevance for our core target, if we were to achieve our objectives of an increase in penetration and thus a share gain which would take us up to 6.9% (we were around the 6% mark).

We knew that with their love of novelty, there was a real danger that our consumers would desert us for the newer brand. Therefore, our brief was to hold onto existing users, as well as seducing new ones, by appealing to their desire for novelty and excitement. We could do this through executional 'games' which surrounded what was essentially an unchanging product message.

This was how 'Spot the Difference' was developed. It was simply a competition based around the TV advertising. Two versions of 'Launderette' were shot, both the same apart from five minor differences. Ten-second trailers and national press ads were also developed, telling people how to enter and when to set their videos to tape the two versions of the commercial. Five prizes of £10,000 were offered to those who correctly spotted all five differences.

Through using the advertising as the heart of an innovative promotion, we believed that we could create a relevant sense of impact and novelty around ICBINB!, while refocusing consumers on the product message.

RESULTS

The idea was extremely successful: 47,000 applications were received (we had been advised by the promotions company that 12,000 would be considered a success). More importantly, the activity did not just protect our share from Utterly Butterly, but actually drove it to a peak of 8.7% (Nielsen weekly data). While this peak has obviously not been sustained, there has been an upward shift in share, as new users stay with the brand. Figure 2 shows share surrounding the activity.

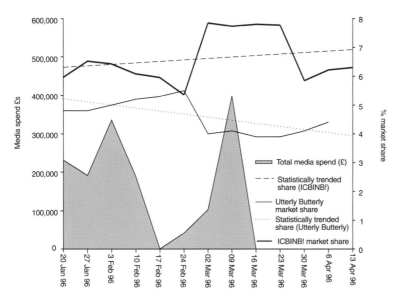

Figure 2: *'Spot the difference' Utterly Butterly and ICBINB! market share*
Source: Register MEAL/Nielsen

The activity has also helped us to drive penetration despite the threat from Utterly Butterly. Table 3 shows how penetration has risen in the last year. Not only are we bringing new people into the brand, but we are also increasing levels of loyalty amongst users.

TABLE 3: ICBINB PENETRATION CHANGES

ICBINB! usage	52 w/e 7 May 1995 penetration %	52 w/e 5 May 1996 penetration %
Overall penetration	15.0	20.8
Solus ICBINB!	0.1	0.3
High loyalty	2.3	2.8
Medium loyalty	2.9	3.9
Low loyalty	9.6	13.8

Source: AGB Superpanel

AGB Superpanel source of volume analysis shows that despite its copycat positioning, Utterly Butterly has taken only 13% of its volume from ICBINB!. Neither has it put an end to ICBINB!'s healthy volume growth, as Table 4 shows. Ignoring the extraordinary rate of the first year, the last three years have seen consistent growth of around 25%. This looks even more attractive when judged within the context of a mature market which is declining by about 3% year on year.

TABLE 4: ICBINB! VOLUME GROWTH

1991 – launch	—
1992 vs 1991	515%
1993 vs 1992	65%
1994 vs 1993	23%
1995 vs 1994	30%
1996 vs 1995 (year to date)	26%

Source: VdBF Best Estimate

Instead of damaging ICBINB!, the combination of two strong, intrusive taste brands has stimulated the butter taste sector, to the benefit of both brands.

ADVERTISING AND GROWTH

ICBINB! is an undoubted success. The question is, how much has the advertising contributed to its success?

Our contention is that the advertising has played a key role in building a strong, distinctive brand which:

— has grown every year since launch in a declining market;

— commands a 28% price premium over the market average;

— is strong enough to support a half-fat variant;

— has fought off strong competition from 'me-too' brands.

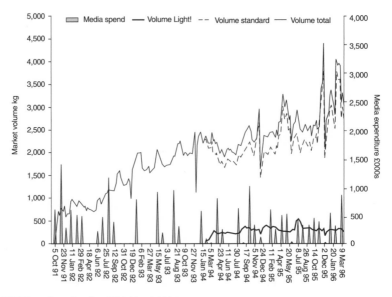

Figure 3: *ICBINB! volume October 1991–March 1996*
Source: Register MEAL/Nielsen

Figure 3 shows total ICBINB! volume against advertising spend. As can be seen, after each burst there is a step change in the underlying volume trend. However, while we can see that something is driving this trend, how can we tell if it is the advertising?

In this case there are relatively few variables. Since October 1992, distribution has remained stable at around 90%. The Light! variant was launched in April 1994 and it too has remained stable at 0.9% share of MLF. The bulk of ICBINB!'s growth has continued to come from the standard variant. There have been very few promotions, as the vast majority of the brand's support has gone behind advertising or price reductions (which run in tandem). Therefore, the key to understanding the effect of advertising must lie with disentangling the effect of temporary price reductions from that of the advertising.

In order to look at advertising effect during the first three years of ICBINB's life, we began by fitting a model of volume using pricing only as an explanatory variable. This model was based on the six months prior to the start of the TV campaign in August 1992. This yielded an adjusted R^2 of 88%.

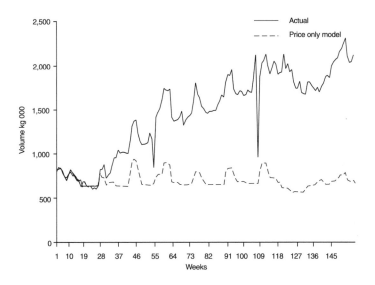

Figure 4: *Volume added by advertising, over and above the effects of price*

The model was then projected ahead by 150 weeks. Although we cannot definitively say that the price model shows what would have happened had there been no TV advertising, the difference between the two lines shows that, from the time of the TV advertising, the consumer's value of the brand had changed. This is after all, one of the main tasks of advertising.

Therefore, looking at the difference between the two lines means that by the end of the period, 52% of volume was not accounted for by the price model, and is therefore attributable to advertising.

ADVERTISING AND A HEALTHY BRAND

Ultimately, the best evidence lies with the demonstration of a strong, distinct brand which is able to grow steadily in an adverse market and which can stand up to the challenges of competitive brands.

One such piece of evidence is provided by two snapshots of the brand's health on a number of key dimensions. The first snapshot is from June 1994, the second from May 1996, with the brand two years older and significantly healthier. This is despite a particularly tough challenge from Utterly Butterly, during the last year.

TABLE 5: ICBINB! BRAND HEALTH

	4 w/e 11 June 1994	4 w/e 11 May 1996
ICBINB! share of MLF %	3.9	6.8
£ distribution %	99	100
Rate of sale (packs)	26.5	43.4

Source: Nielsen weekly data

CONCLUSIONS

Despite the adverse circumstances of its launch, ICBINB! has gone from strength to strength. Advertising has been integral to this growth.

The original high-profile press advertising transformed the potentially disastrous TV ban into a triumphant awareness-and-trial building exercise.

The essence of that advertising was then captured in bold, unconventional TV work which was instrumental in driving penetration and share.

This boldness has been retained throughout four years of the 'Cow-World' campaign. Although the advertising polarises, it has continued to keep the brand top of mind and to drive penetration.

The rewards of this are clear. ICBINB! has grown consistently in a declining market and has out-lived the original gimmick value of both its name and the television ban.

Now a more mature brand, it has proved it can withstand strong competition and continues to draw in new users. What, other than advertising, could have achieved this?

20

'Vive La Clio'

How image leadership created a long-term success story: 1991–95

THE CLIO STORY BEGINS – 1991

The Renault Clio was launched into the small sector of the UK car market in April 1991 in competition with cars like the Ford Fiesta and the Vauxhall Nova.

The 1992 submission, 'Adding Value During A Recession',[1] showed that advertising had contributed to a remarkably successful launch. It helped establish a premium-priced small car from Renault, complementing its well established 'value' offering: the Renault 5.

It also began a dramatic reversal in fortunes for Renault UK. From an all-time low in 1991 its share nearly doubled by 1995.

The advertising that established the car was the first to feature 'Papa and Nicole'. These characters physically embodied the car's proposition: *The small car with big-car refinement.*

The advertising was not only well recalled, well branded and liked but also helped establish a strong image for the car far more quickly than is normal for this market.

THE CLIO STORY CONTINUES 1992–95

The difficulty of isolating the effect of advertising in the car market is well documented.

Arguably, the effectiveness of continued advertising support is even more difficult to isolate – the relationship between variables becomes more complex over time.

We will demonstrate how Clio's performance continued to exceed targets and market expectations in very demanding circumstances. It has been a top-ten selling car in every year since launch and is one of the very few mainstream cars launched since 1980 to have enjoyed a sales increase for five consecutive years.

---

1. See *Advertising Works 7.*

473

We will show that this has been achieved because *the Clio has built and maintained a position as the clear 'image leader' in its sector long after its product advantage had been matched by competitors.*

A famous advertising campaign has been the primary factor in creating and sustaining this image.

THE STORY OF PAPA AND NICOLE

It is unusual for a car manufacturer to sustain a campaign for five years; to do so for just one model is quite remarkable. However, the adventures, assignations and charm of Papa and Nicole provided a potent yet flexible campaign structure.

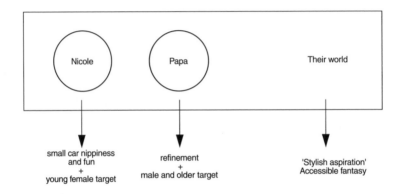

Figure 1: *Campaign structure*

Until Clio, small cars were largely positioned on the generics of 'nippiness' or through hot-hatch performance.

The new car was a step forward in small car design and refinement at launch. The advertising not only communicated this very effectively but allowed virtually all potential drivers of the car to identify with at least one of the characters.

Their 'Provençal' habitat and relaxed lifestyle represented a very attractive, if idealised, aspect of Frenchness, aspirational to many British buyers.

By persevering and developing a familiar campaign, a point was reached where recognition, branding and liking could almost be 'taken for granted'. Any one of a number of familiar elements in the advertising serves to identify it immediately as a Clio ad. This 'structural branding' provided enormous creative flexibility, enabling product features to be demonstrated extremely effectively while building the car's image and personality.

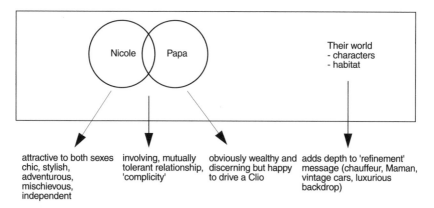

| attractive to both sexes chic, stylish, adventurous, mischievous, independent | involving, mutually tolerant relationship, 'complicity' | obviously wealthy and discerning but happy to drive a Clio | adds depth to 'refinement' message (chauffeur, Maman, vintage cars, luxurious backdrop) |

Figure 2: *Structural branding*

As a result, it has been possible to tailor executions to specific tasks and thus attempt to manage the car's image over time.

CLIO MARKET PERFORMANCE

Market Background

The car was launched at a time of severe market recession. However, it was apparently well placed to move forward as the market recovered.

There were no further new Renault models due until 1994 (Laguna) and 1996 (Mégane).

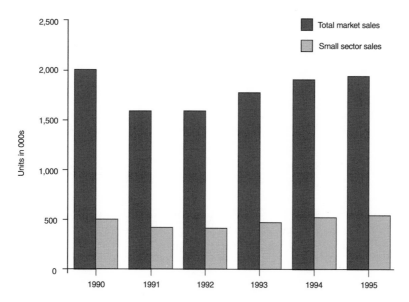

Figure 3: *Small car sector and total market sales*
Source: SMMT

For Renault UK to meet its total market share objective it was insufficient simply to recover with the market. It was essential for Clio to continue to grow its share.

The Competition Hots Up

Continued share growth was likely to be difficult to achieve. Previous papers[2] have highlighted how the cyclical nature of the car market means that product advantage for new cars is held only for two or three years and that this is mirrored in the sales pattern. (An element of fashionability potentially makes this even more pronounced in the small car sector.) The exceptional case is a model representing a dramatic leap forward compared to previous offers from the same manufacturer or its competitors.

The Clio was a step forward but was not the kind of product 'quantum leap' the Peugeot 205 had been in 1983.

The latter car enjoyed a product advantage for several years. Clio, on the other hand, soon had serious competition in terms of product specification.

TABLE 1: NEW CAR LAUNCHES/REVAMPS
SMALL CAR SECTOR 1991–95

	1991	1992	1993	1994	1995
Major launches (Completely new cars)	Renault Clio Peugeot 106	Nissan Micra	Fiat Cinquecento Vauxhall Corsa	Fiat Punto VW Polo	Rover 100 Ford Fiesta
'Facelifts'	Citroen AX Fiat Panda	Rover Metro		Renault Clio Ford Fiesta	Fiat Cinquecento

The Clio was the 'new kid on the block' only briefly. In car magazine reviews it went from leader to just one of the leading contenders by early 1993.

Its core competitors changed over time from relatively lower-price or older models to much newer, more highly specified ones.

TABLE 2: CLIO BUYERS – SECOND CHOICE CAR (TOP 4)

1992	1994
Peugeot 205	Ford Fiesta
Ford Fiesta	Vauxhall Corsa
Rover Metro	Peugeot 106
Renault 5	Nissan Micra

Source: NCBS

The Clio received a mild facelift during the campaign – in 1994. Increasingly these are needed to keep the product competitive and inject some 'news' rather than re-establish any significant product advantage.

---

2. 'The Volkswagen Golf 1984–90', *Advertising Works 7*.

Competitive Advertising

Not only had product advantage been eroded but competitor communication strategies often encroached on Clio's 'small car, big-car refinement' positioning.

For example:

Nissan Micra (relaunch)	'Lives in the city, loves the open road'
Vauxhall Corsa	'The new supermodel'
	'The small car with the big personality'
Ford Fiesta	'It's much more of a car'
	'Not for the small-minded'

One competitor commercial even showed the car beating a thinly disguised Clio being driven by a Nicole 'lookalike' to a parking space in Paris! Others, less subtly, followed the Clio to Provence.

Clio's share of voice has varied over time. This is a highly competitive sector with considerable expenditure behind the launches referred to.

TABLE 3: ADVERTISING EXPENDITURE – SMALL CAR SECTOR

	1991 £m	1992 £m	1993 £m	1994 £m	1995 £m
Clio spend	10.2	12.3	12.4	12.8	14.9
Competitor launches (est)	3.8	5.0	22.0	8.6	18.0
Other	57.3	59.7	75.3	82.7	69.1
Total	71.3	77.0	109.7	104.1	100.0
Clio Sector SOV%	14.3	15.9	11.3	12.3	14.9

* = first-year expenditure, theme campaigns only. Source: Register/MEAL

Sales and Market Share

With only a short-lived product advantage and in the face of substantial competitive activity, Clio increased its volume and its total market share in every year after launch. It also increased its share and ranking within the small car sector over the whole period.

TABLE 4: CLIO VOLUME SALES AND SHARE OF SMALL CAR MARKET

	1991	1992	1993	1994	1995
(000 units)					
Volume	20.80	34.70	45.30	49.30	52.60
% sector share	5.10	8.40	9.60	9.50	9.70
% market	1.31	2.18	2.55	2.58	2.70
Rank in small sector	7	4	4	4	3

Source: SMMT

This remarkable performance even eclipses that of the much-applauded 'exceptional case' Peugeot 205.

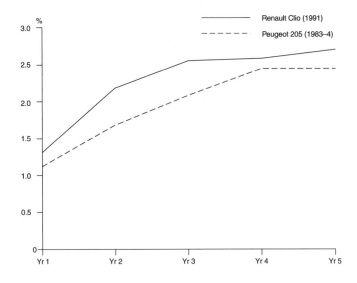

Figure 4: *Total market share since launch*
Source: SMMT

Comparing Clio performance over five years with its closest competitors highlights the strength of this achievement.

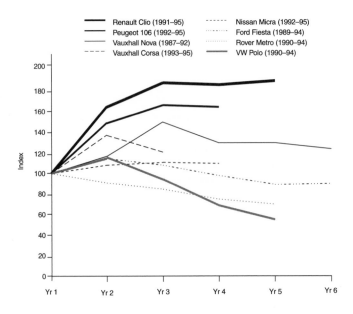

Figure 5: *Sector share development following launch or major facelift (Year 1 = 100)*
Source: SMMT

Further evidence for Clio's exceptional success lies in comparing its UK performance with other European markets. The competitive sets tend to be similar even if the domestic leader differs. Only in the UK did Clio enjoy such consistent sales growth (Figure 6).

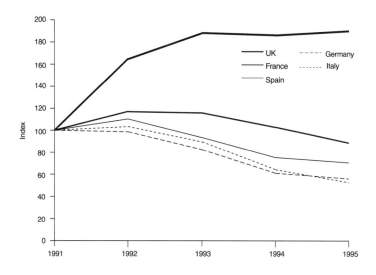

Figure 6: *Clio sector share development in Europe (1991 = 100)*
Source: SMMT and European equivalents

EXPLAINING THE PERFORMANCE

First we will show that this cannot be explained by distribution, price, promotions or changes in model mix.

Distribution

The overall size of the Renault dealer network has been relatively stable for several years. The Clio has grown through rate of sale.

TABLE 5: CLIO SALES PER DEALER

1993	1995
177	219

Source: Calculations based on SMMT and Sewells

It is difficult to compare directly manufacturer's dealer networks. Their structures vary considerably (there is no equivalent of 'sterling distribution'). However, whichever definition one chooses, Clio consistently ranks in the top two small cars in terms of sales per dealer.

It enjoys a higher rate than expected, given Renault's overall rate of sale, although the latter has been improving thanks to Clio and, since 1994, the Laguna.

TABLE 6: SALES PER DEALER 1995

Clio	Small car average	Renault total	All mainstream marques
123	100	96	100

Source: Calculations based on SMMT and Sewells

Price

Despite the entry of other 'classier' superminis, equalising entry prices within the sector, it's *actual* price premium has been maintained.

TABLE 7: PRICE PAID FOR A NEW CAR (£)

	Clio	Small car average	Index
1991	8,910	7,812	114
1992	8,900	7,870	113
1993	9,530	7,780	122
1994	8,950	7,920	113
1995	9,300	8,200	113

Source: New Car Buyers Survey

Promotions

Renault has successfully employed special editions, especially at the lower end of the model range, with finance offers to boost sales tactically. These are frequently advertised.

However, these are used by all major manufacturers. Increasingly, they are an expected part of the marketing mix as can be seen from the amount of advertising support they receive.

TABLE 8: FINANCE AND SPECIAL EDITIONS
SMALL CAR SECTOR ADVERTISING SPEND

	1992 £m	1993 £m	1994 £m	1995 £m
Total	14.2	23.4	29.5	31.9
Clio	1.4	3.6	3.1	5.3
%	10.0	15.0	11.0	17.0

Source: Register/MEAL

Special editions have increased Clio's importance at the lower end of the range, but, significantly, the top-of-the-range 'RT' also enjoyed growth each year. It continues to account for around 35% of all Clio sales.

Also we can show that price and discounts are not key reasons for purchase in the case of Clio nor have they significantly grown in importance.

TABLE 9: REASONS FOR PURCHASE (%)

		1991	1992	1993	1994
Price	Clio	13	13	19	17
	Sector	24	18	20	16
Value for	Clio	8	8	8	9
money	Sector	4	5	5	5
Discount	Clio	0	2	2	5
	Sector	1	4	3	5

Source: NCBS

Model Mix

The only additions to the range have been various performance models (16V, Williams and RSi). The 16-valve first appeared in 1992 since when these models have consistently accounted for only 4–5% of volume sold.

THE IMAGE LEADER

The key explanation for the car's success lies in the strength of its 'image', underpinned by a strong personality.

The Ford Fiesta and Vauxhall Corsa, with much larger dealer networks and model ranges, lead the small car sector in terms of numbers sold, but the Clio has come to lead in terms of image – to a much greater extent than its relative market share would suggest (Figure 7).

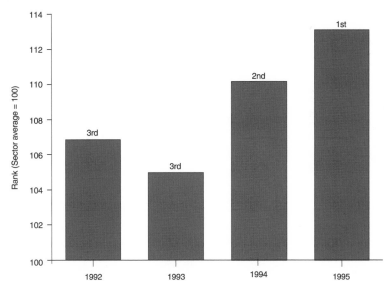

Figure 7: *Image versus sector average – overall opinion*
Source: MIL Car Park Study

Clio has also reached number one position in a number of dimensions that are related closely to the idea of 'big-car refinement' (Figure 8).

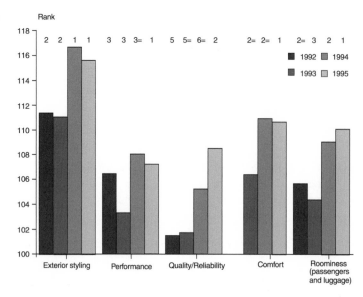

Figure 8: *Clio image – index versus sector average*

The effective introduction of the Phase 2 'facelift' model appears to have contributed to a further strengthening of image.

The image strengths appear to have translated directly into reasons for purchase.

TABLE 10: REASON FOR PURCHASE

	Clio %	Sector average %
Stylish	34	25
Equipment level	24	11
Interior finish	9	5
Roominess	9	6
Size	25	20
Manoeuvrability	13	9

Source: NCBS

'Small car, with big-car refinement' sums up extremely well the main reason for choosing a Clio.

Qualitative research indicates that Clio has more than simply a strong image – it has a real 'personality'.

It was described as being:

classy	reliable, for everyday
quality	fun to drive
nippy	sophisticated
well appointed	attractive
stylish	sexy
individual	'continental'

'It was clear from the research that Clio is seen as being one of the 'smarter' small cars. There was a feeling that Clio was the sort of small car that upper class and well-to-do people favoured.'

Source: Qualitative Research, Roddy Glen – August 1995

HOW HAS ADVERTISING CONTRIBUTED?

Naturally, we intend to demonstrate that advertising has been the key factor in making Clio the image leader.

We will do so by showing how it met a series of carefully defined advertising objectives.

CORE ADVERTISING OBJECTIVES

Objective 1:	To achieve high levels of advertising recall, branding and likeability.
Objective 2:	To establish and maintain a clear, long-term image and premium positioning in the small car sector.
Objective 3:	To help ensure that the car retains a place on the target market's shortlist and thus builds showroom traffic.
Objective 4:	To appeal to a broad target market in terms of age profile.
Objective 5:	To enhance the Renault marque image.
Objective 6:	To motivate dealers.

ADVERTISING STRATEGY

The creative and media strategies were carefully managed over time to meet specific market requirements.

Media Strategy

All manufacturers require a mix of theme and tactical activity. The latter is important for short-term promotions and dealer support.

However, Clio is unusual in having had, from the outset, a much higher proportion of its expenditure behind theme or 'image' TV.

Press and radio have been used mainly to support tactical activity while posters were used in support of TV for the launch of the Phase 2 'facelift'. There has also been some increase in TV support for promotions and special editions.

It is noticeable that the market as a whole has gradually moved towards a mix more similar to that of Clio.

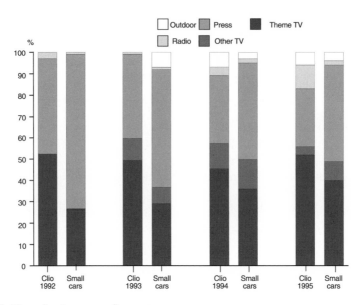

Figure 9: *Clio media mix versus small car sector*
Source: Register/MEAL

Creative Strategy

The broad creative idea was discussed in detail earlier. A strength of the campaign was the ability to develop and deploy executions to manage its emphasis in terms of target market and specific product message.

Most cars in this sector have a broadly young, feminine image, reflecting the purchaser profile. The Clio is no exception – its name being a major contributing factor.

However, men and older buyers have access to the brand through performance models, through 'Papa' and the other male characters. This has been reflected in the copy rotation. All appeal to the core, younger, female-biased target but with different emphasis in subsidiary target markets and product messages.

TABLE 11: EMPHASIS OF THE CAMPAIGNS

	Target emphasis	Product emphasis
'Interesting' 1991/2	Older, male (key in recessionary period)	Core theme
'Date' 1992/3	Younger, male	Performance (16V)
'Ski' 1993/4	Younger, male	Performance (16V)
'Transformation' 1994/6*	Younger (core market)	New 'facelifted' model
'Maman' 1995/6*	Broad appeal	Core theme

* Phase-2 model

'INTERESTING' 1991–93

'THE DATE' 1992–93

'SKI' 1993–94

'TRANSFORMATION' 1994–96

'MAMAN' 1995–96

MEETING THE OBJECTIVES

Objective 1: Recall, Branding and Likeability

Familiarity breeds contentment.

Tracking study data shows that the theme TV advertising featuring 'Papa, Nicole' is among the most highly recalled in any market. It is the most visible, best branded and most liked within its category.

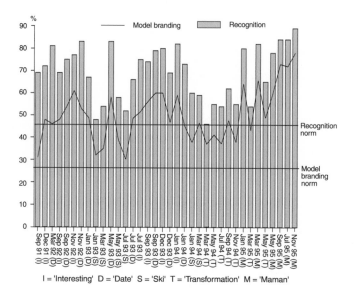

Figure 10: *Renault Clio advertising performance, recognition and branding*
Source: Multipact

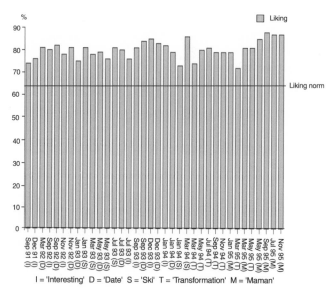

Figure 11: *Renault Clio advertising performance, liking*
Source: Multipact

Individually, different executions have enjoyed different levels of response but all well above average for the sector.

The 'Rotation Effect'

When several commercials were rotated at the same time, even higher levels of visibility were achieved than by airing one commercial alone. This is a tribute to the way the Papa and Nicole stories have managed successfully to engage and involve their audience.

This was an important piece of learning. A well established core idea allows different executions to appeal to different elements of the target group at any one time.

From qualitative research, it also appears that they enjoy comparing and contrasting the individual plots so that, overall, the net effect is greater and wear-out is reduced.

Theme and Tactical Activity

Theme TV advertising dominates recall. This is not to belittle the role tactical activity plays in keeping the car competitive.

Indeed, it frequently works best by exploiting the theme. The most successful special edition commercials borrowed from the main campaign by featuring Bernard, the chauffeur.

Media Added Value

A great indication of how the campaign has captured the imagination is the enormous additional coverage it has generated in the press and on TV. The campaign is frequently mimicked in TV comedy shows. Papa and especially Nicole have achieved more media attention than many soap stars.

Objective 2: Image and Positioning

It has already been concluded that the brand's strong image and the key 'small car, big-car refinement' dimensions were key reasons for purchase.

These key image strengths are consistent with the key communication elements of the theme advertising.

Qualitative research again demonstrates that consumers readily appreciate the 'small car, big-car refinement' from the 'Papa, Nicole' campaign as well as endowing it with an attractive personality. The tracking study highlights the key communication points of individual executions.

TABLE 12: KEY COMMUNICATION POINTS

	'Interesting'	'Date'	'Ski'	'Transformation'	'Maman'
Nippy performance	✓✓	✓✓✓	✓✓	✓	✓✓
Manoeuvrability	✓	✓		✓✓✓	✓
Stylish/chic	✓	✓	✓	✓	
Comfortable				✓	✓✓
For all ages	✓✓	✓✓	✓		✓✓✓
For young people		✓✓	✓✓	✓✓	
Well equipped/ comfortable	✓✓	✓	✓	✓✓	✓✓✓

Source: Based on Multipact

Even though it was not a radical product change, a real sense of improvement was communicated for the Phase-2 Clio – there were noticeable improvements in relative image on a number of dimensions following launch.

We cannot identify any other source for the car's richness of image. Indeed, there is evidence of a direct relationship.

'Clearly, the addition of French sophistication and continental stylishness is of utmost importance to the car. This is provided mostly by the advertising…'

'The majority of competitive owners were actively considering the Clio as their next car and, of these, half stated that it was because of the advertising.'

Qualitative Research, Winstanley, Douglas, Grantham, June 1993

'These commercials appear to succeed in being light in spirit and tone at the same time as being visually very rich, and highly efficient in image creation terms with some intense feature communication segments. As respondents said, "impressive", and well worth preserving.'

'It is a world into which people can quite easily project. As with the interplay between Papa and Nicole, this is an important source of executional durability.'

Qualitative Research, Roddy Glen, August 1995

International comparisons are again useful. The UK was the only market to employ a consistent campaign over a five-year period since launch. Not only was the sales performance stronger but Clio enjoys a relatively better image in the UK than in other 'export' markets (Figure 12).

Specifically, the car is stronger in respect of 'big-car refinement' dimensions (Figure 13).

On 'generic' values the car still scores above average, but the position is much more similar between countries (Figure 14).

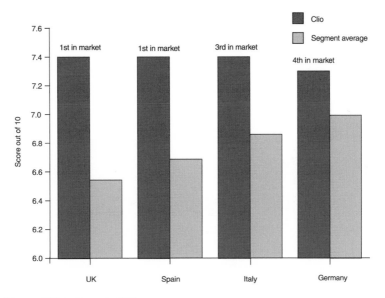

Figure 12: *Overall image of Clio in Europe in 1995*
Source: MIL Car Park Study

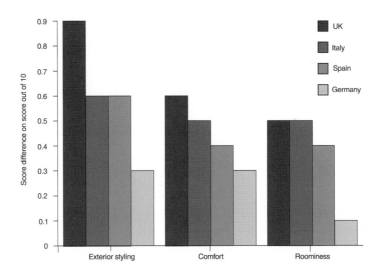

Figure 13: *European comparison on key dimensions, score difference between Clio and sector average*
Source: MIL Car Park Study

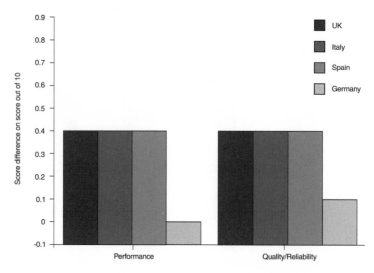

Figure 14: *European comparison on key dimensions, score difference between Clio and sector average*
Source: MIL Car Park Study

Objective 3: Getting on the Shortlist

The Clio is consistently high on potential small car buyers' shortlists – a key measure of relative desirability.

TABLE 13: PERCENTAGE OF SMALL CAR DRIVERS WHO WOULD
CONSIDER A CLIO IF CHANGING THEIR CAR

	Clio %	Sector average %
March 1992	40	33
March 1993	41	31
March 1994	48	34
March 1995	46	32

Source: Multipact

There is direct research evidence that the TV advertising is an important prompt to getting Clio on to the shortlist.

TABLE 14: INFORMATION SOURCES THAT PROMPTED
INCLUSION ON SHORTLIST

	All cars %	Renault %
Word of mouth	21	14
Seen on road	20	22
TV advertising	20	34
Article in car magazine	15	19
Brochure	13	13

Base: All who bought/considered small car (1995)
Source: ICM July–Dec 1994

Objective 4: Appealing to a Broad Target Market

The car does have a more feminine bias overall but changes in profile, reflecting the deliberate changes in targeting emphasis described earlier, can be observed.

TABLE 15: CLIO PROFILE CHANGES

	1992 %	*Index	1993 %	*Index	1994 %	*Index	1995 %	*Index
Male	32	71	46	102	39	88	41	NA
Female	68	123	54	98	61	108	59	
Under 35	26	96	34	136	37	119	30	
35–54	39	102	41	102	39	95	41	
55+	36	102	25	71	24	85	29	

*Sector average = 100
Source: NCBS

Objective 5: Contributing to Renault Marque Image

The relationship between model and marque is a complex one. In the case of Renault this is complicated by the issue of 'Frenchness'. While it has decreased over time, a degree of xenophobia persists in car purchasing (according to the MIL Car Park Study, 29% of potential buyers would definitely or probably not consider buying a French car).

Renault has undergone a considerable reversal of fortune since the launch of Clio. In terms of sales, it has just recorded its highest-ever share (Figure 15).

While the Clio enjoys a distinct image and personality, both the car and the advertising are seen as coming from the Renault 'stable'. Levels of marque attribution on the tracking study are similar to those for the model itself.

The overall image of Renault, both in absolute terms and relative to other European makes, has improved over the same period (Figure 16).

The specific areas that have shown the greatest improvement are those which relate to the image of Clio and which have been communicated by the advertising (Figure 17).

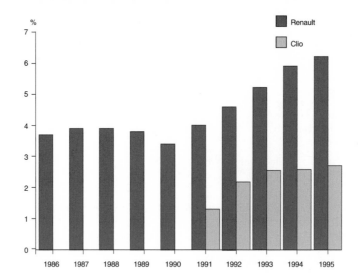

Figure 15: *Renault and Clio market share over the last decade*

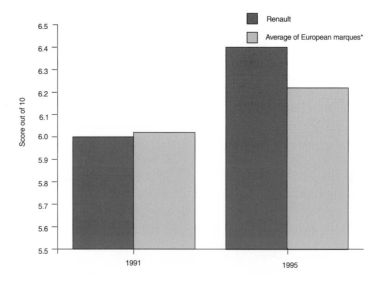

Figure 16: *Renault versus other mainstream European marques: overall opinion*
* Citroën, Peugeot, Fiat, VW
Source: MIL Car Park Study

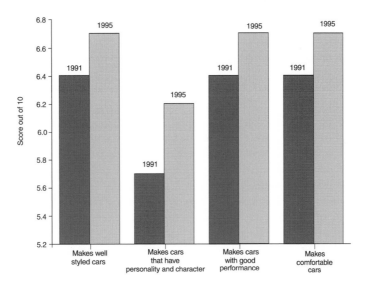

Figure 17: *Renault – strength of agreement*
Source: MIL Car Park Study

Objective 6: Motivating the Dealers

Renault UK regularly receives positive feedback from its dealers about the campaign. It is frequently cited in the car trade press as an example of building a successful image.

A major survey of dealers of all makes showed that its dealers rate Renault very highly indeed for the effectiveness of its product advertising, of which Clio is the most visible component.

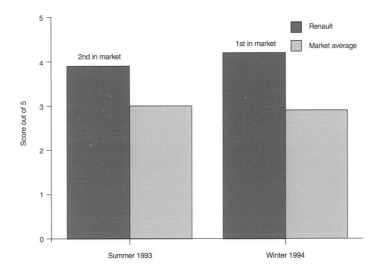

Figure 18: *Effectiveness of product advertising rated by dealers*
Source: RMI Dealer Attitude Survey

CONCLUSIONS

The achievement of 'Papa, Nicole' has not just been to launch the Clio but to sustain its success at a higher level and for longer than could have reasonably been expected.

The Clio was the *product* class leader when it was launched but this was soon matched by competitors.

While product advantage declined, its image advantage began to grow and continued to do so until it became the clear *image leader*.

This has led an increasing number of consumers to continue to choose the Clio over its rivals. Their reasons for purchase clearly reflect the image strengths of the car. They are even prepared to admit it in qualitative research!

The advertising has been the primary driver of this image. The image values of the car clearly match its communication. Its personality is also closely identified with that of the advertising.

Several things set it apart from most other car advertising:

— a consistent, long-running creative approach which has achieved enormous richness of communication and depth involvement

— the ability to 'manage' the communication content over time

— an above-average proportion of support behind theme TV relative to promotional advertising

— a campaign dealers consistently believe in and which achieves high levels of branded visibility – increasing still further when executions are rotated and through the 'newsworthiness' of Papa and Nicole.

The advertising has clearly met its defined objectives. The additional sales over what might have been expected for Clio and the 'halo' effect for the marque have considerably improved Renault UK's overall sales and profit position; more than justifying the investment made.

EPILOGUE

1996 sees the launch of the Phase-3 Clio (the final revamp before a completely new car appears). With the pace of competition intensifying even further – both in terms of cars and their advertising – the challenge is to maximise the effect of the changes to the car.

Nicole is clearly too young for a 'facelift' so the task for the new advertising is to take the success story on, inject news and a sense of change as befits the new car, and make it work even harder, for longer.

Index